W9-ABV-916

Erotic Faith

Erotic Faith

Being in Love from Jane Austen to D. H. Lawrence

Robert M. Polhemus

The University of Chicago Press
Chicago and London

Robert M. Polhemus is professor of English at Stanford University. He is the author of *Comic Faith: The Great Tradition from Austen to Joyce*, published by the University of Chicago Press, and *The Changing World of Anthony Trollope*.

The University of Chicago Press, Chicago 60637
The University of Chicago Press, Ltd., London
© 1990 by the University of Chicago
All rights reserved. Published 1990
Printed in the United States of America

99 98 97 96 95 94 93 92 91 90   5 4 3 2 1

Library of Congress Cataloging-in-Publication Data

Polhemus, Robert M.
    Erotic faith : being in love from Jane Austen to D. H. Lawrence /
Robert M. Polhemus.
        p.   cm.
Includes bibliographical references.
ISBN 0-226-67322-7 (alk. paper)
1. English fiction—19th century—History and criticism. 2. Love stories, English—History and criticism. 3. English fiction—20th century—History and criticism. 4. Love in literature. I. Title.
PR868.L69P65   1990
823.009'354—dc20   89-20438
                                                            CIP

For Patricia

I was well versed in the tender passion, thanks to novels.
ELIZABETH GASKELL

How odd are the love-struck! A hurricane lifts gnarled tree trunks high into the air and flings them down miles away; the creek rushes to the cliff's edge and pours rainbow fish on rocks twelve hundred feet below; a plumed tyrant one morning orders the hearts of twenty thousand captives torn out, and by dusk high priests wade through blood kicking aside surfeited vultures; God radiates sunlight down through rose windows of great stone cathedrals; swift rockets circle Mars, Venus, and the many moons of Jupiter; a nuclear flash turns desert night to day; huge chandeliers sparkle in an opera house, as decibels rise to echo off a gold ceiling; on library shelves, thousands of volumes stand ready to offer readers truth that is beauty and wisdom of infinite variety and use. All the same, I know one who cares only for the sweet crookedness of a woman's mouth and moans of pleasure he has never heard.

Contents

(All figures appear in galleries following pp. 20 and 116, except figure 10, which appears on p. 12)

Preface

A preface is the place to try quickly to explain, disarm, and thank. My complex subject is how love makes novels, how novels make love, how faith makes art, how art makes faith. That topic is so large that obviously I cannot treat it comprehensively. I must concentrate on representative, telling instances and texts, which means that readers will sometimes disagree with my choice of focus and regret my omission of certain themes or works. Love, faith, and fictions are such personal matters that what I say about them will inevitably seem to readers at various times unsatisfactory, wrong, or even offensive. So be it. My premise is that our values, ideas, and what we profess, whatever else they may be, are based on, and part of, ongoing erotic stories that, though they are constructed socially, must be lived out individually. I follow D. H. Lawrence when he says, reviewing another writer, "A critic must be able to *feel* the impact of a work of art in all its complexity and its force." "Literary criticism," he goes on, "can be no more than a reasoned account of feeling produced upon the critic by the book he is criticising." That "reasoned account," however, may take many forms; for me it includes scholarship that relates the object of criticism to cultural history and to the lives of readers, emphasis on the pleasures of the text, and a belief in aesthetic excellence. Its intellectual value comes in showing what might really be at stake—socially, historically, personally, and emotionally—in a work of art. That is my purpose.

I have written this book out of a need for faith, out of the experience of a passionate, uneven faith in love, and out of a deep love of novels; the genesis of my work came when I realized that these things were connected.

On love, everybody is a flailing expert and nobody is original. To write a study about it is to become aware of how dialogic is the mind and how impossible it is to acknowledge contributors and obligations fully and accurately. George Meredith said in *The Egoist* that those who would try to illuminate the mysteries of love must follow "a yellow-dusking path across the rubble of preceding excavators in the solitary quarry." However imperfectly, I have tried to recognize and honor in the notes and bibliography my debts to previous explorers of love and love's artists. One trouble in giving proper credit is that the tossed-off remark of a child, the words and image of an ad, a line from a forgotten movie or song, a friend's anecdote, or a half-remembered conversation may prove as useful and enlightening about erotics as a Platonic dialogue or a brilliant scholar's published insight.

Many people have helped me directly in writing this book, more than I can name. I thank James Kincaid, Susan Morgan, Regenia Gagnier, Ian Watt, John

Bender, Barbara Charlesworth Gelpi, George Dekker, and Herbert Lindenberger for their useful, wise, and generous criticism of large portions of the manuscript. I have also benefited greatly from the suggestions and encouragement of Janeen Duyvestein Barchas, Christopher Cahill, William Chace, Mary Jean Corbett, Simone Di Piero, Suzette Henke, Kelly Hurley, Susan Kneedler, Anne K. Mellor, Diane Middlebrook, Thomas C. Moser, Nancy Packer, Patricia Parker, David Riggs, John Tofanelli, and Sue Zemka. I am indebted for the expertise and advice on specific authors and topics to John Bishop, George Brown, Terry Castle, Bliss Carnochan, Jay Fliegelman, Marsh McCall, Stephen Orgel, Arnold Rampersad, Lucio Ruotolo, and Mary Wack. I thank Mary Lombardi for her fine work in preparing the index. The wisdom, good sense, and editorial exactitude of Linda Jo Bartholomew and Tom Hassett aided greatly in preparing the manuscript for publication, as did the judicious copyediting of Joann Hoy. I wish to thank Doree Allen for her patience and good humor as a research assistant in charge of getting the illustrations, and I owe thanks also to research assistants Jeffrey Erickson, Kelly Mays, Robert Michalski, and Derede Arthur for their time, care, and effort. I want to acknowledge my gratitude to my students, friends, and family at Stanford and elsewhere for the contributions they have made to my thinking over the past decade. The generosity of Marian Polhemus Woessner helped to make the writing of my introductory chapter possible. And I particularly wish to thank Mary Jean Corbett, along with Linda Jo Bartholomew, George Dekker, Ken Fields, Chris Griffiths, Arturo Islas, Herbert Lindenberger, Nancy Packer, Joe Pisano, David and Sue Riggs, and Ruth and Ian Watt for extraordinary acts of kindness on behalf of myself and my family which helped me finish this book.

I have received generous institutional support for my work. A fellowship from the John Simon Guggenheim Foundation allowed me the time to begin this study, and one from the Stanford Humanities Center gave me time to write much of the first draft. I received financial support from the Stanford English Department, and owe much to its administrators, particularly George Dekker, Albert Gelpi, J. Martin Evans, Carolyn Fetler, and Kathy Ganas. The School of Humanities and Sciences and the Division of Graduate Studies, represented primarily by deans Theodore Andersson and Elizabeth C. Traugott, have generously met many costs for illustrations, permissions, and research assistance.

In my understanding of love I am indebted more than I can say to my children, Camilla, Mack, Joe, and Andromeda, and to my stepchildren Matthew and Nicole. My greatest debt is to Patricia Brandt Polhemus, to whom this book is dedicated. Her vision and love enabled me to write *Erotic Faith*.

1   Faith, Love, and the Art of the Novel: "The Feather Plucked from Cupid's Wing"

Behold, how readily are men led into errors and to believe lies! For they believe that Venus, who is dead and without doubt damned, and who never saw Europe while she was alive, is living in the mountains of Tuscany.
    FELIX FABER[1]

The pencil . . . is an old acquaintance. . . . A Venus. I hope it will see me out.
    SAMUEL BECKETT[2]

Purpose

In Norman Mailer's *The Executioner's Song* the murderer Gary Gilmore writes from death row to his incarcerated girlfriend, "What is to become of us Nicole? I know you wonder. And the answer is simple: By love . . . we can become more than the situation."[3] That assertion of the power of passionate love by a despicable wretch exemplifies what I call erotic faith: an emotional conviction, ultimately religious in nature, that meaning, value, hope, and even transcendence can be found through love—erotically focused love, the kind of love we mean when we say that people are in love. (I use the term "erotic" not in its narrow sexual connotation but to indicate broadly libidinous desire and a passionate, sometimes romantic, relationship with, affection for, or attachment to another person.) Men and women in the hold of erotic faith feel that love can redeem personal life and offer a reason for being.

Because doubt about the value of life has been a human constant, historically people have always needed some kind of faith. And with the spread of secularism since the eighteenth century, erotic faith, diverse and informal though it may be, has given to some a center and sometimes a solace that were traditionally offered by organized religion and God. *By love we can change the situation*— that sentiment moves people: love relationships have the highest priority in the real lives of millions as they have had for innumerable characters in fiction.

Erotic faith is not a new thing, a single thing, or a local phenomenon; but, long suppressed or expropriated by Christian and other religious orthodoxies, it has swept the world in modern times as never before. Gilmore's words mark its popular appeal. "Despite the flood of poems, novels and plays on the themes of romantic and sexual love," says one historian, "they played little or no part in the daily lives of men and women of the late seventeenth and eighteenth cen-

turies."[4] That is no longer so. Erotic love became an important basis of everyday
faith in the nineteenth century, and—for good or ill—the evidence of erotic
faith is all around.

In many wedding ceremonies nowadays, for example, brides and grooms opt
to have read Paul's famous "hymn to love": "If I speak with the tongues of men
and of angels, but have not love, I am become as sounding brass or a tinkling
cymbal. . . . Love is long-suffering, love is kind. . . . It covers everything,
hopes everything, endures everything" (1 Corinthians 13:1, 4, 7). The biblical
context, however, contradicts the modern translation and interpretation. Paul,
in this very epistle, denigrates marriage and subordinates it to celibacy as the
preferable condition. The "love" that he extols (and that is rendered as "charity"
in the King James Bible) is not the kind of ideal erotic love that a contemporary
audience witnessing a marriage now projects onto a man and woman; it is rather
a specifically spiritual Christian love of, by, for, and through Almighty God. The
modern performance of the Pauline text usurps the sacred love in Scripture and
transmutes it into the requited love of mating people.

There is in our time a drive to harmonize erotic love with traditional religion;
we long to supplant a remote supernaturalism with a consecrating faith in tangible, personal relationships. Those desires come out of the same tension that
inspires and characterizes so much of nineteenth-century literature and
thought. In many of the best-known nineteenth-century English novels, the
narrative relates the history of characters who find vocation, meaning, fate, and
even salvation in being in love. They tell of the state of being in love in a
particular, realized social milieu. In the 1870s, Anthony Trollope could write,
"It is admitted that a novel can hardly be made interesting or successful without
love. . . . love is necessary to all novelists because the passion is one which
interests or has interested all. Everyone feels it, has felt it, or expects to feel it—
or rejects it with an eagerness which still perpetuates the interest." He goes on:
"It is from them [novels] that girls learn what is expected from them, and what
they are to expect when lovers come; and also from them that young men unconsciously learn what are, or should be, or may be, the charms of love."[5]
Matter-of-factly he thus states the necessity of love as the novel's subject matter
and, just as clearly, assumes the intimate relationship between the rendering of
love in art and the evolving historical experience of love in peoples' lives. Erotic
faith, then, is a predominant motive, theme, and force in the nineteenth- and
early twentieth-century prose fiction that is my subject.

For two centuries English-speaking people have seen and felt love relationships and erotic drives through sensibilities affected, directly or indirectly, by
novelists. Love as faith, and art representing and embodying love, I repeat, are
nothing new, but Victorian and modern perceptions of erotic desire and faith in

love *are* very much formed and conditioned by the fact that the novel became such an influential art form. Love takes shape out of the imagination, and the erotic imagination both creates and is created by art. If La Rochefoucauld's bon mot—"people would never fall in love, if they had not been told about it"—is true, then novels like *Pride and Prejudice, The Bride of Lammermoor,* and *Wuthering Heights* helped bring an erotic gospel to the Victorians and their followers.

I have six broad, interrelated aims:

1. I want to show the reciprocity and integrity of love as subject, the novel as form, and faith as motive in major works by Austen, Scott, Emily and Charlotte Brontë, Dickens, George Eliot, Trollope, Hardy, Joyce, and D. H. Lawrence. The best way I know to do that is to look closely at particular passages and analyze their erotic implications. My focus is on these various books themselves, on their reverberating quality, and on the rich possibilities of knowing and feeling that they offer. Being in love, not marriage, success, piety, or God, is the source and requirement for faith in these novels.

My goal is to interpret and illuminate the interplay between the novels and the perceived reality of actual people—authors, readers, their contemporaries, and their influential forebears. From any number of possible texts, I have chosen ten distinguished erotic visions in British fiction that reflect profoundly on nineteenth-century experience and relate significantly to modern life. Whatever might be said about my choices and strategy, few who read the language of these works carefully would deny that, individually and together, they render radiantly the tensions of being in love and the power and problems of erotic faith.

These novels create and imagine forms of love and faith; love gives them their plot and moral vision; the desire for faith creates their erotic emphasis and narrative forms. As Christian faith caused great Gothic cathedrals to rise, so did erotic faith, or the desire for it, bring into being great nineteenth-century novels; as cathedrals shaped ideas of faith, so these novels shaped ideas of love.

2. I want to explore the historical significance and consequence of the erotic meanings that fiction generates. This study of novels is thus a study also of *erotics*—that complicated individual and social tangle of desire that pertains to the various energies of the human libido. Each work represents and emphasizes some important erotic pattern: for instance, "rational love" in Austen, "repression" in Charlotte Brontë, "fixation" in Dickens, "the politics of love" in Trollope, "sex life" in Lawrence. But every one of these narratives and patterns relates to the others, and each discussion of a particular novel is meant to stand as a contribution to our general knowledge of love.

In the late eighteenth and nineteenth centuries there took place a "novelization" of the arts: poetry, painting, sculpture, and music were deeply influenced by narrative form, which meant in practice by love stories.[6] This "novelization" is thus a kind of eroticization. Not surprisingly, in the Victorian years when the love novel bloomed, we get everything from the full flowering of the love-obsessed arts of opera and classical ballet to the religious eroticism of Pre-Raphaelite painting. Once erotic love had taken hold of popular consciousness, art and artists—if they wanted to please audiences—had to face the subject and render states and histories of being in love.

The stress on love was an attempt to find, establish, and blend metaphysics, moral values, heightened self-consciousness, materialism, and modes of ecstatic psychic and sensual gratification in a time of accelerating change. As everyone knows, the means of production were being revolutionized, social hierarchy and the status of women were changing, science was developing new ideas of determinism, and God, for many, was disappearing. Love stories manifested and sanctioned a sense of individual worth and potential; in love plots, lover and beloved, no matter who they are, are the stars, so the logic of love stories implies that anyone who can fall in love can be a star—one of the elect.

3. I want to develop further my theme in *Comic Faith* (1980)[7] that the British novel is a means for imagining forms of faith that would augment or substitute for orthodox religious visions. The motives for the production and appreciation of art are many, but the religious impulse—the drive, whether personal, social, or both, to express and embody faith in striking form—has surely been one of the strongest. A significant work of art, such as the Mona Lisa or *Great Expectations*, has a multiple existence: it may stand in an artistic tradition as a beautiful form of aesthetic value by which a culture reifies its worth; it may be an instrument of control for the ruling classes or a means of political subversion; it may be seen as mimesis of reality, as a mode of pleasure, as part of the economic system, or as a privileged specimen preserving and focusing a moment of history; it may be a moral force, an expression of gender relationship, or a way of understanding the world and shaping the forms of the future. Whatever its rhetorical function or status, however, art nearly always has to do with the need to put faith in something.

Rooted in such works as Bunyan's *Pilgrim's Progress*, Defoe's *Moll Flanders*, and Richardson's *Pamela*, English prose fiction has sought to fuse religious and erotic desire. Novels were to erotic faith what Bibles, churches, and chapels were to Christianity: the ways, means, and sites for the propagation of faith. Nineteenth-century novelists assumed pastoral roles and took them seriously. Think of some of the main purposes and functions of religion: to honor creation and the mystery of being; to make people feel the worth of their own souls; to reconcile them to their lives and offer an alternative to the pain of daily existence; to justify, rationalize, or sublimate power relations; to exalt by holding out the promise of salvation; to lift people out of themselves, free the spirit, and move them to ecstasy; to transmute and control aggression and violent drives; to sublimate sexuality and idealize gender identity.[8] Some have come to believe that passionate love can do such things; others scoff. But whatever its value or fate, that belief is the product of history and the novel, a heritage that social circumstances and artistic creation have left. Love was once a goddess, a god, or, more precisely, several gods and goddesses, and in the nineteenth century it came again to have the force of deity.

It might be objected that erotic faith is unlike orthodox religion because it is a spasmodic feeling that everyday living wears down, rather than a continuous entity outside the self that lays down the terms for the practice of faith. Faith, however, *is* subjective and often a matter of inward emotion. Novels, which became a primary means for transmitting the forms and terms of eroticism, show the widening gap for many between organized religion and faith in the nineteenth century.

4. I mean to look closely at family relationships and the ways in which fiction works to present them as unfolding erotic narratives in themselves. Most of the novelists I discuss imagine the centrality of family in forming character, outlook, and desire. The nineteenth-century novel has rendered life as a "family romance"—and with great effect in coloring our perceptions not only of the present, but of the past as well. Such figures as Oedipus, Electra, and the Madonna, for example, as we tend to conceive of them, have come to resemble family characters in psychologized narratives, progeny as well as ancestors of novelistic vision.

5. By comparing paintings that portray love to novels, I want to show both the endurance and the malleability of love as subject and motivating force of art. A continuum exists between word, narrative, and visual image. Painters and writers have created and drawn from a common aesthetic and erotic heritage—a cultural flow of ideas, forms, images, and patterns of feeling—that audiences can and do use to illuminate their experiences of love, art, and desire. Paintings can work by analogy to help us identify large patterns of meaning in the contingent life of novels; and certainly, novels have taught Victorian and modern viewers to "read" paintings. Juxtaposing pictures against nineteenth-century texts makes clear the way novels work to develop and individualize common erotic and religious themes. Significantly, this kind of comparison can also illustrate how the novel has influenced not only our perception of painting but of all reality.

6. I want to explore the changing effects of erotic faith in novels, both on gender relations and on the problematic conditions the emphasis on love brings about—especially for women.

The chronology for this study runs roughly from 1800 to the 1930s. This period begins with the emergence of the novel as the dominant literary form and individualism as a predominant, if somewhat vague, ideology. It is a time of industrialization, the spread of literacy, the growing power and influence of the middle classes, and the strengthening and idealization of the nuclear family and its values. In it women come to participate in the literary process—as authors, subjects, and readers—in unprecedented numbers and ways. The period ends with the gradual replacement of the novel as the primary medium of popular art when technology discovers how to fuse writing, sound, and photography. At its close comes the invention of alternatives to print as the chief means of mass communication and the development of the instruments of modern mass culture, such as advertising, motion pictures, telephones, radio, rudimentary television, and cybernetic science. We find a new frankness in various discourses about sex and evolving sexual technologies—for example, the medical alleviation of venereal diseases and the increasing use of contraceptives—that changed or would change sexual attitudes and behavior. And within the period, we see the popular establishment of erotic faith.

Context

To give a history of "love in the Western world" before 1800 and the erotic context for nineteenth-century British fiction would be, to paraphrase George Eliot, like giving a history of lights and shadows; but if we are to understand the achievement of that fiction, its social force, and its relationship to faith, we need to identify some major features and trends in the broad cultural heritage of love in the West generally and Victorian Britain in particular.[9] One way to do that without diluting the subject and becoming sidetracked in reductive or centrifugal theories is to fix arbitrarily, but carefully, on a few representative, resonant art images that can focus erotic subjects, conflicts, instincts, and history. The images that I choose, most of them from or of the Renaissance, when taken together constitute a field and an overture of desire in which and against which we can place, relate, and define the particular erotics of the novels. What they imply about the range of erotic desire—desire for everything from salvation to transgression, from virtue and beauty to power and an inner life—could also provide reference points and a general framework for studying erotic faith in, for instance, French, German, Italian, or American culture and literature; but, as I mean to show, they are especially relevant all together, individually, and in their separate details to the nineteenth- and early twentieth-century English fiction of being in love. Until this century, it is almost exclusively in art—in imagined actions, visions, figures, characters, and forms of language and sound—that the history of love has been made, preserved, and read.

I

Botticelli's *Birth of Venus* (c. 1485; fig. 1), very likely the best-known image of erotic love in the world (and sadly, now something of a visual cliché),[10] illustrates my premises. It shows the interflow of love, religious feeling, aesthetics, and history, but its very fame and the way people perceive it are products of a nine-teenth-century British literary sensibility that was formed under the influence of the novel (the title *Birth of Venus* was first given to it in the last century).[11] After his death, Botticelli fell into obscurity. Though Romantic critics were at-tracted by the religious sentiment in his Christian work, it was not until the 1860s and 1870s, when such English writers and artists as Pater, Ruskin, the Rossettis, Browning, Millais, and Burne-Jones rediscovered his "pagan" master-pieces, that he became famous.[12] These Victorians could see and appreciate the "momentous significance" of these Botticelli paintings that rendered, as E. H. Gombrich puts it, an ostensibly "non-religious subject with the fervour and feeling usually reserved for objects of worship."[13] The artist achieved "the open-ing up, to secular art, of emotional spheres which had hitherto been the preserve of religious worship" (64).

The major reason for the revival of interest in the *Birth of Venus* is precisely that it *does* express religious feeling: reverence for love. John Ruskin said of Botticelli, "He . . . understood the thoughts of Heathens and Christians equally, and could in a measure paint both Aphrodite and the Madonna."[14] In this pic-ture, the love goddess subsumes the Virgin Mother. The artist presents Aphro-dite as a devotional figure, saying in effect, "Here is an image to adore." Walter Pater wrote that *Venus* conveys the "influence over the human mind of the imaginative system of which this is perhaps the central subject."[15] This historic work, conjoining the Madonna and Venus, mystery and realism, calm and tur-bulence, material glory and sadness, makes a good emblem for the enterprise of the novel: the cast of mind that gave the painting renown was shaped by the kinds of imagination and knowing that narrative fiction had brought into play.

Literature and history had to create a public for erotic faith, and Botticelli and his Venus had to be "novelized" before they could be studied and revered. Pater, stressing Botticelli's "poetical" quality, turns the painter into a psycholog-ical novelist of love: "what is unmistakable is the sadness with which he has conceived the goddess of pleasure, as the depository of a great power over the lives of men" (47). He reads Venus as a character from a world older and wider than the Christian world (46). The picture fed a craving to feel, to merge in consciousness religious emotion and eroticism, to seize for the present both the blessings of faith and the sensuous possibilities of life that had supposedly antedated Christian moralism.[16] History and art might open up to the human spirit a means of reconsecrating life through the time-retrieving imagination of both a Renaissance painter and a late-Victorian audience creatively reading his work as a beautiful locus of divine, erotic, and aesthetic faiths.[17]

The rebirth of Botticelli's Venus and all that it signifies was shaped by Walter Scott's influential eroticizing and aestheticizing of history; by gothic novelists who dealt with exotic subjects set in Roman Catholic countries; by Romantic and Victorian narrative poetry; by Jane Austen's rationalization of love; by the Brontës' novels of passion; by Robert Browning's fictionalized monologues of Renaissance artists; by *Romola*, George Eliot's historical novel about Florence; and by thousands of other narrative works featuring love, the past, the changing of faiths, the romanticization of art, and the tension between hard materiality and the quest for spirituality that is the novel's dialogic stock in trade.[18]

Both the production and interpretation of the painting depend on the interplay between image and text. Modern viewers, for example, approach the *Birth of Venus* with its title in mind; and Botticelli, in creating it, was illustrating such texts as Politian's verse, Ficino's philosophy, Lucretius's homage to Venus, and Ovid's poetry—some of which in turn were describing classical works of art.[19] An almost endless chain of interconnecting words and visual impressions forms Botticelli's conception of love as well as ours.

His art, like good fiction, functions representationally, symbolically, and expressively.[20] The *Birth of Venus*, for instance, represents the myth of the goddess coming ashore, symbolizes the fecund power of love coming into the world, and expresses in the emotions it stirs what you might feel when you fall joyously in love. The picture, in the act of viewing, signifies that love is born of art, that art is born of love, and that love is a recurring advent, coming again and again into different lives.

Botticelli brings the subject and precariousness of love into clear light because he renders as well as anyone ever has the desire for erotic balance. A study in poise, the painting makes love the balancing force in life, blending spirit with matter, sexuality with reverence, Venus with the Virgin, sensuality with Neoplatonic idealism, physical with moral beauty, instinct with culture, and the worship of the feminine with objectification of women. Venus, with a haunting, abstract expression on her face, stands between sea and land, naked on a large scallop shell (with its gold-tinged, geometrical fluting, this shell is both a natural vessel and an elaborate artifice). She is also poised between, on the left, the interwined, rose-showered figures of blowing Zephyr and rapt, open-mouthed Flora, those animating natural forces with their prodigal, amorphous tangle of legs, torsos, dishevelled garments, wings, and hair; and, on the right, the cloak-wielding figure of Hora, a handmaiden nymph personifying Spring and Time, ready to cover the nakedness of newly arrived love. Hora wears and holds the apparel of civil life in which floral forms have been embroidered and preserved. The *Birth of Venus* shows that humanity, in portraying love to itself, has felt impelled to include both huff-puffing sexual drive (Zephyr ravished Chloris, turning her into happy Flora) and the care for another's well-being. To come into existence, love, in Botticelli's vision, needs nature's breath of fecund desire; but when it is born into the world, it needs the mantle of civilization to protect it. Both the generating power of nature and of culture appear as devoted satellites to love.

Nowhere is the balance of love more apparent or important than in Venus herself—face, body, hair, and pose. Her enigmatic countenance is detached, magnetic but difficult to engage and categorize. The expression is decorous, independent, touched with melancholy, capable of provoking both sexual fascination and, like the Virgin Mother, moralizing idealism; it stirs desire but seems beyond possession. Her body appears both graceful and voluptuous, and even as she modestly covers a breast and uses her long, golden back-tress to conceal "the apple of her sweetness,"[21] she hardly seems aware of the flesh. Without coyness, she looks at nothing palpable, and that unworldliness adds to her aura of spirituality. Nevertheless, her dramatic hair, delicately fine at the neck and in the blowing strands, heavy and supple as it falls down her left side and snakes across her pelvis to her hand, is alive with sexual allusion. It can suggest Dionysian wildness, flames, fiery desire, serpents, phalluses, Eve, original sin, the appeal of gold—connotations that fly beyond the bounds of Christian virtue and Platonic moral philosophy.[22] The hair, serving as the agent of both modesty and sexual excitement, epitomizes the equilibrium of the work.

Botticelli seems typically to balance the sexual imagery between phallic and womblike symbolism. The visible line of Zephyr's breath points straight through the heart and breast of Venus to the circle of Hora's welcoming cloak, and that same oral line complements the open mouth of Chloris; the upright Venus stands vertical to the vaginal shell, and in the whole composition the figures on either side, and the arching wings, cloak, and trees at the top, form a pregnant space that the Venus fills.

The physiognomy of the three feminine figures also shows a telling balance of the conventional roles of women as they for so long have been imagined by men—and by women too. The hoydenish, sensual look of Flora and the dedicated nurturing expression of the attending Hora play off each other and frame the gaze of Venus, who offers a focal point for adoration. Erotic history has been formed by the desire both to use in every way and to worship the female.

When Gombrich says, "This Venus was to arouse in the spectator a feeling akin to religious enthusiasm, a divine *furor* kindled by beauty,"[23] he indicates how and why the painting has become such a symbol for the hopes that live in our notions of love. It renders in the name of love both that which is desirable and the fulfillment of desire. It presents the erotic spirit that permeates such moving "green" comedies of love as Shakespeare's *A Midsummer Night's Dream* and Mozart's *The Marriage of Figaro*. The advent of Venus seems to bring goodness and pleasure into harmony. It displays a joyful resonance of form and meaning: beautiful shapes, lines, and colors; the sea tamed and made into pleasing shades of green with soft, white, triangular, and scrolling waves; the verdant coast made inviting and aesthetically delightful; radiant gold shed across the land and into reeds and every rose; rich, decorated fabrics, delightful flesh, hair streaming and braided. Imagine the hold of such a beautiful image over a mind, and the consequences that the desire to adapt such an image to the self might have.[24] To make the implications of this *Venus* personal would generate novel plots and characters.

II

If Botticelli can be seen to portray an ideal erotic harmony, two later Renaissance pictures by Bronzino, *The Deposition of Christ* (c. 1543–45; fig. 9) and *An Allegory with Venus and Cupid* (c. 1545–50; fig. 2), can serve when taken together as paradigms depicting desires, conflicts, fluid feelings, and clashing historical conceptions that hover about love and faith in the Christian era. Moreover, they suggest the vital mediating role that art plays in forming common cultural perceptions about the value of religious practice and of eroticism.

Bronzino depicts a "true" and a "false" divinity, Christ and Venus, and thus the works have special relevance for nineteenth-century culture, when the clash between forces symbolized by the two would be renewed so insistently (e.g., in the Brontës, Wagner, Swinburne, Nietzsche, and Freud). Setting at odds eroticism and Christian salvation, these pictures convey a fundamental conflict between two ways of looking at love: seeing it in the emotional radiance of the moment, and seeing and judging it over the course of time. Nevertheless, when juxtaposed, they reveal striking parallels and dialectical connections. Ostensibly they show that the flesh fails and that you need spiritual life; but they also intimate, in heterodox fashion, the power of erotic love to command faith. A strain of hostility to sex runs through the heritage of Christianity—not surprisingly, since the pull of erotic love and its deification were, in Christian eyes, a dormant legacy of paganism and an active heretical threat. Psychologically, however, religious feeling and eroticism run close together.

Bronzino's *Allegory* sums up the thoughtful condemnation of sensual love over centuries: it represents the apparent rapture of an erotic moment as actual disaster. The allegory offers intimations of almost every later assault on the corrupting nature of eros, from Jacobean tragedy through Hogarth's *Harlot's*

Progress, Matthew Lewis's *Monk*, Oscar Wilde's *Picture of Dorian Gray*, and de
Rougemont's *Love in the Western World* to case histories of divorce by contemporary sociologists. One meaning of the "allegory" is that worship of Venus—
and all that such a phrase implies—blinds one to the menace of time and death.
True love for Plato meant desire for the immutable good, and that definition
pervades subsequent Christian thought. To trust and seek the beauty and love
of the world, here imagined as the joy of sexual ecstasy, is to choose what per-
ishes in the flow of time. It means betraying self, God, and humankind as a
whole, which depends for its preservation upon deferred gratification, law, and
control of sensual appetite. To deify seductive eroticism and give way to the
moment is to court destruction and set loose anarchy. The painting shows Time,
the righteous patriarchal figure in the upper right corner, revealing the awful
truth inherent in earthly love.

   The most unsettling thing about the picture is the voluptuous rendering of
mother and son; it flouts taboo, shockingly fusing erotic, maternal, and filial
love. Lascivious Eros is becoming the lover of Venus, kissing and fondling her,
his beautiful body and his obscene stance suggesting both incest and pederasty.
Disarming Venus wields his arrow like a phallus, smiling in her hard, white
loveliness. The image is out of moral control, abhorrent yet fascinating; it conveys both the traditional fear of sex and the excitement of erotic transgression.
It makes sexual intercourse a matter of amoral pleasure-seeking rather than a
providential act of reproduction—libido for libido's sake.

   Sometime in the eighteenth century, church-inspired prurience led to a cover-
up of Venus's genitalia with filmy drapery and of Cupid's buttocks with a spray
of leaves (additions which were removed only in 1958; see fig. 10). That religious orthodoxy insisted on hiding erogenous zones betrays great fear about the
disruptive force that artistic representations of love can arouse.[25]

   Erotic idolatry brings chaos. Holding the golden apple, symbol of her
triumph in the world, Venus is surrounded by her allegorical retinue. To her
right is the heedless rose-strewing cherub Folly and, just behind him, the pretty,
vacuous face of Pleasure. But Pleasure's body, obscured in the erotic present, is
that of a reptilian monster, and in her tail there is a sting. To the left of Venus
and Eros are images of tormenting Jealousy and, above, Fraud, exposed by Time.
The lecherous painting portrays erotic passion subject to the most appalling
ignorance and the most terrible disillusion.

   In contrast to *An Allegory*, we have in *The Deposition* an apparently tragic
event that promises redemption from death. Again the primary relationship is
generational and loving: another mother and son. But the piteous gaze of the
Virgin shows no self-regarding desire, only devoted love for the human-born,
divine agent of salvation. Once more the picture moves its beholder to consider

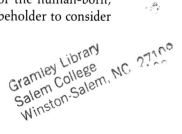

the future that it implies, but here the revelation of time means the promise of eternal life.[26] The Christian God can conquer time, the erotic goddess cannot.

The picture illuminates those deeply influential Christian and classical ideas that insist on moralizing love. Bronzino represents a figure of eroticism in the Magdalene on the right, but her sin is now diffused into Christian worship and spiritual life. Sunk to her knees ("the fallen woman"), she shares with Saint John and the Virgin Mother the weight of crucified Jesus; she repents in time to find timelessness. As Bronzino incorporates Mary Magdalene, so the Bible in-

10. Bronzino, *An Allegory with Venus and Cupid* (before the 1958 restoration). Retouched in the late seventeenth or the eighteenth century with foliage and drapery added. Reproduced by courtesy of the Trustees, National Gallery, London.

cludes the highly erotic Song of Solomon, and both painting and Scripture show the idealizing impulse that erotic feeling generates and the sexual energy that religion appropriates. In *The Deposition* both the Virgin Mary's look and the stare of Mary Magdalene express in context a love that transcends death because it attaches to Jesus. Love bred in the senses, love in the world, is being transformed into a love beyond the sensual realm.

Bronzino includes those most stubborn facts of physical existence, sexuality and motherhood, but he divides them from one another: the reformed whore kneels at Christ's feet and the Virgin Mother takes him on her lap. In the history of love's representation, the three figures of Christ, the Madonna, and Mary Magdalene comprise the most significant group imaginable; they join together notions of sacrifice, divinity, devotion, purity, miraculous regeneration, and an eroticism that must be renounced. The work seems to highlight the difference between the Magdalene's fallen state and the Virgin's immaculate condition, but it also connects them. Not only does the love of both the mother and the whore seem necessary in this sacred vision, Bronzino's art implies that Mary's sinlessness and her transfiguring role in the redeeming passion somehow depend on purging sexuality by projecting it onto a woman who falls and then repents. The prostitute comes to serve a sexless conception of love.

The Deposition illustrates idealism's ladder of love carrying body and mind from lower to higher things. The Virgin's face holds the focus of feeling. What was nurturing, maternal love for one specific person becomes compassionate love for the martyred god who in his regeneration becomes all-pervading good. Her expression works to turn the act of love into the sacrifice of the body for harmony and permanent salvation, a trope that can stand for the essence of all idealism and metaphysical questing. Earthly beauty, good and real as it is, points to something better. Mary may be understood to collapse time by uniting virginity, maternity, and the sympathetic hope for resurrection from death all in one soulful expression. Like *The Divine Comedy*, in which Dante had harmonized love for a woman (Beatrice), Platonic idealism, and Christian faith, this vision makes love transcendent.

III

So the two pictures might seem to represent, in the context of Renaissance ideology, "bad love" and "good love." Their significance, however, far exceeds tame didactic intent and undermines their strict orthodoxy. According to Bronzino's vision, eroticism and Christian love are thoroughly contaminated by one another. Compare, for example, the expression of Eros with the expressions of the Magdalene and the Virgin, or the inviting flesh and homoerotic pose of Eros with the angel at the top left of *The Deposition*. Bronzino insists on the immanence of erotic desire in all areas of the imagination, including theology.

An Allegory verges on the obscene, so insinuating (and creepy) is its eroticism. Conventional relationship and morality are lost in the abandon and eerie beauty of the central figures. Eros's epicene posture, his sexually aggressive hand, and Venus's grasp of the love arrow from his quiver mean forbidden, damnable sex. But the transgressive feeling about the picture has both a perverse glamor and a defiant appeal. One intended message of the allegory is surely "this is not worth it"; but the transport and apparent sovereignty of the couple in the erotic present, the magnetism of their faces, forms and action, the beautiful color in their setting, can send a heretical countermessage, "this *is* worth it."

Thomas Sheehan writes of Jesus that "his role was simply to end religion— that temporary governess who had turned into a tyrant—and restore the sense and immediacy of God."[27] Physical, erotic love with its ecstatic light sometimes acts like Sheehan's Jesus. At face value, *An Allegory* might seem to offer the sinister vision of some Antichrist, but the image of Venus and Amor has a subversiveness that suggests the power of eroticism to defy Christian theology, end orthodox religion's mediation of transcendence, and offer godlike experience.

The painting has such force as a paradigm because it conjoins images of physical love, incestuous desire, and supernatural being. Eros fondles the breast of his mother the goddess: the nipple, whose natural function is to suckle the babe, becomes an erotic object for the sexually mature being. James Joyce in *Finnegans Wake* blasphemously announces the union of the maternal, the erotic, and the holy: "Mater Mary Mercerycordial of the Dripping Nipples, milk's a queer arrangement."[28] That "queer" anatomical "arrangement" signifies the progenerative, two-sexed fate of humanity and also its destiny to be an image-making, memory (mammary)-ideating species that eroticizes the present out of the needs and gratifications of the past. Bronzino's allegory reveals, besides the potential agonies of love, the integrity of the mature sexual libido with early desire. In this way the subliminal meaning in the picture counters the triumph of time over love: erotic love conquers time by making infantile desire and adult gratification synchronous.

Compare the touch of the nipple in *An Allegory* with a telling passage two centuries later from *Clarissa* (1747–48), Samuel Richardson's historic novel of erotic and religious desire: Lovelace, having forcibly exposed Clarissa's breasts, writes, "Let me perish . . . if I would not forego the brightest diadem in the world for the pleasure of seeing a twin Lovelace at each charming breast, drawing from it his first sustenance, the pious task, for physical reasons, continued for one month and no more!"[29] As in Bronzino, the image of desire is the same for lover and child. Lovelace clearly expresses the simultaneous presence in the libido of an unruly generational trinity: erotic seducer, parent, and infant.

In Plato's famous myth of love in the *Symposium*, Aristophanes says that humanity originally consisted of four-footed, symmetrical creatures, but, cut in two by the gods, these alienated beings search compulsively for their missing halves. Love, in other words, is a search for completion.[30] In the logic of *An Allegory*, the key sundering that begins the erotic quest is temporal and generational: one way of interpreting Bronzino's work would be to say that humanity forever seeks impossibly, in love, not only sexual wholeness and soul-mate integrity, but a bonding oneness of the flesh with the parent back to the beginning of the self and beyond that to the beginning of all generation. And one implication of the full-grown Eros's wantonness is that the adult sexual quest grows out of first relationships and is tinged with incestuous longing. In these two paintings Bronzino puts filial and maternal passion at the heart of both religion and erotic desire.

The incest taboo is both a product and a defining feature of human culture, but it is often abrogated in religion, myth, and art, as Bronzino shows. This symbolic or ritual breaking of the ban generally has to do with aspirations for divine potency.[31] Representations of incest and incestuous impulses may serve as warnings of damnation, sin, and utter degradation, but they may also hint at a superhuman freedom and intimacy beyond the lot of men and women. In daily life, the incestuous transgressor is commonly regarded as a despicable outcast. Symbolically, however, incest and sexual transgression have sometimes forged strange links between the erotic and the sacred because the idea of incest can imply a realm of experience on the level of gods whose boundless desires can be satisfied and who transcend human law.[32]

Both of Bronzino's works generalize about life and do not portray its individuality. Their assumptions are, in the one instance, that the audience needs to be cautioned against the perils of sex and that, in the other, it needs to understand that the tribulations and pleasures of earthly life take place within a benevolent Christian order. *The Deposition* pictures the desire to reconcile love of the flesh with a sustaining spiritual faith—the aching desire that, when made personal, would shape the history of the novel. *An Allegory* renders both rational contempt for erotic passion and startling defiance of whatever impedes erotic fulfillment; that fateful tension is what the novel would continually explore and particularize.

IV

The appeal of eroticism comes through even more graphically in Caravaggio's *Amor Vincit Omnia* (c. 1602; fig. 11), an unambiguous picture of brazen sexuality. Though his subject, like Bronzino's, is general, Caravaggio stresses the personal nature of love, the love object, and erotic desire through the sensuous folds of the torso's flesh and Amor's strongly individualized, joyful expression.

The face of Eros is so lifelike and animated that it makes love, in the context of the title, seem finally physical, human, particular, and existential. The wing that, almost like a hand, brushes the thigh, suggests that ethereal, celestial ideologies and flying thought are based on the flesh and the desires it provokes.

The painting is far from conveying the orthodox Renaissance rationale for the theme of love's triumph: love conquers all in the name of the natural regenerative life force that is part of God's larger plan. The amoral, playful charm of Eros and the implicit approval of sexual pleasure in the work do not fit into an idealizing system. And the painting's homoeroticism—the prominent genitalia juxtaposed with the rectal crack—shows, even more strikingly than Bronzino's Cupid, rampant libido, forbidden sexual longings, and private images of erotic pleasure. The picture means what its title says: love conquers all, including Christian and Neoplatonic doctrine. Caravaggio limns heresy and the possibilities of an alternative, worldly faith in an unsanctified love for another individual human being.[33]

At the feet and behind the lower body of Amor lie strewn the trappings of the arts, sciences, and political power—musical and writing instruments, a score, a manuscript, the globe, a square and compass, armor, and a scepter. The message is not only that eroticism is stronger than any other power in the world, but also that Eros infuses and dominates all the forms culture takes. No art, no activity, no will exists independently of personal erotic desire and its influence.[34] Caravaggio's most socially dangerous intimation may be that love equals pleasure. The nineteenth century would recognize the force of this unorthodox, conquering figure, but would try to control it by psychologizing it, spiritualizing it, and making it serious and sacred. One way of understanding Victorian repression is to imagine this socially threatening figure of triumphant erotic joy as always present and always denied.

V

Before love could become a popular faith, three things had to happen: it had to offer some sort of sustaining personal belief; women had to become desiring subjects as well as desirable erotic objects; and the erotic flesh had to become the saving, enduring word. In or about 1665 Vermeer painted *A Lady Writing* (fig. 13).[35] From it we can infer how the subject of love could take possession of life and writing. There is no overt sex or amorous behavior in the picture, but it renders eroticism nonetheless. In the mood of introspection that the woman's expression and the whole painting convey, Vermeer figures the absorbing quality of love. The power both to feel and inspire affection suffuses her face.

The picture comes out of an age when Protestant culture, which in no way privileges celibacy over the married state, had become an established part of

Western civilization, and "affective individualism"—the term Lawrence Stone has given to the historical conditions in which personal feelings and perceptions take on central importance—was taking hold in European life (see note 4). It reflects upon an era when the wishes of prospective brides and grooms were counting for more in the making of marriages, when the middle classes were expanding and encouraging literacy, when more women were gaining more leisure, and when female life in the upper social levels was slowly changing.

Vermeer has portrayed a woman pausing in the midst of writing a letter. No doubt many readings of the painting are possible—that she has been distracted from her project, for example—but her look seems to express concern for the object of her thought and writing. She appears to be in love.[36] But how, after all, can we presume to know that the painting represents a woman thinking about love or a lover? Why not just as well say that she is writing and musing about spices from the Indies, the doctrine of predestination, or tulips? The answer—unless we have the expertise to know that Vermeer worked in a traditional iconographical code that specifically related letters to eroticism[37]—is that, whatever our individuality, we bring a common cultural conditioning to our viewing: Everything about the picture conveys a moment free of triviality, a serious time with the future in the balance, which, for a young lady of her era, would usually mean her erotic destiny. Novels and other literary discourse influence us to judge that such a woman would be thinking and writing about—or to—some man. History, the heritage of fiction, and the rhetorical traditions of art persuade this viewer at least to find narrative subjectivity—a personal story and possibly a marriage plot—in the woman and her picture.

Vermeer's female images are noteworthy figures in women's history, and none is more moving than the lady of this work. The picture says that what a woman writes and the fact that she writes matter. Women have traditionally been fetishized in art, but Vermeer paints them as contemplative subjects as well as objects of contemplation. The subject of *A Lady Writing* does not come out of the Bible or mythology; she is not a sitting object of portraiture commissioned by an aristocrat; she is an individualized woman in the midst of life, the artist's contemporary, who possesses the power of thought and pen—the inner room of her own consciousness. Moreover this figure, in this represented moment of her life, set in the beauty of a composed material world—the sunny morning-jacket trimmed with ermine, the necklace, the shiny studs on the chair, for example—reflects the goodness of being in the world. She looks intelligent, committed to something beyond herself; her face reveals both dignity and kindness. No one could study this picture for long and conclude that men are more important than women or that the inner life of a woman does not have the value or resonance of a man's.

The painting joins the act of writing and the emotion of love. It leads us to imagine that love gives the lady occasion to write, but that writing, as she looks away from the page into the space of her consciousness, directs and feeds her thoughts. This Vermeer depicts the wedding in erotic history of the letter and the spirit of love, whose progeny would include such great eighteenth-century epistolary inquiries into erotic feeling as *Clarissa, La nouvelle Héloïse*, and *Les liaisons dangereuses*. The scriptures of love faith, especially as it flourished in the nineteenth and early twentieth centuries, would be love letters and the public literature whose existence, course, and genres for more than three centuries owed so much to the post-Renaissance custom of private correspondence.

It is a cliché to say that writing empowers, but it may be worth stressing how subjective such power is. Letters are silent, confidential—even confessional— expressions, and they "define a private human space."[38] Reflecting, sifting through images, memory, and experience, choosing words and syntax, one takes on authority—becomes an author. To write is to examine, extend, and populate an inner space, to preserve consciousness, to mediate experience and thought. To write a letter is to give literal substance to a particular point of view. In Vermeer's picture, the lady writing means individualism, means the desire to communicate intimately, means the projected, subjective drama of the erotic self—means, in short, love. The picture has an aura of passion about it, but the passion is private. We cannot see the forms that it takes, we can only see the expression of the woman who sees and feels inwardly. The deliberation over a letter makes it possible for a woman to be clothed, alone, and still, and yet to engage herself fully in a passionate act of love.

Love is as important in Vermeer as it is in Botticelli, Bronzino, or Caravaggio, but the sexual body is not. His picture lets us see how the pen as the instrument of passion could transmute sexuality and flesh into that wondrous, ghostly organ of amorous discourse, the heart. Writing makes it much easier to idealize erotic feeling and make love soulful (see the letters of Héloïse and Abelard); Vermeer's painting illustrates a remark of Terry Eagleton about the letters of *Clarissa*: "Released from the bondage of the body, writing is free to *master* it."[39]

The habits of writing and reading could make love both the discourse of two corresponding selves and also of the single self in touch with its own reflecting, revising imagination. By internalizing the erotic drama, however, literacy may sometimes appear to make the lover's real life invisible. Vermeer's masterpiece can symbolize the mutuality of writing and love, and it can countenance the internal play of erotic sensibility, but it cannot tell definitively the history of a woman, the quality of her mind, or the temporal flow of her personal and social relationships. It would take the novel to open up such a figure and turn her into a character whose love we can read precisely.

VI

The relationship of sexuality, letters, and love lies at the heart of any inquiry into the European novel and the history of erotics. Love letters were a means of sexual seduction and of displaced erotic gratification as well, but they were also a means of sanctifying love and sparking the belief that it is the most important thing in life. Eagleton says of *Clarissa* that what is "unattainable in correspondence is the sexual union of bodies" (44) and goes on, "Letters can be no more than 'supplementary' sexual intercourse, eternally standing for the real thing" (45). That may be true for Lovelace, but it can be misleading when "the real thing" becomes something more psychological and diffuse than acts of genital penetration. Writing may be a supplement to sex, but, in the diversity of desire, sex may be a substitute for writing, and both may be surrogates for idealized love, as love and theology may be surrogates for each other.

An outrageous image from Choderlos de Laclos's *Les liaisons dangereuses* (1782) makes clear how dynamic the interaction of physical sex, writing, and erotic longing could be in the romantic revolutions of feeling that would shape the nineteenth century and its fiction. When the Vicomte de Valmont, that epistolary Don Juan, composes a love letter to the virtuous Madame de Tourvel, he makes his desk the naked body of a whore. To his plotting confidante the Marquise de Merteuil, he describes his seminal pen in action: "I have been using her for a desk upon which to write to my fair devotee—to whom I find it amusing I should send a letter written in bed, in the arms, almost, of a trollop (broken off, too, while I committed a downright infidelity), in which I give her an exact account of my situation and my conduct." [40] His letter to the chaste wife begins, "I come, Madame . . . after suffering . . . the turmoil of a consuming passion," and continues, "Indeed my situation, as I write, makes me more than ever aware of the irresistible power of love. . . . the very table upon which I write, never before put to such use, has become in my eyes an altar consecrated to love." [41]

That double entendre appears to be a piece of what Vico calls "poetic wisdom": the body generates language; sexual lust generates the love letter and, beyond that, the whole sublimating process of making a religion of love. But what at first seems to expose simply, if villainously, the hypocrisy or self-deception of those who would idealize and inscribe love is, in fact, full of prophetic irony. The desire for touch is a source of erotic and religious writing, but the need for such writing is also a source for sexual touch. In a perverse way, the union here of the libidinous body with the language of devotion, with the literary consciousness that produces writing, and with a *plot* makes a perfect symbol for both the nineteenth-century novel and the erotic processes of bourgeois individualism.

What matters most for Valmont, the self-styled scourge of love, is not the body and sexual intercourse, but the rhetorical manipulation of language in his letters to two women whose love, the novel shows, means much more to him than mere sexual gratification: unconsciously he really does love them. Sex and physical pleasure here are not ends, but means to writing and to winning love. Mocking the love religion, the libertine, after all, does dedicate the flesh to a higher purpose—winning the heart of Tourvel and the mind of Merteuil. Valmont, like his fellow schemer the Marquise de Merteuil and like Richardson's Lovelace, is an aristocrat who tries to act as if "love" is a sentimental sham hiding what it really signifies: namely, the determining power in life of sexual instinct, class and gender relations, personal will, and genital possession. These despots of the old regime cannot understand the growing popular appeal of the erotic individualism that their narratives show ruining them. Like others, they fall in love, but they do not believe in it. As the image of Valmont at his "desk" illustrates, they are confused about what they want: is it sexual conquest and pleasure? writing that communicates their power and cleverness? erotic devotion? Since they use love and write in its name, they are shown discrediting faith in love for their potentially loving victims and perhaps for their readers as well. Their sardonic intelligence, a product of privileged-class strategies of exploitation and Enlightenment rationality, undercuts religion and savages illusion, but offers nothing that can fulfill religious desire and the longing for moral self-esteem.

Look at Laclos's image again: a woman as a mass of bought flesh upon which to inscribe the humor of a powerful male; a man as the ruthless rhetorical master of erotic consciousness trying to reduce, with the power of the word, another woman—high-minded, kind, intellectually accomplished—to the whore's status as piece of sexual furniture. What could redress the balance of gender power, honor goodness, dissipate this cynical vision, and still express the truths of the libidinous self in the age of individualism? No wonder writers would try to forge an answer in narratives that bring together erotic love and a sense of faith.

VII

We have this account from the end of the eighteenth century: In Madrid, in the days of the Inquisition, Ambrosio, a charismatic young abbot, alone in his cell after preaching a sermon, stares transfixed at a portrait of the Madonna suspended before him. All admire him, especially lovely women; and, full of spiritual pride, he muses on his superiority to the world and its temptations. Over time, he has come to adore his beautiful image of the Virgin; and now, carried away, he longs for her to come alive, wanting to fondle her golden ringlets and kiss her breasts. He wonders if he would abandon his vocation for such a being.

1. Sandro Botticelli, *Birth of Venus*. Galleria degli Uffizi, Florence. Scala/Art Resource, New York.

2. Bronzino, *An Allegory with Venus and Cupid*. Reproduced by courtesy of the Trustees, National Gallery, London.

3. Jan Vermeer, *A Woman Standing at a Virginal*. Reproduced by courtesy of the Trustees, National Gallery, London.

4. John Everett Millais, *Ophelia*. Tate Gallery, London/Art Resource, New York.

5. Diego Velázquez, *The Toilette of Venus* ("The Rokeby Venus"). Reproduced by courtesy of the Trustees, National Gallery, London.

6. Odilon Redon, *Pandora*.
Metropolitan Museum of Art,
New York, bequest of
Alexander M. Bing, 1959.

7. Odilon Redon, *Pandora*.
National Gallery of Art,
Washington, Chester Dale
Collection.

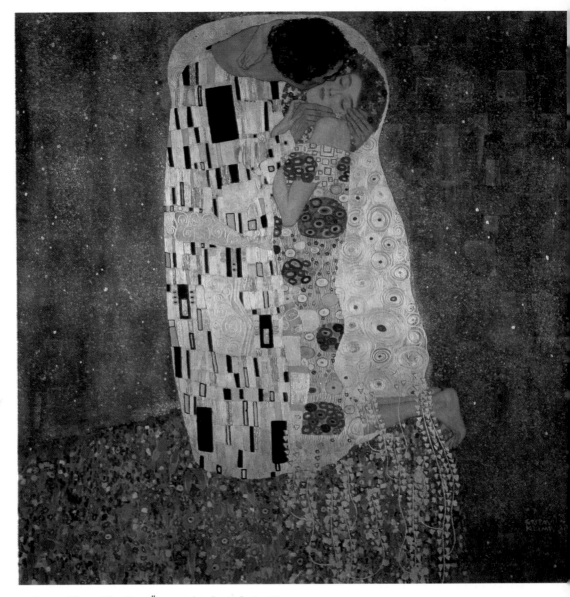

8. Gustav Klimt, *The Kiss*. Österreichische Galerie, Vienna.

Then he checks himself, rationalizing that it is, after all, ideal virtue and the painter's skill he loves. His faith and his dedication to the Virgin are proof, he believes, against any threat to his vows and his calling. But Spain is a place without "true devotion,"[42] where "superstition reigns," crimes are perpetrated by members of religious orders, women are horribly persecuted, matrimony is debased or forbidden, and romantic love is thwarted—all in the name of Christianity.

A novice interrupts Ambrosio's reverie. The youth reveals that "he" is in fact "she," Matilda, a highborn woman in disguise, and she tells him she adores him for his goodness and religious dedication. What she feels for him, she says, is spiritual love, not physical lust. She would give up her life to be near him, but all she asks is that when they die, their bodies shall rest in the same grave. He at first spurns her, but, his vanity flattered and his sympathy aroused, he does not expose her masquerade. Later he is amazed to find that she exactly resembles the beloved Madonna hanging opposite his bed. She tells him that she had her portrait done as the Virgin by "a celebrated Venetian" (I, II, 81) and then conspired to get it to Ambrosio, who prays to it. The seductive Mother of God and Matilda are fused: the painting not only mirrors the monk's desire, it is the means through which he can imagine it.

Soon, she tells him that her feelings have changed and begs for the "enjoyment" (I, II, 89) of his body. Libido overwhelms him, and they have passionate intercourse. The moment is ecstatic, the climax of desire, but he quickly comes to despise her, feeling that he has betrayed his faith and his life. The surge of sexual power, however, makes him delight in the sensual "blessings of Love and Woman" (II, II, 227). He turns hypocrite: wanting the esteem of men and the protection of heaven, he abandons the reality, but not the appearance, of celibacy. This priest can never think of marrying the woman.

After a week of fornication, he loses his desire for her altogether, but not his desire for a lovely virgin. When he begins lusting after Antonia, a pure young woman who takes him as her confessor, he pulls down and grinds to bits his picture of the Madonna, calling her model a "prostitute" (II, III, 244). Antonia's beauty rivals that of "the Medicean Venus," but, with her blonde ringlets, she curiously also seems to look very much like the portrait of Matilda. Eventually Matilda turns out to be an agent of the devil and leads the monk on to commit every sort of moral atrocity, including necrophilia, matricide, incest-rape, murder of his sister, and betrayal of God and the Christian faith. At last he is hurled down by the archfiend to damnation.

All this takes place in Matthew Lewis's lurid novel *The Monk* (1796), which appeared sensationally on the eve of the new century. What crucially bears on erotic faith and being in love in the fiction to come is the novel's displacement of orthodox religious faith by erotic desire and the degradation of organized religion. Erotic vocation can pose a threat to moral piety; but it also follows that, if traditional religious practice and structure can no longer inspire people, then, with a moral reformation of erotics, love might fill the spiritual vacuum.

This morally empty book has precious little faith or love. Obviously Lewis makes a crude attack on Roman Catholicism and, pandering to the prejudices of his English-speaking audience, uses almost anything that will appeal to Protestant fears and indignation—not to mention a prurient fascination with sex. He is a sensationalist, but to understand the biases of British fiction in the following century, we need to concentrate on some of the deeper reasons for *The Monk's* antipopery: namely, the widespread Protestant perceptions that the Church of Rome places its own institutional power and glory above everything; that it is necessarily hostile towards any loyalty to a particular person that might threaten its primacy and control; that, therefore, Roman Catholic influence, directly or indirectly, sets religion and love at odds, disparages romantic love as a dangerous form of individualism, undercuts love as the basis for marriage, and subtly denigrates marriage itself, since its clerisy privileges the unmarried state. The special importance in British novels of the grand matrimonial ideal of a union that would be erotic, romantic, nuptial, moral, and spiritual too thus makes cultural sense, since it grows almost as a religious response out of a clash over the nature of Christianity and faith. The good marriage, which love promotes, could save you from Antichrist. These Anglo-Saxon attitudes, however unfair, shaped nineteenth-century British novels, and they were in large part based on the Roman Church's rule against the clergy marrying and the supposedly terrible consequences of that ban.[43]

In *Violence and the Sacred*, René Girard asserts that religion always needs a scapegoat.[44] In this novel, the old organized religion is itself set up as a scapegoat as if for a new faith, though Lewis cannot imagine that faith. He appropriates the Don Juan myth into the gothic mode, but traditional versions of that myth had opposed the protagonist to orthodox Christianity and set him apart from religion. Here Don Juan is himself a priest of the church, and this internalizing of the tension between erotic and religious vocations, with the implied possibility of merging the two in a single being, signals both the vulnerability of Christian dogma and a new dynamism in the dialogue of faith and love.

VIII

The portrait that so fascinates the monk offers yet another paradigm. Lewis's picture, with its eroticized Virgin, shows how Botticelli's art of love could metamorphose into the English novel; beyond that, it can stand symbolically for the whole body of nineteenth-century fiction that conflates sexual and religious desire. This "Madonna" turning into the love-provoking image of a female character explicitly shows art becoming narrative and religion becoming erotics.

We can read Matilda's plot to manipulate her image—the plan through which she gets her portrait as the Virgin before the monk and sets the story in motion—as a conceit for novelistic fiction. The novel animates a fixed image of desire, sets it moving in time, plots it, brings to it contingency and subjective character, naturalizes and humanizes the supernatural, forms links of cause and effect, and gives specificity to generalized patterns. The use of the portrait tropes the rise and triumph of the novel. The image of the self becomes words in a thick social context.

The Matilda-Madonna in Lewis offers a good rationale for comparing paintings with major novels of the nineteenth century. Our visual heritage is a palimpsest and feeds imaginative language, just as our literary heritage is a record of many voices and texts that shapes the way we see things. In the description of the fictional painting, for example, we can find traces, no doubt unconscious, of a long-forgotten Botticelli, a Bronzino, a Titian, or a Raphael, just as we can see signs of the Bible, Edmund Spenser's False Florimel, and Ann Radcliffe's gothic vision. As a trace of Botticelli's art exists in *The Monk*'s Madonna, so traces of Lewis's Matilda portrait can be found in Victorian readings of the *Birth of Venus*. In Lewis the interactive relationship and reference between the picture and its surrounding life form the narrative reality. Of course the painted female image is part of the linguistic world of the fiction, but within that world, the work of art is brought into being by, and refers to, something beyond itself. The context for Lewis's Madonna shows how narrative pushes us to read a picture (and other artworks) as a vital locus of desire and keeps images alive, erotic, mediative with our world, and freshly charged.

The word "context" here needs emphasis, because it shows the multiple purposes of the complex, fluid process of art. The internal narrative context for the monk's Madonna involves three figures: the "celebrated Venetian," who presumably paints in an artistic tradition with the aesthetic aim of creating a thing of beauty (and a joy forever) and also the economic aim of making money; Matilda, who both commissions the portrait for her own purposes and sits as the object of mimesis; and Ambrosio, the "audience," who has obtained the painting to satisfy certain protean desires, who is deeply affected by it, and whose perception of it changes over time. And beyond the internal context exists the external context of private readers and their desires.

Within the novel, the work of art is evil and idolatrous. Ambrosio adores the icon, and that leads to his damnation. Behind the garish melodrama lies history. The puritan strain in English culture was highly suspicious of the religious heritage of the visual arts, related as it was to the papist tradition. The use of visual

images by continental Roman Catholicism to reinforce its power and to inter-
pose its clergy between Scripture and the laity had led to a Protestant backlash
in Britain that glorified the word and denigrated the image. That in turn would
lead for many reasons to the special moral burdens and expectations of the English novel. The picture in *The Monk* becomes the antipapal word, and the written word of fiction would come to have the moral function of painting and
sculpture in Catholic countries.

The image of a priest lusting after the Madonna turns the Catholic vision of
Bronzino into a moral nightmare. In Christian theology and imagery, as we have
seen, conflicting emotions and tensions cluster around human sexuality and
familial identity. The Church, calling the men and women of its orders "father,"
"brother," "mother," and "sister," expropriates family loyalties and terminology
for its own purpose. Christianity from its first days could not do without both a
Father and Son, and in its second millennium it also had to emphasize the sacred
place of woman, gender, and generation by playing up the importance of Christ's
Virgin Mother (a process that coincided with the emergence of courtly love).
The concept of a virgin mother indicates a religion somehow fixated on sex in
its very obsession with separating faith and love from sexuality. Religion has
often tried to be free of the mortal body by spiritualizing creation and also tried
to revere the generative force by making it divine.[45] Ecclesiastical history reveals
a dogmatic will to idealize or purge the erotic, but Lewis's vision making the
holy Virgin and Mother of God a conceivable sexual partner marks the failure
of that will.

The Monk reads as if the Eros of Bronzino's *Allegory* had become pope. Ambrosio's desire is both heretical and incestuous. Gazing at his holy icon, he
wishes to possess the Mother of Christ and thus identify, through his libido,
with God, usurping His place as both Father and Son. His drive is to be at the
breast, to enter the body that bore God, his own progenitor. The decoded logic
of the scene says that what is consciously repressed in both religious and family
life returns with a vengeance, and it implies a hidden "family romance" in
Christian doctrine. It implies also that in eroticism, there may lurk a will to
displace God—to *replace* Him. On the brink of the nineteenth century, the age
of both the sanctified family and the novel, Ambrosio in front of Matilda's image
previews the erotics in the fiction to come by bringing together religious, incestuous, spiritual, physical, and aesthetic currents and ambitions. One key to
understanding the novels and psychology of the nineteenth century is to see
that Oedipus, Eros, and Christ, like Venus, the Virgin Mother, and the Magdalene, would all blend in the complexes and daily existence of its citizens, its
doctors, its authors and their characters. The ideal *noli me tangere* of Jesus

would change to the great but ambiguous admonition of the novel, "only connect."[46]

"Love and Age," a poem in *The Monk*, honors the source and theme of Anacreon's inspired poetry.

> "Eager He grasps the magic lyre;
> Swift o'er the tuneful chords his fingers move:
> The Feather plucked from Cupid's wing
> Sweeps the too-long neglected string,
> While soft Anacreon sings the power and praise of Love." [II, II, 197]

The lines foretell the relation of love and art in the new century: the feather stands for the implement that makes music, the brush that paints, and, above all, the pen that writes narratives.

IX

In "Fra Lippo Lippi" (1853), the love-struck Victorian Robert Browning turns another picture into a plot and another monk into an artist. Lippi, Botticelli's teacher, must paint ostensibly religious subjects, but he infuses them with erotic meaning. At the end of his monologue, he projects the idea for *The Coronation of the Virgin*, a painting in which he plans to put himself, a "moonstruck" sinner out of place among "the celestial presence," but nevertheless presented to heaven and praised for his art by a passionate young woman he calls "a sweet angelic slip of a thing." Narrative absorbs the work, as Lippi, associating his guardian angel with the prior's affectionate mistress, then imagines an irate husband showing up in his picture, and finally he, the painter, running off hand in hand with her to salvation—his soul and his art saved by their erotic attachment. Love makes his art and his faith, as it did for his creator.

The case of the Brownings, those celebrated nineteenth-century lovers and writers, exemplifies the whole dynamic process that fused being in love, the quest for faith, and novelistic fiction. Two passionate, promising writers, brought up to take Christianity seriously—one trapped by her father and her health in alien maidenhood, the other disappointed in his vocation—read each other's verse admiringly; without having met her, Robert writes Elizabeth Barrett and tells her he loves her poems and he loves her, too. Letters lead to meetings and more intimate letters and mutual love. The correspondents pour out their souls and devotion to one another. Defying the patriarch, they devise a love plot to marry and elope to Italy, which they carry out. Writing thus leads to mating and then to pregnancy and the birth of their child. They fittingly call this son Pen.[47] As Pen grows and matures, his parents' literary careers flourish. Poetry of erotic faith flows from both mother and father. One day, long after

Elizabeth's death and shortly before his own, Robert reverently hands over to Pen (who turns out rather a libertine and fathers illegitimate offspring) a packet of all the letters between himself and Elizabeth Barrett of Wimpole Street. This correspondence, a *locus classicus* of the Victorian love creed, Pen publishes after his father's death. It, in turn, leads to more writing—plays, movies, and scholarship—that mythologizes the Brownings and makes their own love story better known than their poetry.

Pens, penned, more pens, Pen, more pens, and still more pens. Erotic desire, religious training, and repression all motivate the writing that creates erotic desire that expresses itself in writing that leads to love that leads to sexual intercourse that produces a child and more love and writing; and then the child produces the writing that expresses sacred love and reads as a homage to erotic faith. These things are a parable for the recirculation of erotic desire, flesh, the will to imprint a valid faith, aesthetic impulse, and writing that animate the nineteenth-century literary imagination.

X

One more love story will show where this study is going.

A kingdom is in crisis, and its prince sits brooding in his castle. He has been immensely popular with his people, but his first counsellor describes him as now "bewitched."[48] The chief priest speaks out against him for betraying God's trust.[49] It is said that the prince is madly in love, held in thrall by an enchantress who wants to rule the kingdom. His enemies say their love breaches established faith because she has mated with others.

His counsellors give him the choice of giving her up and reigning, or following her into exile. He makes his decision, and then, from the palace, he speaks to the multitudes: "You must believe me when I tell you that I have found it impossible to carry the heavy burden of responsibility and to discharge my duties as King as I would wish to do without the help and support of the woman I love."[50]

The time is December 1936; the crisis is over the British Monarchy; the prince is, of course, Edward VIII, who has just abdicated; and the lady, twice-married and soon to be twice-divorced, is the future Duchess of Windsor, Wallis Warfield Simpson. The abdication speech is a remarkable event in the history of love. The ex-king's words go out on the airwaves—words heard by more listeners than have ever before heeded a royal voice. Around the globe, the abdication and the subsequent marriage are presented as the romance of the century.[51] The news flutters pulses, sells papers, nourishes the new publicity culture, and echoes through distance and time. I vaguely recall, two decades later in the 1950s, some movie star mouthing a lyric for romantic dreamers, "I dreamt that at my coronation / I shocked every foreign nation / By giving up my throne to marry you!"

The way was well prepared for such an act as Edward's and for the huge public response: sympathy from many; comprehension, at least, even with strong disapproval, from almost everyone else. The sentiment, *I cannot live without the woman I love,* touched people, reminded them of the actual power of love, and of their own lives and priorities, be they God, money, comfort, or duty before love, power before intimacy, or love before all.

If the whole affair is not to seem crazy, we must perceive Edward's love as a mode of faith—unlikely as that may now seem, given his subsequent life. His vocation is to "the woman I love." There is, in his language, an assumption that his faith can be known and comprehended by great masses of people: "You must believe me when I tell you" speaks in the imperative of the true believer: *Not only do I believe, but you must come to understand this faith too.* The novel has proselytized for that faith. In the most extensive and elaborate fables the world has ever seen, novelists have embodied some highly debatable, but profound and intellectually provoking, lessons: that people complete themselves and fulfill their destinies only with another; that there is no religious marriage without love; and that in the quest for lasting love and the experience of being in love, men and women find their real worth and character.

The broadcast of Edward's words, however, does mark a change in how love would come to be perceived. After "the love story of the century" had been told, not first in a book, but over the air, in movie newsreels, in the popular press, and in songs and records, the novel could no longer be claimed as the chief site and source for erotic faith. Fiction has had to share with the electronic media, the press, the recording industry, advertising and the whole world of popular entertainment the labor of telling what it means to be in love. It was the novelists, however, who created the job.

2 The Fortunate Fall: Jane Austen's
Pride and Prejudice (1813)

Jane Austen . . . was committed to the ideal of intelligent love.
  LIONEL TRILLING[1]

*Generations of readers have received its love-story as archetypically romantic,
and they have been right to do so.*
  MARILYN BUTLER[2]

I

What does it mean to fall in love? Why does it happen and what do people read
into it? Near the end of *Pride and Prejudice* Elizabeth Bennet asks Darcy "to
account for his having ever fallen in love with her."[3] "I can comprehend your
going on charmingly, when you had once made a beginning; but what could set
you off in the first place?" He muses, unable to be precise: "It is too long ago. I
was in the middle before I knew that I *had* begun." Full of wonder, she asks,
"Did you admire me for my impertinence?" and he replies, "For the liveliness
of your mind, I did" (III, XVIII, 262).

Her curiosity about falling in love and his answer, "for the liveliness of your
mind," matter intensely to our modern culture. No subject could be sweeter or
more useful in establishing a newly engaged couple's intimacy; but Darcy's reason for love does not exactly fit such earlier famous literary lovers as Tristan,
Romeo, Don Quixote, Don Juan, Milton's Adam, Tom Jones, Richardson's Lovelace, or Werther. Love, in this novel, gives a very bright woman a chance for
distinction and relative freedom (in Elizabeth's case, we might say freedom from
relatives), and what wins this love is her energetic intelligence and her individuality. No wonder, then, that *Pride and Prejudice*, as influential as any love story
in English, has been the archetypal romantic novel for countless readers and
imitators.

In it, however, Austen, as she affirms love, alludes to many of the problems
and issues of erotic feeling and being in love that would touch nineteenth-century British novelists. She meditates on the familial relationships that determine the shape of love and desire; she draws connections between love and
ambition for power and money; she shows the relation between love and sex
appeal; and she represents the problematic nature of passion, the necessity of
repression, and the differing functions of love for the two genders. Still, the key
to the optimistic tone and the lasting appeal of the novel lies in the fact that a

woman's mind and lively talents win the love that gives her the chance for a distinguished life.

Pride and Prejudice depends on a rich and influential man falling devotedly in love with a relatively poor and powerless young woman. After *Pamela* such a premise had become commonplace in fiction, but Austen gives it new freshness. She seems to have found the germ of love faith in her reading of novelists such as Richardson, Fielding, Fanny Burney, and Maria Edgeworth; and many of her own novels, which feature the potency of erotic imagination, express both the miracle and the metaphorical reality of the Cinderella myth—that malleable plot whose amazing significance was getting buried in banal formula fiction. It surprises Elizabeth that Darcy should find himself in love with her, and Austen makes it clear how wonderful it is that such a man should fall in love at all. Their match seems perfectly reasonable at the end, but at the beginning there is no very compelling reason why he should fall in love with Elizabeth and marry her. And if we see that the relative status of these two somehow reflects the historical condition of inequality between the sexes, we can understand why such a clear-sighted and skeptical writer as Austen would celebrate love, the pap of novels, even with all its dangers and foolishness. She knows how men can exploit love and women—that's one theme of the book—but she imagines love as a force that can ameliorate that exploitation.

Austen shows how, from her historical perspective on relations between the sexes, men could seem princes and women scullery maids. What sets this story apart from and advances it beyond the Cinderella or *Pamela* pattern (servant girl elevated to sovereign lady) is the active flash of mind that distinguishes Elizabeth and draws Darcy's love. Though she comes to love him by the end, it is not at all clear that she ever falls in love with him. In their romance, man falls in love with woman, and that fall into love is the fortunate fall of Austen's erotic faith.[4]

The world in Austen is often a sordid, dull, menacing, and disappointing place; without love it would be pointless and, despite its polish, quite savage. But the power of love in *Pride and Prejudice* works to generate faith, hope, and charity. Darcy's love for Elizabeth curbs his arrogance and makes him a kinder and better man. The force of this love neutralizes the effects of Wickham's predatory seduction, Mr. Bennet's irresponsibility, Mrs. Bennet's vulgarity, and Collins's and Lady Catherine's class stupidity as well. Because Darcy falls in love, things work out.

II

"Falling in love" is a curious phrase. It connotes something involuntary, a loss of control, a sliding away of sure ground and an immersion in a sea of romantic desire. It suggests the sudden attraction of an erotic gravity that irresistibly seizes one. It means that your state of mind undergoes an abrupt and drastic change. The phrase and image also carry with them the sense of a slippage, a lessening of willpower, and a loss of body control and balance. The words connote a lowering, a movement down, away from the ideal, and they may hint at that original fall of man. And notice—the point is essential in thinking about love and its implications in Austen—what else this phrase might describe if, in a particular culture, a man or his status should be considered, in the typical spatial imagery that inheres in our language, higher than, superior to, or "above" a woman: falling in love would bring him by linguistic logic closer to her, down to her level; but if a woman falls she risks sinking even further beneath the man.

It follows that a woman must be wary about falling in love. Behind Elizabeth's musing about why Darcy fell in love lurk questions and subjects that must have been vitally important to a young woman in Austen's time: "What is especially lovable about me for this particular man?" "How can I make this attraction last?" "How do you know when you're in love with someone?" "Can you love somebody that you have not fallen in love with?" "Am I in love?" "Why haven't I fallen in love with you?"

Characters in *Pride and Prejudice*, especially women in the early chapters, refer often to falling in love. The linguistic constructions "in love" and "in love with" imply the distinction and the separation between the state of love and the object of love. The contrast between the verb "to love" and the prepositional phrase "in love with" points up the difference between doing and being, between will and accident, between choice and fate. The words "in love with" may also connote the mutual positioning of both lover and love object in the same realm of desire, but that realm may be the inner space of subjectivity and psychological projection or an engulfing social space which is larger than, and exterior to, themselves. "In love" might also suggest the possibility of its opposite, "out of love," as the phrases "in office" or "in debt" suggest their opposites, "out of office" and "out of debt." "Falling" is also a word of adventure and suggests narrative, for example, *She fell: and then?* "Falling in love" implies the possibility of turbulence as well as absorbing experience. It suggests both the fixation and flux of romantic desire, and it describes a volatile emotional condition in which need and affection focus on another and commingle for a time. For how long a time and with what end are the implicit questions of a plot. *Pride and Prejudice* shows how the whole enterprise of the nineteenth-century novel might literally "fall in love."

Here is how Elizabeth speaks when Darcy tells her that liveliness of mind drew him to fall in love:

"You may as well call it impertinence at once. . . . The fact is, that you were sick of civility, of deference, of officious attention. You were disgusted with the women who were always speaking and looking, and thinking for *your* approbation alone. I roused, and interested you, because I was so unlike *them*. . . . There—I have saved you the trouble of accounting for it; and really, all things considered, I begin to think it perfectly reasonable. To be sure, you knew no actual good of me—but nobody thinks of *that* when they fall in love" (III, XVIII, 262).

Love in this passage seems both a mysterious and a reasonable thing—like religion—but falling in love transgresses orthodox moral categories.

Reading Austen, you can sense a big change coming: the days of feminine deference are numbered. Elizabeth's speech—playful, teasing, rapid, funny, and progressive—enacts the very liveliness of mind that Darcy loves and desires. Their talk, like the whole of *Pride and Prejudice*, bears profoundly on the erotic faith in the novels and the life of the following century. Singularity in a woman rouses love in a man, and that love offers her hope to satisfy the crying need for distinction that her words express. Her lively mind craves and works to create a distinguished life—distinguished in the precise sense that she wants and has the potential to fly far beyond the mundane level of her mother, her sisters, and most of the other conventionally limited women around her. Austen shows her thinking that gratuitous love from a generous, well-placed man might offer her the leisure and support to protect her and let her further develop her rising consciousness and power. It's an old dream with a new twist.

"For the liveliness of your mind. . . ." It is hard to conceive of a more resonant bit of prose. That liveliness means not just abstract intelligence, but those things that make Austen's own fiction as well as Elizabeth's thought and speech vital: the comic sense, the critical spirit, the drama of trying to learn how to love, and the great personal struggle not to be stifled and deadened by the oppressive folly of daily life and historical accident.

The lively mind conveys the individual quality of a human being that has been called personality, and the idea of the distinctive, unique *personality* is to erotic faith what the concept of the individual soul is to Christian faith. Not surprisingly, the spirit of the "one and only" animates both romantic love and the novel. Austen imagines that a woman could be loved for the particular qualities of her mind, that her mental energy could be the focus of her attraction, that her complex psychological vitality, rather than her mere beauty, her sensual appeal, her wealth, her superior virtue, calculated charm, conventional docility, or any of the other traditional feminine allurements, could provoke the fall into love. That configuration opens up a future.

With "liveliness of mind," Austen, in effect, pronounces *herself* lovable, for that of course is what her novels preeminently offer. The primary desires she animates in *Pride and Prejudice* are the wish to unite the quality of her being with male power and opportunity and the wish to be justly recognized as distinguished. These are the erotic aims of Elizabeth and they are the aims of Austen. In the phrase and in the whole book, she uses fiction as a means of meditating on love, generating it, incorporating it, and creating a community of rational erotic understanding. The real eroticism in Austen's nature shows through in her commitment to fiction as a loving vocation and a form of love.

Look at the exact words of pride she wrote when she received the first published copy of *Pride and Prejudice*: "I have got my own darling child from London."[5] Her love life goes into the novel, and she dotes on the issue of her lively intelligence. Put that gynecological image next to the proud passage from *Northanger Abbey* when she digresses to chide those who condemn novels and the "labour" of novelists:

Let us [novelists] not desert one another. We are an injured *body*. Although our productions have afforded more extensive and unaffected pleasure than those of any other *literary corporation* in the world, no species of composition has been so much decried. And while the abilities of the nine-hundredth abridger of the *History of England*, or the *man* who collects and publishes in a volume some dozen lines of Milton, Pope and Prior, with a paper from the *Spectator*, and a chapter from Sterne, are eulogized . . . —there seems almost a general wish of . . . undervaluing *the labour* of the novelist, and of slighting the performances which have only genius, wit, and taste to recommend them. . . . "And what are you reading . . . ?" "Oh! It is only a novel! . . . only *Cecelia*, [a tribute to her predecessor Fanny Burney] . . . or *Belinda* [homage to Maria Edgeworth]"; or, in short, only some work in which the greatest powers of the mind are displayed, in which the most thorough knowledge of human nature, the happiest delineation of its varieties, the liveliest effusions of wit and humour, are conveyed in the best-chosen language.[6] [italics mine]

She projects her identity, her faith, and her love into her chosen medium. As she pokes fun at pompous men and protests the comparatively short shrift given women novelists, Austen's rhetoric implicitly brands her own novelistic labor as creative, passionate, and maternal. The longing she expresses that the lively intelligence of a woman and a novel might conflate and win the distinction they deserve, finds its form and being in the novelist's "darling child."

III

To make liveliness of mind the primary agent of eroticism is to imagine that love is in the head. Austen does. Before Darcy recognizes Elizabeth's beauty and goes after it, the text shows him falling under the spell of her "uncommonly intelligent" face and her "easy playfulness" (I, VI, 15). He is "bewitched" (I, X, 35) by Elizabeth, and the word stands out oddly in a book where superstition and metaphysics hardly figure. When Austen uses it, she is stressing the miraculous, slightly spooky process by which Darcy or anyone falls in love. Such language points up psychological links between erotic attraction and the uncanny or supernatural. It also shows the tension and potential clash between the institutions of moral orthodoxy and erotic emotion. Furthermore, terms she uses from the lexicon of amorous discourse—like "charm," "bewitch," and "in danger"—reveal the mystery that surrounds female erotic power over members of a physically stronger gender. To Austen there is something both heterodox and extraordinary about Elizabeth's charisma over this man of exalted station— an erotic energy operating beyond either strictly materialist categories or the realm of orthodox religious faith.

Elizabeth, in her taunting, witty way, is "my lady tongue,"[7] verbally and sexually provocative in the tradition of Shakespeare's Beatrice and Rosalind and Congreve's Millamant. In Austen, sex appeal meshes with an aggressive sense of humor. The book conveys how much fun she is to be around and shows, in Darcy's plunge into love, just what a potent love tonic a fine sense of humor can be. Gay and sensible about her humor ("I hope I never ridicule what is wise or good. Follies and nonsense, whims and inconsistencies *do* divert me, I own, and I laugh at them whenever I can" [I, XI, 39]), Elizabeth can teach Darcy a thing or two and fascinate him. Notice how she begins to overcome his prejudice against her with a comic paradox that cuts through sentimental rubbish: "I wonder who first discovered the efficacy of poetry in driving away love!" (I, IX, 30). To Darcy's reply, "I have been used to consider poetry as the *food* of love," she answers, "I am convinced that one good sonnet will starve it entirely away." The point is that she mocks conventional poses that trivialize love or take it out of the complex social context that novels can represent; she comes to it with fresh iconoclasm that energizes the subject. Love is individual. But Austen is also making the subtle point that her "baby," the novel, that linguistic blend of personal and social relations, is the proper new mode for treating love and its particularity.

Part of Elizabeth's liveliness of mind includes her sexual perception and susceptibility. Whenever she sees a man, she notes exactly how much or how little he attracts her. That Wickham can excite her imagination, mistaken though her first impressions about him are, proves her susceptible to sexual attraction. Austen's faith here is that men might love the best and most vital kind of personality, which includes libido; that the richer the woman's inner self, the greater the range and complexity of her being, the more lovable she might be. Darcy desires Elizabeth because she is strong-minded, and he can respect her: she seems to have the most lively mind and libido he has come across. No sycophant, she teases and mocks him. As it is probably a greater honor to be loved by a Ph.D. than by a spaniel, so to be loved and accepted by a relatively free, discriminating and intelligent person is a greater triumph for the ego than to be loved by a nullity. What looks hard to get seems intrinsically valuable.

But something more specific is going on: we can see here the sexual desire that the aura of a particular woman's imagination can excite, that is, a stirring of the male libido that opens to the appeal of a magnetic feminine strength. The idea of attaching and possessing the affections of a rebellious, impudent spirit can be challenging and erotic. Liveliness promises liveliness. Earlier novelists such as Richardson and Choderlos de Laclos had created independent female characters that men desire and even love, but still see as prizes to possess and/or creatures to be broken to their misogynist and sadomasochistic wills. Austen also touches on the erotic power of feminine defiance that would haunt the amorous imagination of the century and reach its apotheosis in the Carmen myth. But the faith of her text is that love can help disarm the impulse to rape the integrity of a woman and work to give an expanding feminine soul the space it craves.

Botticelli's wittiest painting, *Venus and Mars* (fig. 14), which the Victorians rediscovered and brought to London, symbolizes nicely the function and nature of love in this novel.[8] Stupid-looking Mars lies sprawled, gaping in sleep, his weapons of war and his armor scattered beside him. His crude force has been tamed by the beautiful, robed, dominant female figure resting opposite him. This Venus is wide awake, her intelligent-looking, intent, lovely, slightly disdainful face gazing knowingly into the distance. Comic imps, sporting, laughing, looking back at her, like children of her thoughts, play with Mars's destructive weapons, crawl in his armor, and jestingly prepare to sound in his ear the battle-announcing conch. They parody and make silly the antics and trappings of raw force and cavort in mockery of violence and mental torpor. Love has disarmed Mars, put him to sleep and become the focal point of being. He seems to have *fallen in love*. The picture fuses elegant desirability, feminine power, and a pointed, ironic sense of the ridiculous in order to control and satirize brutishness and honor civilized life. So does love in *Pride and Prejudice*.

"Disarming" perfectly characterizes the function and effect of love in the novel. Wickham, would-be follower of Mars, treats life as a campaign of sly combat, seduction, and plunder, but the power of love, acting through Darcy, controls him. As for Darcy, love melts his proud churlishness. It pacifies class conflict, opens the borders of class, saps male chauvinism, and draws a truce in the war of the sexes. It offers the peace that allows the wounds of prejudice, neglect, and disdain to heal.

IV

Darcy and Elizabeth may be famous lovers, but I want to stress another of her relationships, as important as any in the book: the one she has with her father. A remark by him at the beginning shows a cultural hostility that demands a "disarming" counteraction. To his wife who chides him for favoring Lizzy over her sisters, Mr. Bennet says, "They have none of them much to recommend them . . . ; they are all silly and ignorant like other girls" (I, I, 2). That attitude of male imperiousness, so casually uttered, has devastating import. What can begin to change it and lessen its effect? Two things necessary, Austen imagines, are the distinction of love and a rational erotic transference.

"But Lizzy has something more of quickness than her sisters," adds Bennet after slighting his daughters and the female sex. Most serious readers of Austen sense a feminine yearning for patrimony in her novels. The longing for a loving father figure shows through in nearly all of her heroines. Elizabeth, however, *is* distinguished by her father and she very much resembles him. When the critical Darcy picks her from among other women, he only repeats what, in a way, has happened to her before. In her family, she is already the chosen one. Father and suitor love her for the same reason: "quickness," that is, "liveliness of mind."

In the father-daughter relationship, Austen gets at the power of incestuous impulse and sublimation in shaping erotic love—the power that would move the minds and form the art of major novelists in the language from the Brontës and Dickens to Joyce, Woolf, Faulkner, and Nabokov. The bond between Elizabeth and her father is an emotionally charged one. Austen lived, read, and wrote in a time when social history was heightening the desire for the continuity and affectionate relations of family. In Fanny Burney, her early mentor as a novelist, the drive to please the father and embrace his identity stands out, sometimes in sad fashion. Here are Burney's dedicatory verses to her father from *Evelina*— lines Austen read:

> O author of my being!—far more dear
> To me than light, than nourishment, or rest,
> Hygieia's blessings, Rapture's burning tear,
> Or the life blood that mantles in my breast!
> If in my heart the love of Virtue glows,
> 'Twas planted there by an unerring rule;
> From thy example the pure flame arose,
> Thy life, my precept—thy good works, my school.
> . . . .
> Oh! of my life at once the source and joy!
> If e'er thy eyes these feeble lines survey,
> Let not their folly their intent destroy;
> Accept the tribute—but forget the lay.[9]

I quote these lines—worthy of the early Goneril—because they reveal the kind of filial emotion and potential for internal contradiction that a bright, upper-middle-class girl might have to face in the patriarchy of Austen's time.[10] Also, standing as they do at the beginning of a narrative about a girl in search of patrimony, the lines serve as an epigraph announcing the unity of family relations and the bourgeois novel. Moreover they show how, symbolically, the writing of novels, for women, might be an act of dedication to the father and that for which he stands; they also more subtly imply that novels might be not only a means of reaching the father, but of transcending him too. For Austen, as for Burney, the making of books was inseparable from the quest for filial piety and familial love. It is likely that for each of these pioneering authors, writing a novel was a way of trying to find and make love; and, if we consider that likelihood without moral sentimentalizing, it can help us understand the prominence of erotic intention and the theme of the eroticized family in the nineteenth-century novel.

Pride and Prejudice may be the story of a young man in possession of a good fortune getting a wife, but it is also the love story of a young woman's successful psychological transference from parent to mate. Elizabeth is favored and loved by Mr. Bennet but demeaned as a female; empowered by his approval and the wit he sires in her, but hampered by the pull of his identity and his role model of cynicism and detachment. A primary tension in Elizabeth, in the novel, in Austen—and in the modern Western world—is the conflict between the wish to repeat and preserve the pattern in which the father's special bond makes the chosen daughter feel early distinction and the possibility of identifying with male status and ambition, and the strong, contrary wish to break the pattern, since it also has the potential of stifling personal identity and of breeding, in a woman, an insidious form of self-contempt. "Lizzy" (Bennet's pet name for her) needs both to embrace and to break free of her father, to gain independence without losing the advantages his mind and regard give her. Romantic love from a worthy man, Austen imagines, might act to reconcile this conflict.

She writes into her narrative the presence of the parental third person in Elizabeth's interaction with Darcy; and the delicate psychology of this cross-generational, triangular love relationship ought not to be missed. The text shows an almost classical Freudian transfer of feeling from father to lover: first Elizabeth shifts repressed, latent hostility, then respect and affection, from Bennet to Darcy. She appears to have learned the prejudice she first feels towards Darcy at her father's knee. Darcy's early rude words, overheard by her at the dance, express the kind of sexist disdain and cynical irresponsibility that Mr. Bennet shows. When Bingley points to Elizabeth, Darcy says, "She is tolerable; but not handsome enough to tempt *me*; and I am in no humour at present to give consequence to young ladies who are slighted by other men" (I, III, 7). Her delight in the ridiculous proves how much she is her father's daughter, and she seems to live by his words: "For what do we live, but to make sport for our neighbours, and laugh at them in our turn?" (III, XV, 251). In the first half of the book, Elizabeth relishes punishing Darcy's original pride and prejudice, and one reason she does is that they are so like qualities in her father that she, the father's favorite, might resent but could not directly rebel against.

Her feeling of gratitude and esteem, even of humility, towards Darcy in the second half (an attitude that some critics have deplored) marks among other things a transference of respect and love from Bennet, whom she learns to assess in an adult manner, to one who not only is more deserving but also much less inhibiting to her self-realization. She needs to reject the father, but she needs protection and continuity as well. After all, it was by the choice of the father that she first found distinction. Austen describes in Elizabeth a desire to believe in a responsible and powerful male figure together with a drive to be chosen by such a figure. Not surprisingly this wish characterizes Elizabeth's later feelings for Darcy. She needs faith in order, authority, self, and affection. Love for Elizabeth, as it is so often in life, is a quest both to flee and to possess the parent.

Living at the heart of modern love faith and nineteenth-century British fiction, I repeat, lies incestuous feeling. By that I do not mean conscious desire for physical incest, but a romantic desire for intimacy with the relative—a longing for a meeting of minds, a mingling of spirits, a wish to possess and be possessed by the affection of the relative, to love and be the relative's beloved. Nineteenth-century novels make clear that the repression and censoring of sexual discourse actually allowed for a much freer expression of implicitly incestuous material and relationships, since overt sex was taboo and therefore could not creep into the text. The incest exists in the structure of the mind: the *role* of parent, child, or sibling crossbreeds with the *role* of erotic lover. Desire shows itself in an effort to recapture, relive, or represent the intimacy of the imagination of incest. The institution of the nuclear family and "affective individualism" would naturally charge family relationships with strong emotional tensions and longings— some of them highly amorous, some of them murderous towards family rivals for love. What often stirs erotic love is a drive for the most intimate kind of communication with another person and one that cannot be shared by anyone else. Before Freud, novelists did a good job of showing how this drive grows up in the smoldering emotional life of familial groups. Think of the unconscious but definite mother-daughter rivalry between Mrs. Bennet and Elizabeth for Bennet's regard, a kind of muted incestuous cold war of which Austen may have had some firsthand knowledge.[11] Family means familiarity—and familiarity breeds eros as well as contempt. If, in the nineteenth century, literature taught that the child is father to the man, it also taught, as it does in this century, that the family is progenitor of the child's mate.

Austen handles with economy Elizabeth's complex and moving tie with her father. Two conversations between them, crucial to the tone and meaning of the novel, make the father-daughter relationship resonate. When Bingley seems to have let down her sister Jane, and Elizabeth finds herself intrigued by Wickham, we get this dialogue.

"So, Lizzy, . . . your sister is crossed in love I find. I congratulate her. Next to being married, a girl likes to be crossed in love a little now and then. It is something to think of, and gives her a sort of distinction among her companions. When is your turn to come? You will hardly bear to be long outdone by Jane. Now is your time. Here are officers enough at Meryton to disappoint all the young ladies in the country. Let Wickham be *your* man. He is a pleasant fellow, and would jilt you creditably."

"Thank you, Sir, but a less agreeable man would satisfy me. We must not all expect Jane's good fortune."

"True," said Mr. Bennet, "but it is a comfort to think that, whatever of that kind may befall you, you have an affectionate mother who will always make the most of it." [II, I, 95–96]

When people say Austen is a great novelist, that kind of writing is what they mean. This scene flashes with the terrible irony of those supposedly casual encounters between parents and maturing children in which volcanoes of emotion are brewing beneath the surface. Bennet's worldly talk suggests his cynicism, his clever, corrosive sexism, his irresponsibility, and his fear of directly expressed emotion. But it also suggests bitter comic faith, intelligence, and his deep concern and feeling for this one person close to him who can understand him. It shows a distrust of passion and falling in love (the sort of blind plunge that left him mated to a dunderhead) and his ambiguity about Elizabeth's love life—his hopes and fears for her. It also shows his wish, through the conspiracy that ironic form creates, to deepen and strengthen his union with his daughter, not just against the mother, but against the inevitable stupidity and pain of the world. And the passage suggests the strength of Elizabeth's tie to her father, as she follows his lead into irony and a coolness she does not feel. She takes up his style, thus denying her pain and sisterly distress for Jane, and suppresses her own need to examine with someone she trusts her feelings about Wickham. The moving, special closeness of this father-daughter bond comes through in the dialogue, as does the seductive power of irony—that toggle switch of language which proclaims both our sophisticated ability and our inherent inability to communicate precisely and intimately. So too does the violation of her integrity and growing independence—that strategic raid of co-option so common to a favorite parent in dealing with a favorite child—and the corrupting fatalism from which she must free herself. Austen, with her dialogic imagination, conveys such a sense of interesting, reverberating life about these two characters that a discerning reader might want to give a cheer for the privileging of literary texts.

Elizabeth, though she still, like a good little disciple, adopts her father's mode of ironic discourse, is here and now learning that she must consider independently the subjects of distinction in love, her own love life, and marriage—the subjects he raises—since he so obviously minimizes what must matter most to her: a woman's fate. Beneath the ironic insouciance, life is changing.

Different, but as highly charged, is their interview at the end, when Elizabeth tells him that she means to marry Darcy, whom Bennet thought she detested.

> "Have you any other objection," said Elizabeth, "than your belief of my indifference?"
>
> "None at all. We all know him to be a proud, unpleasant sort of man; but this would be nothing if you really liked him."
>
> "I do, I do like him," she replied with tears in her eyes, "I love him. Indeed he has no improper pride. He is perfectly amiable. You do not know what he really is; then pray do not pain me by speaking of him in such terms."
>
> ". . . I have given him my consent. . . . But let me advise you to think better of it. I know your disposition, Lizzy, I know that you could be neither happy nor respectable, unless you truly esteemed your husband; unless you looked up to him as a superior. Your lively talents would place you in the greatest danger in an unequal marriage. You could scarcely escape discredit and misery. My child, let me not have the grief of seeing *you* unable to respect your partner in life. You know not what you are about."
>
> Elizabeth, still more affected, was earnest and solemn in her reply; and at length . . . she did conquer her father's incredulity. [III, XVII, 260]

Most of the irony, that mode of distancing and defense, is gone except for the major irony that just when they have their most sincere communication, the primacy of this relationship is over for Elizabeth. Significantly, this is as emotional a moment as she has in the novel, a moment when she publicly moves from affection to love. Austen has her directly voice that love to her father rather than to Darcy as she might have in the preceding chapter or in the scene that follows. Her tears, her avowal—the passion that she feels—all come out to Bennet, not Darcy. But it is Darcy's love that now allows her to speak self-assertively to her father: "I do, I do like him. . . . I love him." That announcement, echoing the cadence of a wedding ceremony and ensuring a marriage, is an act of faith and a pledge to the future. It also, in this setting, insures continuity with the past.

In turn, Austen has the father talk to Elizabeth with a frank concern that he has never before managed. He shows a responsibility, misguided though it is, that she has always longed for. What Bennet tells her is fascinating. Wrong about her esteem for Darcy and perhaps about her, he still makes the telling point that if she did not love and honor the intelligence of her husband, she would despise him and might fall in love with someone who *would* be her "match." He makes conjugal love the necessary antidote to sexual obsession.

Though all seems changed between father and daughter, it is not: strong identification remains, and identification with another being has erotic undertones and consequences. Notice that she has really accepted just the kind of man

Bennet would choose for her, one who *is* superior and whom she can esteem, one who, in the father's eyes, would play the same role for her that the father has played in her youth. The basic emotions of love as she tries to define them for herself are "gratitude and esteem" (III, IV, 190), and Austen imagines that these typically filial emotions that Elizabeth feels for Darcy and would like to feel for her father are just the ones that Bennet thinks are proper to feel for a mate. We sense, also, the longing that his daughter should feel them for him. In her erotic life, she identifies with his wishes. The flow of love from Darcy, a love that as we have seen was sparked by just those lively talents that Mr. Bennet has generated and praised in her, lets her remain true to her father while transcending him. The new love grows out of the old. Ironically, Austen, who virtually ignores childhood in her fiction, nevertheless here grounds love in a structure of desire based on the parent-child relationship. Love, the young woman's escape from the family trap, is bred in the family.

                    V

Elizabeth sees proper love as companionate, complementary, and forming a fine aesthetic entity. She thinks that she and Darcy would bring to one another just the qualities that each needs. "She began now to comprehend that he was exactly the man, who, in disposition and talents, would most suit her. His understanding and temper, though unlike her own, would have answered all her wishes. It was an union that must have been to the advantage of both" (III, VIII, 214). When Jane near the end asks her how long she has loved him, she answers facetiously, "I believe I must date it from my first seeing his beautiful grounds at Pemberley" (III, XVII, 258), but Austen is getting at a truth other than the desire for wealth. Much earlier, when she first sees Pemberley, after turning down Darcy, she realizes "to be mistress of Pemberley might be something!" (III, I, 167). The reason is aesthetic, as well as materialistic. In the alchemy of love, the material and the immaterial can be transmuted. The estate is a perfect blend of natural beauty with civilized taste and art. It combines utility with real elegance, delightful scenery with lovely architecture, wealth and physical substance with idealistic spirit and the good of its dependents. In all its harmony, it represents for Elizabeth what her life has lacked and what she aspires to have and to be. It becomes for her not so much a fetish for Darcy's love, or even a proof of his excellent qualities—though it is both—as an embodiment and symbol of what their life together might be.

Pemberley is, of course, not real estate, but a property of the imagination which does not exist independently from the erotic attraction between Darcy and Elizabeth. My point is this: novelists of love must make readers sense the power of their characters' amorous desire, and at the start of the nineteenth century, one way to do that was to join the bourgeois dream of owning a landed estate with a thoughtful young woman's hope to marry and be loved by a worthy man. In life, love generates sweet and glorious perceptions in lovers' eyes, and in literature, the need to make palpable the transforming influence and energy of love, that immaterial tidal wave, generates fetishistic description. How do you show what Elizabeth most desires? How do you make clear that love may be rational? How do you make Elizabeth's change of heart towards Darcy plausible, and how do you show the irresistibility of his love? By thinking up and setting down Pemberley, symbol of a distinguished way of life in which the erotic is happily joined with aesthetics and economics.

Theorists of love often deplore the supposed confusion and ambiguity in the word *love*. We say, for example, "I love Patricia," "I love ballet," "I love Big Sur," and "I love peanut butter." The loveliness of Pemberley, however, suggests that such common usage might be more precise and revealing than conventional thinkers, caught up by repression, have supposed, and those seemingly disparate things that we say we love might have a closer connection to our eroticism than we commonly allow. Eros, a deity who lives and works through metaphor, may be, for many, an immanent god.

If Pemberley, the erotic destination of the narrative, always has erotic connotations, so has dancing, which opens courtship in the novel. "To be fond of dancing was a certain step towards falling in love" (I, III, 5), says Austen at the beginning, and in the first volume she uses the custom of dance as occasion, means, and metaphor for amorous relationship. All dances are, more or less, rituals of mating choreographed by Eros. The whole story is essentially told in Darcy's rude refusal to dance with Elizabeth, her subsequent reluctance to dance with him, their teasing quarrel when at last they do stand up together, and their obvious suitability and aesthetic rightness as mutual partners.

In a revealing exchange at a ball, Mr. Lucas exclaims, "There is nothing like dancing after all.—I consider it as one of the first refinements of polished societies." "Certainly, Sir," replies Darcy, "—and it has the advantage also of being in vogue amongst the less polished societies of the world.—Every savage can dance" (I, VI, 16). Both are right: dance is a beautiful kinetic form that signifies a compromise and a mode of harmony between art and nature, between free movement and restraint, between mind and body. It is a way of representing physical attraction and of aestheticizing erotic drives.

In the nineteenth and twentieth centuries, dance would become a principal art form for rendering and paying homage to the exuberance and beauty of love (see, for disparate examples, the ballet *Swan Lake*, the Astaire-Rogers movie musical *Swingtime*, and Gene Kelly's cinematic solo in *Singin' in the Rain*). I stress the link between dance and love in Austen to make clear how close the ties between forms of erotic and artistic expression may be. Notice how closely connected the poise and balance of dance are to Austen's rational conception of love in this novel. I also want to emphasize how novelists and other kinds of artists may seek to convey metaphorically the processes of feeling, such as falling in love, through the representation and appeal of a "sister" art, and how habitual it is for artists working in their particular medium to use and refer to the other arts.

For Austen, love, like dance, ought to be a rational pursuit, leading to what is pleasurable, useful, and beautiful. Elizabeth and Darcy come at last to move in complementary harmony and rhythm—like Fred Astaire and Ginger Rogers, say, in their great number "Never Gonna Dance,"[12] who begin by trying to keep from dancing, but end up joined together in fluid, unified, loving, and lovely motion. If we imagine Elizabeth, her friend Charlotte Lucas, and her wild sister Lydia in a dance, we get a precise image not only of the kind of dancing, but of the kind of love Austen values. Charlotte would move by rote, woodenly, without joy. Lydia would be all tawdry bounce and flounce, without grace. Elizabeth's motion would be both lively and elegantly poised. Like ballet, good and rational love is a balancing act.

VI

Austen sets out her ideal of erotic faith in the process and end that she imagines for Elizabeth. But the contrasting figures of Charlotte Lucas and Lydia Bennet, between whom she places her heroine, show how dubious and difficult the subject of romantic love could be for women in the author's milieu. You may be committed to the idea of intelligent love, but economics and libido can make a mockery of that commitment. Charlotte is all head, Lydia all hormones. One, plain and aging, calculates that she had best marry a fool rather than no one, and the other, ruled by "high animal spirits" (I, IX, 31), falls for a seducer. Austen makes them both in different ways sex objects and slaves to materialism. And though their behavior points up very serious problems surrounding love for women in this society, these characters ironically show why erotic faith could appeal, like most religions, to people who cannot or do not want to live by bread or flesh alone. Without love, the object of marriage tends to become a matter of accounting (Collins) or lust and greed (Wickham).

Charlotte's case must concern anyone who thinks seriously about the history of women:

Mr. Collins to be sure was neither sensible nor agreeable; his society was irksome, and his attachment to her must be imaginary. But still he would be her husband.—Without thinking highly either of men or of matrimony, marriage had always been her object; it was the only honourable provision for well-educated young women of small fortune, and however uncertain of giving happiness, must be their pleasantest preservative from want. This preservative she had now obtained; and at the age of twenty-seven, without having ever been handsome, she felt all the good luck of it. [I, XXII, 86]

Irony shimmers in that prose, and put so baldly, Charlotte's views may look cynical; but her situation is a fearful one, as the unmarried author of those bitter words well knew. Austen sees with more sympathy and ambivalence than her heroine, who quickly condemns her friend, the dilemma facing the woman who cannot get a man of means or promise—a man she might be able to love— to fall in love with her. It's too easy to do as Elizabeth and certain Austen critics do and simply dismiss or fudge the issue.[13] The point is not that Charlotte is a sellout, but that she lives in a narrow, desperate, feminine world of financial constraint, like some poor entrant in a ritualized beauty contest that determines your fate while drying up your soul. Articulate and intelligent, she in fact has affinities with her author, which may explain Elizabeth's sharp intolerance about Charlotte's choice: defensive reflex. Marriage to Collins is a kind of socially respectable prostitution in which Charlotte acquiesces. Love is not going to come to her, and lacking it, she seeks refuge in the security of substance. There is no mystery of life for her, no vision of ecstasy or sweet companionship. She has little chance to do what seems necessary for happiness and faith in Austen's fiction: aestheticize and sanctify life by aestheticizing and sanctifying marriage with love.

What is rational in *Pride and Prejudice* is not merely what is to material advantage. Charlotte's "I am not romantic, you know. I never was" (I, XXII, 88) sounds pathetic when set against Jane's injunction, "Oh, Lizzy! do any thing rather than marry without affection" (III, XVII, 257). The disgusting image of Charlotte censoring her intelligence and shamming her feelings in order to humor her stupid husband makes her so-called worldly shrewdness seem naive. Reason and desire, gazing on the plight of women, would look for something that could change both feminine perspective and circumstances. The institutionalizing of romantic love, imperfect though it was, might begin to help.

Love, however, is dangerous for a woman. Not until much later would it be considered proper for a young woman to fall spontaneously in love and declare her love openly, as a man might. That great eighteenth-century feminist Samuel Richardson wrote, "That a young lady should be in love, and the love of the gentleman undeclared is a heterodoxy which prudence, and even policy, must not allow."[14] That kind of pressure inhibits love, and it comes from the fear of sexuality, a fear that Lydia's case justifies. *Pride and Prejudice* bristles with sexual menace. Seduction and the threat of it abound in Austen's novels, and women, if they want to keep from ruin, must not give way thoughtlessly to erotic feelings.

Austen despises Lydia for her mindlessness and draws her without pity as a nubile candidate for exploitation, like Laclos's Cécile in *Les liaisons dangereuses* or some amoral de Sade morsel. Almost everything about her bespeaks vulgar sensuality, and in one perfectly nuanced exclamation the girl pronounces her character, her passion, her fate, and her author's contempt: "How nicely we are crammed in!" (II, XVI, 151). Born under the star of instant gratification, she is helpless in her lust. To succumb to it is not the same thing as falling in love: sexual infatuation offers no basis for faith because it includes nothing beyond the desiring self. We should note what is sometimes overlooked, that at the book's end, both Lydia and Wickham, with their scandalous sexual reputations, apparently betray each other. Darcy keeps her from total ruin, but through her, Austen gives us a good idea of why sexual passion was so feared and why she felt love should be rational.

Although she draws Lydia as a shallow materialist, at one key point she shifts her tone abruptly and imagines, with startling empathy, Lydia's inner life. Just before Lydia goes off with Wickham, we get this amazing passage:

> In Lydia's imagination, a visit to Brighton comprised every possibility of earthly happiness. She saw with the creative eye of fancy, the streets of that gay bathing place covered with officers. She saw herself the object of attention, to tens and to scores of them at present unknown. She saw all the glories of the camp; its tents stretched forth in beauteous uniformity of lines, crowded with the young and the gay, and dazzling with scarlet; and to complete the view, she saw herself seated beneath a tent, tenderly flirting with at least six officers at once. [II, XVIII, 160]

These words are full of the tension between the creative power of erotic faith and the destructive promiscuity to which romantic desire can lead. No one who pays close attention to this prose would say that Jane Austen did not know the flash of sexual fantasy and the pull of eroticism, and only someone insensitive to language could miss the appeal of Lydia's vision, ironic and insidious as it turns out to be. Suddenly Austen chooses to lay bare the mind of an ignorant girl at the beginning of the nineteenth century—a mind we hardly thought existed—and we see there historically and psychologically revealing imagery of desire. She gets at the impulse behind the pornographic imagination, which seeks for the self a sensually realized, beautiful, but undifferentiated and impersonal *more*. Lydia typically wants an endless supply of lovers. Erotic desire becomes limitless and, without reason or discipline, loses the power of distinction: humanity becomes imaginary, an army of fantasy whose mission it is to make the self feel infinitely desirable. The picture, enticing with its youth, joy, color, bustle, pattern, and amorousness, shows us another, more sinister version of Venus disarming Mars.

Notice here the telltale linking of Eros and power. Lydia's desire and vision are *imperial*. Erotic wish fulfillment tends to appropriate military force in the new age of imperialism. (The Brontës' juvenilia, for example, features the Duke of Wellington as a center of power and erotic desire.) The image says, on the one hand, something not all that different from what the whole novel says: a woman can find power through love, and romantic love can put her at the center of life. On the other hand, in Lydia's context, it says that the irrational erotic appetite can strand you in solipsistic peril, unable to tell the difference between a handsome scoundrel like Wickham and a metaphorical officer encamped in a sexual fantasy. In a wider perspective, the image also means that the novel as a whole can be a good medium in which to test and prove the quality of erotic imagination.

Indiscriminate passion leads to moral and economic degradation, as Lydia's jeopardy shows. Austen of course rejects her image of desire, but it does carry the challenge and dream of erotic passion: The romantic, questing ego, through love, seeks to reach a oneness, for a time at least, of the will and the world; it tries to transgress the normal limits of selfhood and reach a perfect equilibrium between desire and fulfillment. Erotic experience offers the chance of a glorified existence and ecstasy. Austen judges this dream of amorous quest to be a snare, but her prose here conveys something of its seductive force. The desire that brings into being such metaphorical energy and skill in order to communicate itself—whether in the prose of a writer who condemns it or the mind of a silly hoyden—is a historical and literary force to be reckoned with. Jane Austen did not imagine that subjective passion was a mode of transcendence that could change reality and dispense with the social world, but there is a germ of that sort of erotic faith in the Brighton fantasy. It is not far from that officer-rich dream camp to the amorous desire of *Jane Eyre, Wuthering Heights, Madame Bovary, Far from the Madding Crowd,* and even *War and Peace.*

VII

Pride and Prejudice expresses the passion of modern individualism: the need to be noticed and loved for your own distinctive self. For Austen true love is discriminating, and those who cannot discriminate cannot love. For Lydia, falling in love with love is, as the song says, falling for make-believe. You need to love another person whose individuality you distinguish, if love is to be real and good. Abstraction, in this novel, is love's enemy, particularity its friend. Collins wants to marry any suitable woman, and when he finds Jane Bennet taken, he turns to Elizabeth ("it was soon done—done while Mrs. Bennet was stirring the fire" [I, XV, 49]), and finally to Charlotte. Wickham tries to seduce anyone who can provide him money or sexual company. Bennet, who chose a wife without distinction, lumps females together ("They are all silly and ignorant"). Lydia takes up with a handsome officer interchangeable with ones she fantasizes. Fittingly Mary Bennet, idiot princess of abstraction, for whom other people are merely ciphers upon which to hang stale moralisms, winds up loveless at home. These characters do not love other individual beings. But Elizabeth and Darcy, Jane and Bingley, the successful lovers, different as they are, distinguish and honor particular personalities. What Austen keeps showing is her faith that, if love means, as it should, the cherishing of an actual individual, it could be a way out of selfishness.

The famous opening sentence of the novel, "It is a truth universally acknowledged, that a single man in possession of a good fortune must be in want of a wife," neatly satirizes ideas that depersonalize marriage and make it a loveless matter of social structuring. Smarmy Collins, with his "mixture of servility and self-importance" (I, XIII, 44), is an animated comic example of Austen's ironic axiom. Nothing is real or personal for Collins except social standing and power relationships within the community. All is form; there is no moral or psychological content, no genuine feeling, no inner self beneath a social role. "And now," he says to Elizabeth, "nothing remains for me but to assure you in the most animated language of the violence of my affection" (I, XIX, 75). She has no more individuality for this formula-spouting ass than a consumer has for a TV-commercial pitchman. And the voice of Collins, inauthentic, passionless, status-hungry, toadying to authority and money, is heard everywhere in modern lands. But the reality of love within the novel helps to bring out and thus control his mean ambition and his emotional emptiness. It works to make him look ridiculous.

Like Collins, Wickham does not seem able to fall in love. He treats women and their fortunes like booty. Indirectly, the power of love, through Darcy, who *can* fall in love, does control him. Austen treats the sexual exploiter in a new way. He is an avatar of the Don Juan figure that has haunted the Western imagination, but a sleazy one. Amplifying on Richardson, but shrinking Lovelace to midget size, she makes clear how libertinism threatens the well-being of women in the most practical ways and injures the whole family of the victim, especially the females. The seducer corrupts his prey in their relationships with others, and he leaves a wake of social miseries behind him. And the effects ramify. The sin of Austen's libertine is not against God, but against relatively powerless people who cry, suffer, and perhaps remain unmarried—or else marry under squalid and self-demeaning circumstances. What confines and checks Wickham is not God's holy vengeance, the violence of wronged kinsmen, Byronic guilt, or the usual punishments for Don Juan figures, but the influence of love on Darcy.

VIII

"Love can make you a better person." Think how much a part of popular culture that trite sentiment is; and Jane Austen not only imagined it, she seems, with this novel, to have been as influential as anyone in making it a romantic cliché. She imagines love improving the character of both Elizabeth and Darcy, but in ways that differ significantly. Knowledge of being loved deepens her moral sense, and actively loving changes him.

Darcy's love helps to reform Elizabeth's pride and prejudice. In one of the book's moral climaxes, after turning him down and reading his letter, she comes to admit to herself that she has been vain, improper in her arrogance, proud, hurtful to others, and just plain wrong. His love provides the occasion for her to gain self-knowledge and to understand that sin and error are internal as well as external threats: "Till this moment, I never knew myself" (II, XIII, 144).

The reform of Don Juan, a persistent romantic theme, does figure prominently in the novel—not in Wickham's case, but in Darcy's. Darcy is saved by loving a good woman—salvation through the conversion experience of erotic faith. At the very start, he looks bad—proud, rude, with a whiff of the Lovelace predatory rake about him ("She is tolerable; but not handsome enough to tempt *me*" [I, III, 7]). In the end, Austen gives him this passage of lap-dog prose:

"I was spoilt by my parents, who . . . allowed, encouraged, almost taught me to be selfish and overbearing, . . . to think meanly of all the rest of the world, to *wish* at least to think meanly of their sense and worth compared with my own. Such I was from eight to eight and twenty; and such I might still have been but for you, dearest, loveliest Elizabeth! What do I not owe you! You taught me a lesson, hard indeed at first, but most advantageous. By you, I was properly humbled. . . . You shewed me how insufficient were all my pretensions to please a woman worthy of being pleased." [III, XVI, 254–55]

That is dream talk, something a smarter Lydia might imagine and Mary Bennet write down. It would be hard to think of another piece of dialogue in Austen so unconvincing in its particular form and context and yet so revealing about nineteenth-century feminine desire. Not only does love bring Darcy moral salvation, it implies purpose and meaning in Elizabeth's life. Little wonder that Annabella Milbanke, the woman who married and hoped to reform the libertine Byron, so admired *Pride and Prejudice*. If it *is* a man's world, and if, as Marx says, the point is to change the world, then you can only begin to change it by changing men. Love gives a woman redemptive power over a man and thus over the world. That is the hope supporting such a speech, and when we compare its sentimentality with the usual brilliant and tough-minded level of Austen's dialogue, we find evidence of her repressed resentment towards the moral reality of general male behavior. It shows an almost unmediated yearning to find means to transform feminine powerlessness to influence. Desire here overcomes her almost unequalled aesthetic judgment as a novelist.

But that's too harsh. The speech form and blatant wish fulfillment may be wrong, but Darcy's sentiment seems right. Bestowal, Austen realizes, is a lover's pleasure. Acting virtuously on behalf of his love, a man would naturally feel like a better person, and he bestows the credit for his kind action and sense of well-being on his beloved, requiting exactly the gratitude and esteem Elizabeth feels for him. The effects of love on him are clear and convincing.

What remains a problem, and what accounts for the stagy quality of the passage, is Austen's uncertainty about the inner life of Darcy. He plunges suddenly into love, but what does that feel like in a man? How do you represent the psychology of his falling in love? *Pride and Prejudice* is a bible of erotic faith, and the faith hangs on Darcy's conversion; but Austen seems on the outside of that experience, fretting and wondering about how to fill in the blankness surrounding the crucial fall. We know how and why the hero falling in love fits into a proper, reasonable scheme of things, and we know about what qualities Elizabeth has that draw his love, but we can only speculate about the inner process that first moves him to love and what it means to him. For Austen, the coming of love to Darcy seems like a religious election or enchantment, something ineffable.

A man's love and a woman's love in this novel are not the same thing. A woman's love in its society, as we have seen, must be reactionary—reactionary in the sense that she can only respond to men, she cannot initiate relations with them or take the lead in showing feeling without great risk. Austen shows us assembly halls and drawing rooms that, for women, are like disguised mine fields. That's what Wickham signifies. A sensible girl learns that love can deceive and should be rational, but she may also hear or read that it can be a grand, transforming emotion upon which her happiness depends, and that a sure trail to sorrow is to marry without it. When Darcy treats Elizabeth so kindly at Pemberley, though she had rudely turned him down, she ponders on love matters and tries to analyze just what she feels for him: "It was gratitude.—Gratitude, not merely for having loved her, but for loving her still. . . . Such a change in a man of so much pride, excited not only astonishment but gratitude—for to love, ardent love, it must be attributed" (III, II, 181). The faintly mocking singsong of "to love, ardent love," playing with the gentle hint of distaste on a romantic cliché, shows how far she is from his state of mind and yet how intrigued she is by the idea of passion.

In a moving way, the novel lets us see Elizabeth facing up to a strain of coolness in herself and a possible gap between romantic expectation and reality. Here, from late in the book after she and Darcy have engaged themselves, is a piece of such self-scrutiny: "Elizabeth, agitated and confused, rather *knew* that she was happy, than *felt* herself to be so" (III, XVII, 257). For an intelligent woman in this world, knowledge and feeling may often need to be kept separate; the distinction in the prose stresses a tension between them. Trained to beware of passion, Elizabeth cannot just switch on erotic bliss and sexual spontaneity. She wants to feel more—and feel more quickly—than she does, and Austen gets down this pang of disappointment in the midst of her joy. We may or may not sense a strong physical passion in Elizabeth for Darcy, but the wonder in such a milieu is that she's not completely frigid.

One of the larger glories of this novel is that Austen does express unmistakably the dialectical tension between the rationality and the mystery of love. For Elizabeth, love might be summed up as the reasonable desire to marry Darcy and the strong personal affection that makes the desire rational. In the vision of this work such love depends upon something anterior—*being in the power of love*, as Darcy is. It would be hard to claim that she is *in love* with him, though by the end we must conclude that she really does *love* him ("I do love him"). His falling in love is what allows her love to develop. Describing Elizabeth's growing affection, Austen renders the slow but sure aphrodisiac effect of feeling beloved. How fundamentally wise and nice people are, after all, who fall in love with us! Before we can love rationally, somebody must fall in love. That is *the* romantic fact of this novel, and it resonates beyond the bounds of literature.

IX

In an uncharacteristic piece of lumbering prose, Austen offers this significant speculation:

> If gratitude and esteem are good foundations of affection, Elizabeth's change of sentiment will be neither improbable nor faulty. But if otherwise, if the regard springing from such sources is unreasonable or unnatural, in comparison of what is so often described as arising on a first interview with its object, and even before two words have been exchanged, nothing can be said in her defence, except that she had given somewhat of a trial to the latter method, in her partiality for Wickham, and that its ill-success might perhaps authorise her to seek the other less interesting mode of attachment. [III, IV, 190–91]

Something uncertain—some insecurity about love, some drag on clear expression—shows through in that paragraph's rhetorical straw man, leaden irony, misplaced emphasis, clumsy diction, and thudding syntax. The language lacks the "liveliness of mind" that distinguishes Elizabeth and her author. Its conventional wisdom reads as if it had somehow been reluctantly extracted, like the mumbled catechism of a converted heathen.

Why does Austen, the nimblest of stylists, write with awkwardness here, and why, for the moment, does she make love seem so static and abstract? One reason is that she is writing against herself, caught in her own hidden ambivalences and contradictions. Naturally she wants to believe that love is built on the morally benevolent sentiments of gratitude and esteem, but the narrative makes the origin of love the instinctive attraction that Darcy feels. The passage betrays a desire to repress sex, and it questions sex appeal as a good basis for love; but the happy love story she imagines needs first Darcy's libido to push him into the fortunate erotic fall.

Austen's meditation recognizes that feminine love will probably look like a much tamer, more passive thing than masculine love and therefore, implicitly and grudgingly, she tends, in one way, to validate the superior passion of men and thus their superior authority on the subject. But she resents that logic too. Since Darcy has fallen in love with Elizabeth at second, if not at first sight, the text, as I read it, hints at a suppressed dissatisfaction that such experience for a woman is so clearly wrong when it can be so right for a man. Elizabeth does not fall in love with Darcy the way Darcy falls in love with her, and the passage shows signs of envy as well as distrust of romantic intensity. Beyond that, it reveals the author's momentary doubt that she herself understands passion or values it. And if we allow for imitative form, we might see how the words reflect the frustration and epistemological difficulty that an intelligent woman in this society may have in her necessary struggle to perceive erotic matters correctly. Love—alas!—is liable to be life for a woman, but, given a woman's life in this world, it's so hard for her to know anything certain about it.

In this strange discourse, we need to know that Austen is engaging one of her chief predecessors in fiction, Henry Fielding, and that her prose shows the anxiety of influence. In a famous and important digression in *Tom Jones*, Fielding had defended the existence of love against the skepticism of both antinominalist and materialist thinkers and had defined its proper nature as a harmony of moral and sexual desire. Imagine the interest that his language would have for a young woman, like Elizabeth, for whom love is fate, or like Jane Austen, for whom it would inevitably become the subject matter of her vocation:

[W]hat is commonly called Love, namely, the Desire of satisfying a voracious Appetite with a certain Quantity of delicate white human Flesh, is by no means that Passion for which I here contend. . . . I will grant. . . . That this Love, when it operates towards one of a different Sex, is very apt, towards its complete Gratification, to call in the Aid of that Hunger which I have mentioned above; and . . . heightens all its Delights to a Degree scarce imaginable by those who have never been susceptible of any other Emotions, than what have proceeded from Appetite alone. . . . I desire of Philosophers to grant, that there is in some. . . . human Breasts . . . a kind and benevolent Disposition, which is gratified by contributing to the Happiness of others. That in this Gratification alone, as in Friendship, in paternal and filial Affection . . . there is a great and exquisite Delight. That if we will not call such Disposition Love, we have no Name for it. That though the Pleasures arising from such pure Love may be heightened and sweetened by the Assistance of amorous Desires, yet the former can subsist alone, nor are they destroyed by the Intervention of the latter. Lastly, that Esteem and Gratitude are the proper Motives to Love, as Youth and Beauty are to Desire; and therefore though such Desire may naturally cease, when Age or Sickness overtakes its Object; yet these can have no Effect on Love, nor ever shake or remove from a good Mind, that Sensation or Passion which hath Gratitude and Esteem for its Basis.[15]

Compare the two passages. Austen ostensibly accepts and means to support Fielding's meliorist notions about love and its proper basis, but notice the difference in tone, authority, imagistic content, point of view, and nuance. The man writes confidently, asserting truths about the world from a detached, overall perspective; the woman is hypothetical, implicated in the thought process and the contingencies of her heroine. The narrative for her becomes a means of testing theories of love, not a device on which to project them. The man prescribes what love should be; the woman tries to find it in the novel's particular web of circumstances. Love—independent of his novel—exists for the man to generalize about; for the woman it emerges in the individualized experience of the novel. That difference matters. Its logical import is to show love and the institution of the novel bound much more closely than in Fielding's century and to make the novel not merely a genre that represents or reports on preexisting patterns of love, but one that potentially can generate new forms of erotic life.

The authoritative man discourses about love as if it were exactly the same thing for both genders; the woman, self-conscious and tentative, implies—by allusion, by what she omits, and by tying her observation to Elizabeth's experience in the narrative—that love for the two sexes may be different. Her convoluted prose seems to show that she resists exposing such a split, but that she cannot help putting in question, at this moment, Fielding's confident assumption, which the internal logic of his imagery and his mode of argument undercut, that love can be gender neutral. The man speaks of sex directly; the woman, purging from Elizabeth's imagination any overt reference to the sexual desire "for . . . delicate white human Flesh," *has no say about the body.* One conflict I see in the Austen passage is that she both wants to de-emphasize sex and resents having to do so. Despite its jovial piety and disclaiming moves, Fielding's prose, with its image of sexual appetite and stress on sex's potential goodness, definitely features sex in love.

Austen's prose very likely betrays an unconscious resentment against the implicit, contradictory subtext in Fielding that tends to separate and genderize sexual desire (natural and acceptable in men, but unseemly for women, who are its proper objects) and love (good for both sexes, but, modeled on properly affectionate, benevolent, and responsible parent-child relationships and on friendship, most especially fitting for women). Set dialogically against Fielding's text, her own here replicates the condition of women in her world. It is comparatively constricted. It responds and relates to male *authority*. The sexual desire and sexual realities that sometimes menace women, drive them, or objectify them as quantities of "delicate" flesh, are there all the time, but women are not empowered to articulate sex or speculate about it openly. On the other hand, to repress sex in discourse might be a way to help women concentrate on their minds and hearts and to see and define themselves in terms other than their sexual desirability (e.g., "a beauty"), status (e.g., "a maiden," "a virgin," "a spinster"), and function (e.g., "a wife and mother").[16] Austen would like to agree with Fielding that love could arise without depending on amorous desire, but *Pride and Prejudice* indicates the opposite: to find happiness in love, a woman still needs to arouse the sexual appetite of a man. "Gratitude and esteem," the supposedly proper foundations of love for Elizabeth and other women, do not seem to figure equally for men in the general erotic picture, and part of Austen's mind deplores having to suppress the difference. Fielding's passage can seem like lip service to an ideal that only women are expected to live up to. Besides her conditional assent to him, her writing, at this odd moment, reveals a clot of skepticism about faith in love.

And yet, of course, Austen does finally support Fielding and the gist of his assessment about what constitutes the proper basis of love. Two points in her dialectical interchange with this "father of the English Novel" need special stress: 1) She chose to keep silent about the explicitly sexual in adopting his idea of love, and that same choice—the emphasis on the moral, emotional, and spiritual content of love and the *relationship* between men and women, and the hiding away of the delicate flesh—defines the nature of nineteenth-century British fiction and its problematic rendering of love. 2) By responding directly and seeming to accept Fielding's ideas that "gratitude and esteem" are the right qualities for defining love and that true erotic gratification resembles "paternal and filial affection," Austen points the way towards the sublimated incestuous biases of love in Victorian novels. In spite of the fact—or, more accurately in the developing age of the family, *because of the fact*—that the terms express the homage a good girl in early nineteenth-century England might pay to a good father figure, "gratitude" and "esteem" came to seem the desirable, necessary, but somehow troubling essentials for love in narratives.

The question that the syntactical rebellion against her own clear, bright style—that sprawl of prepositional phrases, subordinate clauses, and debilitating qualifiers—poses, and that Austen cannot answer here, is, *Are gratitude and esteem in themselves enough to inspire and constitute that affection people call love?* It is a question that would come to haunt the Victorian novel and Victorian love. Certainly in this novel, they are exactly the terms to describe the author's emergent feelings for the existence of love itself. There is real passion in Elizabeth's and Austen's gratitude and esteem for Darcy's love. They are the fuel, if not the spark, of love. And they make good foundations for marriage. They do not, however, seem strong enough to support the transcendent faith that countless numbers would desire erotic love to be. In her attitude toward love, Jane Austen seems at times like some nominal Anglican who understands Christianity and believes in its doctrine, morality, and influence, but cannot feel, herself, the mystical stab of faith.

X

Austen understands the particular desires and personal lacks that motivate a love relationship and rationally impel two people to union; at the same time, with easy grace and wit, she indicates the general hope for the role of love that men and women were to hold throughout her century and ours. Let's look again at Elizabeth's sense of mating with Darcy: "It was an union that must have been to the advantage of both; by her ease and liveliness, his mind might have been softened, his manners improved, and from his judgment, information, and knowledge of the world, she must have received benefit of greater importance" (III, VIII, 214). Their desires overlap, especially in a mutual wish for affection and camaraderie. And surely desire for liveliness or softening of mind (meaning for him joy, a quicker moral imagination, and a civilizing process), and desire for the benefit of greater importance (meaning for her the possibility of merited distinction and the growth of opportunity) are the main rational ends of love in this novel. Austen imagines reasoned love as being inseparable from a desire to attach the qualities of the beloved to the self.

Pride and Prejudice implicitly distinguishes between "love" and "in love,"[17] between loving someone and falling in love with someone, between a rational blend of affection and desire for a person, and an involuntary, often blind, power of emotion that seizes one (e.g., Elizabeth thinks, "Had I been in love, I could not have been more wretchedly blind" [II, XIII, 144]). Austen sees loving as potentially a rational act, and falling in love as a mysterious, prerational, disruptive process for the individual. This orderly person imagines that some disruption of order is necessary to foster new love beyond familial limitations and bring about a deepened and expanded sense of self, feminine belief in personal progress, and rational marriage. Something novel must enter the Novel. When, therefore, she looks at her world, falling in love appears indispensable.

Her gaze, though, still reminds me of Botticelli's *Venus and Mars*, to which I return. The picture, like the novel, is anything but sentimental, though it is filled with faith and hope. Venus's face looks off beyond the life of the canvas, almost as if she were seeing into the future, and her expression is a mixture of alert authority, resignation, and dissatisfaction. The picture honors love and shows a wonderful faith in it, but that love is not yet fulfilled. Venus lacks ecstasy.

The sentence that follows Elizabeth's description of what a union with Darcy would bring to them is this: "But no such happy marriage could now teach the admiring multitude what connubial felicity really was" (III, VIII, 214). The union, of course, takes place, but the edgy tone and the distancing irony— the strangely nuanced, faint mockery of personal and popular desire, trite-mindedness, frivolous conceit, and pride that the words convey—necessarily accompany Austen's view of love. She tells us near the end that, although her lovers get together, Elizabeth "remembered that he had yet to learn to be laught at" (III, XVI, 256), and that after their marriage he becomes "the object of open pleasantry" (III, XIX, 268). That is necessary lest "respect" overcome "affec-tion." Narratives teach us to imagine the consequences of what we see. Mars will wake again and need to be controlled by love, which, oddly enough, must include liveliness of mind and the imps of comedy. Life and love for Austen and Elizabeth cannot be what they appear to be for Jane Bennet: uncomplicated, sweet, without moral and intellectual contradictions, and smoothly fulfilling. For Botticelli here and Austen—trying to imagine and depict erotic faith—in-telligence, humor, and an indication of the absurdity of the world must accom-pany beauty, if their art is to have any lasting moral value.

About Austen's novels, R. W. Chapman remarked, "[T]hey have nothing to say about the great events that were shaking Europe." [18] Everyone now sees how wrong that is. The growth of individualism and the emergence of romantic love as the heart of private life and a popular expression of faith were matters of world-shaking importance, and *Pride and Prejudice* has profound things to say about them. The book offers a challenge and an alternative to conventional no-tions of what constitutes "great events." "Great events" may be the great events and their meaning in women's lives as well as in men's lives; and novels as well as battles could cause "Europe" to be shaken. A woman's *liveliness of mind*, for example, might shape the future. If the great historical fact of European and American life in the latter half of the eighteenth and in the nineteenth century is the sweep of individualism, the domestication of history which novels enact and the insistent representation of love at the center of things must surely have important consequences. *Pride and Prejudice* is, literally and on many levels, an act of love, and—to paraphrase Hemingway—when people think the act of love is good, the earth moves. The labor of the novelist is now a labor of love: "I have got my own darling child from London."

3   Fatal Love and Eroticizing History:
Walter Scott's *The Bride of Lammermoor* (1819)

"[A]re you come . . . in fatal anger, or in still more fatal love."
WALTER SCOTT[1]

I

The Bride of Lammermoor thrilled the nineteenth-century imagination and fed longings for erotic faith, as these passages from novels by Elizabeth Gaskell, Flaubert, and E. M. Forster show:

"Molly had been in the very middle of the *Bride of Lammermoor*, . . . her mind quite full of 'Ravenswood' and 'Lucy Ashton.'"[2]

"She [Madame Bovary] felt herself carried back to the reading of her youth, into the midst of Walter Scott. . . . [Lucy] begged for love, longed for wings. Emma, too, would have liked to flee away from life, locked in a passionate embrace."[3]

"Harriet, like M. Bovary on a more famous occasion, was trying to follow the plot. Occasionally she nudged her companions, and asked them what had become of Walter Scott. She looked round. . . . Violent waves of excitement, all arising from very little, went sweeping round the theatre."[4]

And in *Anna Karenina*, Tolstoy's love-doomed heroine goes to see a famous soprano sing *Lucia di Lammermoor*.[5] Scott's fiction had a remarkable impact and became a provocative fact of history. His novel and the opera that it spawned became synonymous with the tragic, transfiguring power of love.

In Lucy Ashton, Scott conceived a popular martyr of romantic faith. If, as the framing first chapter tells us, an artwork needs a powerful "original conception" (I, 26) and "interesting and singular . . . events" (I, 25), *The Bride of Lammermoor* offered them. Scott first heard from his mother about a tragic seventeenth-century case of parents coercing their daughter to betray her love and marry against her wishes. Starting from the outcome he imagined for the tale, he composed a narrative backwards, but set the events a generation ahead at the beginning of the eighteenth century.[6] Lucy, forced to break her engagement to Ravenswood and wed Bucklaw, goes mad and stabs her husband on their wedding night: "When she saw herself discovered, she gibbered, made mouths, and pointed at them with her bloody fingers, with the frantic gestures of an exulting demoniac." She taunts her tormenters, then falls delirious and dies (XXXIV, 323).

The text here depicts a maniacal rebellion against a system of legalized rape, and Scott renders the spreading evil set loose by making a woman copulate with a man she does not love. Lucy's gory nuptial chamber stands out as a place of sacrifice to erotic faith. Religion needs texts and images of sacrifice, as does art. Much of Scott's power and influence as a novelist grew out of his realization, intuitive or not, that a secular faith in love and in historical progress, like traditional Christian faith, thrives on the representation of sacrificial violence. The community feeds and consecrates a desire for faith by assimilating an imaginative rendering of sacrifice, and the enthusiastic perception of Lucy as martyr shows how the erotic could verge on the sacred in popular opinion. One effect of the novel is to make sacrilegious that which opposes and destroys the lovers' faith, including orthodox religion, superstition, law, custom, and the authority of kin.

Love novels, as *The Bride of Lammermoor* shows so well, set off an intense dialogic interplay among the arts in the nineteenth century. Scott's "interesting events" gave delighted operatic composers the chance to move audiences eager to hear love's tragic lyricism. Donizetti and his librettist Cammarano turned the tale into *Lucia di Lammermoor*, and across Europe it received at least six other operatic settings, including one based on an adaptation by Hans Christian Andersen.[7] Ravenswood's last words to Lucy foretell that she will become "a world's wonder" (XXXIII, 314), and anyone who has ever heard a great soprano sing "the mad scene" from *Lucia* knows how prophetic he was.

II

Scott's most popular "conception" as a novelist was to marry history—the public events and movement of the past—to the love story. Fusing private romantic experience with epic matter of the Scots and other peoples, he created and institutionalized "the historical novel"; and we need to stress that for him, trying for a new historical integrity, it was virtually impossible to conceive of a historical novel without a prominent erotic interest. "The historical romance" is for him just that: the intrusion of the personal romances of men and women into the past, and the plotting, understanding, and demarcation of history by means of the erotic relationships and destinies of particular characters. In the turbulence of social conflict, love affairs in Scott assert the primacy of the values of individualism and the private pursuit of happiness. The focus of *The Bride of Lammermoor*, in which the fate of two characters who fall in love overwhelms everything else, is not an aberration, as has been argued, but the essence of Scott's historical vision.

We can see also that the historical novel marks the growing consciousness and interjection of women into traditional "history": As female readership expands and women's place in bourgeois ideology becomes more prominent, history, to be popular, must satisfy various demands and begin to include women and what women desire and know. Karl Kroeber has said that for Scott "history was process" and that "he was the first artist to conceive of history as the organic evolution of competing styles of life."[8] If so, think how his conception tends to make individual consciousness the focus of that "evolution" process, how well the conception describes a process of gender relations, and how much it sounds like the process of courtship writ large. In *Waverley* the making of the union between the hero and heroine is inseparable from the process and meaning of the union that made the United Kingdom. In *The Bride of Lammermoor*, says one critic, "the major conflict . . . is carefully connected to the religious and political situation in early eighteenth-century Scotland, and the importance of the national theme is always clear."[9] The historical situation, however, is bound up inextricably with the tragic erotic theme, which stands, among other things, as a cautionary parable about the necessity for the Union.[10]

Scott's genius was to render the past as an immense field of desire. Inscribing love into the past is a way of possessing history, of subjecting it to the moral values of the present and, ultimately, to the desires of the judging self. Scott has often been said to romanticize history, but it would be more accurate to say that—in this novel especially—he eroticizes it.

Figuratively, the love story that Scott weds to history is his own and his audience's. The sometimes long-winded introductions to his narratives—and particularly the first chapter of this book, which features a lengthy aesthetic discussion between a painter and the fictional narrator—drive home the point that *the past is always mediated by art and desire*: aesthetics and erotics. He was the first to realize the possibilities in fiction of mating that whole glamorous cast of *isms* that excited his age: historicism, eroticism, aestheticism, nationalism, and individualism. He knows, for instance, that nationalism is a love story. In history and in its nineteenth-century progeny nationalism, people imagine ways to complete themselves, to find the qualities they want but lack, to project their egos beyond the limits of the self and insert themselves into an immortal but natural process.

To historicize can mean to eroticize. Scott offers a model of the individual conceiving the past and appropriating it for present use. To conceive of history is, as the verbal connotation tells us, a generative act. It produces, like love, an attachment. People find pleasure and vicarious life in the past because they somehow connect with their desire. Imagine such common sentiments as "I love history," "I love the Highlanders," "I love Queen Victoria," "I am deeply moved by the French Revolution." Men and women engage with and aestheticize bits of the past—facts, deeds, and feelings—as they aestheticize loved ones. To seize on a "lost" cause of the past, to find the qualities one admires and desires in history, is much like falling in love.

III

"History," says Joyce's Stephen Dedalus, "is a nightmare from which I am trying to awake." [11] That assessment not only fits the doomed lovers Lucy and Ravenswood, but the whole spirit of *The Bride of Lammermoor* and, beyond that, the tenor of Scott's narrative intentions. To free yourself of a dream, you subject it to your desire: paradoxically you at once put it at a distance and you appropriate it to consciousness; you put it in perspective, interpret and possess it—often by seizing on the elements you want, discarding others, and giving the dream a plot; you relegate it to the past, but also file it for the future use of your own wakeful ego. That is analogous to what Scott does to history.

Life for the most part in *The Bride of Lammermoor* is a Hobbesian horror show. "History" is a melange of blood feuds, economic necessity and coercion, class enmities, religious intolerance, political rivalry, superstitious lore, and the menace of violence. This mixed heritage of custom, genealogy, language, and deterministic forces would be beyond redemption if it were not for romantic love. Critics who condemn as unwise or misplaced the love between Lucy and Ravenswood miss the point. [12] Without fidelity in love, there is nothing worthwhile in the novel's world.

Historically, the conflict in the book between orthodox religion and erotic faith is very important—not just for the history of the early eighteenth century, but for the nineteenth and twentieth centuries as well. True devotion and spiritual value in the tale belong to love, not to formal religion. The moral is surely "Love (rather than God) will not be mocked." Unlike *Romeo and Juliet*, to which *The Bride of Lammermoor* is often compared, or *Clarissa*, Scott's work does not depict a Christianity in harmony with love and the ideals of a virtuous heroine. Lady Ashton expressly makes use of a Presbyterian cleric and Holy Scripture to break the vows of Ravenswood and Lucy; Scott takes care to cite the words from the Bible that negate a daughter's pledged faith: "if her father disallow her in the day that he heareth; not any of her vows, or of her bonds wherewith she hath bound her soul, shall stand" (Numbers 30:5). Ravenswood responds to this "sacred text" with a protest to Lucy that signifies both the clear clash of faiths and Scott's sympathy with the new Eros over Jehovah: "And is this all? . . . Are you willing to barter sworn faith, the exercise of free will, and the feelings of mutual affection, to this wretched hypocritical sophistry?" (XXXIII, 312). Lady Ashton calls him a "blasphemer," but the rhetoric of the novel supports him. I repeat because it is so striking: the practice of orthodox religion in the story is completely at odds with romantic love and offers no proper structure of moral credence or hope.

The passage in which Lucy Ashton first appears resounds with the conflict and change of faiths. Until this moment, "this history," as the author calls his work, has introduced us only to a barbarous life, with Ravenswood swearing vengeance on the Ashtons for ruining his father, Lady Ashton being compared to a latter-day Lady Macbeth, William Ashton engaging in low political scheming, Presbyterians trying to keep Episcopalians from burying the dead, and everyone living in an atmosphere of nasty hostility. Suddenly Scott shows the worldly Ashton stopped by the sound and the sight of his daughter playing and singing. In Lucy's haunting song and the subsequent portrait of her, Scott is imagining the deep human impulse to make lyrical those thoughts and emotions that join beauty and love, and he is using Lucy to represent romanticism's drive to blend aesthetic and erotic faith. Given a lyric voice at the beginning, she becomes for awhile her song and her musical setting (much as *The Bride of Lammermoor* would become *Lucia di Lammermoor*). Like Titian's *Music Lesson of Venus* or the songs blaring from any transistor radio, Scott reminds us how and why music can be the food of love.

[T]he silver tones of Lucy Ashton's voice mingled with the accompaniment in an ancient air, to which some one had adapted the following words:—

> Look not thou on beauty's charming,—
> Sit thou still when kings are arming,—
> Taste not when the wine-cup glistens,—
> Speak not when the people listens,—
> Stop thine ear against the singer,—
> From the red gold keep thy finger,—
> Vacant heart, and hand, and eye,—
> Easy live and quiet die.

. . . The words she had chosen seemed particularly adapted to her character; for Lucy Ashton's exquisitely beautiful, yet somewhat girlish features, were formed to express peace of mind, serenity, and indifference to the tinsel of worldly pleasure. . . . The expression of the countenance was in the last degree gentle, soft, timid, and feminine, and seemed rather to shrink from the most casual look of a stranger, than to court his admiration. Something there was of a *Madonna* cast. . . .

Yet her passiveness of disposition was by no means owing to an indifferent or unfeeling mind. Left to the impulse of her own taste and feelings, Lucy Ashton was peculiarly accessible to those of a romantic cast. Her secret delight was in the old legendary tales of ardent *devotion* and unalterable affection, chequered as they so often are with strange adventures and supernatural horrors.

. . . It usually happens that such a compliant and easy disposition, which resigns itself . . . to the guidance of others, becomes the darling of those to whose inclinations its own seem to be offered, in ungrudging and ready *sacrifice*. [III, 39–41, italics mine]

We seem very far from Elizabeth Bennet and her liveliness of mind here, but somehow close to beauty, religious feeling, and a redemptive vocation. We also sense the potential for woman's victimization. The woman, the song, and the characterization form an overture to love in the novel, the novel as a whole, and the social contradictions it describes. Nominally set in a remote and picturesque past, Lucy symbolically sits smack in the middle of Scott's rapidly modernizing culture and the dynamic forces shaping the future. Like her author she creates a spirit of romance and erotic longing, and like her readers she consumes vicariously the romance, the stories, and the words of others. Shamelessly patronized and genuinely honored, she mediates between the sound-and-fury world of futility that surrounds her and the ironic dream of Christian quietism that her song expresses. Words like "Madonna," "devotion," and "sacrifice" show a desire for reverence and faith not only within this imagined figure, but surrounding her as well.

Look at Lucy's extraordinary lyric. Scott manages to get in those eight lines both the exciting surge of sensual individualism—the mesmerism of personal desire—and the pathos of an appealing but doomed hope of tranquility. Those imperatives to turn away from the earthly pleasures and temptations for a peace which passeth understanding ("easy live and quiet die") sum up a long tradition of Christian teaching (you can find the seven deadly sins and the five deluding senses in the song). But the line "Vacant heart, and hand, and eye"—substitute an "I" for an "eye" and still the sense is the same—reeks of a lost ideal and a moribund faith. Nature, as its growing child Science says, abhors a vacuum.

The dilemma of modern life is here. Carefully set in the faithless, violent world of the novel, the song proclaims vanity's allure but offers "no coherent social faith"[13] to oppose the glamor of materialist ambition—a glamor that can lead to butchery. "Vacant heart" poses the problem inexorably. Human passions *will* be engaged, even if only by greed, lust, or a will to power. Hearts yearn to be filled. Lucy, Ravenswood, Scotland, and Scott are caught between a dead heaven and a deadly, if vital and sometimes glorious, world. In such a situation no wonder romantic love, which appropriates from the past such putative boons as chivalry, idealism, and religious belief, becomes a matter of faith.

The verse, the passage, and the whole narrative pulse with irony. The lyric seems both to embody and to deny the purity and spirituality men had sought and would seek in women. What appears innocent, lovely, and picturesque cannot resist corruption. Lucy offers a vision of serenity that people long for, but nothing could be further from her own subsequent history than "easy live and quiet die." She and the love she gives and inspires miraculously bring hope to life, but that love proves fatal. Playing music, singing exquisite lyrics, sweet-natured and kindly disposed to others, she seems to embody the virtue and beauty of civilization, but her very softness and aura of aesthetic and moral value tempt others to exploit her. The passage gets at the essence of the plot, the conflict that erupts in bloody horror: Lucy is a fetish, but a fetish with a personality.

Scott is imagining what later in his century would become an angel-in-the-house ideal—accomplished, soothing, lovely woman as refuge from the sins of the world. And he makes perfectly clear that this figure does not come out of sentimentality, but out of a culture's profound need and a historical gap of faith. At the core of desire in the novel, however, we find the contradiction that exists in the poem, in Lucy's fate, and in the context of the passage: people think they want to transcend the world, but such is the world's sensual sway that it may turn what seems to promise transcendent quality into a possession, a lovely performing object to do with what they will. There exists a schizoid desire to adore a madonna that can be shaped, owned, and used.

Split desire: it makes erotic history, shapes gender relations, forms novels, moves Scott, and might just drive you crazy. What does a man want? Both a Lucy Ashton and an Elizabeth Bennet (who are, of course, mutually exclusive). In a secularizing society, what is otherworldly may seem "vacant"—in late twentieth-century slang, "spacy"—rather than spiritual. A yielding object of love may not make a strong, free-willed, loving subject. Ravenswood, after he gives his faith to Lucy, betrays a telltale confusion: "He felt that his own temper required a partner of a more independent spirit. . . . But Lucy was so beautiful, so devoutly attached to him, of a temper so exquisitely soft and kind, that . . . he felt that the softness of a mind, amounting almost to feebleness, rendered her even dearer to him" (XXI, 207). He wants contradictory things: a companionate mate and a sacred image to worship; partnership and dependence; a woman's strength of mind and feminine subservience. And contradiction can send you right back to the nightmare of history.

IV

Beauty wakes you up. The aesthetics of love fascinate Scott. Ravenswood and Lucy fall in love with the respective beauty of the other (see V and VIII), and then that beauty for each strengthens and renews their erotic commitment. This beauty at first sight does not provoke lust or even simple desire, but something more akin to instinctive aesthetic appreciation. The sight of Lucy stirs feelings of reverence and even faith. If we think again of her first appearance, we can see how Scott's erotic imagination works. Amid the troubles of life, a person like Ashton or, later, Ravenswood finds a being whose form and bearing bring joy and a sense that *this is good, this is right, this is lovable, this is an image that I like*. That emotion may immediately—or more slowly—trigger desire, but the first response is an aesthetic affirmation producing attraction. In an imperfect world, a positive passion, a *yes*, suddenly fills the heart. And that feeling and the image that arouses it stay in the mind. The first ironic command of Lucy's lyric, "Look not thou on beauty's charming," gives love reign as the world's most seductive offering and merges love with aesthetics. Scott, like Plato, blends aesthetic faith into erotic faith, and that fusion gives the novel much of its power.

To fall in love is often to fall under the spell of aesthetic beauty and find life reflecting some striking artistic ideal or instance. Joyce, in his famous discussion of aesthetics in *A Portrait of the Artist as a Young Man*, calls the aesthetic effect of apprehending beauty "the enchantment of the heart." [14] That accurately describes romantic love in Scott and in much nineteenth-century writing. Love for Lucy and Ravenswood is romantic faith and a moral, intense commitment to aesthetic ideals, not a dialectical relationship. They hardly talk to one another. They are images for each other, images that fulfill the respective desire of each for spiritual value, fidelity, beauty, and goodness.

Ravenswood's vision of Lucy shows how love and aesthetic pleasure could feed the hunger for a new faith to replace the old one that historicism was sapping.

> The exquisite feminine beauty of her countenance, now shaded only by a profusion of sunny tresses . . . cleared, with a celerity which surprised the Master himself, all the gloomy and unfavourable thoughts which had for some time overclouded his fancy. In those features, so simply sweet, he could trace no alliance with the pinched visage of the peak-bearded, black-capped puritan, or his starched withered spouse [Lucy's grandparents], with the craft expressed in the Lord Keeper's countenance, or the haughtiness which predominated in that of his lady; and, while he gazed on Lucy Ashton, she seemed to be an angel descended on earth, unallied to the coarser mortals among whom she deigned to dwell for a season. Such is the power of beauty over a youthful and enthusiastic fancy. [XVIII, 187–88]

That language may now seem overblown, but it expresses the longing in love to fly beyond the limits of worn-out religion, politics, clan, and class, and it bases transcendent feeling on physical presence: a beautiful woman. Erotic, religious, and aesthetic desire and impulse come together to lift Ravenswood's spirit out of the sad bog of his personal and cultural history. If the prose seems slightly ridiculous, the problem of lost faith is serious and real. We cannot understand nineteenth-century angels-in-the-house or love-arias soaring with passion without understanding that people might have a driving urge to keep believing somehow in beautiful angels and the sanctity of passion. Traditional religion cannot, in the world of this book, fulfill that need, but, for the moment, romantic love can.

"It's so romantic!" "How romantic!" Think of that word and how its usage almost always has an aesthetic connotation; for instance, it often indicates a captivating form or a show of passion. The term *romantic* implicitly unites love and art, and in *The Bride of Lammermoor* it does so explicitly. Lucy, "of a romantic cast," steeps herself in music, myth, poetry, legend-haunted surroundings—and in love many fathoms deep. Beholding Ravenswood, she "had never happened to see a young man of mien and features so romantic" (V, 62–63). "Romantic" here means being prone to the combined influences of love and the aesthetic imagination, and it carries a meaning of wanting to transcend the ordinary. Remember Austen's Charlotte Lucas, deciding to embrace the banal Collins, saying, "I am not romantic, you know."

Few novelists before him made more of the relations between art and life or between art and art than Scott. The quotations that head his chapters, the reference to other writers and artistic modes, and his painterly composition of scene all show how aware he was that art gives both the continuity and the forms for the way people perceive experience. He insists that a literary and artistic heritage is an important part of history, like laws and wars, but he also makes clear that no previous art quite fits his particular characters and narrative, because, as the otherness of the past proves, time is always new, love is always particular, and life is always novel. Scott, trying to adapt the resources of other arts into his prose, shows how the novel can better render the social texture and the historical contingency in which love takes place.

The special romance of Scott's novel, this melding in narrative of the erotic subject with particular artistic forms and settings, permeates nineteenth-century aesthetic life. In Calvinist, iconoclastic Edinburgh, Scott tried to incorporate, in novels and words meant to make manifest human love, the images, arts, and aesthetic methods through which Roman Catholics and others had celebrated Christianity and sometimes love. *The Bride of Lammermoor* draws upon other arts, and the associations they carry, to help create its effects; but it also feeds those arts, directly or indirectly.

Music: Though it would be hard to say exactly how music has shaped history, personally and culturally we sense its power and influence. Lucy, beautiful and vulnerable, first appears singing. To suggest why Scott's image matters and what effect it might have, let me juxtapose the words that introduce the scene—"Music . . . affects us with a pleasure mingled with surprise, and reminds us of the natural concert of birds among the leafy bowers" (III, 39)—with an excerpt from William Kennedy's novel *Legs,* in which the legendary gangster Jack Diamond finds himself on a freighter with the famous Harz Mountain canaries. "Canaries," he writes, "are . . . wizards of hearing and love."

> "How's all the birdies?" Jack asked the sailor.
> "Very sad," said the sailor. "They sing to overcome their sadness."
> "That's not why birds sing," Jack said.

"Sure it is."
"Are you positive?"
"I live with birds. I'm part bird myself."[15]

A *piaf* no doubt, like Lucy. The arts inspire and support faith in an otherwise sorry life, and the image of Lucy singing works to illuminate the uncanny mutual interflow between music and a passionate commitment to love. The fact is, no matter how sentimental it seems, the vision of a fragile woman, in the midst of trouble and sorrow, pouring out her feelings in a song really has touched, if only for a moment, the emotional lives of huge numbers of people. Scott's composition claims for Lucy the sympathies we feel for music, but it also suggests and begs for the voice of music itself, the art that, to sensual apprehension, best expresses the immediate feeling and ecstasy of love. Donizetti gave Lucy that voice. The music of operatic characters like Lucia, Bellini's Norma, Verdi's Violetta, Wagner's Isolde, and Puccini's Madame Butterfly, and of real-life singers ranging from Callas to Billie Holiday and Edith Piaf, seems to epitomize, in their apparently tragic affirmation of love, all the desperate, sacrificial beauty of erotic faith.

Painting: Scott's fiction sometimes seems like an album of tableaux through which one slowly shuffles. The power of pictorial composition and images impressed him deeply, and he claims it for the novel. So much of love for Lucy, for Ravenswood, and for their author is image—the image that provokes love, the image that sustains love in the absence of the beloved, and the image that renders the emotions of love. The painter Dick Tinto, in the first chapter, shows the narrator a picture of Ravenswood, Lucy, and her mother at a time, we later learn, when the match is broken off, and says this about his art:

"[Y]ou have accustomed yourself so much to these creeping twilight details of yours, that you are become incapable of receiving that instant and vivid flash of conviction, which darts on the mind from seeing the happy and expressive combinations of a single scene, and which gathers from the position, attitude, and countenance of the moment, not only the history of the past lives of the personages represented, and the nature of the business on which they are immediately engaged, but lifts even the veil of futurity, and affords a shrewd guess at their future fortunes." [I, 25]

Scott wants to combine with narrative the fixing of an image—its abstraction out of time—that we associate with the fine arts. Think how well the phrase "that instant and vivid flash of conviction" fits an art that is going to stress falling in love. The passage also makes clear the emphasis on *focus*, on the artistic transformation of life's flux into an image that minds can and will absorb, preserve, and use.

Scott fixes on erotic fixation. He is cannibalizing the art of painting for the novel and erotics, internalizing the imagination, setting forth objects of desire for the mind's eye, and claiming, in effect, the right to read in pictures the flow of time—the time of narrative and the reader's time too. Take this description of Lucy: "Her locks, which were of shadowy gold, divided on a brow of exquisite whiteness, like a gleam of broken and pallid sunshine upon a hill of snow" (III, 40). That appropriates the painted features of a love goddess or beautiful madonna—figures of reverence—for the love story, and it employs and teaches a habit of aesthetic allusion by which artworks of the past can be applied to the present, released from their frames and set dancing in subjectivity. Botticelli's Venus would soon be born again.

Sculpture: Scott describes Ravenswood bursting in on the Ashtons at the moment they are forcing Lucy to sign a wedding contract with Bucklaw:

Lucy seemed stiffened to stone by this unexpected apparition. . . . for Ravenswood had now more the appearance of one returned from the dead, than of a living visitor.
     . . . His dark-coloured riding cloak, displaced from one shoulder, hung around one side of his person in the ample folds of the Spanish mantle. . . . His slouched hat . . . gave an additional gloom to his dark features, which, wasted by sorrow, and marked by the ghastly look communicated by long illness, added to a countenance naturally somewhat stern and wild, a fierce and even savage expression. The matted and dishevelled locks of hair which escaped from under his hat, together with his fixed and unmoved posture, made his head more resemble that of a marble bust than that of a living man. He said not a single word. [XXXIII, 307]

Scott's prose works to connect our common associations with sculpture to his scene and hero, especially the tactile, weighty sense of frozen emotion and the memorial, sepulchral quality of statues, busts, and effigies. He seems to be trying to carve out an image of the romantic hero both to make us see the impression he imagines it forming in Lucy's mind and to fix it in the pantheon of popular fancy.

Actually, this verbal sculpture forms a wordplay on a famous legendary statue and represents a significant change in erotic history. Ravenswood is "the Stone Guest." The image and legend of Don Juan figures here, for Scott describes his hero as a perfect statue of the traditional, Spanish Don Juan. In that myth, of course, the violator of love, woman, family, religion, and true honor is punished by the sudden entrance of the avenging "Stone Guest," the statue of Anna's slain father. Here it is the family that violates the girl, forcing a de facto rape, and the intruding statue is the Don Juan figure himself, committed to love. The new stone guest makes his dramatic appearance on behalf of erotic faith, not Christian retribution. The family sins against romantic love, and the sworn bond between two lovers has a higher sanctity than ties of kinship. This marble-like figure, like the statue of the commandante, signifies the implacable vengeance of a powerful god, but this god is now Eros.

Though *The Bride of Lammermoor* so often touches the form of other arts, it is a novel: its view of love depends upon the primacy of narrative and the word. Much of the nineteenth-century will to express lyrically and musically pure emotional intensity, to dramatize ecstasy, and to use the power and resources of visual arts to depict love flows from the novel. In the age of individualism, love and romantic faith become personalized myth, and the novel features the subjectivity, and often the interiority, in which love life is experienced.

V

The novel, the medium of private, silent reading, internalizes spectacle, drama, love. The art that most directly relates to Scott's tale is Shakespeare's, and *The Bride of Lammermoor* is inconceivable without it. His trace runs through nearly every page. Rhetorically, Scott uses Shakespeare to claim the kind of importance for his novel that the works of this most esteemed of writers have, and conceptually, he uses him to emphasize the continuity of artistic and historical imagination. And yet, though Scott absorbs *Romeo and Juliet*, *Hamlet*, Ophelia, Lady Macbeth, Lucrece, and other plays and figures into his imagination, his love story's novelty—the way it differs from its Shakespearean influences—is the most interesting thing about it.

Compare the novel to *Romeo and Juliet*: In both, love is fate and fate is love; each honors love and deplores visiting kinship vendettas and other sins of the past upon the young; both works sympathize with the idea of personal choice in marriage; and both sets of lovers become emblems of tragic love. Explicitly referring to the Capulets and Montagues in dramatizing the Ashton-Ravenswood blood feud (see XXXIII, 307), Scott wanted to associate Ravenswood and Lucy with the two most famous lovers in English literature. But his narrative makes the historical impact and changes that the growing popular importance of romantic feeling brings much more critical than they are in Shakespeare, and he much more carefully specifies the economic, religious, and political causes of *his* family feud.

The novel presents a serious crisis of faith as the play does not, and Scott's focus on the perverted marriage with its bloody act of penetration highlights that crisis. Instead of Shakespeare's kindly Christian Friar Lawrence, ally of the love match, Scott imagines the bigoted Rev. Mr. Bide-the-bent, whose faith opposes the marriage of true lovers. Unlike Juliet, Lucy turns murderous, not suicidal, striking out madly at social corruption and faithlessness. Juliet marries Romeo and has a joyful wedding night, but for Lucy the sacrament of marriage itself is horribly profaned. The violation of love looks like a matter of greater social consequence in *The Bride of Lammermoor* than in *Romeo and Juliet* because there seems little else that could be a basis of true value in Scott's world.

Hamlet echoes almost as resonantly here as *Romeo*. Like *Hamlet*, the novel features madness, drowning, and revenge. Ravenswood, like the melancholy Dane, gets caught between conflicting codes and demands, and he finds it hard to take clear-cut action. Like Ophelia, Lucy, much put upon by everyone and disappointed in love, goes mad and dies. She has a Laertes-like brother, Colonel Ashton, who hates Ravenswood and—à la the graveyard scene—quarrels with him at Lucy's funeral, challenging him to a duel which leads to his own death.

In the novel, however, love becomes central; it matters infinitely more to Ravenswood, whose pledged faith to Lucy overpowers every political, economic, or social consideration, than to Hamlet. Ravenswood chooses love over filial vengeance; and Lucy, from passive marginal victim like Ophelia, turns into an erotic avenger. Just as watery as Ophelia, she claims as her own spot the fountain where the legendary nymph who loved a Ravenswood drowned. She seems headed for a similar fate, but instead, erupting into violence, she transforms violated, nuptially unconsummated love—the experience of Ophelia—into the crucial dramatic fact of the novel. John Millais's great painting *Ophelia* (1852; fig. 4), featuring the flower-bestrewn girl floating in a brook, mouthing songs, and about to die, owes much more to the nineteenth-century spirit of erotic faith that Scott's Lucy helps define, than to Shakespeare. (Turn the picture on its side and Ophelia could be Lucia di Lammermoor singing at her fountain.)

Scott also used *Macbeth*: a *Macbeth*-like aura of wild menace hangs over the novel; Lady Ashton has the pride, the ambition, and many of the mannerisms of Lady Macbeth; and three witchlike crones gloat over the carnage. But again the alteration of the adapted features is what tells most. The daughter, not the mother, wields the knife, smears the blood, and goes insane. In the novel the woman stabs out of mad rage at the pollution of love and faith, not out of desire for political power.

His witch figures show clearly Scott's literary and historical bifocalism. They are creatures of superstition, presiding over death and misfortune, representing blind, unredeemed fate, like their Shakespearean ancestors or like the memorable figures in Goya's *Three Fates*. They would seem to be beings out of old times, traditional images of fatalism and evil. But Scott also gives them the function of directly expressing class hatred and political discontent.

"If grit folk gie poor bodies ony thing for coming to their weddings and burials, it suld be something that wad do them gude, I think."

"Their gifts," said Ailsie Gourlay, "are dealt for nae love of us—nor out of respect for whether we feed or starve. They wad gie us whinstanes for loaves, if it would serve their ain vanity, and yet they expect us to be as gratefu', as they ca' it, as if they served us for true love and liking." [XXXIV, 318]

These figures suggest the idea of class warfare and a miserable world in need of some "true love and liking," as Ailsie calls it.

Another Shakespearean heroine, Lucrece, the chaste wife and rape victim in the poem *The Rape of Lucrece,* bears upon Lucy's experience (Lucrece = Lucy). Ravaged and shamed, she also wields a dagger, committing suicide. The parallel with Lucy is obvious, but the real point is surely that Lucy chooses to attack a guilty man rather than kill herself. One simple, broad meaning that emerges when we compare Scott to his Shakespearean sources is this: *Women, exploited and deprived of love, have a new will, motive, and power to strike out and cause devastating harm.*

VI

"Fatal love," says the blind old sibyl, Alice, as she warns Ravenswood off Lucy. His love is fatal in several senses: preordained, historic, doomed, and mortal. Detail after detail, passage after passage, spells out the symmetry of omnipotent fate—and the novelist's plot. But primarily love is fatal in the sense that it decisively makes destiny. Everything else—blood pride, political machination, traditional allegiances, the scramble for place and property, the tenor of every-day life, conventional wisdom, organized religion, intimations of a pagan super-natural realm—pales next to the determining force of love.

That is not to say, though, that all the "thick description" of the book—the store of local legends, a range of characters from the whole strata of Scottish life, Caleb Balderstone's wheedling for food, the old women's witchcraft, ques-tions about the British monarchy and who has the government's backing—is pointless. On the contrary Scott, maddeningly prolix as he can seem, needs a fully imagined, broad social world in which to set love. In all his fiction he finds the details of folkways and "local color" essential in understanding and render-ing both historical process and individual character. But the accumulated, spirit-numbing details of life and economy make inevitable the desire for some sort of transcendent faith. Lucy and Ravenswood can find no value in the mean social clutter without their faith in love. Though the web of alliances, obligations, commitments, and traditions from the past pulls them apart and fatally con-demns their love, we may say also, it fatally condemns them *to* love. Nothing else seems worthy of their idealism.

What are we to make of this story? Some critics of the novel treat the protag-onists as if they were merely unlucky or misguided in their love choices. Others read it as an exercise in the gothic, as balanced and skillful Scottish social history, as a genuine tragedy of fate showing the insignificance of human will. By now, however, it should be clear that in *The Bride of Lammermoor* we are dealing with something almost mystical and religious in nature. This novel says that humanity is fated to live in a world where erotic love demands and commands the faith of some of the best people, and that that fate and faith constitute a fact of the highest consequence.

One of the simple, superficial meanings in this tale is that the past illuminates and often determines our fate. More interesting is another meaning: present events and fate determine the meaning of the past. Nineteenth-century romantic faith might determine how old myths and local traditions are perceived and what they signify. The history of Mermaiden's Well (V, 56–58), where Ravenswood and Lucy pledge their faith, contributes to the sense of fatality hanging over the love story.

The popular legend reports that in olden times a beautiful young lady fascinated and made love to a Ravenswood baron once a week near the fountain, but she could not outstay the ringing of the chapel bell for vespers. Confessing these trysts to the hermit-priest who rang the bell, the baron was persuaded by the cleric that the mistress might be an agent of Satan and that if tricked into staying late by a delay in ringing the chimes she would assume the shape of "a fiend of hell." No change takes place in the nymph's form, but when she was "aware that the usual hour . . . was passed, she tore herself from her lover's arms with a shriek of despair, bid him adieu for ever, and, plunging into the fountain, disappeared from his eyes. The bubbles occasioned by her descent were crimsoned with blood as they arose, leading the distracted Baron to infer, that his ill-judged curiosity had occasioned the death of this interesting and mysterious being" (V, 57–58). Those "wiser than the vulgar," however, explain the legend "as obscurely intimating the fate of a beautiful maid of plebeian rank, the mistress of this Raymond, whom he slew in a fit of jealousy" (V, 58). Others say "the tale had a more remote origin in the ancient heathen mythology" (V, 58). That last phrase has the effect, typical of Scott, of sweeping up everything—here, love, ancient superstition, Christianity itself, and conflicting ideas about faith and fate—into a historical perspective.

One of the marks of nineteenth-century literature and a sign of the amorous faith that infuses it is the use of erotic symbolism in describing place, setting, and landscape. The sexuality and romantic emotion of perceivers flood into what they perceive and then wash back in an eroticizing tide. Lucy, haunting the fountain, becomes its siren, and Scott imagines the romantic spirit joining with "ancient heathen mythology" to show the fatal power of love running through the nature of things: "She sate upon one of the disjointed stones . . . and seemed to watch the progress of its current, as it bubbled forth. . . . To a superstitious eye, Lucy Ashton, folded in her plaited mantle, with her long hair . . . falling upon her silver neck, might have suggested the idea of the murdered Nymph of the Fountain" (XX, 197). The novel is claiming the power of the contemporary imagination to retrieve and expropriate for the self the myths of the past.

Some wag said that what men like to believe about women is that they are wet; if so, literature and art have surely helped to form that idea. Imaginative impressions run together in psyches and artworks about water, sex, fertility, the pleasant sounds of bubbling and babbling, engulfing passions, oceanic feeling, and enticing, dangerous flow. Ravenswood falls fatally in love at a fountain, and he dies at Kelpie's Flow, sucked into the ocean. Again and again in the century to follow, language and narrative join together woman, water, sexuality, countryside, legend, and love.

Says Lucy to Ravenswood, "I like this spot, . . . the bubbling murmur of the clear fountain, the waving of the trees, the profusion of grass and wild-flowers, that rise among the ruins, make it like a scene in romance. I think, too, I have heard it is a spot connected with the legendary lore which I love so well" (XX, 197). Why? At first blush, the grisly legend hardly seems lovable. Notice that the remark about the "lore which I love so well" might fit both author and audience: the writer and reader of historical fiction, oddly enough, do occupy a position very much like Lucy's. What Lucy does is to aestheticize suffering, and that kind of sublimation helps to make not just historicism and historical fiction comprehensible, but religious passion and erotic faith as well, with their various forms of martyrdom. Suffering is perceived as sacrifice, and the perceiver regards the sacrifice as personally redemptive. Also, sinister deeds of the past diffuse into a physical setting of beauty, and the reassuring reality of lovely nature redeems past agony. Moreover, the precedent of the past justifies present desire and belief. The past flows into the self, but the imagination projects itself into the past, and the mental leap out of a narrow present promises the possibility that the future too might be other and better.

Lucy's life and death help us to see the fountain-girl folklore as part of an evolving process that puts fatal love and erotic perception at the center of history. The reference to heathen mythology, in view of Lucy's fate, means that the novel is telling a very important story in, and about, an ongoing clash of faiths. Over time, human fate—the world, personal and social relationships, and how we think about them—has been shaped, and continues to be shaped, by erotic desire. That desire, however, taking many forms, has often been condemned by orthodox religion. The novel sets the clerical and parental use of Scripture to break Lucy's romantic pledge beside the medieval hermit's attack on eroticism.

Scott, like so many nineteenth-century artists who would follow, is fascinated by the collision between love faith and established religion. He wants very much to reconcile them and to isolate the crisis of faith in the past, though in trying to do so he risks sounding either smug or ironic: "The lovers soon discovered that they differed upon other and no less important topics. Religion, the mother of peace, was, in those days of discord, so much misconstrued and mistaken, that her rules and forms were the subject of the most opposite opinions, and the most hostile animosities" (XXI, 206). This language reads like wishful think-ing—the tacit message is, "let us act properly and make these words true"—but it does work to smooth over conflict between orthodox and erotic faith in Scott's age. It also implies that religion can only be a true mother of peace if it joins with the spirit of love, which in this novel offers a living model for future times of redemption through suffering, that is, an example of true passion.

If in light of Lucy's fate we consider the brutal alternative explanation of the fountain legend—a jealous upper-class lover murders a lower-class girl—it no longer seems an isolated crime, but takes its place in an unfolding pattern of erotic terrorism and class rape. Lucy's burst of violence historically refocuses what has come before. It lets us see both continuity and inevitable change, and shows that continuing persecution of love and cultural erotic repression will eventually have uncontrollable consequences. Putting aside her passivity, Lucy becomes a mad defender of a faith that has become a historical necessity. Her attack on the unwanted husband culminates not just a personal history of moral and physical violation, but a social history in which, Scott imagines, Lucy and the maid at the well both take part. Erotic faith can no longer be suppressed with impunity to the suppressors.

The fate of Lucy means that we might reinterpret what has come before and see as crucial those scenes and figures that had earlier seemed contained and marginal. The piercing of the bridegroom, then, comments on the legend of the fountain, and the legend comments on the reasons why the bride stabbed him. So the writing of the novel in the early nineteenth century and its influence on the artists and public of the century are a commentary on the fatal importance of the alleged factual incident that Scott claims to have taken as source material; and that seventeenth-century case, in light of the novel, is a commentary on the reasons for the hold and power of romantic faith on Scott, his disciples in the arts, and their audiences.

The lovers are ravished by irreconcilable historical pressures: victims of his-tory. As a novelist, Scott excels at rendering the conflicting codes and customs from different times that play upon men and women—including the clash of his contemporary ethos with that in the period of his setting. We always view his past with the implicit historical knowledge of what later happened. Each char-acter, he shows, is like a live geological specimen made up of layers of historical stratification, but so are the author and reader. In Scott's vision the dead and their desires live in every self.

VII

The title *The Bride of Lammermoor* calls attention to the subject of marriage. The Christian ministry in the book ironically debases the marriage sacrament, but erotic faith resanctifies it by showing the deadly peril if it is undertaken without loving spiritual commitment. Gothic novels, playing on readers' fears, often portray the degradation of matrimony, with false faith—Roman Catholicism in some perverted form—usually being the guilty agency. Scott's switch is to blame the rabid Protestantism that supports the loveless match. Lucy's debacle broadcasts love propaganda to the nineteenth century: marriage without love is madness.

Scott renders the "fatal" historical moment when the ideal of romantic love as a basis for marriage clashed with older ideals of family loyalty, duty, and honor. The Ashtons, though they take marriage very seriously, do not take erotic love seriously at all. The bride's father and her brother, though not the mother, really do love Lucy, but none of them has real qualms about marrying her, for reasons of family interest, to a man she does not love. They all regard this woman as *disposable*. Ravenswood does not, and that is what makes his love for her and her freely given love for him both disruptive and progressive.

The *Bride*: The ambiguous definition of the word, "a woman who has just been married or is about to be married," puts in question Lucy's virginity, her sexuality, and her relation to the society that sanctions marriage. Making that problematic term the focus of the novel and its title, Scott throws emphasis on the circumstances of her wedding, her would-be bedding, and her woman's fate as a being who is defined by marriage. The pages describing her bridal fate are crucial. They bring to light buried sexual obsessiveness and dramatize one of the deep implicit fears of the collective (un)consciousness in Scott's century—and in many other times and places too: *the wedding night is a stabbing*.[16]

Before Lucy's psychopathic demise, Scott stresses the impersonality of behavior towards the bride. Nothing at the marriage festival has to do with her inner person or consciousness. "It is well known," he writes, "that the weddings of ancient days were celebrated with a festive publicity rejected by the delicacy of modern times" (XXXIV, 321). Ostensibly a historical remark, it actually moralizes in favor of private life, and rhetorically it works to distance the past and meliorate the present. Scott writes that a "ball . . . always closed a bridal entertainment. . . . the gentlemen crowded into the saloon, where, enlivened by wine and the joyful occasion, they laid aside their swords, and handed their impatient partners to the floor" (XXXIV, 321). The effect is to profane and diminish with a slight hint of libertinage the private nature of the marriage.

After Lady Ashton prepares Lucy, she sends Bucklaw off to the bridal chamber: "The instruments now played their louder strains—the dancers pursued their exercise with all the enthusiasm inspired by youth, mirth and high spirits, when a cry was heard so shrill and piercing, as at once to arrest the dance and the music. . . . when the yell was again repeated, Colonel Ashton . . . rushed thither . . . followed by Sir William and Lady Ashton . . . and . . . near relations of the family" (XXXIV, 322).

Scott here gives us an instance of what later would become one of the most characteristic traits of Victorian fiction: sexual concern and activity are featured, but only indirectly rendered. We need to see that this whole passage puts the sexual act at the center of marriage and alludes to the most delicate subject imaginable to a nineteenth-century audience, the erotic act of "deflowering." Scott's narrative art is forcing the issue of whether anyone has the moral right to dispose of another person's sexuality.

This chapter shows how close sex and violence can be in the human psyche and how important it was to Scott and his century to merge sex with love. The scene associates, subliminally at least, sex with pain rather than pleasure, and, not incidentally, makes it a matter of spiritual passion and high moral seriousness. *The Bride of Lammermoor* thus condemns in the strongest terms the trivialization and exploitation of sex. The romantic and novelistic sensibility now finds tragically outrageous what had been commonplace in the past. Specifically Scott raises the question of what exactly happens to a young woman who is coerced into marrying a man she does not love. The details of the text do not let readers easily avoid what is at stake: having to have sex without love amounts to slavery. If marriage is a public and impersonal matter—a violent bending of personal preference to social purpose—then the ideal of individual sexual chastity and fidelity becomes a cynical mockery. If romantic love and personal choice do not form the basis for marriage, then sex in wedlock is just using and being used—violation and pointless sacrifice.

Scott's prose both reveals and conceals. The word "piercing" here reverberates as much as any in the novel. It carries the pain of violated erotic faith and yokes sex to violence; but who lets out a "shrill and piercing" cry, and why? Is the first cry Lucy's when she is being pierced and is the second her cry when she pierces the groom in retaliation? Is one cry his and one hers, or are they both his? Do they both concern the stabbing? What exactly happened? We never know (Lucy dies; Bucklaw, "a sadder and a wiser man" [XXXIV, 325], never tells), and Scott's narrative reticence is one of most important things about the passage. Nineteenth-century middle-class sensibility made it a matter of faith that the conjugal bedroom was private, not public, business.

And yet, as my questions suggest, the whole scene tends to make us more, not less, curious about sex; more, not less, aware of its frightful importance. Its logic moralizes sex and says that a bride and her maidenhead ought not to be regarded as commodities. It implies that sex and love ought not be separate and that, in the end, they cannot be reduced to social convention, law, custom, or biology; instead they remain inseparable from the individual spirit and imagination. The implicit sexual violence and the bloody consequence argue for different proceedings; an attempt to spiritualize sexuality and remove it from public consciousness, far from being an evasive trick of prudish hypocrisy, could be an assertion of human dignity.

We will never understand nineteenth-century repression of public sexuality, sexual discourse, and overt sexual reference if we do not see that 1) it was in some part an effort to enhance personal freedom and the sanctity of marriage by making nuptial sexuality a private matter; 2) it was a means of making sex mysterious—mysterious in the common sense, meaning that it would draw people's imaginative speculation, and mysterious in the religious sense, meaning that its essence and energy could be attached to positive faith and the sacrament of marriage; 3) its premise was that sex has such an awesome potential to influence and disrupt people's lives that it should never be treated casually, nor merely as a means of sensual pleasure; and 4) it was intended, by calling into play sublimating powers, to glorify personal love and make it even more prominent.

VIII

The Bride of Lammermoor does not sentimentalize love. One of the most tragic things about it is that in her madness Lucy loses the virtue of her faith. She learns to hate and strike, like almost everyone else in the book. Her violence, a twisted miming of Edgar's behavior, is a perverse reaffirmation of faith, but she finds no peace or resigned love. Instead she dies in a ghastly betrayal by and of her body, without redemption, *out of her mind*, "convulsed into a wild paroxysm" (XXXIV, 323), as if she were caught up in some morbid pantomime of orgasm: "Convulsion followed convulsion, till they closed in death" (324).

In creating *Lucia di Lammermoor*, Donizetti and Cammarano suppressed the history, the politics, and the older generation, and seized on the mad scene following the stabbing to make it the prime dramatic occasion for the expression of love and its redemptive beauty. They used madness as an opportunity for Lucia to create intense pathos for herself and to recapitulate and display the ecstasy of love. In her crazed, lovely singing, the opera satisfies for the moment an emotion the novel arouses but suspends: the longing to find in romantic love radiance and freedom from the sordid earth. This desire—the desire that Lucy so concentrates and Lucia expresses (and seems for a few soaring instants to fulfill)—is what so moves the sympathies of Madame Bovary, Forster's crowd, and so many other anonymous dreamers of the heart. Like a figure of legend for characters within his tale, Scott's heroine became a catalyst for erotic sentimentality. But for the novelist, the lovers' fall from grace is irrevocable.

Scott sometimes allows his skepticism to play upon the lovers' passion and his style to distance himself from it. The love that Lucy and Ravenswood feel for one another and their attachment are not rational: "he gave his faith to her for ever, and received her troth in return. . . . out of the immediate impulse of the moment" (XX, 198). They love their faith in love more than the other person, with whom they fall in love without really knowing. Not only do almost all the other characters, from all social levels, oppose this union, but Scott takes pains to show that the lovers are not at all conventionally suited to one another. They differ in intelligence, temperament, religion, and politics. Both also worry that the other will break faith.

Which each does. Her "ductile temper" cannot stand up to her mother's tireless will, and he, unable to control his proud spirit, denounces her and throws away the symbol of their faith. Neither is fated to satisfy the deep desires of the other: his, for the possession of peace, beauty, social amity, and family honor; hers, for moral guidance, strength, respect, and disinterested concern. Unfulfilled, they die, victims of fatal love.

But to summarize in this way is, of course, to distort the novel and the force of erotic faith. Scott's story means anything but that these two blindly and foolishly ignore all wisdom and improperly follow deceiving romantic love to their death. Their world offers them no other choice, no way to try to satisfy their desires except through love, flawed though their love may be. The point of the novel is not to demonstrate incorrect procedure, nor to say that the love between Lucy and Edgar is an example of infatuation to be avoided, nor even to say that it is right and good—but to show them "in fatal love." Historical circumstances and personal characteristics, as Scott imagines them, may make their erotic tragedy inevitable, but that just makes the vision of love more powerful. The scholar of romantic love reads about whether it is a good or bad thing, but such discussions finally seem as pointless as talking about whether the weather cycle is good or bad; what counts is that it exists, or has existed, and that it determines fate.

The faith of the lovers falters and fails to save them, but as emblems of faith for others, they succeed. Scott movingly shows them both true at last to their faith, beyond rationality, morality, or aesthetic fitness, each acting out the fate and the faith of the other, struggling for intimacy and erotic oneness even to the point of insanity and death. Lucy's wedding-night behavior recapitulates, in a mime of her unconscious imagination, Ravenswood's words, feelings, and actions during the scene when, beset and confused, they break faith. "Are you prepared to pierce my heart for its fidelity, with the very weapon which my rash confidence intrusted to your grasp?" he says to her, and then throws their gold pledge into the fire and crushes it (XXXIII, 313). That is why we have the piercing cry and the stabbing, Lucy's act of vengeance for Ravenswood. That is why she is found crouched gibbering in the chimney, a human fetish to replace the symbol of his faith. After her death, Edgar, for his part, insists on spending his last night in "the room in which SHE slept the night they were at the castle" (XXXV, 330). By her bed, he, like she, abandons himself "to paroxysms of un-controlled agony" (XXXV, 330). Finally, like Lucy's fountain nymph, he goes out and drowns in love. It is as simple—and as complicated—as that.

Erotic relationship is the only area in this novel's world that allows free play to express and receive personal affection, and reverence for individual worth. Ravenswood says that his "attachment [is] to Miss Ashton *personally*" (XXII, 255; italics mine). Others ally themselves for reasons of party spirit, social obligation, tradition, advantage, kinship, creed, and the like. Only the lovers care deeply about the private, inimitable essence of another being. No wonder that in an age of intensifying individualism, the voice of Lucy would be heard.[17]

IX

The article of romantic faith in the nineteenth century that love is fate made art. Edward Burne-Jones's masterpiece of fatal love, *King Cophetua and the Beggar Maid* (1884; fig. 15), pays homage to Scott's amorous imagination and illustrates the erotic, sacrificial quality and meaning of *The Bride of Lammermoor*. Of course the media of painting and fiction differ, and the effects of these two works, though complementary, are not the same. But Burne-Jones, who once exclaimed, "I love Scott the most,"[18] emphatically does make graphic what we see developing in Scott: the picture, from one end of the nineteenth century, presents the triumph of erotic faith; the novel, from the other, prophesies its coming appeal.

D. H. Lawrence's description of Miriam in *Sons and Lovers* helps me to draw the connection I want between the novel and the picture: "The girl was romantic in her soul. Everywhere was a Walter Scott heroine being loved by men . . . with plumes in their caps. [Ravenswood is wearing a large sable feather in his hat when he drowns (XXXV, 333).] She herself was something of a princess turned into a swine-girl, in her own imagination."[19] The meaning of the picture, as it was read by the late Victorians, is the impetus of the narrative: "the ele-vation of love above everything else."[20]

Burne-Jones took formal inspiration from Mantegna's fifteenth-century painting of the Virgin, *La Madonna della Vittoria*, and his subject from Tenny-son's "The Beggar Maid."[21] The feeling of the painting, however, is much closer to Scott's novel and its tensions than to that poem's sentimental tone:

> Barefooted came the beggar maid
> Before the King Cophetua. . . . .
> So sweet a face, such angel grace,

In all the land had never been: . . .
"This beggar maid shall be my queen."[22]

A young, handsome king dressed in old-fashioned garb—so like Ravenswood he might be his actual illustration—sits, amid the disregarded trappings of power and battle, at the feet of a beautiful maiden in a rich chamber, looking up at her with woeful devotion, totally absorbed. Wearing a thin dress, looking vulnerable and almost naked, her feet, arms, neck, and shoulders completely bare, and details of her torso and thighs visible through her "poor attire," she sits tensely on a pillowed double throne where the king has obviously placed her but not dared to join her. She does not look at him. Absently, she holds in her right hand a shedding bunch of anemones, symbol of rejected love. Wide-eyed, deeply serious, she stares in hypnotic fashion directly out of the picture. Behind and above these two figures, in the background where an orange tree blooms, two boys perform a song from sheets of music, and a window opens out to a lovely, twilit landscape. All these blessings of civilization—music, the skills of art and craft, the charms of wealth and taste that arise out of love and are in the service of love—the man and woman, in their fixation, ignore.

The picture invites narrative reading, and its composition says unmistakably, "Above all else, love matters." It subordinates temporal authority and material pomp to erotic influence. What keeps it from being sentimental or shallow, like Tennyson's piece, is that it conveys passion, sorrow, and sexual power. It also puts in question—like *The Bride of Lammermoor*—the free will and potential subjectivity of the woman as the poem does not. The man and the woman look unhappy and awestruck—stunned by the force and effect of erotic feeling, like the characters in Scott. This is not a rational world, but a place of obsession and idealism—even sacrifice. The figures incarnate and are held by an implacable fate. For half a millennium, painters had found inspiration and subject matter in the suffering, sacrifice, and religious passion of Christianity and its texts. The Pre-Raphaelites, as Christian faith lost its passionate hold, needed to discover fresh subjects of faith and sacrifice, and they found them in women suffering in love.

The maid, like Lucy, is a riveting, sacrificial being—icon and fetish, madonna and prisoner, a dramatic figure and a symbolic one also. As the formal, dominant center of focus, she mediates between the faith that inspires and is portrayed by the work of art, and the life of the audience. We cannot help but join with the lover and, in parallel behavior, focus on her. Sexual vulnerability and the arousing power of latent, but dangerous, sexual desire strongly permeate the work, as they do the wedding-night climax of *The Bride of Lammermoor*. Her strong-willed gaze out beyond material circumstance evokes the force of spirituality and suspends but does not dissipate the menace of concupiscence.[23] The beggar maid has a double function: she is the soulful, beloved protagonist in a very literary painting's love story, and she is the revered embodiment of erotic faith who shows the fatal power of love. She is both a character and an idol on a pedestal in a religion of love, a sacrificial erotic figure who says that the last shall be first.[24] Such a figure is highly problematic; adoration, the novel shows, may turn to sanctioned rape.

Like the novel, the painting is set in the past and, therefore, makes the same implicit claim for love's importance in determining human history and fate: *we are such people as we are because such things have happened in the past, and because we are such people this is how we imagine the past.* Both works pose a tension between the otherness and the contemporaneity of the past and render the paradoxical truth that it is both present and absent.

And they have one more thing in common: novelist and painter transform the paraphernalia of the past into romantic images and use them to fulfill erotic and aesthetic desire. History itself is made subservient to the purposes of art, and a belief in the fundamental priority in life of the erotic relations between individual men and women inspires artists. If we say that Scott—like Burne-Jones and so many other Victorian artists of all kinds whom Scott deeply affected—loved history, we need to say also that in history he found an old testament to love which they could read and use. But any faith and the art that renders it sooner or later raise the problem of who or what becomes the beautiful sacrifice and why.

The madness of Lucy is one of the fine achievements in British fiction, but it may be that only a comparative few, in the heyday of the exploded canon, will take the trouble to read of her fatal love, her carefully imagined erotic revenge, and the finely rendered logic of her mania. Nevertheless, even people who know nothing of Scott's Lucy may have honored or still be honoring her memory and his faith.

4   The Passionate Calling: Emily Brontë's *Wuthering Heights* (1847)

There are staggering similarities and even corresponding or interchangeable characteristics in the two systems, erotic and mystical.

GEORGES BATAILLE[1]

With a human love replacing the divine, Emily pursued in the novel the theme of spiritual union that can be made to triumph over the divisions of physical existence.

WINIFRED GÉRIN[2]

If the mystic says: "I am because I am God," or if Descartes says he is because he thinks, Cathy must say: "I am Heathcliff, therefore I exist." Her hyperbole is the climax and endpoint of the long tradition making love a private religion in which the loved one is God and there is a single worshipper and devotee.

J. HILLIS MILLER[3]

I

In 1842, the year that Emily and Charlotte Brontë went to school for a time on the Continent, *Giselle* was first performed in Paris. Like *Wuthering Heights*, that enduring ballet is one of the nineteenth-century testaments of erotic faith. Though the story lines of ballets and operas often read like the sport of drunk comedians, details of *Giselle's* plot bear looking at. A morally flawed hero capable of evil loves a girl of the country. These two, though very much in love, separate for reasons of class, and pathetic Giselle dies in a mad passion at the midpoint of the piece. The man visits her grave and her spirit haunts him; without her love, he is a damned and doomed man. A supernatural spell hangs in the atmosphere. The two lovers call and reach poignantly to one another from the opposite sides of death. He is willing to join her, but, as it happens, their mutual love gives each a form of life. For a time they dwell together in a night world of cruelty, erotic longing, loneliness, and extraordinary beauty. It's a hard, enchanted world where love's fatality literally gives you the Wilis. At the end, Giselle, a sacrificial figure, is absorbed into nature—into earth, grass, and flowers—where, the dancers mime, her beloved will join her in immortal love.

The fragile intensity of their love can be profoundly moving. Betrayal, bad faith, resentment, erotic victimization, sadism, and revenge fill the ballet; but, if the dancers' skill is good, all that fades in the audience's mind. The two lovers have a special calling. The motions, figures, and patterns of their love can make their experience appear worthwhile, lovely—even transcendent.

I push the comparison between Emily Brontë's novel and the ballet to point up how erotic faith permeates the art of the century. This ballet is a composite, synthetic work, so it reflects what's in the air.[4] In both works love is the most important thing, and it is all-consuming for the man as well as for the woman. Its frustration causes anguish and guilt, which then motivate behavior and haunt life. In both we sense a powerful erotic paganism clashing with a tepid or unsympathetic Christianity. Love is the true vocation. Other pursuits and concerns—like normal marriages, occupations, and worldly calculations—though inescapable, seem trivial, or the mere gathering of so many sour grapes. And both *Giselle* and the novel imply that lovers in death can find immortality.

There is one great difference, however, between the protagonists of these two works. Giselle's lover is a count; Heathcliff is as common as a Liverpool slum. Before Brontë, the great lovers—the devotees, in their various courtly and romantic fashions, of erotic faith, such as Tristan, Troilus, Romeo, Don Juan, Lovelace, Valmont, Werther, Emile, Fabrizio, Darcy, Ravenswood, and even the real-life Marquis de Sade and Lord Byron—had almost always been upper class, or, in the rare cases when they were not, at least they were of noble mind. Brontë mongrelizes Heathcliff, gives him a plebeian origin, makes him a dirty, degraded boy, shows him scrambling for money. Her passionate lover is a base-born marauder of bourgeois manners and morals, a true underdog. In creating him, she thus imagines love and erotic faith as potential motivating force and solace for the despised. To understand the power of *Wuthering Heights*, we need to grasp this idea: As divinity could appear in a stable or strike a persecuting tax collector in the road, so transfiguring passion might come to a manic, miserly sinner amid squalid conditions. As no figure had quite done before, Heathcliff—bad, impossible person—holds out the hope of erotic redemption.

Georges Bataille writes, "The lesson of *Wuthering Heights*, of Greek tragedy and, ultimately, of all religions, is that there is an instinctive tendency towards divine intoxication which the rational world of calculation cannot bear."[5] Heathcliff, showing how, in the modern age, romantic intensity and the capacity to love and attract love, like religious fervor historically, were becoming means for asserting self-worth and superiority, puts the case of erotic individualism this way: "If he [Edgar, Cathy's genteel husband] loved with all the powers of his puny being, he couldn't love as much in eighty years as I could in a day. And Catherine has a heart as deep as I have. . . . It is not in him to be loved like me."[6] Heathcliff seems to be describing an alternative capitalism of the heart, where subjective feeling and defiant devotion are wealth. Through him, Brontë gets at a revealing tension in nineteenth-century culture, for Heathcliff, in fact, has a genius for amassing property. His acquisitiveness, she shows, sublimates frustrated love, but she also shows that the amazing force of his erotic desire coexists with his passion and talent for appropriation. Thus erotic faith could both defy the quantifying money society and teach the necessary paradigms of desire that would make the system work. Heathcliff, in whom Emily Brontë makes the religion of love more catholic and democratic than it had ever been, stands between the religion of Christianity and the religion of capitalism, a rebel against the values of both, but with obvious ties to each. A grubbing messiah of unlimited spiritual desire, a miser who would rescue love from death, he looms as a figure of world-historical significance.

II

What happens to you after you die? Many people find that religious faith helps them face that question without falling into despair. Desire for transcendence, not just of the self but of the self's mortality, has motivated the will to faith since the first syllable of recorded time; and, if love is a faith, we ought to find that some of its devotees see it as a hope in confronting—or avoiding—the problem of personal death and annihilated consciousness. Death haunts Emily Brontë's *Wuthering Heights*, as it so terribly haunted the Brontë family, and in its pages she imagines a mystical, passionate calling as a way of facing the immanent and imminent mortal agony. The book, as earthy a piece of Victorian fiction as there is, grounds grand romantic passion in the gross texture of everyday life. Nevertheless, it is a crucial text of mystical erotic vocation, raising and forcing most of the critical issues that swirl about romantic love in the post-Renaissance era.

Emily Brontë's characters talk repeatedly about afterlife. No novelist's imagination has ever bound love and death more closely together, and no nineteenth-century writer more clearly shows the relation between the menace of unredeemed, meaningless death and the rise of popular faith in romantic love. Hating and fearing death, people have often professed to welcome it as a release into eternal joy. If you are good, you may go to heaven when you die; you may find "peace." Some form of that idea has been a traditional solace of religion. In one of her famous speeches, Catherine Earnshaw, to the chagrin of conventional Nelly Dean, rejects such orthodoxy. "If I were in heaven, Nelly, I should be extremely miserable. . . . I dreamt, once, that I was there. . . . heaven did not seem to be my home; and I broke my heart with weeping to come back to earth; and the angels were so angry that they flung me out, into the middle of the heath on the top of Wuthering Heights; . . . That will do to explain my secret" (IX, 72). It will do also to explain the novel's title: "Wuthering Heights" means the rejection of heaven. Reject heaven and you reject angels—even angels-in-the-house. We have here the complaint of romantic individualism that Christian heaven—theocratic authority called bliss and made perpetual—does not seem to be an inviting place or a satisfactory consolation for death.

But it is one thing for advanced poets like Blake, Byron, and Shelley to side with Satan's rebellion against heaven, and another for a Yorkshire parson's daughter to find the dogma of afterlife wanting. We are confronting a growing crisis for orthodox faith. *Wuthering Heights* is filled with a religious urgency—unprecedented in British novels—to imagine a faith that might replace the old. Cathy's "secret" is blasphemous, and Emily Brontë's secret, in the novel, is the raging heresy that has become common in modern life: redemption, if it is possible, lies in personal desire, imaginative power, and love. Nobody else's heaven is good enough. Echoing Cathy, Heathcliff says late in the book, "I have nearly attained *my* heaven; and that of others is altogether unvalued and un-coveted by me!" (XXXIV, 259). Even Cathy II and young Linton imagine their own ideas of the perfect heaven (XXIV, 198–99). The hope for salvation be-comes a matter of eroticized private enterprise.

Faith tries to reconcile what, to reason, is irreconcilable. Consciousness of death and of the self defines us as human, and yet human beings try to deny the death of the self. Catherine and Heathcliff have faith in their vocation of being in love with one another. Says she, "If all else perished, and *he* remained, I should still continue to be; and, if all else remained, and he were annihilated, the Universe would turn to a mighty stranger. I should not seem a part of it" (IX, 74). He cries that "nothing"—not "death," not "God or Satan" (XV, 135)—has the strength to part them. They both believe that they have their being in the other, as Christians, Jews, and Moslems believe that they have their being in God. Look at the mystical passion of these two: devotion to shared experience and intimacy with the other; willingness to suffer anything, up to, and including, death, for the sake of this connection; ecstatic expression; muti-lation of both social custom and the flesh; and mania for self-transcendence through the other. That passion is a way of overcoming the threat of death and the separateness of existence. Their calling is to *be* the other; and that calling, mad and destructive as it sometimes seems, is religious.

Wuthering Heights features the desire to transgress normal limitations, and that desire accounts for its violence and for the eccentric, fascinating flow of libido in it. If we think of the three major acts and areas of erotic transgression for the nineteenth-century imagination—sadism, incest, and adultery—and then consider how the Cathy-Heathcliff love story touches on them, we can see why the novel has had such a mind-jangling effect. It's a very kinky book, re-plete with polymorphous perversity, sadomasochism, necrophilia, hints of pedophilia, and even a bent towards polyandry, as well as incest and adultery. All this, however, figures in the urge to free the spirit from social conventions, the world, and the galling limitation of the body. That dispersed eroticism, shocking as it is, connects with an underlying drive for the breaking of boundaries—transgression as a means to transcendence.

Consider the question of Brontë's pervasive sadism: she seems to revel in rendering pain. One of the first things we find out about Cathy, even before Heathcliff comes, is that when her father asks her what present she would like, she opts for a whip. That choice characterizes her life. Like Heathcliff, she behaves with a prodigal disregard of physical well-being, almost as though will and love could turn pain to pleasure—which is the point of libidinal sadism. The lovers' sadism ought in part to be seen in the same light as disdainful war on the flesh by early Christian ascetics. Their erotic faith claims a passion superior to physical circumstances. The pain that figures so deeply in the novel's view of erotic psychology impinges upon Christianity's emphasis on the Christian Holy Passion. Few writers get so directly at the petulant fury of love—that anger at a limited state of being that frustrates free and timeless erotic connection. The author, like Cathy and Heathcliff who starve their bodies, seems furious at fleshly matter because it confines souls and keeps beings apart from one another and from nature. Bearing pain—or even inflicting it—tests lovers and the strength of love; it helps induce heightened states of ecstasy and insight, proves one's spiritual devotion, and defies the way of the world. Mortifying the flesh for being mortal, Emily Brontë rebels against materialism for confining love.

Spiritual quest shapes the life of the book. Says Catherine to Nelly, "I cannot express it; but surely you and everybody have a notion that there is, or should be, an existence of yours beyond you. What were the use of my creation if I were entirely contained here?" (IX, 73–74). Those are the words of religious seeking. She is talking about the difficulty and the necessity of making manifest the ineffable but common inner mysteries of spiritual desire, talking about the wish for an immortal soul. The Christian characters—Joseph, the brimstone-ranting fundamentalist; Nelly, charitable voice of conventional, pragmatic Anglicanism; and even Lockwood, tepid defender of orthodoxy—could all subscribe to those two sentences of Cathy's.

That is not true of the famous enunciation of her creed that follows: "My love for Linton is like the foliage in the woods. Time will change it, I'm well aware, as winter changes the trees. My love for Heathcliff resembles the eternal rocks beneath—a source of little visible delight, but necessary. Nelly, I *am* Heathcliff" (IX, 74). Here Brontë is setting out a heretical erotic creed. Being so much in love, Cathy imagines abrogating the physical boundaries of bodies and souls, as if she *were* a heavenly creature. Freud would later psychologize Cathy's miraculous feeling: "At the height of being in love the boundary between ego and object threatens to melt away. Against all the evidence of his senses, a man who is in love declares that 'I' and 'you' are one, and is prepared to behave as if it were a fact."[7]

"I *am* Heathcliff" proclaims the erotic vocation—to dissolve the limits of the self by achieving absolute intimacy with the beloved. Notice the language: for Cathy, Heathcliff is like a "rock of ages," a "rock" upon which she founds her identity and faith. And the passionate assertions of Cathy and Heathcliff in their moments of transport dismiss conventional religion. In death, they seek union with one another, not with God.

III

The Christian text becomes an erotic text. Brontë, in an early passage, uses imagery that symbolizes a major theme of my study: Scripture turns into the novel, and the novel is haunted by being in love. Letters preserve the spirit of the dead, and what starts as a marginal form of literature, a gloss on holy writ, becomes, in itself, a means to immortality: Our first knowledge of Catherine Earnshaw comes when the narrator Lockwood, spending the night at Wuthering Heights, finds her name written all over the ledge by his bed. When he closes his eyes, "a glare of white letters started from the dark, as vivid as spectres— the air swarmed with Catherines" (III, 25). (The mind jump between writing and ghostly figures, as we shall see, is anything but random: both preserve the past.[8]) He then peruses her margin-annotated "library," including her defaced "Testament," in which she, as a girl—notice that one of the most renowned lovers in fiction begins as a marginal figure—recounts the disgust she and Heathcliff feel for Sunday services and Joseph's long-winded, sanctimonious bullying. They rebel against religion, and, ripping up Christian books, they run away for a romp on the moors. Lockwood falls asleep reading some bitter sectarian tract, which gives him a nightmare about a chapel congregation falling into a violent free-for-all. From the start, Christian practice appears harsh and life-denying, a form that has degenerated from sacred mystery.

What then follows is, literally, erotic vocation: the callings of Cathy and Heathcliff set in a mediated, dreamlike atmosphere of pain and absurd chaos that epitomize the world of *Wuthering Heights*. Lockwood, the gentleman, mixing dream and wakefulness, reaches out the window and feels the grip of the long-dead Cathy's ice-cold hand:

> "Let me in—let me in! . . . I'm come home. . . .'
> As it spoke, I discerned, obscurely, a child's face looking through the window. Terror made me cruel; and, finding it useless to attempt shaking the creature off, I pulled its wrist on to

the broken pane, and rubbed it to and fro till blood ran down and soaked the bed-clothes:
still it wailed, "Let me in! . . . I've been a waif for twenty years!" [III, 30]

Lockwood, in his dream, piles up books to keep the ghost out; but, when the
specter threatens to enter through the massed words, he cries out, rousing
Heathcliff. Half awake, they argue, and Lockwood, babbling the language of
dessicated faith, exclaims, "Catherine Linton, or Earnshaw, or however she was
called—she must have been a changeling—wicked little soul! She told me she
had been walking the earth these twenty years: a just punishment for her mortal transgressions, I've no doubt!" (III, 31–32). Such a remark in the context of
his sadistic nightmare indicates how big a part sadism can play in religious feeling and doctrine. Later, when Heathcliff thinks himself alone, Lockwood ob-
serves him: "He got on to the bed and wrenched open the lattice, bursting, as
he pulled at it, into an uncontrollable passion of tears. 'Come in! come in!' he
sobbed. 'Cathy, do come. Oh, do—*once* more! Oh! my heart's darling, hear me
this time—Catherine, at last!'" (III, 33).

Out of banality, cruel hallucination, and stumblings in the night come the
mysterious calling and desire that spell love for Emily Brontë. "Let me in!" and
"Come in!" are signifiers of the lovers' vocation. They express the longing for
infinite vulnerability to the other. *Their calling is to call to the other, to desire
impossibly, trying, through passion and imagination, to overcome physical and
temporal reality.* Through love, they seek identity even in, and beyond, death;
they strive to nullify natural law and merge in oneness, but a oneness that is
personal, distinct, and unique—not abstract.

Heathcliff's outburst, a genuine prayer if there ever was one, is an important
piece of narrative strategy. It wins sympathy for him, sympathy he cannot entirely lose, despite his many sins, because he appears early on so naked and
helplessly sincere in his love. Such feeling is impressive. Readers who remember
nothing else about the book remember Heathcliff, Cathy, and their love because—no matter what Nelly Dean, Lockwood, or conventional moralists say—
passion is the star of the show.

Later in the book we find out that Heathcliff has prayed to Cathy once before,
just after her death. That prayer and his passion help us to understand this
narrative introduction to Cathy's presence/absence and to Heathcliff's love: to
Nelly Dean's trite sentiment, "Her life closed in a gentle dream—may she wake
as kindly in the other world!" he answers, "May she wake in torment! . . .
Where is she? Not . . . in heaven—not perished—where? . . . I pray one
prayer—I repeat it till my tongue stiffens—Catherine Earnshaw, may you not
rest, as long as I am living! You said I killed you—haunt me, then! . . . Be with
me always—take any form—drive me mad! only *do* not leave me in this abyss,
where I cannot find you! Oh, God! it is unutterable! I *cannot* live without my

life! I *cannot* live without my soul!" (XVI, 139). Heathcliff's prayer to the beloved, deceased *other*, his "God," again spells out the opposition between orthodox and erotic faith. It also gives one plausible answer to the question of what
happens when you die, which is that you might haunt the living. Immortality,
at least figuratively, might be a diffusive and lasting, if various, haunting—
through memory, image, spiritual infusion, word of mouth, legend, and writing.
And haunting might depend upon alienated love and the desire to overcome
erotic separation.

IV

Two things seem especially puzzling about this episode: Why does Cathy appear
in the reserved Lockwood's dream, and what is that awful piece of torture, the
bloody wrist-rubbing incident, doing there? The answer would seem to involve
"the return of the repressed" and the rhetorical status of Lockwood, the un-
imaginative principal narrator with whom the story begins and ends. (Though
Nelly Dean narrates much of the time, she tells her tale to and through him.)
He mediates the novel for us, assumes common social conventions, gains our
general credence; thus we are implicated in his dream and its cruelty.

I want to suggest a trope: As the dream-waif Cathy is to the dreamer Lockwood, so *Wuthering Heights* is to its readers. His dream enacts the agonizing
internal war of the self on the past and past love—love that might threaten
present life. It renders the spooky hunger for love of the enduring, importuning
child within—battered and rubbed a thousand wrong ways—who is the past
self's denial of love to others and also the self denied love in the past. Cathy is
not only the passionate lover; she is also the erotic history of childhood—the
needs and urges formed back then and inefficiently suppressed later—that so
terribly and inexorably haunts consciousness, all consciousness. This child is
mother to the man and the woman too. Erotic desire is the mother of imagination and the shaper of fate. How else account for the hold of this odd book, not
just on the romantic temperaments of the passionate and young, but on some
much closer to Lockwood and Nelly than to Cathy and Heathcliff? One more
trope: This chapter and dream can stand for the continuing creative process of
life and literature. Language plays upon memory and emotion to make new
forms and images which create new combinations of language for the imagination.

Dreams matter intensely to the mystical Emily Brontë. Cathy, later, makes
two notable comments on the subject: "I've dreamt in my life dreams that have
stayed with me ever after, and changed my ideas; they've gone through and
through me, like wine through water, and altered the colour of my mind" (IX,
72); and "my dreams appal me" (XII, 106). Both apply to Lockwood's dream.

The first statement asserts that dreams are in some sense true and have consequences. Recall Cathy's dream of rejecting heaven or think how Lockwood's
blood-red dream colors the novel and you see how strongly Brontë supports that
idea. Dreams shape and are shaped by how we perceive things, and, as psychology now stresses, the reporter of dreams reconstructs them in the waking context of present urgencies. They display, as phenomena, in extreme form, the
force of individualism: the self, like a god, orders—or disorders—a world. And
they give glimpses of a realm of wonder, of supernatural possibilities where
normal limitations do not hold. Dreams, like fiction, tell us that, however we
try to repress the knowledge, life is partly out of control and fantastic. It *is*
mysterious; we are all touched truly, if unconsciously, by the visionary power
of imagination.

Foppish Lockwood, in the first chapter, reports that he had recently fallen
"over head and ears" in love but was too shy to communicate his feelings to the
woman and, driving her away, thereby "gained the reputation of deliberate
heartlessness" (I, 15). His dream, then, makes good psychological sense. His
repressed guilt at spurning love and his repressed need for love haunt him. The
"characters" of Catherine's name and writing swarm into his brain with his
memory of lost love to give dream life to a girl-child imploring him to let her
come in from the cold world of the dead.

But the unconscious imagination of a dreamer may receive impressions that
the rational daytime mind cannot precisely catalogue or comprehend. Any number of separate reasons can be given why Lockwood dreams the dream he does,
or why the whole novel is as it is: indeterminacy is Brontë's queen and the
critic's chance. Dorothy Van Ghent has plausibly suggested, for instance, that
the oak-panel closet is like a coffin and thus its occupier would be open to a
death-haunted dream (Heathcliff, in fact, will die here at the end).[9] One possibility is that the amorous drive to overcome the separation of death inevitably
touches and infects to some degree the lives of almost all people, even if they be
as passive and mediocre as Lockwood. The strength of love might be so intense
and at the same time so diffuse that it can in effect produce an intersubjectivity
of imagination, even though we cannot trace exactly how. Emily Brontë, for
example, might imagine that the force of the Heathcliff-Cathy erotic desire
might—through the words of Cathy and Heathcliff's bearing—sink into Lockwood's dreaming mind.

The dream, however, *is* appalling. It previews the pain and violence to come.
It quickly establishes that the panorama of cruelty that defines life in the novel
is not something alien to a "civilized" person, nor some weirdness beyond the
pale in the wilds, but an inescapable part of "normal" reality. "Terror made me
cruel," says Lockwood, this conventional filter of our knowledge, and then in his

mind he commits what may well seem the most sadistic act in this compendium of sadism. A desperate quality of hurt the hurt (i.e., if you can't stop the pain, revel in it!) comes through in his dream act, and that spirit permeates the narrative. It is as though Brontë were trying, by rendering the bleeding dead flesh, the hanging dogs, the slaughtered rabbits, and all the other acts great and small of bestial cruelty in the book, to retaliate against existence for giving us the excruciating knowledge of death and loneliness; as though, in suppressed rage, she were saying, "If you think cutting a girl's wrist on a windowpane or destroying puppies is terrible, what about an earth and a life in which you and every person you ever love will die, and you can never really repress the fact of your own unquenchable loneliness?" In *Wuthering Heights*, the impulses and effects that arise from the love-frustrating, death-plagued conditions of existence flicker in the consciousness of all souls, be they mild-mannered, colorless, well-meaning, or savage and vengeful. That is the kind of world Emily Brontë lived in and imagined.

Of the interpretation of dreams there is no end, but let me make four more suppositions about the dream scene.

1. A paradox in Lockwood's dream is that the dead can bleed. That might suggest that there is an unending flow of consciousness in which people have a kind of immortality. It can also suggest that imagining pain is one way of overcoming the blankness of nonbeing that threatens us. If losing the power to feel is one of the terrors of modern life, then contemplating and feeling pain at least proves some sort of emotional vitality. That notion might help us to understand the strange link between sadism and eroticism, a connection that often appears in this novel. Sadomasochism would seem to be a desperate strategy to break through the wall of numb otherness, a fanatical attempt at intimacy and abnormally intense communication through the sharing of pain—the inflicting and the bearing of it. In Brontë, spiritual strength comes from a resolve to disdain the flesh by mortifying it and, beyond that, a will to mortify death itself. John Donne, the Christian, says, "Death thou shalt die."[10] Brontë, the erotic mystic, imagines that if we can't make death die, at least we can make it bleed.

2. The intrusion of death upon the living, a permanent feature of psychic and social life, terrifies people and provokes violent reactions. We hate and instinctively want to punish the knowledge of death, and we want no part of it. But, of course, we want exactly the opposite too: information and witnesses from beyond that tell us that death is an illusion. Hence we get the ambiguity and tension in the dream and the novel about the barrier between life and death which the recurrent liminal imagery symbolizes—here, the reach from outside to inside, the grip of the dead hand, the attempt to "cut" oneself off from fleshly connection with death, and the penetrating voice of the girl insisting on a return

to mortality. The blood is sacrificial—homage to the power of imagination and love, both of which are bound up with the knowledge of suffering. It proclaims that human life as we know it rests upon the reality of cruelty and death. Culture and civilized comfort require their toll of blood, as does vital fecundity.

3. We will later learn that Lockwood's closet was the place where Heathcliff and Cathy slept together until, to her chagrin, Hindley separated them when they reached thirteen and twelve, respectively—approximately the age of puberty. This blood that "ran down and soaked the bed-clothes," therefore, could be imaginatively fused with the menstrual blood that causes painful alienation and loss of innocence. One meaning of the image might be: *blood shuts out childhood.*

4. Another is: *the privileged and the civilized are willing to shed the blood of others to protect themselves.* Rich tortures poor; male tortures female; insider tortures outsider. Brontë's imagination does associate blood with transitional states of being. The dream also shares the color and violence of an event that separated Cathy and Heathcliff. Going for their run on the fatal Sunday that Lockwood reads about before his dream, Heathcliff and Cathy look in at the refined elegance of Thrushcross Grange: "We . . . saw—ah! it was beautiful— a splendid place carpeted with crimson, and crimson-covered chairs and tables, and a pure white ceiling" (VI, 47). When the Lintons, the "civilized" insiders, hear them, they loose a bulldog, and Cathy, this time a living child outside the window, suffers bloodshed that connects with Lockwood's image: "The dog was throttled off, his huge, purple tongue hanging half a foot out of his mouth, and his pendant lips streaming with bloody slaver" (VI, 48). The result is that she is drawn away from Heathcliff into the Linton world, class distinction, and womanhood. There is such hurting and mindless torture loose in this world—and it is so ingrained in the texture of things—that pride in refinement and virtue looks like the wildest delusion, if not hypocrisy.

Putting an act of violence in Lockwood's mind prepares us for Emily Brontë's overall vision. All are brothers and sisters in the collective agony of human fate. Her world cries out for some sort of redemption and expiation. Hence the vocation of love. In the words and actions of Heathcliff and Cathy, Brontë creates a love so strong and a passion so interesting that she imagines they could break through into the Lockwoods of the world by the sheer force of energy they generate.

V

The calling of Heathcliff and Cathy is to seek oneness. That sounds like a single-minded, if mystical, quest, but it is not, since living in time gives them disorderly, destructive character traits and contradictory desires that hold them apart. When they grow up they both betray their calling. Their passion for each other gets mixed up with secondary obsessions about class, culture, wealth, and vengeance. They never, however, lose their vocation.

In nineteenth-century fiction, the condition of motherlessness, or a deep and special alienation from the mother, seems repeatedly to motivate passionate love. Brontë locates the germ of erotic faith and grand passion in childhood. In their respective states of literal and figurative orphanhood, Cathy and Heathcliff immerse themselves in each other and in nature, where they find instinctive intimacy and an antidote to motherlessness. *Wuthering Heights* gives us an eroticized and unsentimental version of a Wordsworthian vision. These two are not trailing prenatal clouds of glory. Deprivation and fierceness—especially in the victimized Heathcliff—mark their lives from the beginning, but their early years together call to them in retrospect as paradise lost.

Their vocation points in two directions. Sometimes it seeks to recover lost time by regression to childhood intimacy; sometimes it moves towards a longed-for unity in death. Emily Brontë deserves more credit than she usually gets as an explorer of juvenile experience and its decisive psychological importance. There is, as critics have noted—sometimes disparagingly—an infantile quality about the love between Heathcliff and Cathy;[11] but the novel is onto something. These two seem to experience a sadistic joy in love for each other. Everyone senses the lack of inhibition in these characters. In *Wuthering Heights* we seem often to be in a realm that is not so much *beyond* good and evil as *before* them. The lovers have in them a spirit of infantile sexuality that antedates moral system, a trace of erotic aggression that we might fathom if we could recall the libidinous pleasure of *biting*. When Heathcliff exclaims famously, "I have no pity! I have no pity! The more the worms writhe, the more I yearn to crush out their entrails! It is a moral teething, and I grind with greater energy, in proportion to the increase of pain" (XIV, 128), the words may sound insane. But if we consider the impulses behind the words, if we try to imagine where we have encountered anything like them, we may remember tremendous emotions and transgressive acts of narcissistic rage against otherness and alienated existence that spring from childhood. Infantile erotic desires for absolute freedom to use everything—any and all flesh, blood, and animated spirit—for pleasure may not be noble, but they are formative emotions and demand outlet.

Part of the fascination of Cathy and Heathcliff lies in their high style of verbal and physical cruelty. They touch on basic erotic desires of omnipotence, but Emily Brontë knows that such desires have a history that reaches back to the time when the processes of socialization are just beginning and children resent them. Like Wordsworth, she knows growing up can bring deplorable loss; but unlike him, she offers no moralized innocence of first years. She does, however, show how a moment of quiet in Cathy's young life becomes a spot of time that the lovers—soon separated from one another—long ever after to recapture: "[S]he leant against her father's knee, and Heathcliff was lying on the floor with his head in her lap" (V, 43). Heathcliff's whole existence, right up to his attempt to merge with Cathy's spirit, can be seen as a frustrated longing to recapture that lost time.

Cathy, fevered and terminally ill, gives one speech that sounds just like a prolegomenon to the great twentieth-century fictional study of eroticism and early life, Proust's *A la recherche du temps perdu*.

"Nelly. . . . I thought . . . that I was enclosed in the oak-panelled bed at home; and my heart ached with some great grief which, just waking, I could not recollect. . . . I was a child; my father was just buried, and my misery arose from the separation that Hindley had ordered between me and Heathcliff. I was laid alone, for the first time, and, rousing from a dismal doze after a night of weeping. . . . memory burst in—my late anguish was swallowed in a paroxysm of despair." [XII, 107]

For Proust's narrator the critical trauma is the nighttime separation from the mother; for Cathy it is the ban on sleeping with Heathcliff that biology, social custom, and kinship structure dictate. For both, primary, semi-incestuous urges for closeness fix vocation and make it strong.

In her delirium, Cathy imagines a supernatural state of eternal childhood in roaming the moors: "It's a rough journey, and a sad heart to travel it. . . . We've braved its ghosts often together. . . . But Heathcliff, if I dare you now, will you venture? If you do, I'll keep you. I'll not lie there by myself; they may bury me twelve feet deep, and throw the church down over me, but I won't rest till you are with me. I never will!" (XII, 108). Her vocation, asserting the power of erotic faith even—and expressly—over Christian faith, carries her backwards in memory and forwards to death, which paradoxically liberates her into past time.

In the lovers' calling, death appears both as the dreaded severer and as the unifier of loving souls. Cathy and Heathcliff at times wish for death because earthly life keeps them apart. In a sense they, with their fasting, both commit a kind of suicide. Yet they fear and rant against death, too, and have no consistent view of what it is or what sort of existence they want in death. The different, contradictory views of death that emerge are projections into the future of their passions. (Cathy says, "Heathcliff! I only wish us never to be parted," but in her very next speech, "I'm wearying to escape into that glorious world" [XV, 133–34]). They imagine that the dead lover can haunt the living, that they can find some sort of unified tranquility, that the moment of death can bring the desired release, that the grave will and will not part their souls, that they will both keep and lose one another.

Let us take one phase of Heathcliff's vocation: after Cathy's death, he lives possessed—first by impulses of necrophilia, then by his long perception of her tormenting presence just beyond the reach of his senses, and then, near the end, by his jealous concern about the fate of his own and her material remains. He tells Nelly, "I could *almost* see her, and yet I *could not!*" (XXIX, 230). He has the man who digs Edgar Linton's grave open Cathy's coffin. After seeing "her passionless features" (XXIX, 229), Heathcliff bribes the sexton to arrange it so that he will be buried next to Cathy with the sides of their coffins removed. Though Edgar's coffin on Cathy's other side will disintegrate, says Heathcliff, "by the time Linton gets to us, he'll not know which is which!" (XXIX, 228–29).

The morbidity of this burial scheme actually shows the fantastic power of the erotic imagination. Heathcliff's love is so strong that he simply must project through eternity an intimate physical connection and identity with his beloved. Think of the animating force of a creature who can *imagine* and rejoice in a scene in which two corpses thoroughly molder into one another so that their simple material essence is indistinguishable, while a third moldering corpse, completely disintegrated but somehow retaining consciousness, finds that the remains of his wife and his rival have become one. An eternal triangle indeed! It would be wildly comic, if it were not so pathetic and oddly moving. In Heathcliff's vision, Emily Brontë really does try to confront the physical inanimacy of a dead beloved and a dead self, but she shows that the force of human attachment is so great that it overcomes the idea of death as an impersonal nothingness and imbues even mortal dust with fiery, amorous spirit.

Generalizing from Heathcliff, we can say that the passionate vocation of love depends upon desire that separation creates; and death, the great divider, makes this vocation all the stronger. Love and death so often flow together in the human mind, not because romantic passion is world-hating or life-denying and thus seeks death,[12] but because death, changing and removing the material presence of the beloved, is the ultimate obstacle and test for lovers. Love is what makes the diffusion of death personal and creates an afterlife, though that afterlife exists in the minds of particular people. Heathcliff does not wish to have no life; he wants a permanent life identified with Cathy. Her death, by which she loses corporeal reality and becomes identical with his love—that is, his own spiritual desire, memory, and projection of her—transforms her into his own enduring perception of her desirability and his agonizing, frustrated longing to be at one with her. His state is like that of a religious mystic conscious of, and constantly seeking, oneness with God: "In every cloud, in every tree—filling the air at night, and caught by glimpses in every object by day, I am surrounded with her image!" (XXXIII, 255).

Why doesn't Brontë have Heathcliff kill himself soon after Cathy's death, feeling as he does? A logical answer would be that his love, that is, his passionate need for her, lives within him, even though it torments him; he knows her very existence depends upon his own agony and separation. She has been translated into his passion. For two decades, he does not want to risk destroying his love, even though her physical absence parches his spirit and makes him terrible to himself and others. She exists after death in his suffering.

VI

In Heathcliff's confrontation with death, the pattern his vocation of love follows is this: personal grief and crazed desire to possess unchanged the body of the deceased; frustrated and tormenting quest for sense communication with an existent but intangible spirit; acceptance of material transformation to impersonal matter, and physical, objective—*not* subjective—integrity with the beloved; seeming consciousness of perfect identity at the moment of his own death (he dies in triumph, according to Nelly, a "frightful, life-like gaze of exultation" in his eyes [XXXIV, 264]); fusion into the imagination and legends of others; and finally, a peaceful unity with nature and all being which, however, mysteriously depends upon erotic faith and diffusive subjective perception.

Heathcliff and his fate show how being in love, rendered in art, has a modern, specialized vocational impact as a calling that serves other people's lives and needs. On Nelly, on Lockwood, on the neighborhood folk, on readers, the professed passion leaves its mark. The country people feel the presence of the lovers as ghosts who together rove the area. In the minds of some, the two have overcome death and joined together in eternal youth, specters—as Cathy foretold— of the continuity of past and present and of the power of love. The text suggests that for Lockwood, both as a typical nineteenth-century bourgeois man and as a surrogate for a romance-hungry audience, Heathcliff performs the function of an erotic surrogate through whom the splendid agonies of love can be experienced vicariously and the sins of love taken away; *as for passionate loving and suffering, the characters in our novels will do that for us.*

Nelly finds and describes him dead in the panel closet where he slept with Cathy as a child: "Mr. Heathcliff was there. . . . His eyes met mine so keen and fierce, I started; and then he seemed to smile. . . . he was perfectly still. The lattice, flapping to and fro, had grazed one hand that rested on the sill; no blood trickled from the broken skin, and when I put my fingers to it, I could doubt no more—he was dead and stark! . . . I tried to close his eyes—to extinguish, if possible, that frightful, life-like gaze of exultation" (XXXIV, 264). Flowing blood signifies corporeal life and suffering. Lockwood's dream of Cathy, who bleeds, and Nelly's final view of Heathcliff, who does not, fit together in a perfect symmetry of image, narrative, and the wish fulfillment of dreams. Private erotic desire and obsession fuse with public erotic imagination, and we seem to have at last both Heathcliff's individual perception of identity with Cathy—and thus his triumph and self-transcendence in death—and the immortality of the lovers in the perception of others.

The much-noted ambiguous ending of the novel shows how reverberant the lovers' vocation and afterlife can be. Lockwood, with stories of ghostly rovers in his head, visits the graves of Heathcliff, Cathy, and Edgar: "I lingered round them, under that benign sky; watched the moths fluttering among the heath and hare-bells; listened to the soft wind breathing through the grass; and won-dered how any one could ever imagine unquiet slumbers for the sleepers in that quiet earth" (XXXIV, 266). To a sensibility like his, they have become memory and consoling moral *exempla* who reconcile us to personal death. The violent lifelong passion finally ends, and contemplating it all, in the lovely wholeness of nature, we can feel that the mortal fate of dreamless sleep, where there is no pain, nothing to fear, no hellish desire, constitutes a practical happy ending.

But, as many have pointed out, this last complex paragraph is deeply ironic.[13] Language gives us social areas where meanings coincide while at the same time calling up uncontrollable personal associations. For example, the moth that flut-ters about the heath might remind a reader of the lover who flutters about the flame of Heathcliff, and such an association might mean that the passage would connote something different for that reader than for Lockwood. I prefer to take the question and expressed wonder as literal rather than rhetorical. As the local folk—not to mention their author—prove, the easiest thing in the world is to imagine "unquiet slumbers" for Heathcliff and Cathy. The rhetoric of their speech and actions have such power that it is hard to imagine them peacefully contained. The novel, in the formal structure of its telling from the point of view of unreliable narrators and in the way it features the force of private emo-tions, stresses subjectivity and personal vision. We know that for some those lovers can rise right out of the grave.

The evocative beauty of the final sentence, however, cannot be missed. Heathcliff and Cathy are once more, as in childhood, immersed in nature, death now replacing love as the unifier. The end suggests Wallace Stevens's line, "Death is the mother of beauty";[14] but my corollary would be, after Emily Brontë, that "the expression of love is the mother of death and beauty." Love creates death as many men and women come to know it because it makes them conscious of its primary meaning for them: the agony of loss.

Behind the traditional sentiment of Lockwood—in effect, "rest in peace"— Brontë is working out in her prose a faith in transubstantiation that points to continuous life. She chooses to write *heath* and *hare-bells*, words that denote flowering life, but also conjure up, in a mode of verbal magic, associations with Heathcliff, Hareton, the heather that Cathy loves, and the erotic history that she has just imagined. The imagery and the diction bring out the connection and continuity of all natural life in a world whose matter, though it metamorphoses endlessly, is finite. For Emily Brontë, the power of metaphor and metonymy do actually mean that we live in a world of transubstantiation. Fusion and mutual interflow between characters, their passions, inanimate matter, growing and living things, language, and imaginative perception *take place* in this final passage. Within the novel, when death comes, love has the power of transubstantiating the dead into continuing life—spirits, flowers, or circulating words, for example. Erotic faith does, therefore, meet the test that we said all religions face: it offers a dissolution of death.

I want to suggest something more: in Brontë's imagination, the moving force creating metaphor is the drive for love. Set next to the novel's ending those most famous words of Cathy: "My love for Linton is like the foliage in the woods. . . . My love for Heathcliff resembles the eternal rocks beneath. . . . I *am* Heathcliff." The basic condition of our being is to live in the metaphorical, metonymical medium of language; to understand and become part of the world, we say one thing is like another; we want to attach this or that quality or constellation of being to ourselves. Language, then, is the means of seduction and expropriation, and by mutual expression we merge with the other and join a process that extends beyond our death. The desire for attachment beyond alienated being manifests itself as love. The maddening imperative of the erotic calling in *Wuthering Heights*, to transcend the self and join in the identity of another, is really the involuntary vocation of being human. Being in love and trying to say it epitomize the human condition.

VII

Emily Brontë enunciates the vocation of love mainly in the speeches of Cathy and Heathcliff to Nelly Dean or to each other. These erotic professions have such frenzied force that, though they can make some people feel ill at ease, they go through the minds of readers, staining them, if not changing them. They always grow out of the pain of threatened or real separation. Cathy's cry, "I *am* Heathcliff," for example, comes when he has already gone, and nearly all of Heathcliff's eloquence comes when Cathy is dying or dead. Nelly, as a professional servant who depends upon stable social arrangements that violent erotic feeling can upset, deplores these verbal displays of passion, and often appears as a sensible skeptic of socially unsanctioned love. But Nelly's prosaic mentality cannot address the most profound needs and problems of individual existence that the lovers try to express. In their context, these manic, engulfing speech acts proclaim the drive to mate spiritual with physical being. The lover's cliché "soul-mate" points out one of the strongest of all human longings and the obsession of *Wuthering Heights*: the desire to be at the same time a bodiless spirit and a material creature too.

Wuthering Heights renders directly the problem that love and its representation in the arts of "the Western world" pose: is the emotional exaltation of romantic eroticism worth the human waste and sorrow that it seems to cause? Many theorists of love, including Freud, Denis de Rougemont, Ortega y Gasset, and even Irving Singer, often appear to bemoan overwhelming amorous passion.[15] They see that it violates common sense, bends nature, mistakes another person for projected internal desires, kills tranquility, and often ends in tragic misery. Few philosophers would agree with the Judgment of Paris; most, it seems, would like to award the apple to a goddess of piety, wisdom, or power. That myth, however, conveys the magnetism of erotic love. Emily Brontë, especially in the frenzied last meeting of Heathcliff and Cathy (XV), dramatizes the case for transfiguring passion. The wild, sadomasochistic love that spews out in the dialogue and action of this chapter—a love that harms the perdurance of life—can work rhetorically to persuade readers that erotic experience brings existence to its highest pitch, that it is the most sacred thing life has to offer.

Brontë composes for the dying Cathy a shrewd speech to Heathcliff in which she mocks practical attitudes towards love:

"I care nothing for your sufferings. Why shouldn't you suffer? I do! Will you forget me—will you be happy when I am in the earth? Will you say twenty years hence, 'That's the grave of Catherine Earnshaw. I loved her long ago, and was wretched to lose her; but it is past. I've loved many others since—my children are dearer to me than she was, and, at death, I shall not rejoice that I am going to her, I shall be sorry that I must leave them!' Will you say so, Heathcliff?" [XV, 133]

She actually frames the essential argument of almost all who distrust erotic love and insist that the tedious "long run" matters more than ecstasy, whose subjective and unquantifiable value time always dilutes. But the whole scene—and it is largely the inscribed passion of this chapter, a touchstone in the literature of love if there ever was one, that has propelled Heathcliff and Cathy into popular consciousness—renders the counterargument.

Brontë imagines for Heathcliff and Cathy what I shall call *the individualism of two*. In their climactic interview, they express themselves completely in all their rage, pain, self-contradiction, and vitality, and then they close together in a momentary, doomed embrace. The extremity of their situation allows a wonderful candor. They can say anything to each other—do anything—without disguise, and thus they can, even if just for a short time, *be* themselves completely. One of the great appeals of eroticism is that it offers a chance for open-ness, no holding back of the self. It allows a liberation from the repression that social life demands, and we mistake its force if we think only of sexual repres-sion. We long to be known wholly by another being in all the savage need, inconsistency, and passion of our being—known and *still* loved—in fact loved all the more for this knowledge.

Cathy says to Heathcliff things like, "I shall not pity you, not I. You have killed me—and thriven on it. . . . How many years do you mean to live after I am gone?" (XV, 132). He berates her for "infernal selfishness" (XV, 133) in this time of her dying—never pretending to her that she *isn't* going to die: "I have not one word of comfort. You deserve this. You have killed yourself. . . . You loved me—then what *right* had you to leave me?" (XV, 134–35). They can talk this way because they identify so closely with one another that nothing the other says, nothing the other reveals, not even those flashes of hatred and pure aggression that boil in lovers, can threaten their love. In their shameless state, Emily Brontë then imagines the kind of atoning, ecstatic communication that such a relationship can induce.

> "Let me alone. Let me alone," sobbed Catherine. "If I've done wrong, I'm dying for it. It is enough! You left me too; but I won't upbraid you! I forgive you. Forgive me!"
> "It is hard to forgive, and to look at those eyes, and feel those wasted hands," he answered. "Kiss me again; and don't let me see your eyes! I forgive what you have done to me. I love *my* murderer—but *yours*! How can I?" [XV, 135]

If we think of the impassioned speeches of this chapter as the most vitally charged expression of desire, faith, personality, and being for these particular depicted characters, Catherine Earnshaw Linton and Heathcliff; if we see Emily Brontë pushing, like Wagner in *Tristan und Isolde*, to find artistic utterance that conveys the complexity of desire and the resourceful power of the self to engage with another, to merge oceanic emotion into an oral epiphany of the most in-tense consciousness human beings can feel—we can begin to comprehend the consecrating function of the lover's vocation.

Violent love in this operatic scene shows forth in action as well as in speech. The two grab one another, kiss madly, go into breathing paroxysms, tear hair, cause bruises, squeeze the life out of each other, and altogether behave fero-ciously. Nelly witnesses their final, shocking union: "An instant they held asun-der; and then how they met I hardly saw, but Catherine made a spring, and he caught her, and they were locked in an embrace from which I thought my mis-tress would never be released alive" (XV, 134). This is a very pregnant woman who would rather die holding the man she loves than live comfortably with the nice husband who has impregnated her. Fighting and shrieking to hang on to her lover while her husband approaches the room, Cathy cries, "I shall die!"

(XV, 136) and passes out in Heathcliff's arms; she gives birth to her daughter and dies without regaining consciousness.

Without reproducing the whole chapter, it is almost as hard to convey the force of this scene and its passion as it is to convey the erotic force of Wagner's *Tristan* without playing the music. Nelly reacts to it all with bewilderment, like a Christian watching heathen rites, "in great perplexity" and "very uncomfortable" (XV, 134, 135). The erotic energy and the mad eloquence overwhelm the decent social convention which helps to sustain everyday life—and drain it of its mystery. The expression of requited, cruel, anguished love is so fully imagined and suggestive that the scene embodies and challenges readers with the primary claim of romantic faith: that the value of life lies in the quality and intensity of feeling.

Something Edward Albee writes in *The Zoo Story* illuminates this chapter and the whole novel: "I've learned that neither kindness nor cruelty by themselves independent of each other creates any effect beyond themselves. And I've learned that the two combined are the teaching emotion. And what is gained is loss." [16] This "teaching emotion" Emily Brontë knew. "Cruelty" and "kindness" provoke the dialectic that inheres in being; *Wuthering Heights* renders it. "The teaching emotion" inheres in eroticism and points to the idea of *sacrifice*— sacrifice, the act upon which religion is founded. And a feeling of sacrifice, the painful beauty of violent passion, is what makes love religious in the novel.

I go back to my hackneyed phrase for what astonishingly happens in the episode: Heathcliff truly and in a double sense *squeezes the life out of* Cathy. I suggested before that the phrase, "love is the mother of death and beauty," characterizes Emily Brontë's vision. Fierce love provokes Cathy's death and the premature birth of Cathy II, who, in the plot of her happy, melioristic love with Hareton, will redeem normal, worldly life in the novel. (The text suggests that had not Cathy been stunned into labor, she would have died without giving birth to a living child.) I sense here also a trope—intended or not—for the violent, cruel, erotic process of regeneration. Human reproduction, regarded historically, is a system of propagation so dangerous, painful, and melodramatically charged that it almost defies belief. Another subliminal message here might be, "if you think this chapter is emotionally overwrought, consider the circumstances and conditions in which women have given birth; or think of the act of crazy fury, gentleness, selfishness, pleasure, intimacy, and physical wildness that leads to birth!"

VIII

Cathy and Heathcliff alike reject "the real world" if it denies them the love they want. She, for example, turns the "double standard" on its head and professes to be in love with two men at once, who both love her. Brontë, through Cathy's polyandrous feeling, is getting at the limitlessness of desire and a feminine will to power through erotic drive. Wanting to be infinitely lovable—"I thought, though everybody hated and despised each other, they could not avoid loving me" (XII, 104)—she dreams of herself as a mediating redemptress. She embodies the need, in love, for both identity and complementarity, claiming Heathcliff as her true self and Linton as the not-self which draws her. The contradictory logic of desire is both "like with like" and "opposites attract."

An ambiguity and ambivalence about sexuality in the book has puzzled critics.[17] Some have wanted to see the plot's first triangle in conventional Freudian terms; that is, the idlike Heathcliff is sex, and cultured Edgar Linton is civilization with its repression and discontents.[18] And yet Cathy early on finds Edgar physically attractive, wants his person as well as his status, and chooses without ado to become his sexual partner; loving Heathcliff soulfully, she seems much more interested in claiming Heathcliff's spirit than his flesh. Near her death, she tells Edgar, "What you touch at present, you may have; but my soul will be on that hilltop before you lay hands on me again. I don't want you, Edgar. I'm past wanting you" (XII, 109). Soul and body play out their usual bitter debate in the novel, but both refuse to speak their conventional lines. The soul seems earthy and sexy, the body ethereal; and each partakes of the other in the complexities of erotic vocation. The passionate current of libido in the novel does not especially seem to have a genital focus.

Though there are moments when the author seems at war with sex, in general the text neither condemns conventional sexual feeling nor exalts it. Sex is a worldly process leading to both reproduction and destruction of the flesh (Cathy's, for instance); in itself, sex is not transcendence. Brontë conveys intense desire and physicality—much more so than most Victorian novelists—with lots of violent, polymorphous touching and animal spirits; but much of the sexuality expresses pre-adult impulses. The grown-up Heathcliff has an obvious erotic magnetism, but his sexual maturity means for Cathy that she can no longer sleep with him. Sex also means here the curse of gender definition, with its fixed roles, functions, and desires channelled by custom, and thus more boundaries to curb the spirit.

There is a specter haunting *Wuthering Heights*, the specter of incest. The novel, with the original love bonding of Cathy and Heathcliff, eroticizes childhood and floats this ghost. It ties love to children's history and dramatizes, without the usual repression, the erratic libidinal spirit, combining the feeling of a hothouse and a Roman arena, that so often marks the emotional atmosphere of the close, nuclear family. As so often with Emily Brontë, she creates a powerful effect by heightening—not downplaying—the contradictions of profound desires. The historical development of family life and affections in a world of change could make memories of early sibling affinities a reassuring psychological refuge in the face of the uncertain, alien nature of adult existence. But as familial relationships became increasingly close, emotionally charged, and idealized, the culture would more urgently feel the threat of incest, the force of the incest ban, and the need to stress it. The subject would naturally take on the glamorous mystery of taboo and transgression. Brontë makes Heathcliff an outsider who looks like a gypsy child, but she also poses the question of Earnshaw's paternal relation to him and imagines him growing up like a brother to Cathy. She thereby holds in provocative tension the strong attraction and repulsion of the impulse to sibling incest that emerges in nineteenth-century literature, psychology, and family life.

Her conception is brilliant. It allows Heathcliff to be 1) an intrusive figure of exogamy at odds with the semi-incestuous Earnshaw-Linton harmony, class smugness, inbreeding, and potential spiritual degeneration; 2) a subversive tempter showing the dangerous appeal of incestuous transgression; 3) a mystic defier of time and social reality who desires a pregenital existence where there is no such thing as incest or the adult preoccupation with sexuality. One reason for the nineteenth-century cult of childhood is that it honors the erotic intimacy of the family, even as it denies the threat of incest by focusing on a period that predates it. If Cathy's wraith could come to Heathcliff in the flesh, they would be children again, and incest would be out of the question.

IX

There are many ways of being in love in *Wuthering Heights* besides the passion of Heathcliff and Catherine. They range from Lockwood's trivial crushes and Isabella's disastrous infatuation, through Hindley's brief and pathetic love match with Frances, Edgar's real but unsatisfactory love for Cathy, and the puppy love of Cathy II and Linton, to the civilizing, happy-ending love of Cathy II and Hareton. The high drama of Cathy I and Heathcliff, however, overwhelms all the rest of Brontë's anatomy of love—even that constructive, redeeming love at the end.

The Cathy II–Hareton love match promises a well-adjusted erotic union attuned to the reality principle and social continuity, the would-be goal of almost all "love" experts since the middle ages.[19] Though some find it pale and contrived, it seems credible enough. Even its admirers, however, tend to see it in the shadow of a greater love. J. Hillis Miller calls the primary process of the novel's action "the establishment of a valid community based on mediated love"; but even stressing the rational, benevolent love that develops in the second generation, he writes, "The love of Hareton and the second Cathy appears to be possible only because Heathcliff and the first Cathy have broken through life into death, and have liberated energies from the region of boundless sympathy into this world." [20] Getting at the mystical nature and intentions of the book, he concludes, "The breakthrough into God's world of Heathcliff and Cathy has not only made possible the peaceful love of Hareton and the second Cathy; it has also made institutionalized religion unnecessary. The love of Heathcliff and Cathy has served as a new mediator between heaven and earth, and has made any other mediator for the time being superfluous." [21] That sounds a bit too sanguine, and the phrase "God's world" seems questionable; but it reinforces the idea that when we talk of Heathcliff and Cathy we are talking about serious religious feeling, aspiration, and function, and that the effect of their vocation touches others.

Brontë chooses to stress that the Cathy II–Hareton love is mediated by reading and books. Again she imagines a symmetry with the novel's beginning: Cathy I's writing plunges Lockwood into the love story, and in his dream he shores up books to keep out her ghost; Cathy II teaches Hareton to read and gives him books as a sign and a means to love. Cathy I and Heathcliff throw their religious books away and become erotic demons; Hareton, taught by Cathy II, picks up books suffused in love, and, being in love, they read together. We have a true Brontë-sisters and Victorian wish fulfillment. The woman's power over the word leads the man to love. The importance of the nineteenth-century myth of cultural and moral redemption of men by women that recent critics and historians, for example, Nina Auerbach and Ann Douglas,[22] have been analyzing gets strong support from the Cathy II–Hareton relationship. The image of a loving, competent, pert woman training the savage beast to read and be a gentleman says a lot about the history of women and the faith in the reforming power of love.

The fusion, in a book, of love and developing literacy offers a paradigm not only for "the rise of the novel" but for the English novel itself, one motive for which might well be described as "the establishment of a community based on mediated love." The union also shows the socializing power of the word and the laying to rest, in a book, of the ghosts of erotic desperation. One strain in Brontë is a hope that the novel can teach proper love, as, say, *Pride and Prejudice* does. But *Wuthering Heights* is much better at starting erotic ghosts than at containing them. Conflict exists between the mediation of love through literacy and books—reading and writing—and the drive, erotic in itself, for unmediated love.

Hareton, happy graduate of Cathy II's course, is not the hero of love. Heathcliff is. Brontë gives him what Hareton lacks—the charismatic quality Blake names when he says, "energy is eternal delight." Charlotte Brontë, whose notorious 1850 preface sometimes reads as if Nelly wrote it, says of her sister's hero, "Whether it is right or advisable to create beings like Heathcliff, I do not know: I scarcely think it is. But this I know: the writer who possesses the creative gift owns something of which he is not always master—something that at times strangely wills and works for itself."[23] What Emily wills to express through Heathcliff is the insatiable need for permanent love and a furious resentment against a moral, social, and natural order that inevitably creates impossible desires and thwarts personal freedom. Through imagined love, she wants to identify with and expropriate domineering male power and also to show this power devoted, finally, to a woman who, in this fantasy of real but conflicting desires, is both separate from and identical with the man. Through Heathcliff and his relationship to Cathy, she renders the human imagination of love violently at war with "objective reality."

The trouble with the Cathy II–Hareton match is that it, like literature for this novelist, may contain, but cannot requite, the deepest desires in her text: *the longing for a pre-incestuous world, for self-assertive transgression of boundaries, and for the transcendence of personal death.* Unlike the other love relationships, even the paltry ones, the surviving couple is not threatened by time and extinction. The heart of Emily Brontë's vision is a passion to confront and overcome—through totalizing, immediate love—the separation of death that she sees inexorably testing human relationship. The basic contradiction in *Wuthering Heights* is that faith in such love can only be formed, expressed, and sustained by writing and narrative.

X

Love, like religion and politics, is power—often the power that destroys. In her own reading, Emily Brontë found that out mainly from Walter Scott and Byron. She owes much to the erotic subtexts of gothic fiction and the stark fatalism of the Scottish ballads, but much more to Scott, the novelist who manifested history and country as areas of desire. He feeds her text. As a child, she chose him as one of her heroes,[24] and as a novelist she formed the names Heathcliff and Earnshaw from his hero in *The Black Dwarf*, Earnscliff, a figure caught between love and family vengeance. As Lucy Ashton read and absorbed romance, so, no doubt, did Emily Brontë read of Ravenswood, Lucy, the sexual politics of the Ashton family, and the latent force of love passion. Absorbing Scott's eroticization of history, she went on to make the fatal significance of erotic desire in the world unmistakably clear. And she learned from him how to mix romance and earthiness. From his matter-of-fact portrayal of common life in novels like *The Bride of Lammermoor* comes the hurly-burly and physical detail of day-to-day life at Wuthering Heights—Balderstone and Ailsie Gourlay would be right at home there. The pattern and direction of the novel can even be seen to follow Scott's overall perception of history: glamorous, exciting, but deadly passion in the past that gives way to the more rational, if less emotionally compelling, compromises and civilizing process of the present.

But Scott, important as he is, was not the major outside literary influence on the Brontës. Behind Heathcliff, and behind the love and lovers in much Victorian literature, looms the figure of "Byron," that is, the amalgam in the popular imagination of Byron the man, the poet, and the Byronic hero. "Byron" conjures up the heroics of eros and an erotics of individualism. In him flow together the romanticized, positive conceptions of Milton's Satan, Prometheus, Don Juan, and other defiers of orthodox authority. For the young Brontës, and for thousands of other romantic young people in the nineteenth century, "Byron's name was synonymous with everything that was forbidden and daring."[25] He was the embodiment of the Romantic movement, and his name, work, and example set libidos swirling. If Heathcliff is Emily's brother, Branwell, romanticized, he is equally "Byron" fantasized—"novelized" we might better say—in the gritty Yorkshire world.

Traces of the Byronic figure show up in nearly all British literary renderings of love down to our own time, so we must pay attention to him. Helen Moglen writes definitively,

Byron's hero was modeled upon the role which the poet himself had chosen to play. Misanthropic and adventurous, he also defined himself as rebel. He not only rejected the ugliness of the new world he saw coming to birth, but also the old repressions of the world from which it had descended. Central to his rebellion was the assertion of a self freed from external limitations and control. Without religion, he proclaimed himself his own God. . . . Emerging from a mysterious past, he was without apparent familial ties. . . . Because his isolation is unbearable, he undertakes the romantic quest: to resolve aesthetically or erotically the subject-object conflict—obliterating the division between the "I" and the "not-I" by fusing the two in a redemptive state of feeling. To those who were part of Byron's cult, the drive for integration was focused in eroticism.[26]

The persona "Byron," in the popular mind, offered a cult of youth, a cult of art and the imagination, a cult of self-assertion, and skepticism about stultifying creeds and customs.[27] Notorious as a seducer who would transgress any erotic ban in the pursuit of love, he—"mad, bad, and dangerous to know"—was most sensationally of all the breaker, with his half-sister Augusta, of the incest taboo.[28] For the Brontë children—Charlotte, Emily, Branwell, and Anne—given the circumstances of their physical and psychological isolation and the intensity of their relationship, "Byron" expressed the drive for psychic, social, and erotic freedom. To read him and study his life and work in their formative years was a heady moral teething, and their writings—from the juvenilia of Angria and

Gondal to *Jane Eyre* and *Wuthering Heights*—would be inconceivable without his example.

But Emily Brontë is, to borrow Harold Bloom's term, a "strong" writer who moves beyond the vision of Byron or anyone else to her own; and Heathcliff, as we have seen, is a revolutionary figure. He's no gentleman, and he gets dirty. Byron writes, "Man's love is of man's life a thing apart,/'Tis a Woman's whole existence."[29] Brontë insists—it is the point of her narrative—that it is Heathcliff's whole existence, too. The novel gets rid of Byronic posing, abstraction, and self-pity. It is the least self-righteous and pretentious, but the most mystical, of Victorian novels—descriptive terms that do not fit Byron at all well.

XI

At the end, Heathcliff speaks of his "one universal idea" to be ecstatically united with Cathy: "I have a single wish, and my whole being and faculties are yearning to attain it" (XXXIII, 256). Nearing his goal and death, yet not there, he says, "I'm too happy, and yet I'm not happy enough. My soul's bliss kills my body, but does not satisfy itself" (XXXIV, 262). That is like Saint Theresa's "I die that I can not die."[30] Think of his final "life-like gaze of exultation" and of Catherine's last moment of consciousness holding desperately onto her lover with "mad resolution on her face," crying "Heathcliff, I shall die! I shall die!" In *Wuthering Heights*, love as vocation is literal, not metaphorical. It seems fitting, then, to use one of the most famous representations of mystical transport, Bernini's sculpture *The Ecstasy of Saint Theresa* (1645–52; fig. 17),[31] to help illustrate and understand the passionate calling in the novel.

The face of Theresa, rapt, by love possessed, matches the passion of Heathcliff and Cathy. It does not fit the emotion of Cathy II or Hareton, and that negative fact tells us why irrational, ecstatic love sometimes drowns the appeal of rational affection. Theresa's visage, the scene and image of blinding love, not only expresses faith, it somehow countenances it and calls it up in beholders. Her eyes are closed, her vision inward and subjective. The experience belongs to her, and the world cannot judge its value. We know the strength of emotion from the open mouth and the general demeanor of one transported. This woman's status and social relations in the world are beside the point. The suggestion of orgasm, the bare flesh, the sensuous folds of the drapery, the handsome angel who so closely resembles Cupid (he has been compared to Caravaggio's Eros in *Amor Vincit Omnia*[32]), and the phallic imagery all point to the high tide of libidinous energy in religious experience. The golden arrow that the angel wields, the smile on his face, and the expression of the woman encompassing joy, agony, and worldly oblivion stress the inseparability of suffering and pleasure, hope and cruelty in the time of true passion. Two particularly striking features of

Bernini's art set up a reverberating tension: first, the integration of the group—Theresa, the angel, his wings, the clouds blending both heaven and nature and supporting the figures, all flow into one another to make a unity; and, second, the individual passion on the love-struck human face upon which wonder fixes. We see the whole process and the rendered balance—we see how things fit together—but the intensity of personal emotion itself is what seems miraculous. So it is with *Wuthering Heights*.

In a celebrated religious text, Theresa describes "the Transverberation": "In his hands I saw a long golden spear and at the end of the iron tip I seemed to see a point of fire. With this he seemed to pierce my heart several times so that it penetrated to my entrails. . . . The pain was so sharp that it made me utter several moans; and so excessive was the sweetness caused me by this intense pain that one can never wish to lose it, nor will one's soul be content with anything less than God."[33] Being in love is something like this for Cathy at the end of her life, and for Heathcliff: an amazing experience and an excruciating calling. If we avoid the temptation to read the passage and the art it provoked in the reductive terms of crude Freudianism (i.e., it's just a sublimated wish for genital sex), we can see how they and Brontë's novel bring into focus the complex, irresistible human drive for ecstasy that comprehends and makes use of both theology and sexual activity.

Yes, some might say, but the comparison is all wrong: Theresa is a saint; Cathy and Heathcliff are selfish, cruel characters; and juxtaposing the blindingly beautiful love of Christ with one sinner's erotic love for another is either trivializing speciousness or blasphemous special pleading. One work of art depicts experience leading to beatitude, the other describes destructive, juvenile, antisocial behavior. But surely both express the heartbreaking compulsion to get beyond the physical self through love and identification with another being, and that drive is religious as well as erotic. Being in love for the novel's characters is rendered as an experience of comparable magnitude to Theresa's rapturousness: *that* is the heresy of the age of individualism.

Heathcliff and Cathy enact a quest for salvation, a quest to make and keep something they (and perhaps *we* as well) struggle to name in the word *soul*. Cathy: "Whatever our souls are made of, his and mine are the same" (IX, 72). Heathcliff: "I *cannot* live without my life! I *cannot* live without my soul!" (XVI, 139). We can read this kind of emotion on the face of Bernini's Theresa, as we can find there the ecstasy of their last living embraces and the passion of Heathcliff's own countenance at the moment of his death. In light of *Wuthering Heights*, his expression conveys the passionate faith of both its lovers. The comparison can help us with the ontological questions, why does this figure of Saint Theresa exist, and why does the last meeting of Heathcliff and Cathy exist? The works, in conjunction, make it obvious that there is something erotic about religious faith and something metaphysical and sacred about libidinal love; and, when erotic and religious feeling come together, we can sense the full aesthetic power of each.

Bernini's *Ecstasy* bears on *Wuthering Heights* in another way. Let me take the face as a metaphor, not this time for Heathcliff, Cathy, or their experience, but for a humanity that has been prodded and pierced repeatedly by the shaft of insistent, obsessive, pain-dealing love. Heathcliff and Cathy come together to goad one another and their audiences to erotic consciousness. The vocation of love might appear sometimes to ravish the world. *Amor vincit omnia*, "love conquers all," and that could mean that many get killed, wounded, and sacrificed. But the hope in Brontë's text is that the faith somehow evolves by touching others.

Just as religious rhetoric might persuade many normal people that Christian faith is good and that it would have been a fine thing to be a fanatically devoted follower of Christ wandering in the desert or out from Avila, so the rhetoric of Emily Brontë's fiction might also persuade some with romantic tendencies that love is good and that it would be a marvelous thing to be a possessed lover like Heathcliff. To many the mysterious frenzy of the lovers' last interview might seem as bizarre as the flaming heart of Saint Theresa, but to others that ecstatic devotion might arouse as much sympathy as does the religious passion of god-struck saints. What counts for others about the seekers of transcendence is not their personalities—in social context, mystics are liable to be difficult, crazed, highly unpleasant people—but the power of their emotion, the form of their expression, and the example of their faith.

Heathcliff and Cathy would continue to haunt the modern imagination as they were reported to haunt the countryside. Laurence Olivier, arguably our century's most distinguished actor, stars as Heathcliff in the 1939 William Wyler film of *Wuthering Heights*, and Luis Buñuel, one of the greatest of all filmmakers, makes the novel into a movie, *Los abismos de pasion* (1954), focusing on the conflict between religious orthodoxy and erotic passion.[34] You can hear, in the transistor age, Kate Bush's keening lyrics "Wuthering, Wuthering, Wuthering Heights! . . . Heathcliff! It's me! Cathee! I've come home."[35] A high school student in the 1980s writes to his brother, "I love *Wuthering Heights*! It's so powerful for me. Just imagine the strength of that love. Wow! I love it because I feel that I could love someone that much myself and I know you have the passion, the sensitivity and the desire to love someone as Heathcliff and Cathy do. . . . P.S. Here is my favorite line: 'Be with me always—take any form—drive me mad! Only do not leave me in the abyss, where I cannot find you! Oh God!'"

The question to all this again is, why? What gives Heathcliff and Cathy such a continuing fascination? I suspect that the attraction of erotic passion, especially for the young, comes not so much out of lust as out of a longing to gain identity and feel important. One of the appeals of love is the implicit promise of most faiths: that the last shall be first and live at the heart of things. People long to believe that the miracle of significance, of ecstasy, of felt passion might strike anywhere—even where they stand (or thrash about). Emily Brontë has imagined intercessors for erotic faith. If Sartre can write "Saint Genet," we can certainly proclaim, after nearly a century and a half in the canon of love, "Saint Catherine, Saint Heathcliff"!

5   Faithful Repression and Erotic Enchantment:
Charlotte Brontë's *Villette* (1853)

A lily prisoned in a jail of snow.
SHAKESPEARE[1]

[W]here were they, and where was I? In a land of enchantment.
CHARLOTTE BRONTË[2]

I

Everyone knows that love can be a thudding, humbling disaster, no matter what
Austen, Heathcliff, or youthful glands say. And in historical perspective, doesn't
it often seem an especially bad thing for women? In *Villette*, Polly Home de
Bassompierre quotes from Schiller: "Oh, Holy One, call back your child, I have
known earthly happiness, I have lived and loved!" (26:389).[3] To Lucy Snowe,
the first-person narrator, she then muses: "Lived and loved! . . . is that the
summit of earthly happiness, the end of life—to love? I don't think it is. It may
be the extreme of mortal misery, it may be sheer waste of time, and fruitless
torture of feeling. If Schiller had said to *be* loved—he might have come nearer
the truth. Is not that another thing, Lucy, to be loved?" "I suppose it may be,"
says Lucy, in her characteristically repressive mode, "but why consider the subject? . . . we will not talk about love" (26:389). But she will write about it—in
fact, about little else.

   This dialogue gets to the crux of the novel and expresses the need that made
love a nineteenth-century faith despite its ravages. The problematic relationship
between love and the power of expression, between desire and repression, between love and identity, love and the sacred, love and the novel, all figure
throughout the book. The repressive, enchanting "holy one" is the erotic god
as well as the Christian God, and *Villette* shows as well as any text the continuing, oscillating displacement between the one and the other in nineteenth-century sensibility. Charlotte Brontë knew all the arguments against romantic
love—they lived in her nerves—but she imagines it as a necessity. The holy
trinity of her being, like Lucy Snowe's, consists of love, Christian faith, and
writing; and though the parts are finally inseparable, the greatest of these is
love. Without erotic emotion, there is no faith and no lasting word of God.

   The controversial logic of *Villette* says that the self, until it is loved, lacks definition, reality, and voice; only by feeling love from another or being in love can the personality take form in the world. Only love can repress the power of death and bring the word that gives sanctity to being. "You're nobody," goes the song, "until somebody loves you." You're also nobody if you do not find a means to express love.

Charlotte Brontë's sorrowful, wonderfully original, but demanding novel is as suffused with desire as *Wuthering Heights* and just as important a testament of love and erotic history. *Villette*, however, is the most inward and Protestant of fictions. Unlike the flamboyant *Wuthering Heights*, it avoids violent outbursts of passion or ecstatic dialogue. It has inspired no songs, operas, or movies; it has no witty, lively heroine like Elizabeth Bennet, no self-dramatizing fireball like Catherine Earnshaw, no image of beauty and sacrifice like Lucy Ashton.[4] Instead it features neurotic Lucy Snowe who lacks beauty, charm, health, wealth, and family. Shabbily genteel, she is one of those nineteenth-century "relative creatures," women fated to flutter on the periphery of middle-class life and notice.[5] Lucy must work as a paid lady's companion, a governess, a school teacher and school keeper. What have such marginal, apparently self-effacing people to do with love? Brontë, who once *was* such a creature, tries to render a story that will make readers know and care. Her unconventional heroine's repressed mien and emotional displacement hide a monomaniacal lovesickness. Love is to Lucy as money is to a pauper: something whose absence and need define her. The condition of her life is erotic hysteria and what she calls "heart-poverty" (13:186).

Villette is as somber and uncompromising as a Samuel Beckett novel—*love* "how it is," not "as you like it." Brontë, like Beckett, insists on the terrible, drab compromises and the compulsive fictionalizing that the hunger for love foists on people. She questions erotic faith, even while she subscribes to it. Charlotte Brontë is a Calvinist of the heart. Some are saved and some are damned on earth by love, and erotic providence and its signs show everywhere. On the one hand, the novel deflates romantic illusions about some one-and-only, Mr.-or-Miss-Right kind of love coming beautifully along; but on the other, no novel more insistently slashes away at the opposite sentimentality, the naive who-needs-*them*, I-can-make-it-on-my-own school of sublimation and pseudopragmatism. In its bitterness and honesty, *Villette* pushes readers to focus on just what they seldom want to face, especially in times when the ideologies of quantification, individualism, and equality flourish: namely, the inevitably demeaning conditions of dependency—the radical imperfections and insufficiencies both in themselves and in those they love that make love so imperative, fragile, and death-haunted.

II

As love becomes faith, Scripture feeds the Novel. "Many waters cannot quench love," says the Bible, "neither can the floods drown it" (Song of Solomon, 8:7). Charlotte Brontë's imagination takes those canonical words and forms from them her controlling imagery and her narrative of being in love. The intention of the text is to reconcile human love and Christian faith; but in *Villette*, as in *Jane Eyre*, faith in love both conflicts and fuses with Christian calling. This novel of religious yearning reads like a *Pilgrim's Progress* of Victorian love. Charlotte, proudly Protestant and much more orthodox than Emily, steeps her book and her protagonist-narrator Lucy Snowe in the language, typology, and cadence of the Bible, religious tracts, sermons, confessional narratives, and moral testimony,[6] but she uses the tone and forms of religious writing to explore erotic faith. She also uses personal erotic experience to breathe life into these old forms of Christian testament.

Doubt and strain permeate the text: if faith, hope, and charity are to have a chance in hearts and in the world, then Christian idealism must blend with erotic love; but Jehovah and the god of love may not be reconcilable. The dilemma Charlotte Brontë faced was awful: How do you keep erotic longing and faith from being a curse to some poor hapless souls and bodies, as Christian belief is to those who believe themselves damnable? *Villette* struggles with that predicament.

Everything in it exists in a double context: Christian and erotic. It is no accident, for example, that the first man Lucy loves has the same name as the herald of faith, John the Baptist, or that her true lover and savior, whose epistles from afar inspire her, is called Paul Emanuel. Moving through Lucy's text is like traveling through some land whose people and ethos are shaped by the accretion of two powerful religions. Her narrative needs to be read like a passage from Revelations, an evangelical autobiography, and a Freudian case history all in one.

III

The novel's meaning and structure may be complex, but the basic story is simple. Lucy Snowe, pathetic ugly duckling, suffers many trials, including an unrequited love for the handsome Dr. John. By the end, however, at a boarding school in the mythical foreign city of Villette, she wins the love of a fellow teacher, a good, if flawed, man, Paul Emanuel. Through their faith in one another, she achieves both vocational success—a career as head of her own school—and the power of imaginative expression. Though it seems clear that Paul dies at sea before they can be married, Lucy finds the strength to articulate her vision of the world out of her experience of being in love and being loved.

The shadow of death and loss, however, chills even requited love. She tells the chronological story of her life only up to the time she comes to possess love, and then stops. Even though the "first person" who sets down this account refers to herself as a white-haired older woman (5:105), she tells nothing of the thirty years or more between the ocean storm that presumably drowned Paul and the time of writing. *Villette* is not the story of a life, but the story of love and its inscription.

The novel, in its images of love life, raises bitter questions. If love makes life worth living and a person cannot bloom without it, what then is an unattractive, unloved, and apparently unlovable woman to do? *Villette* offers no solution except to pursue and imagine love in a way that makes it possible to go on living, and there is no guarantee that the pursuit will bring anything except a renewal of suffering. Lucy Snowe must follow both her erotic and her professional vocation. Working hard, aspiring morally, fighting for good in the immediate circumstances of life are for Charlotte Brontë ways of bettering the world and the self, gaining esteem and self-respect, and thus possibly making oneself lovable. Another tactic is to repress and discipline hopeless erotic desire, so that the deflected energy can find new possibilities for love and make one's inner life glow with enchantment—the kind of enchantment that can turn disparate material into art and, as happens in *Villette*, a frog into a prince. Lucy has to undergo the kind of humiliating ritual that eros usually requires: she has to switch her love from a man who loves someone else to one who can love her. And then she has to try to preserve that love when physically it no longer exists. If you can't be with the one you love—to paraphrase the modern lyric—then find a way to love the one you're with (even if you can only be with that one through the power of imagination and art).

Equivocal Thackeray, sincere admirer and cruel patronizer of Charlotte Brontë, wrote, "That's a plaguy book, that *Villette*. How clever it is! and how I don't like the heroine. . . ."[7] That is just the point. The heroine is not a type who can gain easily the liking of men on which women's life and fate so much depend. In a letter to a young woman, Thackeray set out, with nasty, sexist shrewdness, a great problem of the author and Lucy—and the whole age:

The poor little woman of genius! the fiery eager brave tremulous homely-faced creature! I can read a great deal of her life as I fancy her in her book, and see that rather than have fame, rather than any other earthly good or mayhap heavenly one she wants some Tomkins or another to love her and be in love with. But you see she is a little bit of a creature without a penny worth of good looks, . . . and no Tomkins will come. You girls with pretty faces . . . will get dozens of young fellows fluttering about you—whereas here is one genius, a noble heart longing to mate itself and destined to wither away into old maidenhood with no chance to fulfil the burning desire.[8]

Though a Tomkins (Arthur Nicholls, her father's curate) afterwards *did* dismally come, Thackeray rightly sensed that the book grew out of Charlotte Brontë's thwarted desire for love.

She suffered from her hopeless love for Monsieur Héger and made the novel out of her life. Héger was her teacher and the proprietor, with his wife, of the school she and Emily attended in Brussels to prepare themselves to teach, to which she returned alone, and from which she had to leave in sorrow and mental confusion, forced out by Madame Héger and an impossible situation. This love and the agony of both knowing and trying to deny that it was obsessive, humiliating, unrequited, and morally wrong—and that she was condemned to go on fantasizing about it in her loneliness—shaped her mind and art for the rest of her life.

Other men and experiences fed into the eroticism of the novel. Charlotte seems to have fallen in unrequited, if not all-consuming, love with her publisher, George Smith, a "prototype" of Dr. John.[9] (She displaced the rejection of love from the Héger figure to the Smith figure, and that transferral indicates, among many other things, just how excruciatingly difficult and shameful it can be to imagine that the person you love most passionately—the love of your life— really does not love or want you. Brontë can render John's rejection, and she can drown Paul, but she cannot write that Paul would not find her lovable.) Also she turned down a proposal of marriage—à la Paul's—from ugly little James Taylor, Smith's partner, on his way out to India for five years.[10] And behind these unconsummated relationships lay the kingdom of death which the world, taking her family one by one, showed itself to be.

IV

Lucy Snowe writes about providence—erotic providence. For her, erotic providence is world, life, and destiny ordered and given meaning by the desire for human love; and the force of love and desire is what allows her to regard Divine Providence with stoic faith. Lucy is one of the great case studies in the fiction of repression, and what she represses is whatever threatens to close off or delimit the working of a mystical providence. She undertakes to do through her text what religion and religious institutions try to do: to repress death, control desire, and show that individual life matters. Her first-person narration—the first-person world—is the creation of providential erotic desire, and she represses what would separate her perception from the creative energy of that desire.

This repression works both negatively and positively. When, loveless, she equates the idea of self with hopeless desire, then she suppresses her personality and memory. Her repression, however, though it makes her an unreliable narrator, leads her to project her frustrated desire and patterns of imagination everywhere. She fears the pain of exposure, but she also fears being cut off and alienated from the outside world. The tension disorients her being. In her prose and psychology, she displaces, transfers, and fuses her self into other characters, objects, places, sights, nature, and even providence itself. The overriding pattern—a pattern, I need hardly say, we find in the life of her author—is to sublimate desire into language.

Disorientation: Villette, the little city of competing faiths, the capital of a small Low Country, lies to the east of England and within the fluid boundaries of Lucy's mind, an erotic New Jerusalem where the walls between self and not-self quietly come tumbling down. Inner and outer life have no fixed demarcation in *Villette*. Lucy's repression helps create the erotic enchantment of her vision and works to idealize love or preserve the possibility of forming and holding onto such an idealization. It also helps to blend her libidinous desire into her labor (including her narrative) and her vocational ambitions. The book therefore presents a small-scale version of the way Victorian sexual repression was ideally supposed to work in large: faith in love would be preserved and great quantities of energy would flow into good and constructive works.

Repression, displacement, and enchantment characterize *Villette*, where nothing can be taken at face value because all appears through Lucy's words and eye. The novel reads like the testimony of a voyeur: deflected, displaced desire, skewed self-regard, and passion eroticize everything. A concert, a painting, a play, an actress performing, clothing, a king—all are tinged, framed, and inscribed with personal meaning by a love-hungry mind. Erotic desire expropriates anything—art, architecture, public ceremony—to tell its tale. And almost everything magically connects, as in a land of pure enchantment, which Villette is. The characters who live in England are sure to show up years later in Villette; the Dr. John who saves her and who tends the sick at the girls' school is sure to be the Graham Bretton of the opening, and so on. This is a world of romance ordered and composed by Eros, for that is how Brontë imagines Lucy's ordering and composition of her text.

The Low Country novel that Brontë made out of her Low Country experience can be illuminated by a Dutch painting: *A Woman Standing at a Virginal* (1670; fig. 3) by Vermeer, portrayer of women in love, has much in common with the treatment of love in *Villette*.[11] In the picture a young lady with prominent brown eyes stands at the keyboard gazing enigmatically at the beholder. Her subtly nuanced, shadowed expression shows a mixture of stolid reserve, preoccupation, intimidating perception, and inward knowingness. On the wall behind her hangs a huge picture of a domineering, admonitory Cupid with glowing hair. His brown eyes and steady gaze are exactly the same as the woman's. In his right hand he grasps his bow, which, since she stands in front of the lower corner of his frame, appears to pierce right into her head. Vermeer composed the painting so that Cupid's foot brushes the woman's cheek. Her hand rests idly on the keys of the instrument, its name, its symbolism, and the iconographical link between music and Venus telling us that it stands for her virginity and connotes love. To the left of the oversized painting-within-a-painting of Eros, next to the high casement through which the sun streams, hangs a smaller picture of a landscape enclosed by a brilliant, radiating gold frame.

The whole complex painting has a myriad of other features worthy of comment, for example, the empty blue chair in the foreground; the comparable mountainous landscapes, one painted on the instrument, one within the gilt frame; and the dazzle of Cupid's hair complementing that shining frame. Detail after detail reinforces the idea of displaced subjectivity in enchanted surroundings. But what stands out is the reverberating erotic triangle formed by the woman's face, the blatant Cupid, and the glittering frame of the picture: *expression, love, and radiance.*

The work is both mimetic and symbolic: Vermeer portrays a woman of his time, and yet he sets her in a charmed context of displaced emotion and high erotic tension. In the objects about her, and the composition of the whole picture with the relationship of its different parts to one another, the woman's interior life and passions are externalized. Everything that surrounds her and impinges upon her is projection. There is no real discreteness to the apparently discontinuous parts of the work. Vermeer's form persuades us that all is continuous with the woman's erotic being. The various framed, delimited spaces can be read as psychological mirrors reflecting on the woman's thoughts and life. What appears on the wall, for example, since it rules her mind, is a part of the portrait of the lady. The picture is mediated by the subject's desire, and it holds a tension between revelation and concealment. It suggests a world of amorous implication and meaning, but it draws on us to make interpretations. The impassive, deceptively calm face of the woman tells little by itself, but the whole composition proclaims eroticism and demands explication. The art is psychologized and eroticized, as is Charlotte Brontë's. The subjectivity and thus the resulting indeterminacy of these works necessarily engage the subjectivity and intuition of their audiences. Like Vermeer's masterpiece, *Villette* is a portrait of a woman's inner life and amorous enchantment.

V

To be enchanted is to be caught in a spell, and Lucy Snowe's story lies in the spell of writing that seeks to express love and repress death. That spell transfixes time, so that Lucy's narrative, though at first it may seem to move chronologically, is actually synchronous, like the hundred dormant years for Sleeping Beauty after the prince's kiss awakens her, or like our past when we recollect it. The idea of enchantment, as in fairy tales, Vermeer's painting, or *Villette*, often features the absent figure of an awaited lover and stresses the power of love to overcome the threat of death. Charlotte Brontë, the last survivor of her siblings, kept learning all her short life the lesson that anything she loved or attached herself to would die or be denied her. In *Villette* she is trying to imagine—as Emily so differently does in *Wuthering Heights*—how and whether love could be stronger than death.

The novel is both progressive and circular. Time as well as emotion and experience is repressed and displaced. For example, we find the most probable allusion to Lucy's state of mind, life, and faith as an older woman not at the end, but near the beginning in her account of Miss Marchmont; and this report comes immediately after Lucy has displaced the repressed emotion of her own traumatic childhood and apparent motherlessness by projecting it onto Polly Home, the only child we see in the novel. Thus in this "heretic narrative" (15:235), we seem to have the essential beginning and end of Lucy's autobiography, but they take place in other characters' lives and almost before the story gets started. Not only does the action on the last page precede the setting down of the words on the first page—the usual convention of first-person narratives—but also the events, the images, the very language of the last chapter are necessary to understand and appreciate the novel from the beginning. Anyone trying to grasp the full significance and power of *Villette* comes eventually to see that it must, in effect, be read backwards as well as forwards.

Nothing does more to cast a singular spell over the novel than Lucy's fusion of past and present at the end and her refusal to tell Paul's fate directly or mention her own after his final voyage. In the last chapter, Paul, having engaged to marry her, must leave Villette to spend three years working in the Caribbean. Anxious for his return, Lucy, when his time is up, moves her prose from past tense to present, her eager memory making all contemporaneous. Brontë imagines her writing these pregnant words: "I thought I loved him when he went away; I love him now in another degree; he is more my own" (42:595). On the last two pages she describes, in vivid present tense, the killer storm that strews wrecks and corpses, but she does not say explicitly that Emanuel drowned.

We need to look carefully at the book's penultimate paragraph: "Here pause: pause at once. There is enough said. Trouble no quiet, kind heart; leave sunny imaginations hope. Let it be theirs to conceive the delight of joy born again fresh out of great terror, the rapture of rescue from peril, the wondrous reprieve from dread, the fruition of return. Let them picture union and a happy succeeding life" (42:596).

This is complex, ambivalent prose. Brontë plays with "the happy ending," that sentimental heaven of popular novels. Sardonically, she edges near parody of the conventional courtship novel which, after all, narrates the match of lovers, but then stops the story before they have to live together. With a bitter twist, she makes explicit the void that is implicit, for example, in Austen. But the paragraph also fuses the language and imagery of love with that of Christian faith. It can be read as an orthodox vision of immortality and resurrection as well as a rosy romantic ending. Lucy's wish for those "sunny imaginations" accords nicely with Christian hope and doctrine. Her narrative and experience cast doubt on the efficacy of institutional faith, but the irony and weight of the passage are demeaned only if we think of those "sunny imaginations" belonging to mere sentimentalists who cannot face a mortal fact. These sunny ones can also be seen as the conventionally faithful. Charlotte Brontë struggles against despair by trying to imagine a blend of traditional and erotic faith that would avoid the deceptions of each, but she also sees the cant of mush-minded optimism.

Lucy Snowe is not "sunny." She has the imagination of moonlight—romantic, melancholy, slightly distorting, misty, and "loony"—a light in shadows and darkness, a light depending upon a nineteenth-century womanly process of visionary experience and reflection. ("Imagination," she reports, showed her "a moon supreme, in an element deep and splendid" [38:547].) We know that Brontë had planned to kill Paul, but her father wanted a happy ending, and we know that she simply could not imagine a happy marriage for Lucy without distorting her sense of truth.[12] The main point, however, about the climax is surely the repression itself. Everything that has come before is connected to her radical strategy of avoiding closure.

Muting the fate of the man and the relationship shows both the extraordinary reticence and the willpower of Brontë and her narrator. For all we know from the text, Lucy Snowe lives her life—a life that, from the only evidence she gives, has been devoted to love—as a virgin, never knowing the intimacy of the flesh. The final pages confirm as her lasting reality her idealization of love: "I love him now in another degree; he is more my own." Karen Chase calls this process "the lover denied, the love affirmed,"[13] and it shows the reason for the prevalence and force of erotic faith. In *Villette's* metamorphosis of a male lover into a woman's spiritual love, the novelist and the novel show how idealizing love is not some abstract, precious phenomenon but action that grows out of desperate need and deprivation. "I love him . . . in another degree; he is more my own": I find, in the oddly brave repression of what might be called *carnal knowledge*—in order that an erotic present can be possessed lastingly in words and memory—the full religious aspiration and power of the erotic imagination.

9. Bronzino, *Deposition from the Cross*. Musée des Beaux-Arts et d'Archéologie, Bensançon, France.

10. See p. 12.

11. Caravaggio, *Amor Vincit Omnia*. Staatliche Museen Preussischer Kulturbesitz, Gemäldegalerie Berlin (West).

12. Giovanni Baglione, *Divine Love*. Galleria Nazionale d'Arte Antica, Palazzo Corsini, Rome. A photo of the Istituto Centrale per il Catalogo e la Documentazione, Rome.

13. Jan Vermeer, *A Lady Writing*. National Gallery of Art, Washington; gift of Harry Waldron Havemeyer and Horace Havemeyer, Jr., in memory of their father, Horace Havemeyer.

15. Edward Burne-Jones, *King Cophetua and the Beggar Maid.* Tate Gallery, London/Art Resource, New York

16. Edward Burne-Jones, "*King Cophetua and the Beggar Maid*, in the Style of Rubens," pencil, from a decorated letter by Burne-Jones. Reproduced by courtesy of the Trustees of the British Museum, London.

17. Gian Bernini, "The Ecstasy of Saint Theresa." Cornaro Chapel, Santa Maria della Vittoria, Rome. A photo of the Istituto Centrale per il Catalogo e la Documentazione, Rome.

18. Claude Lorrain, *Landscape with Psyche outside Cupid's Palace* ("The Enchanted Castle"). Reproduced by courtesy of the Trustees, National Gallery, London.

19. Claude Lorrain, *The Judgment of Paris*. National Gallery of Art, Washington, Ailsa Mellon Bruce Fund.

20. Odilon Redon, *The Birth of Venus*. Ville de Paris, Musée du Petit Palais, Paris.

21. Jan Vermeer, *Officer and Laughing Girl*. Copyright the Frick Collection, New York.

By idealizing romantic love and suspending questions about its physical, time-doomed nature, many Victorians and others have sought to transcend the finitude of particular flesh and affections and make of love an open-ended creed and comfort.

The prose of Lucy's key paragraph both does and does not cede authority: it gives direct responsibilities to the readers to define themselves, but it wraps itself proudly—even arrogantly—in mystery, and glorifies the writer and writing. It suppresses material fact and, what is more, death. Paul's letters, she tells us in this last chapter, were the "living water" that sustained her life, the spring of her energy: "He sat down, he took pen and paper, because he loved Lucy and had much to say to her" (42:594). As she moves to the end, she is reciprocating, trying to inscribe herself with him in an epitaphic text, and to make their love live in narrative.

Lucy offers words that carry many meanings and connotations, some of them contradictory. That paragraph says that some lucky people do not know the deadly unfairness and sorrow of life, and that telling them would do no good. It says that true believers can imagine that no matter what the tragedy of earthly life, they will rejoin their loved ones and God in eternal life. It implies both that love might create an enchanted world where there is no death and that such belief is Pollyannish. It says that by refusing, in narrative, to make death the end of things, the writer might throw emphasis on life and preserve it through memory. It says also that as the world seems to promise intimacy, but then withholds it, so I, Lucy Snowe, shall withhold the intimacy I have implicitly promised you readers. And what it unmistakably says to careful readers is that what is here denied or omitted through repression here breaks through elsewhere, that is, *what I don't say now, you will find coloring what I have written before.*

VI

By suspending the question of Paul's death, Brontë gives priority to the unspoken. Death and the loss of love, unfixed and unlocated in the text, haunt Lucy and show up everywhere. Only with the climax of reticence on the last page can we realize the displaced significance of another key passage from early in the book, when the girl Lucy leaves Bretton.

It will be conjectured that I was of course glad to return to the bosom of my kindred. Well! the amiable conjecture does no harm. . . . I will permit the reader to picture me, for the next eight years, as a bark slumbering through halcyon weather . . . —the steersman stretched on the little deck, his face up to heaven, his eyes closed: *buried,* if you will, in a long prayer. A great many women and girls are supposed to pass their lives something in that fashion; why not I with the rest?

Picture me then idle, basking, plump, and happy, stretched on a cushioned deck, warmed with constant sunshine, rocked by breezes indolently soft. However, it cannot be concealed that, in that case, I must somehow have fallen over-board, or that there must have been wreck at last. . . . To this hour, when I have the nightmare, it repeats the rush and saltness of briny waves in my throat, and their icy pressure on my lungs. I even know there was a storm, and that not of one hour nor one day. . . . a heavy tempest lay on us; all hope that we should be saved was taken away. In fine, the ship was lost, the crew perished. [4:94]

Repression means obsession. Two famous dicta, "in my beginning is my end" and Freud's assertion that the unconscious is timeless, fit *Villette*. Putting together the excerpts from the start and finish of the narrative makes clear its spellbound quality. The result of the final storm and the fate of Paul show up displaced in the early passage, as the fixation of the woman in Vermeer appears in the figure of Cupid. The word "buried" and its morbid force redound throughout the book. The type of audience capable of "amiable conjecture" in the beginning reappears as the "sunny imaginations" of conclusion; a drowning storm has devastated Lucy before, and she represses direct information about both these calamities. What at first reading seems a local conceit both to express and conceal Lucy's painful early losses turns out not only to imply exactly Paul's fate—drowning—but also to show how her entire narrative perception is shaped in light of shipwreck, impending death, and the need to control through repression the menace of losing love. Language can be used for control and its properties can be manipulated to transmute perception and direct response, but the hidden force of passions ironically can and often will govern the selection of language. The text becomes a model of mental life; it asks for an intensive process of rereading to give it wholeness and resonance, as her life requires of her a constant rereading and recycling of experience to give it significance and purpose.

The two passages taken together limn Charlotte Brontë's anatomy of love. To crave love and need it desperately and then to find someone who loves you and whom you can love is to have your being and self-image in that lover. As the prose shows, Lucy identifies closely with Paul, and the language she uses is *ghostly*. It aims at bringing back the disembodied spirit from the dead and shows the mental mingling of two selves that love can generate. She has projected his fate into her text and feels what it is to drown. In her writing she unites with him, his watery fate becoming hers, and he goes on living in her, as Cathy goes on living in Heathcliff's desire—an absence that is a haunting presence, love kept alive through painful vocation. And the earlier passage deepens the pathos and resonance of "leave sunny imaginations hope" because it shows—as in reflection it identifies Lucy and Paul with times of Caribbean sunshine and imagination—that people, even the victimized, need and sometimes feel the hope of love, not only in their future, but in their living memories of the past. Love, I said before, creates "death" because it makes us feel the terrible sadness that the person who cared for us is no more, and it gives us partial knowledge—since that which affirmed our identity has itself ceased to be—of our *own* death. But death, or its shadow, absence, creates love too because it tells us of the tempestuous hollow of emptiness in consciousness that requires the company and affection of the other to make us whole and reflect our being.

The reciprocal passages also suggest an erotic pattern for Lucy, for they make clear that the loss of Paul repeats and fuses with earlier experience. In love, says Freud, "the object selected is never the original one, but only a surrogate for it."[14] For Brontë, something like that also holds true for the choice of love stories and how you tell them. There is never a time when Lucy Snowe does not seem to be keeping back vital information about losses of loved ones, never a word before some first, unknown, alienating storm has already left her a stranded survivor, never a page that does not seem haunted by absence and frustrated desire. The drive for lost love seems to inaugurate the narrative, collapse time, and infuse everything with reiterated libido. Brontë filters Lucy's perception through "Auld Lang Syne," a chapter title and a key umbrella concept that for her shapes a life. The tone and feeling of the novel are, as Joyce puts it, that "all that has been done has yet to be done again."[15]

VII

The book begins, as it ends, with passive-aggressive reserve. The pre-Villette chapters stand as an overture to all that follows, but we cannot realize their art and meaning until the end. Lucy, already in her fourteenth year, says nothing about her family and antecedents. Childhood, a kind of perverse Eden in *Wuthering Heights* and a nightmare in *Jane Eyre*, does not exist in Lucy's history, except by indirection as an ominously silent chasm. In the first chapter, at her godmother's, Lucy tells about the arrival of little Polly Home, the unhappy marriage of Polly's parents, and the disgraceful history of Polly's mother, but gives not a line about her own parentage or early life. Polly, at the start and throughout the text, usurps Lucy's place in the affections of the Brettons—mother and, especially, son—but Lucy also projects onto Polly, as she does with other characters to come, her own repressed desires and concerns. Let me repeat, because the text's implicit claim for the power of love and libido to determine perception (and, in novels, the first-person point of view) lies in this fact: *There is no absolute sense of a discrete, objective other who can be known and spoken of outside of the observer's conscious or unconscious erotic desire. When we talk of others, we talk of ourselves and what we want and love; we can't help it.*

Lucy's vision oscillates; other figures—Polly for example—reflect both projections of her self and detached images of the not-self. Right from the start, Polly's grief over separation from her father and her role as the one who alienates affection from Lucy look like reenactments by Lucy from her own "unspeakable" childhood. The whole episode of Polly in the first three chapters smacks of a screen memory for a sensitive girl traumatized by the arrival of a younger sibling. Lucy swings wildly between expressing strong hostility to others, especially females, and vicariously identifying with them—two basic, common strategies in sibling relationships. René Girard's general theory of mimetic desire as the heart of erotic love—the idea that love is mediated and we love what another loves—finds good grounds of support both in the relationship of Lucy and Polly and in the existence of sibling rivalry and incestuous impulses that comprise for us original, if not eternal, triangles.[16]

For much of the novel, Polly-Paulina is what Lucy would like to be, but is not. To understand Lucy, her narrative, and love in *Villette*, we need to watch her watching Polly: "I, Lucy Snowe, plead guiltless of that curse, an overheated and discursive imagination [just what *does* characterize her]; but whenever . . . I found her seated in a corner alone . . . that room seemed to me not inhabited, but haunted" (2:69). Lucy is herself possessed by the spirits of others, and through Polly she imagines *herself*. "Papa!" cries the small girl when her father goes off: "It was low and long; a sort of 'Why hast thou forsaken me?' . . . I perceived she endured agony. She went through, in that brief interval of her infant life, emotions such as some never feel; it was in her constitution. . . . I, Lucy Snowe, was calm. The little creature . . . contended with an intolerable feeling; and, ere long, in some degree, repressed it" (3:79). We cannot tell the watcher from the sufferer here. Lucy's daring, almost blasphemous words tie religion and God to a specific need—and lack—of human love; they show her fascination with martyrdom and sacrifice; they feature repression, and they repeat her formulaic denial of emotion, the defense mechanism that casts its dislocating spell over the text.

Lucy then gives a moving account of Polly's transferred love for sixteen-year-old Graham Bretton, one of the few places in literature where we find expressed with delicacy the common, but rarely discussed, passion of a young child's falling in love with an older person. But what Lucy does not report until many years later is that she too at that time was in love with Graham—that the whole story, in fact, starts with her being in love and that she provoked and mediated Polly's love. Ten years after, in Villette, Lucy recognizes in Dr. John's house "a portrait."

It seemed a youth of sixteen. . . . Any romantic little school-girl might almost have loved it in its frame. . . . Ah! that portrait used to hang in the breakfast-room . . . . : somewhat too high, as I thought. I well remember how I used to mount a music-stool for the purpose of unhooking it, holding it in my hand, and searching into those bonny wells of eyes, whose glance under their hazel lashes seemed like a pencilled laugh. . . . I hardly believed fancy could improve on the curve of that mouth, or of the chin; even *my* ignorance knew that both were beautiful. . . . Once, by way of test, I took little Missy Home, and, lifting her in my arms, told her to look at the picture.

"Do you like it, Polly?" I asked. She never answered, but gazed long, and at last a darkness went trembling through her sensitive eyes, as she said, "Put me down." So I put her down, saying to myself: "The child feels it too." [16:242–43]

Lucy, the writer of narrative, like Brontë, begins by showing another her love, and she keeps on, even if she tells her story by reflections. Being in love frames her life. This would-be disdainer of emotionalism, in fact, was mooning over Graham's picture like any other "romantic school-girl." She offers readers the vision of her life and desire almost in the same way as she offers the vision of her love to Polly. The image of the older girl holding the younger up, watching her reaction, teaching her—by fanning mimetic desire—to love the same person she does, suggests the unpredictable wonder in love and the forms it takes. Such a scene deflates that cynical *mot* of La Rochefoucauld, "People would never fall in love, if they had not been told about it," because it says that to be human *is* to tell people of love, by word, deed, gesture, and art. It makes a good symbol not only for what Brontë does in *Villette*, but for what distinguished Victorian fiction does so well: namely, to hold unawakened erotic nature up to a mirroring art of desire.

If Polly is Lucy's surrogate as a child, Miss Marchmont, the "maiden lady" Lucy tends for two claustrophobic years before going to Villette, previews her later life. The chapter "Miss Marchmont" rereads like an abstract of the plot, the tone, the matter and manner of the book. Marchmont dies, but on the night of her death, she tells Lucy of her tragic love. By the end of the book, we see that her experience is completely fused with Lucy's text and fate. Nearly all the radiating symbols and images by which Brontë organizes the novel show up first in Marchmont's tale: "I . . . feel," says she, telling of the night her lover died, "the . . . firelight warming me, playing on my silk dress, and . . . showing me my own young figure in a glass. I see the moon of a calm winter night, float full, clear and cold, over . . . the silvered turf of my grounds. . . . The flames had died in the fire, but it was a bright mass yet; the moon was mounting high, but she was still visible from the lattice" (4:100). We have in these lines the moon, that shining satellite—symbol of fertility, flow, imagination, feminine being, and bonding, and more particularly, symbol of Lucy, light bringer in the night. We have also frozen water, clothes, images of fashion, fire—representing passion and love—and the reflecting mirror and the lattice, devices for looking and spying. The prose gives us in imagistic form the very name of Lucy Snowe and it tells us that her identity may be projected through the entire text.

Of her long-dead lover, Marchmont tells Lucy, "[I]f few women have suffered as I did in his loss, few have enjoyed what I did in his love" (4:99). Nearing death, she says, in words that Lucy will later echo, "I can say with sincerity, what I never tried to say before—Inscrutable God, Thy will be done! And at this moment I can believe that death will restore me to Frank. I never believed it till now" (4:99).

Erotic faith is here regenerating Christian faith. That is Charlotte Brontë's project in the novel. Like her sister Emily, she makes the idea of a desirable heaven depend on the strength and endurance of individual human love. But Marchmont ends on a typical nineteenth-century note of doubt: "You see I still think of Frank more than of God; and unless it be counted that in thus loving the creature so much, so long, and so exclusively, I have not at least blasphemed the Creator, small is my chance of salvation. What do you think, Lucy, of these things? Be my chaplain and tell me" (4:101). In other words, can God and Eros be reconciled? The tension that exists between them, the feeling that "salvation" is impossible without both, the hope and doubt that both can bring light within the single soul—that is what Marchmont is articulating, what Lucy is projecting into her, and what Charlotte Brontë is rendering. To comprehend the function and enterprise of the nineteenth-century novel we must take these words of this overture to *Villette* seriously: the writer of the text—the new scripture—is to be the chaplain of erotic faith, and significantly here the chaplain, that is, "one appointed to conduct religious services for a society," is a woman.

Lucy says she "had no words" then; but later, near the end, when her own life parallels Marchmont's, she does. Speaking of God's blessing on the lucky, Lucy turns to her own misfortune and takes up both her old mentor's questioning of God's motives and her resigned faith ("Thy will be done!"). Rhetorically Lucy asserts the orthodox creed:

His will be done, as done it surely will be, whether we humble ourselves to resignation or not. The impulse of creation forwards it. . . . Proof of a life to come must be given. In fire and in blood, if needful, must that proof be written. . . . In fire and in blood does it cross our own experience. . . . Pilgrims and brother mourners, join in friendly company. Dark through the wilderness of this world stretches the way for most of us: . . . be our cross our banner. . . . Let us . . . keep the faith, reliant in the issue to come off more than conquerors: "Art thou not form everlasting mine Holy One? WE SHALL NOT DIE!" [38:534][17]

Faith means a way of preserving life. Though this Christian exhortation verges on pietistic rant (Charlotte Chaplain?), few who consider the agony out of which Lucy writes or the reality of Brontë's own experience will fail to find it moving. With all of her siblings dead and her love life at nil, the author must have felt proud to write such words and hopeful that they could touch her readers. As for Lucy, she has just told the life story of Polly and her old love Dr.

John, who—she quickly summarizes—live a full and happy life with many children, much love, and all the good things that the world can offer. And she is about to inform us that her new love, Paul, is leaving Villette without declaring his love for her.

I want to stress two points:

1. God, in Lucy's sermon, is an author much like her; they both follow the same pattern. He brings to his creation fierce discipline which tests faith, generates mystery, and issues in a form of afterlife. The pattern of this Christian faith, like the pattern of erotic faith in her text, features repression and displacement, and offers a somber hope of undying enchantment.

2. Brontë immediately undercuts, even blasphemes, her onward-Christian-soldiers piece with an astounding juxtaposition. These words directly follow it: "On a Thursday morning we were all assembled in classe, waiting for the lesson of literature. The hour was come; we expected the master [Monsieur Paul]" (38:534). "The lesson of literature" and "the master," the term of the faithful for Jesus, used just at this point and shortly after followed by other references to "M. Emanuel," casting him typologically as the awaited savior, intimate Lucy's true faith in love and show that she just cannot separate religion, writing, and love.

One of the primary images of the novel, the mysterious "ghost" nun who appears from time to time to Lucy and others, provides an apt symbol for love's impersonation of Christianity in the novel: "she" turns out to be de Hamal, the lover of the coquette Ginevra Fanshawe, in masquerade. The image can stand for my whole subject, and it takes us back to "Monk" Lewis's portrait of the erotic Virgin. The nun's costume sums up a meaning that Brontë reiterates in passage after passage: love walks in the guise of religion; it takes over religious habits and vocabulary; it is life even if it takes the form of death; it moves with sacral aspect through the enchanted atmosphere of the novel.

VIII

When Lucy enters Villette and Madame Beck's school for girls ("Pensionnat de Demoiselles"), the primary setting, she moves, as always, in both an internal and an external world. The text projects outward the emotional life within a single being, but it also tells of a young Englishwoman's observation and adventures in a foreign school, a Roman Catholic city, and a nineteenth-century cultural institution for training females. We are, like Proust, "within a budding grove" ("à l'ombre des jeunes filles en fleur"), and that grove is both Lucy's self and an academy for budding girls. The garden, the hidden *allée defendue* where Lucy walks the straight and narrow path, the cluttered, gothic attic of the house, and the haunted dormitory are psychological as well as physical loci. The place of feminine education, discipline, and surveillance throbs with erotic desire and intrigue.

I want, again, to compare a Brontë novel with ballet in order to stress how cultural repression can work to create an enchanted art that renders love. The choreography for a late nineteenth-century corps de ballet in *Swan Lake*,[18] for example, epitomizes aesthetically the Victorian educational ideal of molding modest, beautiful, accomplished, and soulful young women. *Swan Lake*, in fact, directly presents a vision of enchantment—women turned to graceful swans by ruthless male power. For spectators, the pain, discipline, and devotion generally of young female dancers can produce an overwhelmingly powerful rendering of romantic love. In much the same way, the painful repression of Lucy Snowe within the budding grove of Villette—and of Charlotte Brontë in the Pensionnat Héger (she called M. Héger "the black swan"[19])—leads to a passionate expression of erotic desire. *Villette* and *Swan Lake*, like so many works of nineteenth-century art, depend upon the suffering of courageous women and dedication to erotic faith. And both take place in an enchanted voyeuristic atmosphere inimical to women's independence where, nevertheless, love, dangerous as it is, is the only way to salvation.

Lucy, I said, is a voyeur—like so many others in this narrative of voyeuristic sensibility. She gratifies her desire by effacing herself and watching others, appropriating their experience, and ascribing to them what is in her soul. Voyeurism, the use of the field of vision for erotic pleasure, blurs the limits between the self and others; it seeks out forbidden or unconventional intimacies. Lucy watching Polly gaze at Graham or Madame Beck spying on Lucy's love life seems to break taboos of modesty and leave the observed vulnerable.

The word *surveillance* appears again and again in Lucy's text, and spying is the way of its world.[20] What interests all the watchers is the erotic life of others and how it relates to their own. *Villette* makes clear how closely connected art and voyeurism are. Both make available intelligence and a knowledge of others that the reality of social life does not usually allow. They offer the pleasures of vicarious experience without risk of self-exposure—in the short term, at least. The voyeur and the artist long to strip humanity naked and take in the sights. They make what they see the object of speculation—speculation in the sense of thoughtful contemplation, but also in the sense of something that will pay off in emotional capital.

Lucy as narrator as well as character incarnates the repressed, voyeuristic atmosphere of Villette: One day in the school, she is typically watching Dr. John: "I was observing the colouring of his hair, whiskers, and complexion. . . . when I saw that his notice was arrested, and that it had caught my movement in a clear little oval mirror fixed in the side of the window recess—by the aid of which reflector madame often secretly spied persons walking in the garden below" (10:163). That is typical: eyes spying reflections of eyes spying. Some hundred pages later, Lucy tells us that this was the moment she realized that Dr. John was one and the same as Graham Bretton; but, she remarks here, "I did not speak." Knowledge is power—or, more precisely, knowledge amassed and withheld gives one a sense of control. Voyeurs, concealing themselves, seize intimacy from others without being willing to give it back.

One reason why spies capture the public fancy is that their activity has something sexual about it. Espionage—what we now call "intelligence"—voyeurism, art, and eroticism all in some degree offer delight in the exposure of the other— as, sometimes, does religion in its confessional modes. To an extent, Charlotte Brontë creates a Protestant satire attacking totalitarian Roman Catholic practice. When the good Catholic Paul Emanuel tells Lucy that, as a moral guardian, he takes pride in spying on the school and even uses a telescope, she chides him. But of course, as a dedicated moral spy, she is just as bad.

The voyeuristic imagination finds a way of claiming the beautiful and erasing material boundaries. Brontë shows, with brilliant prescience, how important it is in smoothing various ways to make love possible and popular. It works complexly, absorbing what it sees into the viewer's fantasy life. It can identify vicariously with its object, but it can also give viewers a sense of superiority to what they see. It offers the joy of forbidden knowledge, and it works to debase, dispelling the awe that surrounds its object and thereby overcoming psychological inhibition so that libidinal energy can be aroused in the viewer.[21] That may not be an ennobling truth, but it helps account for the existence of all kinds of art, novels, movies, TV shows, videos, and other popular entertainment.

Ever since people have been thinking about love, they have associated it with beauty. From Plato to *Playboy* cruel ideas abound that tell people that only the physically beautiful are worthy of love. Slang breaks right through politeness to talk about "good looks" and "good-looking." But such terms, dehumanizing and demeaning as they are, also show how looking at "beautiful people," watching their erotic behavior, attaching them to the self, can be a way—degrading or not—of claiming the world and spirit of love.

Lucy, though she despises pretty Ginevra Fanshawe, loves to look at her, be near her beauty, and follow her love life. Ginevra is an antiself for Lucy, the opposite who somehow attracts even while repelling. Dr. John loves Ginevra, who doesn't love him. Lucy loves Dr. John, who doesn't love her. Looking at Ginevra is the way Lucy begins to internalize the social fact and effects of *the pretty girl* and of beauty in her culture, and then gradually to deal with what they signify. She who would believe in love must come to terms with the unfair cultural linking of the beautiful, the good, and love. In a resonant moment in both this novel and in erotic history generally, Ginevra makes Lucy join her before the school's great looking glass. Exulting in the contrast ("I know I am beautiful: I feel it, I see it" [14:214]), Ginevra expresses all that Lucy has repressed: "I *am* pretty, *you* can't deny that; I may have as many admirers as I choose. . . . There is *me*—happy ME; now for *you*, poor soul! . . . you have . . . no beauty. As to admirers, you hardly know what they are. . . . I believe you never were in love, and never will be" (14:215). Lucy coolly agrees, but says sincerely that she still would not give sixpence for Ginevra's life or place. Through Lucy, Brontë gets at that astonishing bit of evidence that makes personal love possible and proves the metaphysical reality and subjective value of people: they say and *they believe* that they would choose to have the integrity of their own being rather than trade places with others who are physically superior and materially better off. And upon such thought and feeling depends the lover's faith in the unique qualities of the beloved ("my one and only").

Seething at Ginevra because she toys with Dr. John, Lucy poses questions that have made countless women—and men too—resent love and erotic desire: "Have you power to do this? Who gave you that power? Where is it? Does it lie all in your beauty—your pink and white complexion and your yellow hair? Does this bind his soul at your feet?" (14:218–19). Those words call in doubt the moral worth of love. And only the smug can think they touch merely shallow people; Lucy, for instance, who has just called John "handsome as a vision," regards him in much the same light as he regards Ginevra. The larger question hovering over the novel is: given the link between love and looks—that staple of romance—how can one find or maintain erotic faith? Brontë imagines an aesthetic solution issuing out of the diffusive voyeur mentality in this radically unconventional love novel: by the authority of the narrative itself.

IX

Voyeurism and vicarious passion initiate Lucy into being in love and into perverted erotic vocation; but, leaving her sick with desire, they provoke a religious and hysterical crisis. She breaks down when, left during the school vacation with only a deformed cretin girl, a warped parody of her own life, she projects herself completely into the absent Ginevra. "By True Love was Ginevra followed. . . . I imagined her . . . loving now with reserve; but purposing one day to show how much she loved. . . . Ginevra gradually became with me a sort of heroine. One day, perceiving this growing illusion, I said, 'I really believe my nerves are getting overstretched: my mind has suffered . . . —what shall I do? How shall I keep well?'" (15:230–31). Lovesick and hallucinating, she takes to her bed.

Brontë wrote the chapter "The Long Vacation" out of her own experience at the Pensionnat Héger during the holiday in 1843, when, in love with M. Héger, she felt both abandoned and worse—cut off from talking to anybody about what obsessed her.[22] The episode gives us as agonized an account of depression as nineteenth-century fiction offers, but it also constitutes one of those Victorian set-pieces of prose—Ruskin's "The Storm-Cloud over the Nineteenth Century" is another—that brings home the terror that the idealistic conception of a benevolent God without the certain conviction in his existence could cause.

For Lucy here, religious affliction and erotic affliction are the same. Her suicidal despair comes from loss of faith that she could matter to any entity whom she could love—including God. Trying to pray, all she can utter is, "From my youth up Thy terrors have I suffered with a troubled mind" (15:232). The climax of the night of her soul is this: "Methought the well-loved dead, who had loved *me* well in life, met me elsewhere, alienated" (15:231). The words, in fact, point to a telling gap in Lucy's narrative. They lack the specificity of her usual revelations of previously repressed memories, though they do apply to her deepest fears late in the story and of a future *beyond the text*. So far she has told us nothing at all of anyone who *has loved her well*. The statement has the ring of Charlotte's own autobiography about it, and it seems to mean more than Emily's complaint about the insufficiency of the orthodox conception of heaven. M. Héger was the love of the author's life, and that love was illicit. We see Lucy here doubting that her religious faith can preserve love or dispel the shame of being unlovable, but we also may be getting the particular state of mind of Charlotte in Brussels, who had no hope that *even if there is an afterlife, it could be anything but terrible*, since, by Christian convention, she could never be united with the being she most loves, even in eternity. The words are Lucy's, but the sentiment is Charlotte's as well.

The crisis of the chapter, the narrator, the book, and the author focuses on confession and the temptation of the Church, for what is at stake is the choice of vocation and form of life. Fighting hysteria and the death wish, Lucy leaves the school, finds a church, and, on an impulse, goes to Catholic confession, that psychologically satisfying ritual of institutionalized voyeurism. The scene had its genesis during Charlotte's "long vacation" when she herself, fierce anti-Catholic though she was, went to confession. It is likely she told the priest her feelings for Héger, insofar as she could articulate them.[23] In the novel, Lucy's motive is the need for counsel and comfort, but her words are interesting: "I had a pressure of affliction on my mind of which it would hardly any longer endure the weight" (33:233). There exists in Lucy, as there existed in Charlotte, in her Protestant culture, in her nation, in the socially conditioned lives of women generally, and in the whole Victorian age, a tremendous desire and impetus both to repress and, inevitably, to confess the drives, the thoughts, and the complexities of erotic being. A faith must rest on the hope that the need for confession, absolution, and communal understanding can somehow be met.

Many traditional literary and religious themes converge in *Villette*, but the novel transforms them. As we saw in *The Monk*, gothic novels had laid stress on the evils of Continental Catholicism and its diabolical agents. Brontë makes use of various gothic conventions: for example, the seductive priest, inquisitory spying, the legend of a nun supposedly buried alive for some sexual transgression, Jesuitical plots, and that nun's black-and-white ghost; but she does so in order to symbolize and then demystify psychological and social realities in Lucy's world. Despite her anti-Roman prejudices, she decriminalizes Papism and exorcises its devils. That allows her to bring to light the serious problems of loneliness and the confessional impulse that the church addresses, to expose what she sees as its real danger to freedom-loving women, and, beyond that, to weaken the subtle, emotional hold of Christian paternalism of all sorts.

The kind priest Père Silas, giving Lucy solace, tries to lead her into the "true faith" of Rome and offers her a nun's life of moral peace and devotion. The temptation in this chapter and scene has the import of the classic novelistic Roman Catholic temptations in *The Brothers Karamazov* and *A Portrait of the Artist as a Young Man*. In Dostoyevsky the Grand Inquisitor offers the world for the spirit; in Joyce the Jesuits offer Stephen Dedalus the power to manifest God in people's lives if he will give up artistic freedom; in Charlotte Brontë the father, in essence, offers her pious serenity, a corporate family, and a loving afterlife (see 15:234) if she will cede erotic desire and the control of her love life to ecclesiastical authority (i.e., the rule of the fathers in Mother Church).

Knowing the appeal of such a life and faith, Lucy says that had she gone to see the priest again, "I might just now, *instead of writing this heretic narrative*, be counting my beads in the cell of a certain Carmelite convent" (15:235; italics mine). "Heretic" is not just a coy term for "Protestant" here, not just ironic anti-Roman sentiment. The chapter has a delicate balance. Lucy does not want to confess and give over her eroticism either to priests or to the stern God the Father of puritanical conscience. She rejects the lure of Rome, but the individualistic, rigid Protestant religion has failed to give her the means of love and its expression. Ultimately her choice is an erotic faith that tries to incorporate Christian faith and word. The agency of that faith is not the Roman Church's public and visual ritual, not even private prayer and communication with the Bible God, but that "heretic narrative," the novel.[24]

Villette gives strong support to Foucault's ideas about the role of institutionalized confession and surveillance as instruments of control in modern life, and his theory evolves primarily out of a similar Catholic culture.[25] Charlotte

Brontë, a product of the Protestant tradition, opposes the Continental system with the less formally mediated system of conscience that features the literate imagination and rules by Scripture—by bringing people "to book." She poses the intellectual crisis for Lucy as a choice between church and Scripture, but she explicitly calls Lucy's scripture heretical. She elects imaginative literature to perform the office of confession, and the novel as the form *to bear witness*—that apt phrase connoting suffering for faith—and to find redemption. As Lucy (and maybe Brontë) looks back at her life, she sees that desire for love brought her to crisis. In retrospect, however, the choice was not between being a nun or a good Protestant woman, but between being either a religious devotee to the pieties that others have formulated or a writer of a new testament, "the heretic narrative."

X

In *Villette*, writing and love feed into each other, even become interchangeable. Faith must be legible. Love becomes the occasion for writing, and letters have an important part in the story. To write with creative freedom and power you need love, but writing itself inspires love, and love generates imagination that makes faith possible.

The goal of a human being, as set forth in this novel and in much nineteenth-century thought, is to imagine, create, and live a love narrative. That is why the heroine must leave the church, lose all consciousness, and then awake in the house of her love, a place that, figuratively speaking, she never again leaves, though its owner changes. One project of Lucy Snowe's text is to transcribe a demystifying and then a remystifying of romantic love. We see that she can love more than one man, that she can switch her passion from a girl's notion of a romantic paragon to a man she knows has obvious faults, and that such a man's love can animate her creative spirit. But before she can be refreshed by love, she first must come to acknowledge that she feels it and can value it. John prepares the way for Emanuel.

Letters, for Lucy, are fetishes of love. Ink is the blood of her erotic life and faith. The free and open correspondence between Paul and herself in the final chapter is what enables her to survive, and the letter she gets from Dr. John first gives her identity and hope because it tells her that someone she loves could actually care about her. She treats John's letters as if they were living beings, and when he stops writing her, she prepares a funeral and actually *buries* them. No act could better symbolize the powerful erotic charge that letters carried for the Victorians or what they meant historically to women.

When Lucy meditates on how she might reply to a letter she thinks, "[W]here the bodily presence is weak and the speech contemptible, surely there cannot be error in making written language the medium of better utterance than faltering lips can achieve?" (21:307). Look at the implications of that sentence: Writing might allow a despised, plain woman to equal or better a privileged man's force of expression. It might compensate for all kinds of physical and social inferiority through genius, and it might be a way of making one's vision last.

Lucy's repression must have an end, in the sense of both a finish and an aim. Her self-censor leads her to one of her most perverse acts. Thrilled by Dr. John's letter, she writes him back, pouring out her "sincere heart." If anything is to come of her love, this is her opportunity. But she tells us then that "Reason" makes her "snatch the full sheets, read, sneer, erase, tear up, re-write, fold, seal, direct, and send a terse, curt missive of a page. She did right" (23:335). The monosyllabic diction and blunt syntax hammer out these self-mutilating blows to the heart and show the terrible split in Lucy. Being in love for her means, as it often did for nineteenth-century women, both a striving for intimacy and a withholding of intimacy for fear that the dignity and fragile selfhood that signs of affection nurture would be swamped in a sea of rejection. Lucy's repressive reason, in Brontë's prose, bludgeons any hope of a serious romance with Dr. John. The absence of the letter of love kills the spirit.

Repression's end comes in the outpouring of her heart to Paul in their last meetings, in the freedom of their letters, and in the narrative she writes. What Lucy calls "Reason" is, she says, "envenomed as a step-mother [the simile offers a clue to her early sorrow and the repression of her childhood]. If I have obeyed her it has chiefly been with the obedience of fear, not of love" (21:308). Her imagination, however, eventually flourishes, making even Belgium fascinating and the experience of a drab teacher in an undistinguished school wondrous. But this imagination depends on some requited love if it is to become what Lucy calls "intercommunion," the mysterious rite of inspired communication with others by the "kindling" word.

Strangely, the horrible repression by "Reason" works, and the eerily disciplined will that makes her tear up and bury precious letters brings her to conquer romantic myth and win the rational love of Paul Emanuel. But how flat that sounds. The full human and historical relevance of this novel will only come through if we try to understand the genuine hunger signified in the term *love-starved*. "Heart-poverty" means what it says: an absence of sustenance that can destroy well-being as surely as the penury to which it so often is related. To the pitiful little epistolary tomb, Lucy speaks final words that bring home again the awful power of erotic providence. "Good night, Dr. John; you are good, you are beautiful; but you are not mine" (31:452). To subsist, this woman Lucy Snowe needs, as the imagery specifically tells us, the coin of reciprocal love: "The love born of beauty was not mine; I had nothing in common

with it: . . . but another love, venturing diffidently into life after long acquaintance, furnace-tried by pain, stamped by constancy, consolidated by affection's
pure and durable alloy, submitted by intellect to intellect's own tests, . . . this
Love that laughed at Passion, . . . in *this* Love I had a vested interest" (39:567).
That is the language of erotic economics. She is describing the indispensable
exchange of love—love that the imagination must once more somehow enrich.
Lucy fits Paul typologically into her religious framework as a miraculous Christian agent of salvation (e.g., "Emanuel," "He was come" [38:540]; "Be ready
for me" [38:542]; "He was my king" [41:587]; her "Pauline" epistle), but as a
human savior.

Villette presents a revealing analogy between the structure of erotic faith and
Christianity. Brontë shows us the force of love in Lucy's world, that love made
manifest in the flesh of Paul, and the power of erotic imagination to inscribe
itself and make love live in her narrative. That trinity parallels the popularly
understood Christian trinity of nineteenth-century Protestant sensibility: God
the immanent ruler of all things; Christ, divinity in the form of human flesh;
and Scripture, the Holy Word of God and manifestation of the Holy Ghost.[26] In
the phantasmagoric, psychedelic night journey through Villette's illuminated
park (chs. 38, 39), Lucy finds her Holy Ghost, "Imagination": "With scorn she
looked on Matter, her mate—. . . . 'this night I will have *my* will. . . . Look
forth and view the night!' was her cry" (38:547). The personification of imagination not only tells us that there is no disjunction here between Lucy's inner
and outer life, no clear divisions between what exists and what she perceives; it
also shows her becoming conscious of the power that can translate matter to
spirit through language—that can, in other words, achieve through the mode
of writing her desire to transform an absent lover into present love. This power
is religious, erotic, and narrative.

The narrative subordinates the forms of Christian belief and the religious
conflict between Lucy and Paul to their relationship. Both Lucy and Paul come
to choose love for one another over their respective Protestant and Roman Catholic convictions. Brontë sets out clearly their religious differences (see chap. 36,
"The Apple of Discord") and then makes the subject of their last communication
a belief in love so strong that it acquiesces in tolerance for the other's brand of
Christianity and dismisses their conflict. Her scripture, therefore, imagines
nothing less than a shift—a displacement—in the priority of faith from God
and the interpretation of his will, to love.

XI

As we have seen, the rise and triumph of the novel meant that other arts were
often displaced into narrative. In *Villette* artworks and the occasions of witnessing art reflect on love, on women's fate, and on male-female relationships. Dra-

matic performances and paintings especially become "sites" in the text where Lucy's desires and values are defined, and Brontë shows her strong Victorian penchant for stressing and judging the moral content of art.

Acting: In England, a stage can seem all the world, and some say that the nation especially loves and patronizes the drama because its people need a way of acting out their emotional repressions. Says Lucy, "[A] keen relish for dramatic expression had revealed itself as part of my nature" (11:211). She first shows passion in public when, in a much-discussed episode, Paul conscripts her to act as a male lover in a play featuring Ginevra and Dr. John. She refuses to cross-dress fully, insists on retaining items of female clothing, but gives a warm performance as a man in love. The scene suggests any number of meanings: e.g., Brontë's androgynous sympathies; a metaphor for her willingness to take up the masculine-tinged identity of Currer Bell without giving up her real feminine identity; a play within a play miming the lovers and their fates in the novel; sublimation of Lucy's fierce erotic consciousness; a perfect example of triangular desire; and a conceit for the multiplicity of erotic desire.[27] The role features a narrator who projects the passion of her inner life into her writing acts.

One of these is a stage performance both "real" and symbolic. Dr. John takes her to see the actress Vashti (seeing the world-renowned actress Rachel doing Corneille in 1851 had electrified Brontë[28]), and Lucy's deflected, stifled emotions erupt. She compares Vashti to her own cosmic totem, the moon, "half-lava and half-glow." Her description of Vashti portraying the wronged woman pulses with conflicting feelings—admiration, condemnation, anger, a love of drama, and a puritan fear of it. Brontë uses the occasion to burst out with her own burning, frustrated drive to love. Her metaphorical imagination literally sets the house on fire. What the madwoman in the attic is to *Jane Eyre*, Vashti as the raging cast-off mate is to Lucy Snowe and *Villette*.

The idealization of love by nineteenth-century women and men was, in part, a revolt against the tyranny of matter and its seemingly inflexible physical laws (e.g., death obliterates your individual life; the property you can amass determines your personal worth; the arrangement of your natural features decides whether you are desirable or not). Vashti's resentment boils against materialism which inhibits her passion and denies her desire for lasting, faithful love. Bataille has defined the erotic as the assertion of life up to the point of death,[29] a definition that exactly fits Lucy's description of Vashti's orgasmic art: "an inordinate will, convulsing a perishing mortal frame, bent it to battle with doom and death, . . . sold dear every drop of blood, resisted to the latest the rape of every faculty, *would* see, *would* hear, *would* breathe, *would* live, up to, within, well nigh *beyond* the moment when death says to all sense and all being—'Thus far and no farther!'" (23:342). The Theresa-like ecstasy that Emily had imagined does, after all, figure in *Villette*, but projected into the artist's life.

Painting: In the most comic chapter in the novel, Lucy visits a gallery, sees the Rubens-like picture, *Cleopatra*, and scathingly calls it so much "butcher's meat" (19:275). Brontë uses the grossly sexual image of a woman to portray forms of male chauvinism. De Hamal, the sensualist, simpers before it like a porno fan. Dr. John, loyal son, amiable companion, and conventional, unthinkingly racist Victorian, finds "the mulatto" not as good-looking as his mother or the blond Ginevra. M. Paul, a moralist with a weakness for sexist diatribe, announces that he would not have this figure for wife, daughter, or sister, and drags Lucy away. He makes her look instead at *La vie d'une femme*, four pictures of a pious girl, a bride praying, a young mother "hanging disconsolate" over a baby, and a widow looking at a grave. The series is male, Catholic propaganda, prescribing female uniformity, and Lucy denounces it: "What women to live with! insincere, ill-humoured, bloodless, brainless nonentities! As bad in their way as the indolent gipsy-giantess, the Cleopatra, in hers" (19:278). One painter offers the slavery of sex and the other the slavery of dogma—both forms of role bondage for women.[30]

"Cleopatra," even as Lucy slanders her, does proclaim the primal facts of sexuality and the body's appeal. But how could Charlotte Brontë, whose personal and cultural history cut her off from the joys of sensuality, help but detest such an image? Lucy gloats over Vashti's vengefulness: "Place now the Cleopatra, or any other slug, before her as an obstacle, and see her cut through the pulpy mass [with a] scimitar. . . . Let Paul Peter Rubens wake from the dead . . . and bring into this presence all the army of his fat women" (23:340).

Like so many Victorians, both Brontë and Lucy, religious devotees looking for signs of moral grace, wanted flesh to be animated with a consecrating spark of holy love, and Rubens and his followers gave them underdone rump roast.[31]

XII

The three couples of *Villette*, Lucy-Paul, John-Paulina, and Ginevra-de Hamal, offer several perspectives on love. Brontë imagines Ginevra and de Hamal as Vanity Fair's pretty, amoral, faithless flesh that is grass—mere erotic materialists. "Happiness," says Lucy, "is not a potato, to be planted in mould, and tilled with manure" (22:330), but it is for these potato-head hedonists. John Graham Bretton and Polly-Paulina, good-looking, moral, intelligent, and rich—the elect of romantic faith—reflect ironically on both the charm and the irrelevance for most people of sentimental, happy-ending love fiction. They have everything. Brontë gives them each a rich, doting parent and shows how close, in the Victorian erotic ideal, filial affection and married love could be. Polly has her protective papa; Graham, his devoted mama. The nice problem for each is to transfer love: not to break the parental bond, but to stretch it and marry each other—to substitute the other for the dominant parent and take parental roles themselves. Their "problems," therefore, now look like mild forms of the Oedipus and Electra complexes that the retrospective Viennese analysis of nineteenth-century privileged-class life would make famous. Lucy calls them providentially blessed and sees their conventional life as good, but we can read in them a gently satirical subtext about the pampered classes and their naive notions of trouble.

Unlike the other couples, Lucy and Paul have terrible money worries. The logic of Lucy's text—like Austen's novels—argues that the winning of love is first of all a material necessity for most women of the time. In the political, social, and psychic economy of life, nineteenth-century women not only had to seek love, they had to compete for it. That aura of erotic competition, which Lucy's hostile relations with the other females—mistress, teachers, and students—at the school bring out, is one of the most disturbing things about the book. Love, however, is too important to lie about, even if the lies you want to tell about it make you feel better. Paul first falls in love with Lucy out of mixed motives: mimetic desire—he's jealous of Dr. John; a will to power over a vulnerable, strong-minded woman; loneliness; a longing for intellectual companionship; and a desire to play the Pygmalion as a heroic part. As for Lucy, she finds in him a frame for self-love, a being much like herself—small, not goodlooking, fiery in spirit, intellectually curious, bookish, a good writer, sexually eager, and idealistically devout—but also a man, older, more confident, less repressed, someone as interested as she in vocation who can help her and teach her that she matters.

Faith—and love, though it tormented her, was Brontë's faith—must finally be strong enough to face hard truths, if it is any good. Thus Brontë takes pains to show that Paul and John both fall in love with other women before they find their "true" loves, Lucy and Polly. And she demolishes any double-standard idea that men here differ from women by insisting that Lucy herself loves two men at once: not only did she love John passionately before Paul, she never stops loving him. When, heartsick in love with Paul, Lucy goes on her night trip to the fête, she and John Graham see one another: "I believe in that goodly mansion, his heart, he kept one little place under the skylights where Lucy might have entertainment. . . . I kept a place for him, too. . . . All my life long I carried it . . . yet, released from . . . constriction, I know not but its innate capacity for expanse might have magnified it into a tabernacle for a host" (38: 555). Religious idiom and eroticism flow together here in confessional candor.

From the beginning, Brontë's rendering of love in *Villette* has been controversial, and Harriet Martineau's 1853 review set out the issues for critical debate:

An atmosphere of pain hangs about the whole. . . . All the female characters, in all their thoughts and lives, are full of one thing, or are regarded by the reader in the light of that one thought—love. . . . and so dominant is this idea—so incessant is the writer's tendency to describe the need of being loved, that the heroine . . . leaves the reader at last under the uncomfortable impression of her having either entertained a double love, or allowed one to supersede another without notification of the transition. It is not thus in real life. There are substantial, heartfelt interests for women of all ages, and under ordinary circumstance, quite apart from love.[32]

A split between these two friends was inevitable, given their different allegiances. A dedicated novelist for whom writing is a sacred vocation must sometimes represent erotics otherwise than would a person whose ruling passion is to lead a broad political movement and advocate directly the betterment of women's lives. From the Brontë sisters' perspective, like that of so many modern writers, righteous priority to even the best of causes risks promoting art that can become the equivalent of that deceiving *La vie d'une femme*: simplistic, constricting work inspired by, and serving doctrinaire views of, political and moral correctness—views that, of course, may be perfectly valid.

Exactly what Martineau objects to—that awful telling of the raw need for love and the compulsive nature of erotic desire as it shapes perception—is what burns *Villette* into memory. People who have known sufficient requited love may plausibly claim that it is overrated, as prosperous people may claim that money can't buy happiness. Lucy Snowe, writing her narrative, was not such a figure.[33]

In a preface to *Villette* the novelist Mary Ward, at the end of the nineteenth century, explained how and why, for women, the subject matter of love, which later would seem to many a dependency drug, could mean the chance for literary achievement and the opportunity to combine, in the novel, feminine religious insight and feeling with feminist aspirations:

What may be said to be the main secret, the central cause not only of her [Charlotte Brontë's] success, but, generally, of the success of women in fiction, during the present century? . . . As a rule, so far, women have been poets in and through the novel. . . . they are here among the recognised 'masters of those who know.'. . . For the one subject which they have eternally at command, which is interesting to all the world, and whereof large tracts are naturally and wholly their own, is the subject of love—love of many kinds indeed, but preeminently the love between man and woman. . . . The modern novel reflects the craving . . . for that feeling which expresses the heart's defiance of the facts which crush it, . . . and brings up, or seems to bring up, the secrets of the infinite.[34]

Ward is describing the inner city of Villette, scene of expanding consciousness.

Harriet Martineau wrote to Charlotte, "I do not like the love, either the kind or degree of it; and its prevalence in the book."[35] Brontë replied, "I know what love is as I understand it; and if man or woman should be ashamed of feeling such love, then is there nothing right, noble, faithful, truthful, unselfish in this earth, as I comprehend rectitude, nobleness, fidelity, truth, and disinterestedness—Yours sincerely—To differ from you gives me keen pain."[36] That is religious sentiment—pure and not so simple. She was trying to establish a faith that would be true to her experience. Erotic faith might not bring happinesss, but it could offer a reason for being and an incarnation—an inscription—of meaning. It could make the flesh into word.

Brontë is imagining how, for a woman of religious feeling, a lover's vocation can merge with an artist's vocation—erotic faith with aesthetic faith. In *To the Lighthouse*, Virginia Woolf, deeply influenced by Charlotte Brontë,[37] delves into the mind of the unmarried artist Lily Briscoe and, for me, nicely sums up the feeling and nature of love in *Villette*:

[F]rom the dawn of time odes have been sung to love; wreaths heaped and roses; and if you asked nine people out of ten they would say they wanted nothing but this—love; while the women, judging from her own experience, would all the time be feeling, This is not what we want; there is nothing more tedious, puerile, and inhumane than this; yet it is also beautiful and necessary.[38]

Charlotte Brontë, with her death-cursed family history, knew that erotic faith, like most religions, finally rests on the principle of sacrifice; and faith in the sacrificial effect of displaced love was her link to immortality. How else can we account for these heartfelt words in Lucy Snowe's narrative? "Proof of a life to come must be given. In fire and in blood, if needful, must that proof be *written*" (38:534; italics mine).

The Fixation of Love: Charles Dickens's
     Great Expectations (1860–61)

Begotten by despair upon impossibility.
ANDREW MARVELL[1]

I

In a scene late in *Great Expectations* Dickens shows the huge pull of a secular erotic faith for the Victorians and the weakening of faith in Christian salvation. Pip's convict benefactor Magwitch is about to die when Pip, comforting him, decides to tell him what he thinks the wretch would most want to hear: "Dear Magwitch, . . . You had a child once, whom you loved and lost. . . . She lived and found powerful friends. She is living now. She is a lady and very beautiful. And I love her!"[2] Magwitch dies in peace.

The master of popular emotion was trying to touch his audience by having Pip send the condemned man off with a happy love story. Modern readers have taken this passage for granted, but a devotee of old-time religion wouldn't. It explains why Dickens, even though he wrote one, could not publish an ending that kept Pip and Estella apart. It may seem kind and natural to make Magwitch believe in the end that his vicarious dreams of gentility and love were being fulfilled. Pip is not being quite honest, but, Dickens assumes, his deception will seem fitting: a bit of deathbed charity. Dickens is counting on a massive shift in public opinion. Pip, in effect telling lies, implies that the union Magwitch would most desire will take place, but in fact Estella has married a brute, and Pip himself is miserably lovelorn. Just two pages before, when Magwitch is sentenced, Dickens gives us a passage of Christian doctrine: "[the condemned] . . . and the Judge . . . both were passing on, with absolute equality, to the greater Judgment that knoweth all things and cannot err" (56:467). If there is eternal life and judgment, according to Christian belief, and if Pip, Magwitch, Dickens, and his readers really have faith in God and afterlife, what good would it do to mislead a dying man who, once beyond the world's border, will quickly know the truth? Why does Dickens, who so prides himself on being in tune with his public's feelings, have Pip deceive the man? The answer must lie in the inherent cultural strength of erotic devotion and a slipping commitment to orthodoxy.

Pip's final prayer shows the conflict: "I knew there were no better words that I could say beside his bed, than 'O Lord, be merciful to him, a sinner!'" (56:470). The mercy, however, comes not from hope of a divine heaven, but from faith in the love story of Magwitch's daughter and adopted son. Dickens, in a moment of high feeling and moral climax, stresses the regenerating power of erotic love through which the old man can connect with the future. That is how he chooses to present here the customary solace of religion: go to your death with great expectations still intact. He knows that such a dramatized sentiment, playing on a popular need to embrace some self-transcendent but earthly faith, would touch his readers.

But erotic doubt marks the text, too. The split in nineteenth- and twentieth-century life between the felt need for faith and the knowledge that faith leaves you vulnerable to agonizing disillusion shows through in Dickens's rendering of love. The conflict between love as redeemer and love as a destroyer gives the novel much of its force and character.

For Pip, "I love her!" expresses the truth of his life: his erotic fixation. He is still in love with Estella, as he has been since their first meeting as children. The story that Magwitch takes to the grave begins with the child Pip at the grave. Pip's soothing words bring together and underline the thrust of his own desires and the realities of his first-person narrative. Orphanhood is there, then the wealth that makes possible great expectations—including, in Pip's imagining, the greatest of all: love. And there is also, in little, the compulsion that has been in him from the beginning to trace out in language a story and an identity that will make atonement for suffering and deprivation. The hold of an informal ideology and religion of love on the Victorian imagination looks very strong when we see how easy it is to mesh and classify novels by people as radically different as Charlotte Brontë and Dickens. *Villette*: an orphan's first-person narrative testament of want, erotic fixation, and faith (*female*). *Great Expectations*: an orphan's first-person narrative testament of want, erotic fixation, and faith (*male*).

II

The opening of *Great Expectations*, famous for Pip's coming to consciousness, tells a lot about perception. What is repressed in *Villette* is quickly expressed in Dickens: the nightmare of childhood, the lack of love, and the fact of death. As the narrator performs the revolutionary act of becoming as a little child again and remembers in words and images his first impressions, we seem to be not just at the start of one small boy's life, but at a symbolic beginning of the modern age of individualism, literacy, economics, and intense self-consciousness.

Dickens opens with the identifying, alienating word "Pip," the name the boy makes for himself out of "Philip Pirrip." Identity depends on the distinction of language and on a dialectic between what is heard and what can be said; the human animal begins by trying to express its own being through words, and it must keep on. The first glimmer of mental sentience means the loneliness of language.[3] But more than that, the opening soon shows a dialectical synthesizing process not only between what can be said and heard, but what can be written and *seen* as well.

As I never saw my father or my mother, and never saw any likeness of either of them (for their days were long before the days of photographs), my first fancies regarding what they were like, were unreasonably derived from their tombstones. The shape of the letters on my father's, gave me an odd idea that he was a square, stout, dark man, with curly black hair. From the character and turn of the inscription, *"Also Georgiana Wife of the Above,"* I drew a childish conclusion that my mother was freckled and sickly. [1:35]

Notice: 1) the statement "I never saw . . . my mother," strictly speaking, cannot be true and must really mean, "I do not remember seeing my mother"; 2) it implies therefore that memory and the storing of images must be tied to linguistic impressions and development; 3) the generic means by which people in a given society imprint memory and make images, such as photography, epitaphs, or novels, *and the interplay of these means,* determine how and what they see; 4) imagistic consciousness and linguistic consciousness are not discrete or separable: language is part of what we see, subjective images are part of what we say and write; 5) inscription—writing—for Dickens and Pip, is also a crucial part of the subjective imagination and indistinguishable from perceived life and relationship: "Where's your mother?" (1:37), the convict who has "started up from among the graves" (1:36) asks Pip. "There, sir! . . . Also Georgiana. That's my mother" (1:37). In Pip's and Dickens's imagination the missing mother first makes her impression in engraved form.

The child learns of his family from letters on stones, first becoming aware of life in a *grave*yard, the place where the names of the dead are written and earth is engraved with flesh. He imagines his ties to the past—his *relatives*—through signs marking death. Great expectations begin ironically with the consciousness and fused impressions of death, language, orphanhood, the need to imagine relations, and the fixation of desire for the absent (m)other. Out of them love will develop.

This book, like *Villette* and so many other nineteenth-century novels, seems to grow out of—and to express—an era of orphanhood. Dickens and other novelists populate the booming age of individualism with parentless figures who cry for love. The new world of capital and accelerated change brings ambition and opportunity, but fearful alienation as well. The beginning conveys symbolically what being cut off from the past can feel like: father, mother, siblings turned to stone. The child finds himself musing upon a rock which he must try to read, inscribe with a fiction, animate, love, and transform to flesh. Metaphorically, that is Pip's story, but its meaning extends outward to the whole modern world of great expectations. In *Vanity Fair*, for example, Thackeray says of Becky Sharp's son, "Mother is the name for God in the lips and hearts of little children; and here was one who was worshipping a stone!"[4] Dickens, imagining that metaphor literally and taking the materialism of the modern era one step further, has reversed the Midas myth. Flesh and blood have turned to hard matter, the generators of destiny have become inanimate substances; and in this world of materialism, people try to take property and with it make, know, and possess a rich, full life—try to touch and revivify it into love.

Everything for Pip is a shaping, a fixing, and an intricate elaboration of early consciousness. Key words, images, and experiences permanently inscribe the developing psyche when the fresh self undergoes menacing trauma; and, in later times of high emotion, these memory images recur, forming and screening new perception. Here is Pip's first view of the world and his place in it:

> My first most vivid and broad impression of the identity of things, seems to me to have been gained on a memorable raw afternoon towards evening. At such a time I found out for certain, that this bleak place overgrown with nettles was the churchyard; and that Philip Pirrip, late of this parish, and also Georgiana wife of the above, were dead and buried; . . . and that the dark flat wilderness beyond the churchyard, intersected with dykes and mounds and gates . . . was the marshes; and that the low leaden line beyond, was the river; and that the distant savage lair from which the wind was rushing, was the sea; and that the small bundle of shivers growing afraid of it all and beginning to cry, was Pip. [1:35–36]

Identity begins in an anti-Eden for Dickens with the horror, hostility, and lovelessness of the other, the not-self. He sets out here the phenomena that will haunt Pip, images that will help determine how he sees and what he tells: the bleak overgrown place, the burial ground, the marshes, the river, the sea, the wilderness, the mounds, the low leaden line broken by the tiny jut of life— the terror and tears in things and in personality. We are located in a half-lit, fabulous, scary landscape situated just above the realms of death.

Dickens is trying, as no other novelist before him, to get at the origins of memory and personal desire. In conscious, "memorable" life, Pip's first human encounter is with the ravenous Magwitch: "'Hold your noise!' cried a terrible voice, as a man started up from among the graves" (1:36). It is as if the convict *were* Pip's father popping out of the earth to roar at him. The whole scene between them looks like a case of displaced infant terror at the raging father. Psychologists report that one of the most common fears of small children is the loud noise of the father, and Magwitch handles and whirls Pip the way a furious parent might yank a baby around. He threatens to eat Pip, to sic a cannibal killer on him, to have his heart torn out from him and devoured. Pip, at first consciousness, takes from the escaped prisoner a patrimony of guilt, terror, hunger, and implicit violence.

The "vivid impression," the imagery and experience of this opening, work on Pip like the formatting of a floppy disk. Not only is he impressionable, but the kinds of impressions he can take in, remember, and set down have been pre-scribed. When the boy has pledged to help him, Magwitch moves off: "As I saw him go, picking his way among . . . the brambles that bound the green mounds, he looked in my young eyes as if he were eluding the hands of the dead people, stretching up cautiously out of their graves, to get a twist upon his ankle and pull him in" (1:38). The power of that image as a symbol of life requires little comment, but the phrase "in my young eyes" needs stressing. What strikes us "in" our "young eyes" lasts because it shapes imagination and organizes reality. "In my young eyes" can even be regarded as the setting for all of *Great Expec-tations*.

Dickens ends this chapter by impressing upon Pip's mind the idea of *hanging*: "The marshes were just a long black horizontal line then, as I stopped to look after him. . . . I could faintly make out the only two black things in all the prospect that seemed to be standing upright; one of these was the beacon by which the sailors steered, an ugly thing . . . ; the other a gibbet. . . . The man was limping on towards this latter, as if he were . . . going back to hook himself up" (1:39).

The fact not only of death, but of criminality, institutions of punishment, and man's inhumanity to man comes through. The image of the gibbet, or gallows, will stay with Pip and so will the image of the guiding fire of the ugly beacon warning of danger. We are at the beginning of the life of the book, but in a sense all the rest is just a working out of its symbolic logic. Man is a terrified child, with whom we are brought to identify, set down in the midst of death where he must trace out meaning and identity and come to terms with his paternity and the terrible rule of the father figure; man is a prisoner of hunger, shackled by scarcity; man stumbles over the mounds of the dead, evading their grasp; man limps towards the gallows to hang himself; man is the creature whose head is full of such visions. Even when he is writing in retrospect, there is a small, shivering child from the past who lives in him still.

I deliberately use the word *man*. This is, I said, a male's narrative. No woman, no mother figure, no kindness, no beauty appear in the first chapter. It is "a man's world," a phrase whose brutal irony will be appreciated by those who, like most men if they could admit it, having had some scary version of manliness early impressed on them, must live with their own terrible visions of woman-less, dog-eat-dog, masculine existence rattling around somewhere in their psyches. No wonder the deprived boy later seeks love compulsively. The father figures for him—Magwitch, Joe, and Jaggers—do not appear as desirable mod-els, but as freedom-robbing beings, different as they are, who threaten his identity. The absence, the gap in Pip's life, helps to generate erotic desire; the missing woman in the opening is the space for love in the novel.

III

The atmosphere and vision of *Great Expectations* find almost uncanny parallel and complement in Claude Lorrain's painting, *Landscape with Psyche outside the Palace of Cupid* ("The Enchanted Castle") (1664; fig. 18).[5] Each work features obsessive, melancholy love. Each has a remarkably similar landscape and atmosphere of amorous fixation and enchantment, even down to details such as the evening light, the small, intimidated form of the love-struck being in an overwhelming space, the setting at the edge of water, the inhospitable house of love, "the horizontal line," and the eroticizing of vista. In the picture, the solitary figure of Psyche, hopelessly in love, sits brooding, chin in hand, under an expansive sky of twilight amid low green mounds in the foreground. Behind and above her, separated from her by dark thickets of undergrowth on one side and an inlet of choppy water on the other, stands an impregnable-looking stone palace at the rim of the sea.

The subject is taken from Apuleius's tale of Cupid and Psyche in *The Golden Ass*.[6] Psyche, heartsick with desire for the mysterious Eros, has been excluded from his dwelling, banished for her unavoidable guilt. It is as romantic a painting as there is, and Pip's words describing his impression of visiting Satis House and meeting Miss Havisham and Estella—"it's . . . so strange, and so fine— and melancholy" (8:89)—fit it perfectly. So does the mood and feeling of his growing consciousness of romantic longing, when the new ache of love and his sense of alienation from that love begin to suffuse all he sees.

The imposing castle, without a sign of life about it, stands at the center of the picture, dominating it and intimidating the lonely Psyche. The wide sky, caught at a moment before the dying of the light, gives the canvas an elegiac feeling. So does Psyche's attitude of thoughtful remembrance and also the retrospective nature of the subject which, like Pip's story, has taken place in the past. Musing sadly beneath the wide evening sky, Psyche looks pathetically small and abandoned before the vast world, the sea stretching out to a far distant, engulfing horizon. Nature—the large dark trees on the right and the jumbled boulders, the mountains, and the trees on the left—diminishes her stature; and the mammoth castle appears deserted, inaccessible, and oblivious to personal desire. The dilemma is clear: How can she make an impression on that solid mass of matter? How can she get inside those walls and find love? Psyche, like Pip's psyche, finds love petrified and seeks a way to animate it. Pip calls the unreachable, beloved Estella "the innermost life of my life" (29:257), but he cannot penetrate the core of his being. He is kept out. Dickens's world is fiercer and more turbulent than Claude's, but *Great Expectations* could be the handwriting on Eros's wall.

It seems especially fitting to juxtapose Dickens's novel to a work of visual art because of the unusual importance, semiotic power, and consistency of his imagery from beginning to end. He may work in an art of linear time, but in his representation, the human personality takes its shape from the imprinting of visual forms on the mind. As life goes on, the self preserves those images, superimposes newer ones on them, and thus grows while maintaining an integral identity. Life for Dickens is a palimpsest as well as a narrative, and we have to visualize the recurrent imagery and how he modifies it to see the deep line and multiple meanings of the text.

IV

In *Great Expectations* the palace of Cupid collectively consists of the various mental, social, and physical walls, jails, structures, impasses, barriers, and hard surfaces that separate people and keep them from love—the class structure, the prison of the past, and the incest taboo, for example. Specifically it is Satis House, bizarre labyrinth of erotic fixation where Pip meets Miss Havisham and Estella, and love for him pitches its crazy mansion.

The first live female in Pip's story, his sister Mrs. Joe, one of many bad parent substitutes, sends him up to play for a rich woman's warped amusement in hopes of being paid money. Mrs. Joe (she doesn't even have a feminine name) complains of "being . . . mother" (2:41) to him; but, hard, barren, and plain as the rock "Georgiana Wife of the Above," she has no motherliness, and she gives and inspires no love. Dickens often makes brother-sister relationships focal points of affection and love—sometimes they even seem charged with latent incestuous feeling—but between Pip and Mrs. Joe, the least loving of all his brother-sister pairs, there is no kindness whatever. The lack of loving familial feeling impoverishes life in the novel.

I want to concentrate on Pip's first visit to Miss Havisham's when the visionary Dickens explores the genesis of class feeling and conflict in the boy. Not incidentally, it also renders the painfully weird process that falling in love can be. Dickens can make you see the abject need and the twisted motives that spark love, and he shows the power of love—love, sour love—to be, among other things, a plague on the human spirit.

Like the bride of Lammermoor, Miss Havisham, the bride of Satis House, haunts the erotic imagination as a victim turned victimizer. A figure of erotic paralysis, her image embodies Dickens's psychology of obsessive love. He is always trying to make you see. What would disappointed love look like? What does living neurotically in the past look like? Like Miss Havisham in Satis House. In Pip's first sight of her, she is posed, "her head leaning on [her] hand," in the attitude of Claude's Psyche:

> She was dressed in rich materials—satins, and lace, and silks—all of white. Her shoes were white. And she had a long white veil dependent from her hair, and she had bridal flowers in her hair, but her hair was white. . . . I saw that everything within my view which ought to be white, had been white long ago, and had lost its lustre, and was faded and yellow. . . . I saw that the dress had been put upon the rounded figure of a young woman, and that the figure upon which it now hung loose, had shrunk to skin and bone. . . . Once, I had been taken to one of our old marsh churches to see a skeleton in the ashes of a rich dress, that had been dug out of a vault under the church pavement. Now . . . [the] skeleton seemed to have dark eyes that moved and looked at me. [8:87]

This scene, like Lucy Ashton's wedding night, is a grotesque comment and parody on the happy ending for love and marriage, but it shows just how all-consuming the idea of being a bride could be. Put it next to the deaths of Lucy Snowe's and Marchmont's respective fiancés in *Villette*, and you can see the psyche-jangling social pressure on nineteenth-century women to marry, and the compulsive, widespread fear that something would go wrong.

The sight is full of wonder, decay, wealth, threat, and subjective meaning for Pip, and it is inseparable from his whole narrative vision. Dickens, reiterating the theme of death in life and life in death, shows how this experience fuses with the impressions of the first chapter—the graveyard, the marshes, the church, the pavement, and death. As Magwitch is to his father, so Miss Havisham, figuratively exhumed "in his young eyes," is to his mother (in the wordplay, she is compared to a *mummy*).

She quizzes Pip, "What do I touch?" "Your heart." "Broken!" (8:88). In an extreme form, she, like Pip the character, Pip the narrator, Lucy Snowe, Heathcliff, and all of us, lives in double time: time both does and does not stand still at the moment long ago when she was jilted. The unchanging past is the reality of the present, but the aging process still turns fabric from white to yellow and hair from yellow to white; the heart breaks but, bypassed, brokenly beats on, seeking other hearts from a new generation for breaking (or transplant) in turn.

Estella becomes Miss Havisham's tool of erotic vengeance, and the two merge inseparably in Pip's emotional life. Erotic patterns and desires of the past blend and flow into those of the present. "'Call Estella,' says Miss Havisham, and her light came along the dark passage like a star. . . . 'Let me see you play cards with this boy.' 'With this boy! Why, he is a common labouring-boy!' I thought I overheard Miss Havisham answer—only it seemed so unlikely—'Well? You can break his heart'" (8:89).

That is the stuff of an anti–fairy tale, not realism, but it rings with awful metaphorical truth. Out of disappointed love desires and their pain grow sadistic impulses which then shape erotic desire and behavior in the young. And erotic hurt is bound up with social injustice, erotic power with the power of social hierarchy, erotic vulnerability with class powerlessness. Dickens makes explicit what Emily Brontë and Heathcliff imply.

He, in this chapter, is trying to get at exactly how, why, and when the bent of a particular being's erotic desire is fixed, and at the same time he wants to show the social significance of that fixation. His social vision associates the particular formation of erotic desire with the knowledge of class distinction (whatever form, historically, "class" may take). The disposition to love, he sees developing as an antidote to the pervasive sadism of class pride. He learns the nasty lesson of exclusion whose hidden horror is that, being shut out and disparaged by some sort of "elite," men and women often tend, on some deep level, to accept this evaluation: they come to envy and desire what oppresses them.

When Estella feeds him like an animal, Pip writes, "I was so humiliated, hurt, spurned, offended, angry, sorry—I cannot hit upon the right name for the smart—God knows what its name was—that tears started to my eyes. . . . so bitter were my feelings, and so sharp was the smart without a name, that needed counteraction" (8:92).

The kind of counteraction that becomes mandatory for Pip touches society and history. The need for counteraction against perceived social deficiencies determines the direction of being. This emotional crisis concentrates and epitomizes all the misery of Pip's love-starved childhood, and Estella becomes the object of his repressed feeling. What stands out and takes on general significance is that nameless lack—that inability to find words to express and thus define the agony of unattached being—which makes a vacuum in the self. Pip's coming love, life, and certainly his narrative can be seen as projects to fill out a self and counteract not only "the smart," but the chaos and nothingness that his inarticulation signifies. This gap takes us back to the beginning when Pip tries to comprehend in inscription the absent family, but now he cries for an unnamable failing, a pain that civilization has refined beyond the sense of primal deprivation. This lack defines itself as the compulsive need to imagine and project love and to attach himself to Estella and Miss Havisham and what they mean to him. Dickens is imagining in the boy, who has never seen genteel females or richness before, the common male identification of women with great expectations and wealth. The "counteraction" that will take the form of ambition, love, imagination, and writing grows out of inarticulate resentment, and Dickens sees that impulse to counteraction as the kind of thing that shapes and shakes the world.

I reiterate: movement and meaning in the novel rest on fantastic scenes that grow out of, and build on, earlier scenes and images. Dickens senses that love, inner and outer personal life, society, and even history develop this way—by accretion, like a coral reef. Estella now becomes the name of Pip's desire in one of the novel's most important scenes: "[there] was a rank garden with an old wall: . . . I could . . . see . . . that Estella was walking away from me even then. . . . So, in the brewery itself. . . . I saw her pass among the extinguished fires, and ascend some light iron stairs, and go out by a gallery high overhead, as if she were going out into the sky" (8:93).

Estella, meaning star: she, Dickens the imagist shows, is far above him, the star that Pip will follow. Impressionable, he makes her his heart's desire, everything he lacks. This vision is a definitive image of the star system, the longing to catch a star—to love, unite with, and be a star—that comes out of some psychic or social disability and often fixes on a human fetish.

That passage binds together erotics and the germ of ambition, and the imagistic consciousness that follows is essential to the novel.

> It was in this place, and at this moment, that a strange thing happened to my fancy. I thought it a strange thing then, and I thought it a stranger thing long afterwards. I turned my eyes—a little dimmed by looking up at the frosty light—towards a great wooden beam in a low nook of the building . . . , and I saw a figure hanging there by the neck. A figure all in yellow white, with but one shoe to the feet; and it hung so, that I could see that the faded trimmings of the dress were like earthy paper, and that the face was Miss Havisham's, with a movement going over the whole countenance as if she were trying to call me. In the terror of seeing the figure, and in the terror of being certain that it had not been there a moment before, I at first ran from it, and then ran towards it. And my terror was greatest of all when I found no figure there. [8:93–94]

That is fearful symmetry indeed. The image of the gibbet and convict from the trauma of the opening blends with his traumatic visions of Miss Havisham and Estella. Pip's isolated psyche, in crisis, fuses impressions in a fantasy that contains and animates much of its history and emotional content. The self always must see the present in light of its own past impressions. The buried life, at a time of stress, is unearthed: the fire of high emotion and associative psychology welds together the graveyard beginning, the missing parents, a coarse father figure, the child's longing for the inscribed but absent mother, the murderous intimations of violence and hanging, the disinterred woman, the crazy old bride, and the pretty, cruel figure of high station. In the forge of Pip's mind, Miss Havisham and Estella are joined, and that fusion, bridging the generation gap, is crucial for Dickens's view of love. In Pip's imagination, he cannot separate his feelings for one from the other. (Nor can he separate his present writing self from his memory's vision: "like earthy paper.") Dickens, in as complex and infinitely rich a piece of literary imagery as I know of, shows exactly how in Pip's male unconscious the child's unfulfilled desire for an older woman coexists with the boy's desire for the young woman. (The missing shoe in this vision suggests that one meaning of Cinderella's slipper is that a would-be prince of love might be looking for someone who can wear his mother's shoes, a very delicate fit.) He also shows how the cliché, "love is close to hate" (*odi et amo*), comes to be true. And he is trying to express something that cannot be paraphrased wholly or shown in discursive language: what the simultaneous progress and timelessness of experience and the multifariousness of selfhood feel and look like.

Rhetorically, this vision does to readers what it does to Pip: it disorganizes conventional response. It gets at the hallucinatory nature of ordinary life. It conveys the young self's charged energies, its contradictions, its terror at its own distorting and creative insight, and its fear that what it perceives may not be real, may not matter at all. The prose captures the whole ambivalence of Pip's attraction and repulsion for Miss Havisham and everything she stands for. It pushes us to imagine the psyche's fallibility, its twisted inventiveness, its need to destroy and to rescue, and the fantastic shapes of its desire.

V

The visit to Satis House determines Pip's erotic fixation. Of that experience the narrator writes, "Pause you who read this, and think for a moment of the long chain of iron or gold, of thorns or flowers, that would never have bound you, but for the formation of the first link on one memorable day" (9:101). Dickens's express aim is to make people see the correspondence of the life on the page to their own lives. His project here is psychoanalytic—to focus on the origins of desire and memory—but overtly the text is meant to function like Scripture: that is, *for your own good, see how these words apply to your lives.* Whatever we may think about the relation of fiction to reality, for Dickens and his fellow Victorians, the nineteenth-century novel has become the medium and place to find and meditate on the links of fatal love (*links* in two senses of the word: what joins and what imprisons).

In *Great Expectations*, the need to love and be loved precedes both ambition and the definition of desire. As he moves into adolescence, Pip can only articulate his sense of incompleteness; but in the mix of his mind, he must find a way to give shape to his desire and find images to "counteract" the void. In a key passage, he writes of his dreamy younger self, "Whenever I watched the vessels standing out to sea with their white sails spread, I somehow thought of Miss Havisham and Estella; and whenever the light struck aslant, afar off, upon a cloud or sail or green hill-side or water-line, it was just the same.—Miss Havisham and Estella and the strange house and the strange life appeared to have something to do with everything that was picturesque" (15:137). Notice the striking conflation of Miss Havisham and Estella, and the way the mood and content of the passage exactly fit the feeling of Claude's *Psyche*. The boats with their lovely sails, the light on the water touch Pip with a sense of remote beauty, and his mind moves to embody his hovering desire. The psyche is a poet, continually seeking out metaphors for love.

According to Dickens, what influences personality most deeply—what motivates and shapes the direction of adult life—is not formulated, rationally chosen goals of growing maturity, but mysterious moods and images that we conjoin with the early strata of our psychic lives: a sail, the memory of a house on a hill, the smell of rich leather, the flicker of torches in a musty room, a view of water. These kinds of things move and drive us.

The word *picturesque* carries great force in Dickens's art and his understanding of the mind. (Its connotation here also makes very clear why it is important to compare pictures of love to words, forms, and plots of love in a study of eroticism in the novel.) Pip must translate his desires and energies into something he can see. People fix on mental images and objects in pictures that might fill in the blanks of their personality and then turn these objects into fetishes of desire. Ambition is ignited by some vague but powerful sense of dispossession that calls for love, and by affecting, but private, images that reach back beyond reason and conscious memory.

Stendhal calls the birth and course of passionate love in early nineteenth-century polite society "crystallization,"[7] a word that seems just right for Estella. (Glittering with light and jewels, "Estella"—as is so often the case of the beloved for the lover—is for Pip, during most of the novel, not so much a person as a fetish.) Stendhal's theory of love and its unfolding psychology seems too formulaic and too limited to the Continental upper classes of his era to be of much general use. He emphasizes the lover's idealization of the beloved, whereas Dickens more acutely stresses the particular bent and mind-set of the lover. But Stendhal's extended *metaphor* of falling in love does shed light on the erotic process in *Great Expectations*. Look at his imagery: "Leave a lover with his thoughts for twenty-four hours, and this is what will happen: At the salt mines of Salzburg, they throw a leafless wintry bough into one. . . . Two or three months later they haul it out covered with a shining deposit of crystals. . . . The smallest twig is studded with a galaxy of scintillating diamonds."[8] Pip's psyche crystallizes Estella into an object of magic value, one to which cluster qualities that, he feels, could he possess them, would give him the wholeness he lacks.

Dickens sees the schizoid nature of this love. For Pip, Estella is both pure, crystallized desire and a young woman whom he judges realistically. He writes of the day years later when, having been made a gentleman, he goes back to Miss Havisham's to meet the dazzling grown-up Estella: "But, though . . . her influence on my boyish life and character had been all-powerful, I did not . . . invest her with any attributes save those she possessed. . . . I knew to my sorrow . . . that I loved her against reason, . . . against peace, against hope, against happiness. . . . I loved her none the less because I knew it, and it had no more influence in restraining me, than if I had devoutly believed her to be human perfection" (29:253–54). That is the irrational erotic force that gives romantic love a bad name among priests and psychologists, but it shows how love can come involuntarily with the force of a deity.

Why, like Pip, do so many so often fall in love with people they don't much like? The answer, of course, is that desire is stronger than critical or moral reasoning. But even an apparently simple specific reply, such as "availability," "physical beauty," "power," or "sexual gratification," turns out to be highly subjective and to beg other basic questions, for example, why is this available person so sexually desirable and not another? what, subjectively, does beauty mean? and why would anyone choose a hard person over someone soft? The imagination discovers or endows some figure with just those associations and attributes that might seem to offer satisfaction to appetites and wants from a previous time.

Dickens's anatomy of love assumes, but goes beyond, the idea of simple mimetic desire—that we desire what another desires, that others mediate our desire—and makes of people artists, or at least artisans, of love, unconsciously making images and symbolic equations out of the negatives of early life and stressing the complexity of our desire. In *Great Expectations* we might call love *metaphorical desire*. The sexual desire of adolescence clearly gets sublimated into money desire, a change that points to economic reasons for sexual repression. Dickens eroticizes the passion to be rich and equates capitalistic passion with a form of being in love, and he unequivocally puts being in love at the center of life: "Truly it was impossible to dissociate her presence from all those wretched hankerings after money and gentility that had disturbed my boyhood. . . . In a word, it was impossible for me to separate her, in the past or in the present, from the innermost life of my life" (29:257).

"The innermost life of my life": that phrase, with its mystical overtones, tells why love becomes an obsession. The psyche, excluded from the inner sanctum of love, is not only kept from its desire, it is alienated from itself. Pip reads Estella as the signature of his identity. If we ask what Pip's career or vocation is, we see that, as surely as with Heathcliff, it is as a lover whose reason for being is to unite with his beloved. But the split identity of the beloved makes the

quest to satisfy erotic desire impossible. There is the inner Estella, a project of
Pip's ego, and the outer Estella, a separate being made ice-hearted by Miss Havisham, who exists independently of Pip, as he well knows. The erotic vocation,
focused partly on an expression of the inner self and partly on an external subject-object, must always run up against the wall between desiring consciousness
and separate physical matter.

The erotic faith of a Pip or a Heathcliff seeks, through the agency of the
beloved, to end separateness and merge with all it sees and imagines. Says Pip
to Estella, in words that recall Heathcliff,

"You have been in every line I have ever read, since I first came here, the rough common boy
whose poor heart you wounded even then. You have been in every prospect I have ever seen
since—on the river, on the sails of the ships, on the marshes, in the clouds . . . in the
wind. . . . The stones of which strongest London buildings are made, are not more real . . .
than your presence and influence have been to me, there and everywhere, and will be."
[44:378]

Love, then, comes often, as it does in this novel, as a wail of the articulate
imagination seeking an impossible oneness and protesting the alienated nature
of being. It comes as a mighty regression, an impassioned strategy to return to
the calamities of early life and counteract them. Pip's imagery for the ubiquity
of Estella—the "line," the "marshes," the "stones"—goes right back to the first
chapter and reiterates developing consciousness. His love looks like a craving for
the preconscious unity of the self with nature and the not-self, together with
the personal consciousness and individuation that linguistic power brings, and
with the nurturing and requited affection he missed. Erotic faith, for Pip—
and many others—presents itself as a miraculous chance to hang onto, redeem,
and transcend all at once the adorable, victimized bundle of shivers that the
older self sees in its past life.

Miss Havisham, seeing Pip's passion for Estella, pours out to him the amorous schizophrenia that can divide love from the person loved: "If she favours
you, love her. If she wounds you, love her. If she tears your heart to pieces . . .
love her! . . . I developed her into what she is, that she might be loved. Love
her! . . . I'll tell you . . . what real love is. It is blind devotion, unquestioning
self-humiliation, utter submission, trust and belief against yourself and against
the whole world, giving up your whole heart and soul to the smiter—as I did!"
(29:261). This fixation, like primitive religion, significantly demands sacrifice.
It splits apart affectionate kindness from passion, and it makes of children objects to fulfill the desires of their elders (desires that may ultimately have erotic
causes). Such fanatical words may read like the testimony of a flagellant to a
god that failed; but, however perverse they seem, they express genuine, common religious and erotic sentiment. The bitterness that unfaithfulness in love

spawns comes about when and because the other, whom one has idealized as a kind of god, betrays one's "faith," in the exact religious sense of the word. But betrayal does not necessarily mean the end of erotic faith; it may just turn Eros into a jealous, avenging god.

In spite of the the emotional serfdom that plagues Pip and paralyzes Miss Havisham, passionate love, Dickens shows, offers these boons: *intensity of feeling and a starring role*. In Pip's love affair, in Miss Havisham's, in Dickens's love story or in the reader's—sad or happy—they are the heroes or heroines. Emily Brontë, like Dickens, gets at this: When we were children, we were sometimes the center of the universe; we did not know our own unimportance by the alienating standards of social perspective. Love recreates that state of living at the world's heart. Even the extreme dependency and vulnerability of love recreate childhood conditions and offer the illusion, if not the reality, of another chance to fulfill the unmet desires of the past. In being in love, according to Dickens, we either reexperience those miseries or we overcome them; and the condition, like some creative neurosis, elevating drug, or martyr's life, has its strange rewards.

VI

Nevertheless, there is no denying or minimizing the crisis of erotic life that *Great Expectations* portrays. Disjunctions appear everywhere (and are epitomized by the two different endings that Dickens wrote). Affection separates from desire; morality and love divide; sexuality is sundered from love; and love seems very different for the rich and poor, romantic passion looking very much like a class privilege.

The onset of passion in the novel has nothing to do with moral goodness. In the rendering of Estella and Biddy, Pip's teacher and "the girl next door," we get the common nineteenth-century split between erotic desire and goodness. Loving Estella, Pip has no desire for Biddy until the end, when, morally reformed, chastened, and wanting a good person and a mother figure as a companion, he decides to offer himself to her, "like a forgiven child" (57:481).

Freud's brief, uneven, but provocative inquiry into the nature of modern eroticism, "On the Universal Tendency to Debasement in the Sphere of Love,"[9] owes much, directly or indirectly, to Dickens and to other nineteenth-century novelists. In it Freud stresses how typical is the failure of men to unite affectionate feelings with the libido, and he states the famous formulation, "Where they love they do not desire and where they desire they cannot love" (183). Pip's dilemma pertains to that syndrome, though it is not quite the same thing. Where he loves, he desires, but he does not esteem, and where he likes and esteems, he does not much desire or love. Dickens, once a poor boy himself, puts greater emphasis than does Freud on the role of social ambition, class, and the appeal of "portable property" (24:224) in creating erotic desire, but he also represents the inhibiting effects of virtue on desire (and not just in the male; Estella and Miss Havisham are like Pip in this); and he hints at the sexual attraction of the forbidden.

Freud attributes in part the gap between liking and desire to "the influences of strong childhood fixations and of later frustration in reality through the intervention of the barrier against incest" (184), something that Dickens in the novel makes graphic. "If I could only," says Pip to Biddy early on when he confesses being in love with Estella, "get myself to fall in love with you" (17:158). This conflict is like the Carmen-Micaela split in both Mérimée and Bizet, the classic nineteenth-century instance of the "whore-virgin" syndrome (Carmen is sex; Micaela carries the letter and seal of the mother), except that Estella's sensuality has been frozen by a Midas touch. Biddy, like an idealized maternal figure—finally and fittingly she *does* become the mother of a new "Pip" (59:490) by Joe—serves for young Pip as the moral imperative of dutiful, dependent love that wilts the libido. Estella, whom Dickens's imagery ties to Pip's deepest primal longings, but also to sexual maturation, is for him the maternal stone named desire.

Freud daringly generalizes on the subject of love's dichotomies: "It sounds not only disagreeable but also paradoxical, yet it must nevertheless be said that anyone who is to be really free and happy in love must have surmounted his respect for women and have come to terms with the idea of incest with his mother or sister" (186). The very cultural situation to which Freud reacts is one that Dickens, a half century earlier, for reasons we will later see, morally favors and imaginatively projects: namely, a strong Oedipal, incestuous fixation with severe sexual taboos. As usual, the solution for one age becomes the problem for the next.

The novel displaces and personifies the libidinous impulse. The lack of union between tenderness and sensuality shows up in bestial male figures who plague and rival Pip. When Pip reaches the age of puberty, not a word is said about sex; but Orlick, the phallic blob of id, suddenly appears.[10] This slouching rough beast "likes" Biddy (17:159) and, when Pip is with her, slinks about and "dances" (17:159) out at her, much to their chagrin. Bentley Drummle, Estella's lover and then husband, though highborn, is a similar figure. "Like some uncomfortable amphibious creature" (25:226), he inhabits the marshy ooze of the psyche's lower depths; Dickens describes him as a social and sexual parasite. Estella, in self-contempt, chooses to "fling" (44:377) herself away on this most worthless suitor who, Dickens implies (by carefully comparing Drummle to a blotchy spider eating out the fungus of Havisham's wedding feast), will and does make an obscene sexual feast of his bride.[11]

Great Expectations downplays and tries to purge love of overt sex. In its happy love matches (Herbert-Clara, Wemmick–Miss Skiffins, Joe-Biddy), physical desire seems to play little part. Sexuality in the novel lurks at the edges of consciousness and in the murk of nature, symbolized by low forms of life or rotten matter—rank instances of parasitism sapping some ideal. The meaning that emerges in these deflected sexual images and most of the other allusions to sexual desire (e.g., Magwitch's infidelity with the gypsy woman whom Estella's mother murders) is that *women and their bodies are menaced and exploited by the force of the sex drive*. Unsublimated sexuality leads to corruption and violence; it needs squelching.

Passion seems to be a soulful, but bent, vocation in the novel—a vocation of leisure. It can be destructive, but also a proving of the self. Romantic love, to flourish, almost always needs people with time for idealism and imagination. The noble tradition of courtly love, that nineteenth-century rediscovery (and reinvention) of upper-class medieval erotic sentiments and concerns, seeped into the thinking of the Victorian bourgeoisie, the men and women with "great expectations." Notice that while happy love flourishes in the novel, it does so in its companionate, utilitarian form, generally among hard-working people too busy for passion. Erotic faith and fixation have a touch of class about them, appearing to the privileged as a passionate, noble calling. (People madly in love often, in their own eyes, do have class.)

Frederick Goldin identifies the perverse elitism and religious ideology that motivated medieval love faith: "Ordinary men cannot love unless they get something in return—something they can get hold of. . . . In this wilderness of carnality and domesticity, nobility declines; there is no reason, and no chance, for the longing, exaltation and self-discipline of true courtliness. This is one of the creeds of courtly love."[12] As Edmund White puts it—in a passage that pertains to Pip, Miss Havisham, and the prevalence of erotic faith—for such a lover, no matter when he lives, "love is useless, painful, unfulfilled, obsessive, destructive, and his very allegiance to this peculiar, seemingly unnatural ideal is proof of his superiority to ordinary mortals."[13] Says Pip to Estella: "[T]o the last hour of my life, you cannot choose but remain part of my character, part of the little good in me, part of the evil. But, in this separation I associate you only with the good, and I will faithfully hold you to that always, for you must have done me far more good than harm, let me feel now what sharp distress I may" (44:378). That sounds like cant, and it is, except that the need to sustain an ideal and find some path to integrity has the anguished ring of sincerity. Love for

him is a discipline—a creed even—that holds the hope of moral, spiritual betterment no matter what the world brings. Such love, independent of the beloved, is a triumph over material circumstance. It rests on a combination of
devotion, sublimated narcissism, and a veiled spirit that claims election: a real
and important, if odd, psychological noblesse oblige. But to indulge such a faith,
of course, it helps to be rich.

Love, then, in *Great Expectations*, tends to be either tender companionship
or passionate fixation, two things almost impossible to reconcile; but in either
case—as friendship or emotional scourge—Dickens imagines that it can open
up the possibilities of faith. Without heart, however, it is a holy terror.

The heart is the soul in love. Located halfway between the mind and the
sexual parts, it is the official organ of love in the nineteenth-century novel.
The metaphysical concept of the heart, as their literature shows, was one of the
Victorians' dearest popular articles of faith. Estella keeps saying that she has no
heart. She, the product and reverse image of Miss Havisham with her broken
heart, is frigid. Together they constitute a Dickensian dialectic of lovesickness.
Estella, trained to embody value and arouse male desire, behaves like a whore of
crystallization, a lovely piece of portable property. Her function is to arouse and
then frustrate desire so that her "Mother by adoption" (38:322) can vicariously requite her suffering upon men. Through the career of the heartless
daughter substitute, Miss Havisham can also identify with the male victimizer
of her youth and play with sexuality. She uses Estella both to sap and imitate
male power. But Estella, trained to despise all men, to use them, to fascinate
them with sex, is filled with joyless self-loathing; she has no more capacity than
a diamond to love anyone, even herself. Miss Havisham, used as a thing herself,
ironically turns Estella into an object to be used and despised, a material girl
who gives herself over to the grossest sexual body, Drummle. Thus frigidity, her
heritage, would seem to grow out of a passionate hatred of passion and out of
the erotic fixations and phobias passed on from one generation to the next. A
broken heart may lead to something even worse, heartlessness and the tyranny
of dead cold matter: life in a wilderness of stones signifying the absence of
familial feeling and love.

VII

I want to look closely at the climactic scene from chapter 49 when fire engulfs
Miss Havisham and Pip acts to save her. It represents an Oedipal coming together of stunning resonance in which Dickens does indeed "come to terms with
the idea of incest." (I use here the standard, if loose, definition of incest: "erotic
intercourse between persons related in certain prohibited degrees of kinship.")
The cry that rings out in the book and echoes beyond it is Miss Havisham's

Oedipus-like wail, "What have I done! What have I done!" (49:411). Pip's whole first-person narrative is one answer to "What have I done!" The climax of the novel's moral fable and of its love story too begins when Miss Havisham realizes the mess her fixation has made of Estella and sees in Pip "a looking-glass" (49:411) of her own miserable love. "What have I done!" is a questioning of the past, and it sets the scene for one of the great visionary erotic passages in literature.

Whoever considers the subject or word *love* for even a moment, sees the differences between what we feel for someone we want to mate with and what we feel for our parents or children. But Dickens, examining life from the beginnings of perception, looks for the integrity of love and life, even if that integrity makes a mockery of conventional distinctions. By going back to the beginnings of love, he finds union in its disparate strands, and Pip's love life has integrity, even if it is sometimes a grotesque one. Dickens imagines his novel's one instance of passionate physical contact between a man and a woman taking place between old and young, Miss Havisham and Pip; and he finds a way of showing, *of inventing imagery that will force you to see*, the interpenetration of filial and parental desire with erotic desire.

When Pip and Miss Havisham meet—alone and without Estella—each begins "compassionating" (49:408) the other. The woman asks him for forgiveness. The stage looks set for a final condemnation of erotic fixation and assertion of the traditional principles of Christian charity and rationality. That very likely is what Dickens intended. Perhaps it is even what he somehow renders. But the outbreak in the prose of energy and vision are so original and fully realized, that to describe the action and meaning in that way is as misleading as to call Aphrodite's emergence from the sea, a day at the beach.

When Pip parts from Miss Havisham, he walks around the grounds and soon finds himself right back in the living past amid the "wilderness of casks" (49:413), the dying light, the ruined gardens, and the ironic emotions of the great expectations of the opening and the first visit to Satis House. His psyche still mourns outside Love's palace.

A childish association revived with wonderful force in the moment of the slight action, and I fancied that I saw Miss Havisham hanging to the beam. So strong was the impression, that I stood under the beam shuddering from head to foot before I knew it was a fancy—though to be sure I was there in an instant.

The mournfulness of the place and time, and the great terror of this illusion, though it was but momentary, caused me to feel an indescribable awe. [49:413]

Traumas set off alarms in childhood and reverberate through involuntary memory to the last breath. Pip's "indescribable awe," a phrase that takes us back to "the smart without a name," results once more in the illusion of Miss Havisham hanging. Again, as so often in the novel, Estella and Miss Havisham flow together for Pip. In his prosperity and in his fantasy-life, Pip had projected on Miss Havisham the role of an eccentric fairy godmother who fulfilled his desire and turned out to be the bountiful mother he never had. Now, that inexpressible "awe" comes from seeing again the depth of his homicidal impulse toward her and Estella for their hardness, but beyond that, it comes from realizing the full force of "childish association" to rule personal life. And yet there are differences. A purge is taking place. Instead of running away at first, he runs towards her, as if his unconscious were telling him to rescue her and embrace her fate. It is as if he were trying to unravel the compulsions of the past by dredging up to the light the images and symbols of his buried life. His text moves towards, not away from, Oedipal feeling and desire.

"Bright flaming people in a roundelay of accidental life that alters the world." That phrase by William Kennedy nicely characterizes what follows. Dickens's spontaneous combustion, composed just at the time of Freud's childhood, could be the blazing sign of an Oedipal second coming: "I looked into the room where I had left [Miss Havisham]. . . . I saw a great flaming light spring up. In the same moment, I saw her running at me, shrieking, with a whirl of fire blazing all about her, and soaring at least as many feet above her head as she was high" (49:413–14). That vision means an emotional conflagration and a time of reckoning.

> I had a double-caped great-coat on, and over my arm another thick coat. That I got them off, closed with her, threw her down, and got them over her; that I dragged the great cloth from the table for the same purpose, and with it dragged down the heap of rottenness in the midst, and all the ugly things that sheltered there; that we were on the ground struggling like desperate enemies, and that the closer I covered her, the more wildly she shrieked and tried to free herself; that this occurred I knew through the result, but not through anything I felt, or thought, or knew I did. I knew nothing until I knew that we were on the floor by the great table, and that patches of tinder yet alight were floating in the smoky air, which, a moment ago, had been her faded bridal dress. [49:414]

This strange coupling makes tangible the intercourse of old and young and shows metaphorically the erotics of parent-child relationships. The elaborate, open-ended symbolism of the prose has almost unlimited centrifugal power to convey and imply meaning. We need to see that Pip clutches, amid all the emblematic trappings of sex that the imagery communicates, a pathetic woman whom he has imagined as the mother of his desires. That fire, the searing outblast of repressed feeling, is purifying as well as deadly, sacrificial as well as infernal. Pip, for once, finds himself joined here to another being, as he is later joined to Magwitch, and in this instant of heroism, instinctive love, and the burning away of self-consciousness, he no longer is an orphan alone. The image of these two, the disillusioned youth and the crazy old lady, on the ground "struggling like desperate enemies," must surely be one of the most grotesque in literature, but it has its own weird beauty. As he upsets the rottenness of the past, Pip fights to save one who has hurt him. For them both it is a moment, such as they have never known before, of all-consuming passion, of union and atonement—at one in hell.[14]

Dickens takes care to show that her bridal dress has burned off, which means that she is at long last naked with a man, the bride of fire and death. He is touching the core of being, summoning it up, as he phrases it, "from no shallow place." Oedipus and Jocasta, Hamlet and the Queen, Freud the theorist of incest and the interpreter of dreams, Marx the incendiary, and Bosch and Goya with the amazing illuminations of their grotesque art all meet here. Images of meaning and association shoot out of the textual fire like pyrotechnics: love as a smoldering embrace with a mother substitute; orphan mating with his desire; son saving, lying with, marrying sere and withered mother; the bared, ugly, scorching honesty of the body and its pain; child forgiving and redeeming the sinful parent; the burning away of *have-is-sham* and the desiccated costume of wealth and class; the inevitability of personal, social, and erotic trial by fire; the all-embracing delirium and apotheosis of the libido; the binding together of generations, classes, and the sexes in love, hate, danger, and death; and redemption through suffering.

We have a mental landscape:

Then, I looked round and saw the disturbed beetles and spiders running away over the floor, and the servants coming in with breathless cries at the door. I still held her forcibly down with all my strength, like a prisoner who might escape; and I doubt if I even knew who she was, or why we had struggled . . . until I saw the patches of tinder that had been her garments . . . falling in a black shower around us. . . .

Though every vestige of her dress was burnt, as they told me, she still had something of her old ghastly bridal appearance. [49:414–15]

That is a tragic, parodic fantasy of a wedding night for both. Remember that Estella is the creation of Miss Havisham's desire and the two mingle together indiscriminately in Pip's psyche. His love and desires have turned to ashes. (Again and again, Dickens's imagistic art refreshes clichés, e.g., "turned to ashes," "fiery embrace," "burning passion.") The bride he has wanted to mate with turns out to be a searing phantom of the past. The text renders a spiritual and physical consummation for these two whose greatest expectations have been for marriages that failed to happen.

The contact between these two is the most important Pip has known and the closest to peace either has come.

Towards midnight she began to wander in her speech, and . . . said innumerable times in a low solemn voice, "What have I done!" And then, "When she first came, I meant to save her from misery like mine." And then, "Take the pencil and write under my name, 'I forgive her!'" . . . At about six o'clock of the morning, therefore, I leaned over her and touched her lips with mine, just as they said, not stopping for being touched, "Take the pencil and write under my name, 'I forgive her.'" [49:415]

That moving kiss is—if I'm right in laying stress on the erotic tie between pseudoparent and child—the key that, for Dickens, frees Psyche to enter the Victorian house of love. Sexual passion and the megalomania of desire and resentment are burned away, leaving compassion, penitence, and the benevolent touch of frail flesh. Miss Havisham's rosarylike chant of self-scrutiny, confession, and the beseeching of mercy means a giving up of the violent will to inflict erotic pain on others and a recognition of her kinship with other suffering and madly loving people. And Pip's kiss means the granting of pardon and the recognition of his own need of forgiveness and his intimacy with her desire, her sin, and her change of heart. Being in love, for Dickens, is a condition that necessarily involves and bonds past and future generations. So the kiss signals a continuity that reaches across time and proclaims the communal nature of erotic fate. It signifies the end of the old and young using each other as means to fulfill selfish erotic desires. It also connotes and honors the healing powers of the sympathetic imagination.

Notice how Dickens imagines this imagination. For him, as for Charlotte Brontë, the act of writing brings atonement and the transubstantiation of love: "Take the pencil and write under my name, 'I forgive her.'" We have come full circle from the cold inscription on the tombstone, "Also Georgiana Wife of the Above," to the request from the burning "Mother by adoption" to make mercy and intimacy real by writing. It's writing that proves and makes lasting charity. Being in love leads to the inscription of love in the novel. The words of the epitaph that announce the absence of love and the unreachable mother in Pip's childhood give way to his necessity to love Estella and counteract the dearth of love in his young life; and that love leads him finally to close with Miss Havisham and, in a sublime act of love, write forgiveness. Pip's narrative does just what Miss Havisham asks him to do.

Let us be clear about what happens in *Great Expectations*: Erotic love, in all its complexity, leads to the saving imagination issuing forth its consolation in the act of writing. Impressions lead to inscriptions and the fixation of love—but not fixation in the sense of compulsive mania. Dickens projects here through the burning of Miss Havisham the function of writing as a plea for forgiveness for oneself and others by creating and communicating imaginative wonder, understanding, and flaming passion and compassion.

Moreover it's tempting to see the image of Miss Havisham here as Dickens's muse. He deeply resented his mother's insensitivity to his talents and feelings, and when he finally got out of the blacking factory, he never forgot that his mother was "warm" for sending him back.[15] The scene forms a sweet personal metaphor for him; writing is his way of pardoning her and finding his way back to maternal love and bounty. And beyond the personal significance, the old, dying woman, desperately imploring him over and over, "Take the pencil and write under my name, 'I forgive her,'" makes a perfect figure of the muse for anyone who ever needs to find the means for forgiving self or life for not giving enough love. Many interpretations are possible. We might even read this section as a parable for the genesis of literature.

VIII

It would, however, be a shame and a distortion of the novel to become pious about this chapter, since it so clearly shows Dickens getting at forbidden topics and unsavory, controversial aspects of love: specifically, the ugliness of sex and the incestuous bias of his culture and personality. The episode obviously has the rhythm and feeling of violent sexual encounter, but I do not mean that it straightforwardly represents an act of sex. In fact, that it cannot be simply reduced to a "normal" sexual coupling is one thing that very much matters about it. That sex cannot be represented directly in the Victorian novel in part defines the nature of Victorian life. In Dickens's world, as we have seen, the sex drive and act are disguised, suppressed, displaced, and dispersed in consciousness. Direct sexual expression is censured and censored. Sexual impulse and activity are either repressed and kept in tight check (e.g., Pip, Joe, Jaggers, Wemmick, Pumblechook), so that sexual energy spends itself in deflected ways, or, after infesting people's lives (e.g., Joe's father, Orlick, Magwitch), it erupts with sudden violence, like a subterranean explosion that spews out poisonous vapors.

If we look at the scene again, we might see in it a sudden outbreak of fire, a rushing together, a desperate, animal-like embrace, nudity amid nuptial rottenness, a shrieking woman struggling to free herself from the man's hold, repulsive, time-honored symbols of depraved sexual activity (i.e., little creepy crawly things), insensibility, impotent exhaustion, the spent mood of postcoital *tristesse*, and the longing for that symbol of sublimated phallic potency, the creative writing-stick. Dickens, in *Great Expectations*, can imagine sex only as a quick burst of flame that throws people into hideous conjugal postures and leaves them in agony and weakness.

Pip's narrative, a flare-up and a burning away of desire, manifests the kinds of contradictions that would lead doctors of the psyche to perceive widespread erotic conflict and crisis by the end of the century. A cynical, but plausible, reading of the passage might find a poetically just mutilation of the flesh, with Miss Havisham, the bad-mother figure, confessing her maternal sins and burned to death, while Pip, punished for his amoral desire, is unmanned and reduced to the status of a dutiful child (not unlike Rochester at the end of *Jane Eyre*). The sublimity that the chapter attains and the degraded vision of the physical intercourse that it presents both stand out. Two facts when taken together seem especially revealing: first, that Dickens was the most popular novelist of his age; and, second, that the split between love and sex is, on the whole, more pronounced in his fictional world than in that of any other great novelist. He touched those—and their name is legion—who wanted to believe in the redemptive force of love between men and women, but who felt that the sexual libido was the disruptive enemy of fidelity and religious idealism.

Civilization progresses or, at least, survives by the wedding of one generation with the next in forbearance and sympathetic concern for mutual suffering. The "burning," in all its radiance, sheds light on an observation by Freud: "Thus we may perhaps be forced to become reconciled to the idea that it is quite impossible to adjust the claims of the sexual instinct to the demands of civilization; that in consequence of its cultural development renunciation and suffering . . . cannot be avoided. . . . The very incapacity of the sexual instinct . . . becomes the source, however, of the noblest cultural achievements which are brought into being by ever more extensive sublimation."[16] The union of Pip and Miss Havisham would seem to relate to and epitomize much of Victorian culture, with its bizarre mental contortions and its magnificent accomplishments.

The vision of love and the whole thrust of the novel—maybe even, hyperbolically speaking, our whole understanding of Victorian erotics and the aftermath of various sexual revolutions and reactions up to the present—depend on Dickens's choice of having Pip lie with the old woman rather than with the young one. After all, he could have set Estella on fire had he wanted to. He opts for the chaste filial kiss over the tumultuous flail of fiery *young* bodies. It is the naked intimacy, permission, and charge of the mother figure that enable him to lift the fertile pen(cil) of creation. He chooses, like his culture, moral incest with the mother figure.

What I mean by that glib statement is this: In fairy tales and legends, the attractive, ambitious young figure must embrace and accept the pathetic old figure at the fountain, or wherever, before he or she can win the princess or prince: first sympathy for the figure of the past, the affectionate acceptance of the pseudoparent; then the blessing and the happy transformation of the present becomes possible. Victorian sensibility largely agrees. The Victorian Oedipal complex—and I use the term loosely as an umbrella for being in love with the parent figure and all that she or he represents—was a strategy and fixation of the nineteenth-century imagination evolving in particular historical conditions that we have seen: for example, the growth of religiosity and simultaneous undermining of supernaturalism; the transmission of religious reverence to women (in a time when the death rate for childbearing females remained high); the spreading popularity of romantic love; new social awareness of the destabilizing nature of sexual desire; the cults of kindness, benevolent sentimentalism, and childhood innocence; the elevation of marketplace and biological competition into an ideology; and the faster pace of change in all fields. Above all, as Mark Spilka puts it, there occurred the strengthening of "intensely insulated affections for members of the family, especially those of the opposite sex, and severe censure for sexual expression of any kind."[17]

In the age that glorified and popularized the family as a moral, stabilizing institution, the Victorian ban on writing sex directly is linked with the symbolic eruptions of incestuous desire in novels and the fascination with the incest taboo in late nineteenth-century anthropology and psychology. Sexual repression might flow into, and shape, images and fantasies that betray incestuous fixations, and they in turn might control sexual impulse.

The burning of Miss Havisham has such a rich indeterminacy that it can never be satisfactorily "interpreted"; its inherent conflicts cannot be entirely reconciled. For instance, you can argue that erotic faith and Oedipal desire lead to moral redemption or that they both must be renounced before redemption is possible; that the victimized woman is, in effect, designated as the "burnt" sacrificial offering upon which culture and love redeem themselves, or that she finds peace and fulfillment in inspiring the forgiveness, devotion, and accomplishment of the young; that Pip frees himself from mother hunger and sick incest, or that he seizes onto a healthy familial faith. It seems, however, to be so forceful as art and to concentrate such significance that it calls for some hypothetical speculation.

Is it really farfetched to read the coming together of Pip and Miss Havisham as a complex symbol of incest, incest taboo, and their multiple implications? If we look closely at the scene as Dickens set it down, with its specific rhythms, words, details, and images that he did not have to inscribe, but did—the wedding dress burned off, the disrobing of Pip, the clutching bodies, the "breathless" cries, the sudden eruption and quiet ebbing of passion—an Oedipal interpretation makes sense.

Let us suppose the following conditions: In the age of the greatest social mutability the world had ever known, people longed for emotional continuity. They wanted a steady safe love lasting through life and, as pure conviction in otherworldly salvation ebbed, secure ties to the material past and future of this world. The way to bolster shaky egos whose immortality was menaced and to hold onto civilized values and make them flourish, so middle-class moralists thought, was the kind of attitude and action they found in affectionate filial responsibility and in loving parental concern—"familialism." If such drives to-

wards familial benevolence could include potential sex partners, if an erotic desire to want to marry someone who would be a good mother or father could be
inculcated, if people's libidos could be moralized and rhetorically shaped, they
might desire altruistically. If the incestuous urge could be desexed but preserved,
if erotic love could be idealized, and if people would project their incestuous
drives and tendencies onto suitable mates or goals, then the Oedipus-Electra
complex and erotic desire could themselves be mated and the deflected libidinous
energy might be safely gathered, embraced, and used. Incestuous feeling controlled and transferred could become the friend of marriage, love, and family—
not to mention literature.

Art, we said, often grows out of great tensions that, for various reasons, are
difficult to express conceptually and explicitly. We can see why a society, a nation, and particular authors living with the traditional taboos surrounding incest
but also in circumstances that promote close, cloying family feeling, would produce a literature permeated with incestuous conflicts and affect. Personal fulfillment and identity, in a time of change, might depend on finding a way to be
true to early desires, the figures that animate them, and the images to which
they attach themselves.

We need to see that "incest in the novel" is as important a subject in thinking
about love and fiction as "adultery in the novel" [18]—more important in the tradition of British fiction. Lovers are often literal or spiritual orphans, like Pip,
trying to find a way back to a mother (or father, in the case of characters like
Fanny Price, Jane Eyre, Lucy Snowe, or Romola), trying to reimagine—to *represent*—their basic desires, and fulfill them through some mode of transference in the present so that they can find a coherent self and creative relationship.

Suppose that in the erotic behavior of humankind we find two tendencies
moving in opposite directions that threaten social stability and health. Let us
call these impulses, on the one side, adultery, which threatens the communal
structure of kinship, property, and tranquility, and, on the other, incest, which
menaces people with inbreeding and, thus, impossibly volatile and violence-
provoking intrafamily passions. The course, if not of true love, then of socially
acceptable love and marriage, has seemed to lie between these two, the Scylla
and Charybdis of love life. In exploring the two great taboos of love, the British
nineteenth-century novelists, because of their historical heritage, chose to put a
heavier stress on incest than on adultery, unlike many of their great Continental
contemporaries. They stress marriage as an end. Marriage takes place because
society wants and must have mothers and fathers. There is an impetus to bring
society and the individual into harmony in nineteenth-century life and novels,
to blend the collective need with the personal motive by writing into the love-
story plot: *You* marry because *you* want a mother or father. Control the sexual

impulse, but keep incestuous energy bubbling, and you might release a potent force sustaining social coherence and ethical loyalties.

IX

Thackeray's *Henry Esmond* (1853), a novel that broadcasts a bent for idealized incestuous feeling, had a strong impact on *Great Expectations*. It might be called *The New Oedipus*, à la Rousseau's *La nouvelle Héloïse*. Esmond's first-person narrative tells how he, a poor eighteenth-century orphan, after compulsively loving for years an Estella-like hard-heart and would-be adulteress, marries instead his foster mother, who also happens to be the girl's mother. By marrying the woman who mothered him, Esmond rejects sexual compulsion and chooses for his love filial and reverent emotion. In essence, he weds the supposedly libido-curbing, socially responsible values of Victorian morality. For Thackeray himself, fixated on his own mother and cynical about passionate love (*Vanity Fair* wickedly satirizes erotic faith), Esmond's solution to his life's riddle was simply to follow Oedipus.

Dickens would render, among a hundred other things, the ghastly aspect of embracing the mother. But that these two most famous and influential of Victorian novelists, in fictional autobiographies, imagine, respectively, son marrying pseudomother and son lying with pseudomother, would seem to show the Oedipal preoccupations and bias of nineteenth-century love. "Coming to terms with the idea of incest" might mean, as Dickens and Pip show, finding a way to accept the reality of primal attraction to the being that has helped to form and constitute your very system of desire; and it might also—and simultaneously— mean recognizing the reality of primal aversion to the ugly, domineering, and deteriorating body, mind, and will of the figure who gave you life. It might mean accepting and rejecting the narcissistic desire to use children as physical extensions of your ego; and it might mean recognizing the appeal and the tyranny of making women's only sanctioned vocation the fulfillment of maternal desire.

And there is something more that needs to be said about the burning scene, and the idea and taboo of incest. Incest has symbolic meaning—perhaps the deepest symbolic meaning of all. Coming to terms with incest might finally mean symbolizing it in communal, personal, or institutional fantasy life. Incest and the incest taboo would both seem to be defining features of human culture and invention, products of the blessed, cursed ability to abstract and conceptualize human relationships. Symbolizing incest in literature, therefore, is a purgative metasymbolizing of humankind's symbolic erotic nature. It means human love can never be "natural."

The burning of Miss Havisham and Pip, like Bronzino's *Allegory* and like the whole of *Great Expectations*, shows that the alienation that begins the drive for love is born out of humanity's symbolic structure and generational fate. Incestuous desire itself must be accepted, figured, forgiven, and inscribed in and by the burning imagination.

X

The contradictory endings for the novel, printed in most popular editions now, show there are two kinds of love stories in it: one about erotic fixation and its cure, the other about the power of love to rule the psyche. They also show how deeply *Great Expectations* is riven by the will both to deny and affirm belief in the goodness of passionate love. They give evidence of the muddled conflict that a bias towards spiritual incest and sexual taboo creates for Dickens. One of the revelations of the plot is that Pip and Estella have the same parent figures in common, which gives an incestuous tinge to his love for her.

Like Pip's last words to Magwitch, the ending Dickens published stands as a testament to the strength of erotic faith. It reunites Pip and Estella in the ruined garden. Had he chosen his original ending, the meaning of the narrative would be changed. In that ending, Pip, after many years, meets her by chance in London. They look sadly on one another, shake hands, and part. Pip concludes, "I was very glad afterwards to have had the interview; for, in her face and in her voice, and in her touch, she gave me the assurance, that suffering had been stronger than Miss Havisham's teaching, and had given her a heart to understand what my heart used to be" (Appendix A, 496).

Period. That was going to be it. The end of great expectations would mean giving up youthful fantasy and adjusting to the reality principle. Pip—single, hardworking, no longer fixated, able to face the past and move quietly beyond it—resembles, in this end, an old-fashioned psychoanalyst's dream of the cured analysand. The downplayed meeting with Estella shows moral progress for them both. It rests on understatement, and its starkness implies that maturity *is* a kind of understatement—an anticlimax for the romantic that exists somewhere in most psyches. It is a considered, tough ending, and it confirms the burning away of phantom illusions and obsessive eroticism that the Havisham fire had signified. But Bulwer-Lytton and other friends objected to it, and Dickens, agreeing, composed in its place "as pretty a little piece of writing as I could, and I have no doubt the story will be more acceptable through the alteration" (Appendix A, 494).

George Bernard Shaw, who put out an edition with the first ending, called the second "psychologically wrong" (Appendix A, 496). Shaw, however, had little use for religious feeling, and faith—not some spurious sellout to the public—was the real issue for Dickens. The first ending offers erotic agnosticism and Pip's rational, abstract adjustment to the world, but it somehow deflates the life of the narrative. It may have verisimilitude, but it leaves the reader with no passionate reason for being and no antidote to the spiritual paucity of a bourgeois life of small expectations that the flat prose of the penultimate chapter captures perfectly. "Many a year went round, before I was a partner in the House; but, I lived happily with Herbert and his wife, and lived frugally, and paid my debts. . . . We were not in a grand way of business, but we had a good name, and worked for our profits, and did very well" (58:489). Desire is tamed, but desire is what makes hope, plots, and the future. Erotic faith may be warped, but it is something; and you can't beat something with nothing.

The two conclusions show, just as in *Villette*, how difficult or arbitrary it is to end love stories and how ready the modern romantic imagination is to endow love with a metaphysical quality, as if belief in the happy union and afterlife for lovers in a story were like belief in heaven. David Lean's film of *Great Expectations* shows us a third ending, a truly happy Hollywood one. In it, Estella has taken Miss Havisham's place in Satis House and lives shut up once more amid darkness, disappointment, and all those same nasty trappings of decay around her. Pip walks in, throws open the curtains, grabs her by the hand, and runs with her out into the sunlight, like Robert Browning whisking Elizabeth Barrett off to fertile Italy.

If we set the discarded ending and the film ending next to the actual ending, we can see what was at stake, why it mattered, and what Dickens's problem was. The moral imperative for the health of a culture is to keep personal desire from running wild. Religion and religious feeling have been human stratagems for controlling desire while giving people faith. The Victorians longed for a religious sense of life and were disposed to find it in love. But love arises out of potentially dangerous eroticism. Therefore we get continuing efforts to apotheosize love while separating it from desire. And what is true in Victorian love is an instance of a contradiction in religion generally. Faith depends upon personal desire, but religious feeling must transcend the will of the self if it is to command moral authority and general credence. Dickens's superseded ending purges desire but leaves no basis or need for faith; the film fulfills desire completely but in doing so denies the human reality that gives rise to both faith and moral quandary. The conflict between desire and morality is the crux of the dilemma for Dickens and for erotic faith, and his conclusion is a hard-put improviser's compromise.

Pip's narrative ends with his return to Satis House, after eleven years, for "Estella's sake" (59:490), and the scene stresses the integrity of personality and love by reiterating that life moves backwards as well as forwards in one whole: "I saw that some of the old ivy had struck root anew, and was growing green on low quiet mounds of ruin" (59:491). In the innermost life of his life, Pip has never gotten out of that graveyard at the beginning: "I . . . was looking along

the desolate garden-walk, when I beheld a solitary figure. . . . 'Estella!'"
(59:491). That is the externalized vision and inner spirit that has guided his
life. The parallel with *Villette* is striking: the long-lasting obsession with love
enchants the vision of the first-person text and narrator. Far from being able to
deal once and for all with past love and move forward, early erotic longing floods
into every impression: "'I am greatly changed. I wonder you know me.' The
freshness of her beauty was indeed gone, but its indescribable majesty and its
indescribable charm remained. Those attractions in it, I had seen before; what I
had never seen before, was the saddened softened light of the once proud eyes"
(59:491).

Everyone, even Shaw, praises the artistry of this chapter. Notice the word
indescribable, the precise term that takes us back to the "indescribable awe" Pip
had felt when hallucinating just before the burning scene, back to the nameless
lack that mothered his love for Estella, back to the time of his first impression
of the identity of things, and even before. And the saddened, softened light
takes us back to Pip's views of Miss Havisham and to the vision of Estella when
she passed among extinguished fires into his soul's eye. Estella appears as a fair
penitent of erotic faith here, and the importance of penitence in Pip and his
whole narrative shows how love and the novel had become structures whereby
the old religious offices and sacraments, such as penance, confession, and even,
on the part of novelists, informal ordination, could be rendered in an increasingly secular culture.

The last words have a resigned Miltonic dignity about them, "calm of mind,
all passion spent," and they echo the feeling at the end of chapter 49, the quiet
kiss of the twilight mood: "I took her hand in mine, and we went out of the
ruined place; and, as the morning mists had risen long ago when I first left the
forge, so, the evening mists were rising now, and in all the broad expanse of
tranquil light they showed to me, I saw no shadow of another parting from her"
(59:493). This union, if it is a union, has a chaste, unworldly feeling about it.
Estella the morning star has become the evening star, still Venus, but ethereal
and insubstantial.

Repression, as in Charlotte Brontë, makes the enchantment of love possible.
The same gap that exists in Lucy Snowe's narrative exists in Pip's: we are not
told about the present circumstances of the fictional writer's life, nor of the
period between the time when the last represented intimacy of the lovers takes
place and the time when the narrator writes. The accent is thrown on feeling
and the integrating imagery.

Dickens makes moves here of great significance: He tries to fuse and leave
intact both moral faith and erotic desire. He does not renounce or transcend
desire, but he lets a mood of moral atonement and resignation cover it. He

eroticizes nostalgia and basks love in an elegiac tone, making love inseparable from knowledge of the past and contemplation of the meaning of death. The suffering of love and its integrity prove faith.

No one sensitive to language could call the ending conventionally happy. The tone and vision suggest a mood of approaching death, the only place where the desirous heart senses no partings, no shadows, no mistiness. What Dickens finds in the consistency of erotic focus is not happiness, not transcendence, but a wholeness and consistency of personality. His erotic faith turns out to be not really a devotion to another person, but to the idea and power of the integrating imagination. The fixation of love claims for the single human life an emotional coherence, a *character*, no matter what the self's disappointments, no matter how violent the tides or flames of erotic desire may be beneath the surface of the public self. In *Great Expectations* Dickens imagines that we are always in touch with an inner visionary child inscribed with fiery desire, that offspring and veteran of the passionate force that brings us into the world.

7   In Love with Moistness: George Eliot's *The Mill on the Floss* (1860)

The relationship between a man and a woman was to her as important as the relationship between human being and God had once been—the centrally serious business of life. . . .
   PHYLLIS ROSE[1]

[T]he psychic pattern which was to direct her course throughout life was formed almost exclusively by her relationship with her mother, her father, and—most observably—with Isaac.
   RUBY REDINGER[2]

I

Venus is born from the sea. Wetness and flow are inseparable from the erotic imagination. George Eliot gives us a mind-catching expression of being in love and the fluidity of erotic faith when she says, at the beginning of *The Mill on the Floss*, "I am in love with moistness."[3] The narrator who makes this astounding statement is like a ravishing goddess of love herself, eroticizing nature, turning it into a partner of her desire and intimate knowledge; her words both intensify and diffuse at the same time the drive of the individual libido. The goal of her love story will not be marriage but regenerative faith.

The opening of *The Mill on the Floss* projects a vision of immanent amorousness on the world and claims as reality an erotic version of the so-called pathetic fallacy: "A wide plain, where the broadening Floss hurries on between its green banks to the sea, and the loving tide, rushing to meet it, checks its passage with an impetuous embrace" (I, I, 7). This setting of the scene means that love and sexuality can determine how life is perceived and color everything the novelist writes. Eliot continues, "On this mighty tide the black ships—laden with fresh-scented fir-planks, with rounded sacks of oil-bearing seed . . . —are borne along." Animated moistness, fluidity, fertile forms of matter—they, like language, which writers are always showing is to humanity as water is to life (see, for example, Shakespeare, Charlotte Brontë, and James Joyce), are the agents of circulation, fecundity, and metamorphosis. Eliot's streaming consciousness uses them to set out an image and a narrative about being in love and the effort to sustain love in the world. She starts and ends by imagining a symbolic baptism and dissolution of the self in erotic faith.

The faith that she portrays, however, is in even more serious crisis than love in *Great Expectations* (published in the same year). The incestuous bias is even more overt and dangerous. We can see now that the words of John Ruskin's casual dismissal of the novel, if even partially true, would actually attest to its cultural importance: "There is no girl alive, fairly clever, half educated, and unluckily related, whose life has not at least as much in it as Maggie's, to be described and to be pitied."[4] Maggie Tulliver is faithfully in love from start to finish—in love with her brother Tom. That love kills her. Family ties and family-induced desires keep her from fulfilling love exogamously; she has no good way of getting what she needs from outside. Her plight implies a general conflict and dilemma. The intense love and desire for a forbidden relation must be rendered, purged, and diffused. Eliot connects and renders in the tale of Maggie the common impetus towards incestuous love in the century, the renunciation of keenly felt sexual desire, and the communal, collective nature of life; she stresses the binding of love and language as a mode of faith and a means of progress. Everywhere in the novel, in George Eliot's thought, in her sense of personal and social history we find this pattern of desire: relationship, renunciation, diffusion.

II

Diffuse: "to pour out and spread, as fluid; to disseminate." Eliot says of Dorothea at the end of *Middlemarch*, "[T]he effect of her being . . . was incalculably diffusive."[5] Life and literature are flow. George Eliot loves and trusts the flow from personal experience to generalization, from sense impressions to artistic creation, from ink to page, from self to narrator, from narrator to character to reader—the flow back and forth through time and space between fiction and life.

The book presents Maggie as a sacrificial emblem—a saint—of erotic faith, just as Saint Ogg, the charitable oarsman of olden times who ferried the Virgin, was a Christian saint. But in the modern story, the virgin drowns. Eliot can be seen to sweeten, broaden, and conceptualize the sacrificial and consecrating function of Emily Brontë's rude saints of love. If erotic faith is to flourish, Maggie's martyrdom for the love of her brother must be diffused: it must spread and flow into others; she must be transfigured into the being and consciousness of that lover of moistness, the dream-prone narrator of chapter 1 (and the novel), and into the imagination of the audience.

For more than a century, *The Mill on the Floss*, in its spirit and details, has been approached and read as an autobiographical novel, and much of its interest lies in the light it sheds on the shaping of Eliot's creative life. I want to use it to speculate upon the role of love in her mind and fiction, but primarily to stress its social significance and its close relationship to the expression of love in the nineteenth-century tradition of erotic faith. George Eliot, like Maggie Tulliver, adored Sir Walter Scott, and her novel assumes the fateful eroticizing of history that *The Bride of Lammermoor* enacts. She develops a bourgeois, provincial, more modern version of the conflicts in Scott's novel. Both see erotic faith as a historically conditioned process; but Eliot, like Dickens, renders in detail the origins of individual love patterns and the deep conflicts within the single personality that belief in love could bring. Her work explicitly concerns itself with the personal quest for faith.

The discursive chapter "A Voice from the Past" (IV, III) still stands as a classic statement about the necessity and difficulty of finding faith in the modern world. I quote from it to show why erotic faith matters so much in this novel and why it has taken hold of so many people in latter days who may never have thought about it. Meditating on Maggie Tulliver's adolescent gloom, Eliot expands her vision to uncover spiritual poverty and class arrogance of historic consequence.

> In writing the history of unfashionable families, one is apt to fall into a tone of emphasis which is very far from being the tone of good society. . . . But then, good society has its claret and its velvet-carpets, its dinner-engagements six weeks deep, its opera and its faery ball-rooms; . . . [it] lounges at the club, has to keep clear of crinoline vortices, gets its science done by Faraday, and its religion by the superior clergy. . . . how should it have time or need for belief and emphasis? But good society, floated on gossamer wings of light irony, is of very expensive production; requiring nothing less than a wide and arduous national life condensed in unfragrant deafening factories, cramping itself in mines, sweating at furnaces, grinding, hammering, weaving under more or less oppression of carbonic acid—or else, spread over sheep-walks, and scattered in lonely houses and huts. . . . Under such circumstances, there are many among its myriads of souls who have absolutely needed an emphatic belief. [IV, III, 255–56]

Eliot renders and bemoans the absence of such essential faith in the world of Saint Ogg. In the chapter "A Variation of Protestantism Unknown to Bossuet" (IV, I, 238), she makes it clear that Christianity no longer provides the needed belief and force: "one sees little trace of religion, still less of a distinctively Christian creed." She goes on, "I share with you this sense of oppressive narrowness; but it is necessary that we should feel it, if we care to understand how it acted on the lives of Tom and Maggie" (IV, I, 238). Maggie is a romantic seeker, like the young Mary Anne Evans, "with a blind, unconscious yearning for something that would link together the wonderful impressions of this mysterious life, and give her soul a sense of home in it" (III, V, 208). Love rushes into a vacuum of faith.

The Mill on the Floss ends where *Great Expectations* begins, in a churchyard, with an epitaph: "In their death they were not divided" (VII, "Conclusion,"

457). That inscription matches the feeling and tone of Pip's last words, "I saw no shadow of another parting from her." These two books, written at the same time, are like great mirrors on opposing walls in the Victorian house of love, reflecting on erotic faith and being in love from different but mutually reverberating perspectives. Moral rescue and saving forgiveness, not happiness, are the ends of both plots. In Eliot, an oceanic, not a fiery, embrace marks the climax of erotic desire. In one book, inscription determines the direction and action of love, and in the other the course of love issues in inscription and the inscribing imagination. One is a first-person narrative, presumably of moral redemption; the other, except for chapter 1, is a third-person narrative about a tragic figure who, however, somehow miraculously metamorphoses into that very third-person narrator herself. Like Dickens, George Eliot gives us childhood, youth, and their erotics, but—crucially—from a feminine point of view. Like him, she imagines an incestuous drive shaping life, but an incestuous passion for the brother, not for the mother figure—in the sociology of taboo, sibling rather than parental incest. Love is the counteraction to lack and exclusion, but exclusion by gender rather than class, a shutting-off from male opportunities. Unlike Pip the orphan, Maggie Tulliver finds herself mired down among relations. Repressed, sublimated sexuality bursts out in metaphor and image in both novels, but Eliot sees sexuality as a much more attractive and potentially positive force than Dickens does, and she puts more emphasis on the problem of frustrated sexual need in a repressive society. Though both main characters risk their lives for others, Eliot explicitly stresses sacrifice rather than personal redemption and gives us a martyr's life.

III

The story of Maggie bears eerie resemblance to the image of another Victorian saint of erotic faith, *Ophelia* (1852; fig. 4), that masterpiece of Pre-Raphaelite painting by Eliot's friend John Millais.[6] In both we see beautiful women drowning, victimized by fatal love and a deadly conflict of loyalties, in a lovely setting haunted by nostalgia and sorrow. Both offer iconic images of sacrifice. Millais took this "relative creature"—brother to Laertes, daughter to Polonius, sometime beloved of Hamlet, favorite of the queen to marry her son—and made her fate the tragic center of things.[7] What Tom Stoppard did for Rosencrantz and Guildenstern, the painter's act of composition had long before done for Ophelia, giving her "an equivalent centre of self."[8]

Millais created his vision from the news of Ophelia's offstage demise "in the glassy stream": where "a willow grows," she "Fell in the weeping brook. . . . like a creature native and indued / Unto that element" (*Hamlet*, IV, vii). Shakespeare's description and Millais's setting are comparable to the key watery site in *The Mill on the Floss*. On the first page of the novel, the narrator remarks, "How lovely the little river is. . . . I remember those large dipping willows," and goes on to talk of this place in terms that apply exactly to the painting. In Maggie's childhood, she and her brother Tom go to a "wonderful pool . . . framed in with willows and tall reeds, so that the water was only to be seen when you got close to the brink" (I, V, 36). There she has a definitive experience with her brother, the gist of which will stay with her and enthrall her unto death: she feels his approbation for once, and the serenity of a oneness with him, with nature, and with her imagination. In this time and place she feels the relationship that makes possible the transformation, as Eliot says, of "perception into love" (I, V, 38). At the time of their death, Maggie and Tom relive the intimacy and feeling of this place.

In her fashion Eliot had in mind the character and predicament of Shakespeare's Ophelia.[9] Innocence drowning, the clash of love and kinship, Laertes and his warnings to his sister about her chastity, his desire to avenge his father, his family pride, and the odd sense of doom surrounding his relationship with Ophelia—such things figure in the making of Tom and Maggie. But it is Millais's vision of Ophelia's preeminence—the picture of her fate without any overshadowing or diminishment by Hamlet, or any implication of the greater importance of men and their concerns—that drives and helps to explain *The Mill on the Floss*.[10]

Millais's configuration, like Eliot's, reveals woman, love, sexuality, helplessness, the rich profusion of nature, the coming of death, fluidity, and tension between personal and impersonal life. The face is rapt, love-struck, expressive of desire and even quiet ecstasy; the hands and underwater arms gesture with openness, ready for communication and embrace; the posture of the form could be that of a woman during, or ready for, intercourse. But she lies in a liquid grave, not on a marriage bed. The upper part of her body shows precisely detailed, personal features, but the lower part of the body, submerged, indistinctly outlined, fusing with flowers, dress, water, and mud, remains mysterious, an undifferentiated part of nature, its full humanity denied, like the lower part of a mermaid. From one perspective, the expressive face and hands seem the epitome of human culture, unique in the field of nature the painting depicts; the appearance of the woman is startlingly out of place, like the appearance of the Virgin at Lourdes, but here a disaster. How does that refined figure relate to the setting? That she floats there in the passion of dying proclaims lonely fragility and failure.

From a different perspective, however, you might see a moving, beautiful suffusion of a self into the world. This graceful human being seems to grow out of the mud and water, like any other blooming thing. The water and the mysterious sexual underbody appear to mediate between nature and humanity, to relate and blend them. Ophelia looks like an earthborn flower in harmonious relationship with a pantheistic all. On her countenance, there is both madness and immersion in love. If it were not for the jarring appearance of the flesh of her left hand and her enchanting face in the midst of the pretty landscape, then her relationship to nature might appear soothing. Few artworks better illustrate the long-standing custom of the formal imagination to populate, personify, and equate bodies of water with lovely female beings.

But the picture, in its very appeal, demands renunciation. Like the novel, it's full of contradictions. The same figure shows both nurturing and destructive love. Look again at the Millais and you find morbidity. Beneath its uncanny beauty, the painting is deeply disturbing; imminent death is too pretty. It's as if you were shown a noble figure of human sacrifice, and then persuaded to focus on the innocence and the lovely features of the woman, rather than the horror of her fate.[11] It has something of the quality of a snuff picture for aesthetes.

That is the point. Millais's painting shows that his times are out of joint. It not only insists on depicting the victimization of Ophelia, it also gets subtly at the complicity and acquiescence—even in the figure herself—to such victimization. Though the artist creates a distinguished portrait of great sympathy and appeal, he is portraying both madness and suicide. He imagines a prodigal and melancholy waste. A death wish haunts the picture and, as Eliot shows, the Victorian sensibility out of which it grows. The woman is mortally objectified. (The aesthete Philip Wakem's words to Maggie, "I shall make a picture of you . . . —you, among the Scotch firs and the slanting shadows" [V, I, 267], could be the caption for this Millais.) The moral hope of the painting is that the skill of the artist, the malleability of the artistic tradition, and the collective process of art can rescue and diffuse the potentially sweetening influence of such an Ophelia for others. She is above all an image of love, a sign of love—but not a model for love. And in the light of Millais's portrait of her sacrifice I see the impossible love of Maggie Tulliver.

IV

Most serious readers of *The Mill on the Floss* have found it a flawed work of very great power. Its structure is skewed, as Eliot noted, too much time being spent on Maggie's growing up, not enough on her experience as a young woman. "Dissatisfaction with the catastrophic ending," says Gordon Haight, "is almost universal."[12] The flood that allows Maggie to save Tom, renew her childhood love, and die with him in an apotheosis of self-sacrifice is so obviously an overdetermined wish fulfillment and a way out of Eliot's dilemma about what to do with Maggie that it ruins the end as plausible mimesis. Nevertheless, at some

level, the novel, including its ending, which everyone remembers, works. Its
force comes from the basic issues about desire and love that it raises, the relent-
less logic of its dominant imagery, and its vision of sacrifice. Though it makes
little sense in the end as realism, as a parable of particular faith—why it exists
and what it demands—it has great rhetorical power.

There is a disjunction in the novel between the narrator's equanimity and
Maggie's smoldering rebelliousness and hunger for male approval. So much of
Maggie, we know, comes out of the experience of Mary Anne Evans that a major
question becomes, how did the wise narrator who identifies with Maggie in the
first chapter develop out of this resentful, brother-crazy girl? How, to put the
question in her mentor Wordsworth's terms, does the unhappy, doomed girl
become the mother of that contemplative woman whose creative text, with its
"mother tongue of . . . imagination" (I, V, 38), is pregnant with the largeness,
the fertility, and the meaning of the world?[13] One unavoidable answer is that
Maggie had to be renounced and sacrificed. Eliot repeats her dialectical formula
over and over: stressing relationship, renouncing the object of relationship, and
then finding a medium, symbolized by various forms of moistness, for diffusing
the experience of relationship into the wider world. A less abstract way of putting it would be to say she casts off former selves and relationships into the flow
of her fiction.

One of the achievements of this novel is that the narrator conveys how much
she cherishes and feeds upon the memory of Maggie's early life while making
clear how oppressive that life really is (was). Great strain exists between the
twin necessities of wholeheartedly relating to and renouncing the past, between
understanding and incorporating it on the one hand and transcending it on the
other. For Dickens, the story is the integrity of the writer and the child; for
Eliot it is the distance between them. And yet the parochial girl in the narrow
world of her perception and the author with her spacious discourse and consciousness *are* intimately related. Three pivotal scenes establish the fluid identity of Maggie and the narrator:

1. In the first chapter George Eliot defines her persona as an eloquent, farseeing visionary, but also as a dreamer whose imagination breeds in absent-
minded reverie. The opening panorama of the water, the world, the mill on the
Floss, and the little girl with whom she empathizes—a magnificent, brooding
evocation of love for the very *being* of things—turns out to be an armchair
dream of a narrator who, before her dreaming imagination took over, was going
to begin her story.

2. In the fifth chapter, at a high point in her childhood, Maggie goes fishing
at Round Pool with Tom.

He threw her line for her, and put the rod into her hand. . . . But she had forgotten all about the fish, and was looking dreamily at the glassy water, when Tom said . . . "Look, look Maggie!". . .

Maggie was frightened lest she had been doing something wrong, as usual, but presently Tom drew out her line and brought a large tench bouncing on the grass. . . .

"O Magsie! you little duck!" [I, V, 36–37]

This is the moment, except for the ending, of Tom's greatest affection for her. We later see, when she grows up to be beautiful, that this epithet establishes her as the ugly duckling who becomes the swan. But the "little duck" also establishes her kinship with the narrator, whose "I am in love with moistness" is followed directly by "and envy the white ducks that are dipping their heads far into the water" (I, I, 8). Ruby Redinger[14] has shown convincingly how this scene and the variant on it that Eliot made the heart of her later sonnet sequence, "Brother and Sister," fused her love for her brother, her capacity for loving the world, her creative imagination, her daydreaming, and her guilt.[15]

3. When Maggie grows up, she floats unconsciously in a boat with Stephen past their destination into the wide water of passion and fate: "Every influence tended to lull her into acquiescence: that dreamy gliding in the boat . . . helped to bring her into more complete subjection to that strong mysterious charm" (VI, XIII, 410).

In all three passages, Eliot gives us a figure in love—with moistness, with Tom, and with Stephen—gazing at the water, plunged abstractly in her imagination, who suddenly finds the object of her desire and whose drifting state of mind seems the same: "Look, while I was dreaming, I got just what I wanted— a fish and my brother's approval; a rich, handsome lover and sexual adventure; a way into a vision for a great novel."

Maggie and the narrator share patterns of reverie and resentment. *The Mill on the Floss* is a much angrier, much more militantly feminist book than has commonly been thought.[16] One of the first lessons Maggie has drummed into her is that boys are more important than girls. Even before we see her adoration of her brother, George Eliot has the father bemoan the fact that Maggie is smarter than the boy and say girls have no business being clever. Her bright bookishness just makes the father think, "It's a pity but what she'd been the lad" (I, III, 18).

Eliot's view of childhood, like Dickens's, is that the adult self is programmed to repeat the patterns of early experience. Thinking of the narrator and George Eliot, we can see how telling Maggie's defiant acts are in book 1, "Boy and Girl." Struck by "the picture of Jael destroying Sisera" (I, IV, 26), she drives nails into her red-cheeked doll to ease her fury. She also hacks off most of her own hair, shoves goody-goody Lucy into the mud, and runs off with the gypsies. These are parables. The famously tolerant and understanding writer reflects the girl. She took upon herself masculine authority, name, and role; told Victorian feminine propriety to go jump in the lake; and, taking up with freethinkers like Bray, Chapman, Spencer, Lewes, and the Pre-Raphaelites, she not only escaped to the gypsies, she lived to become their queen. But it's the doll, fictional fetish and primitive evidence of the metaphorical mind, that best shows her relationship to the girl. Maggie is to Eliot what the doll is to Maggie: a memorial image of deflected pain and sacrifice to the paralyzing, hopelessly muddled desire of girlhood.

V

The Mill on the Floss sympathetically portrays, but finally renounces, the incestuous nature of nineteenth-century familialism. In nineteenth-century art, where an implicit theme of sibling incest often appears, the Maggie-and-Tom story stands out along with the Sieglinde-Siegmund episode of *Die Walküre* as one of the most resonant expressions of incestuous feelings. Its very domesticity and tone of responsible moral striving make the sibling passion convincing as an important part of everyday life. We all know women who look for their fathers in men, and men who want to marry people just like their mothers, but we also know women and men—though the pattern gets less notice—who keep trying to love someone who could live up to the image of a beloved brother or sister. Eliot's coup was to go back to the homey details of *girl*hood to imagine the reason why such a thing might happen and what such desire might mean.

From the start, Maggie is mad about Tom. Why? We know Mary Anne Evans felt this way about her brother Isaac, but that just begs the same question. The answer that the novel gives is that Maggie's love for Tom is born from the need for complementarity, from self-sacrificing desire, and especially from admiration for power of various kinds. Maggie loves Tom for his *potential*, for being at the center of concern rather than on the periphery. He is the right sex, can do things she cannot, can go where she cannot; he is bigger, more mature. No wonder Eliot makes her a *tomboy*. In her imagination, to be with him offers escape from female impotence, even if she has to pretend to like what interests him. She hungers for close relationship, and she can identify with neither her father nor her mother; one seems too remote, the other too passive. But she learns to take Tom's part, to stick up for him, and to live, at moments, through him. One of the sweet secrets of love we discover is that it can seem to put us on the inside—or else the person we love and identify with seems to be inside, to belong, to be at the heart of the matter—and it is in childhood that we first learn what *does* matter. Says Tom to Maggie, "I always have half-sovereigns and sovereigns for my Christmas boxes, because I shall be a man, and you only have five-shilling pieces, because you're only a girl" (I, V, 32). If, as a paunchy statesman supposedly remarked, power is the best aphrodisiac, this novel points out why that might be so.

The sister's impetus towards sibling incest in nineteenth-century literature and life is a specific, if desperate, psychological strategy against gender liability and limit.[17] It shares with the incestuous impulse of brothers in nineteenth-century literature the will to defy and break with the past. It is also, like incestuous feeling generally, a sublimated mode of narcissism. In discussing *Great Expectations*, I said that the Victorian bias towards incest was a means of conserving energies and talents to develop one's society and, in fact, one's own inner circle; since the taboo against outright incest was so strong, it was a way of diffusing libidinous drives into what were considered culturally and morally constructive channels. But in *The Mill on the Floss*, the urge is anything but abstract: Eliot, calling the "need of being loved, the strongest need in . . . Maggie's nature" (I, V, 34), shows how the girl gets both physical affection and attention from the boy, though never enough. "[They] were still very much like young animals, and so she could rub her cheek against his, and kiss his ear in a random, sobbing way; and . . . he actually began to kiss her in return" (I, V, 35). This girl craves touch and the bonding of physical intimacy, which she associates with the brother. Eliot intimates a motive for the incestuous fixation in childhood in both her self and culture: in a repressive society, the polymorphous relations of children and their memory could appeal as a sign of sexual freedom and desire—compare *Wuthering Heights*.

Maggie as a child says, "I love Tom so dearly . . . —better than anybody else in the world. When he grows up, I shall keep his house, and we shall always live together" (I, IV, 28). As for him, he "meant always to take care of her, make her his housekeeper, and punish her when she did wrong" (I, V, 36). Note the irony here: the girl is always to keep the boy's house. Facing unsentimentally the insidious desires that power relationships reveal, Eliot represents their mutual attraction but their different motives. The little man wants a servant, dominance, and someone to nurture and torment. Maggie wants secure relationship and a structure of feeling and identity transcending the self; but there is also a hint that she—and all she represents—seeks and expects some kind of punishment and discipline for not being born male. Eliot, thinking of Isaac, was being very personal here, but the mutual wish for union and the tinge of sado-masochism in these candid desires no doubt express feelings common in Victorian life and afterward.

She has Maggie, feeling alien from the dominant "Dodson" part of her family, seize on Tom as a way of knowing and claiming her own blood and being.

The girl wants to appropriate what is foreign to her nature but part of her inheritance. She loves passionately what would complete her. Eliot explicitly makes Maggie and especially Tom—she, a "Tulliver," rash, magnanimous, imaginative; he, a "Dodson," conventional, scrupulous, moralistic, industrious, literal-minded, narrow, joyless, and grasping—stand for strains in English national life.

Relationship—"the large vision of relations," "the ascertainment of a unity which shall bind the smallest things with the greatest" (IV, I, 239)—is a project of Eliot's creative imagination. The narrator makes the point over and over that fascination with relationship cannot be separated from Maggie's love for Tom. Understand that relationship, its passion, history, and fate, and you understand vast life, as a scientist who understands the attraction of atomic particles understands the coherence of all physical being. Eliot's love for the world is incestuous, a love for, and an assertion of, the kindredness of the brother universe which is the Dodson being and spirit (endurance and law over idealism and mercy) writ cosmically large. In the narrator's ranging consciousness that claims knowledge of the workings, order, ties, and meaning of the world—surely Eliot's voice is one of the proudest and most presumptive voices in literature—we find a tone of the mediated narcissism and boundlessness of incestuous relationship: Eliot having intercourse with the meaning of things. The compulsive love that the girl feels for the brother, the literal desire for and embrace of the brother, become the author's embrace of the world through the metaphor and diffusion that they provoke. But that is getting ahead of the story.

What the children's romps and play on the moors are to Emily Brontë, or the child's longing for the mother's kiss is to Proust, the brother and his presence with Maggie about the water are to Eliot and her vision of love. Philip, Maggie's first lover, says to her, "[Y]ou would never love me so well as you love your brother." "Perhaps not," she replies, "but then, you know, the first thing I ever remember in my life is standing with Tom by the side of the Floss, while he held my hand: everything before that is dark to me" (V, I, 268). No words could make clearer the permanent fixation on the brother. That first memory holds the subjective link between love and water, with all its protean connotations in the "mother tongue of our imagination" (I, V, 38). It registers the traumatic nature of that first experience for both Maggie and the narrator. Moreover, if Maggie has the representative quality that Eliot claims for her, the words also make clear the obsession with childhood developing in her culture, the neurotic fixation on the past, and the growing belief in the erotic determinism of infantile experience.

No one, no other relationship, can replace Tom for Maggie. Even the intellectual and religious passion of her miserable adolescence—her discovery of

Thomas à Kempis, Christian humility, and self-abnegation—comes to her as "the voice of a brother" (IV, III, 255) with the right proper name. In the last two books of the novel, when the grown Maggie has her ill-fated romance, her brother seldom appears; but his influence is still decisive. After she and Stephen drift out to sea together and go on board the Dutch vessel, she has a telling dream: in a boat with Stephen, she sees a star that fades into the Virgin seated in Saint Ogg's boat. The boatman is at first Philip, but he turns into Tom, who rows past ignoring her; in her distress she capsizes, then awakes to find that "she was a child again in the parlour at evening twilight, and Tom was not really angry" (VI, XIV, 413). When she "truly" wakes, she determines to renounce Stephen and go back without marrying.

In the love scene between Maggie and Stephen as they drift down the river, Eliot writes of "the sweet solitude of a twofold consciousness that was mingled into one by that grave untiring gaze which need not be averted" (VI, XIII, 407). A moment of true love, it is nevertheless superseded at the end by her stronger love and bond with Tom. Again she is in a boat, and we get the triumph of erotic regression:

> It was not till Tom had pushed off and they were on wide water—he face to face with Maggie—that the full meaning of what had happened rushed upon his mind. It came with so overpowering a force . . . that he was unable to ask a question. They sat mutely gazing at each other. . . . [Eliot changed the word *looking* in her manuscript to *gazing*, which strengthens and makes clear the intended parallel to the boat scene with Stephen.] But at last . . . the lips found a word they could utter: the old childish—"Magsie!" [18]
>
> Maggie could make no answer but a long deep sob of that mysterious wondrous happiness that is one with pain. [VII, V, 455–56]

A sob of happiness that is one with pain?[19] That pun sounds like sex, like an indelible sadomasochistic strain in the novel—like an old-fashioned pornographic "deflowering" even; but in context, and from this author, it has the ring of felt religious passion too, and it also sums up the emotion of Maggie's entire relationship with Tom. Whatever the sexual implications of this passage, Eliot has obviously written it as a love scene to be compared to the one with Stephen. It fixes unmistakably Maggie's erotic priority in the novel.

VI

I recall a lyric from the 1960s about the ban on mentioning drugs in songs that said, in effect: "But if the radio won't play it / I guess I'll just have to lay it between the lines." The Victorian writers did that with sex. Though badly hampered, they did gain some distinct advantages, as we have seen, from the taboo. For one thing, censorship is a mode of looking for something, and what people seek, they find. The novelists became aware—and found ways to make readers aware—of how deeply sexuality permeates "ordinary" life and how erotic desire shapes perception. If there were no acceptable "site" for sex, then libido, as in a "harmless" dream, might be anywhere and everywhere. The boundaries between sexual and nonsexual activities become blurred when all physical eroticism must be implied and inferred. I want to stress a point that helps account for the power of fiction in the last two centuries: as well as explicit symbols to get at erotic life, novels might carry layered meanings and messages that depend upon unconscious intentions and wishes of *both* author and reader. That fluid subtext could make for intimacy in the reading process—something private going on between writer and reader which was full of meaning, but which could not be made public or perhaps even articulated. More and more, it appears that psychoanalytic understanding is the narrative-making child of that vehicle of communication, transaction, and transference which was and is the nineteenth-century novel.

In discussing erotic content and motives in *The Mill on the Floss*, we treat matters of importance, but ones that do not lend themselves to certain knowledge. We *must* speculate, but we can *only* speculate. Who can prove definitely that George Eliot meant Tom's sword practice, or the chapter title "In the Red Deeps," or Maggie's interlude on the water with Stephen, or the final climax to have direct sexual connotations, or that we are right to interpret these episodes in erotic terms? Nevertheless, I do want to maintain that she did and we are. Eliot is everywhere alive in her fiction to sensual delight and desire. She takes pains, as we have seen, to describe the physical intimacy of the little brother and sister. She grounds love in material reality, conveying throughout the body of her fiction the force of sensual appetites. Moreover, she has little of the puritanical bias against sex per se that Dickens and Thackeray often show; she seems more aware of the joys of libido.

Eliot's problem, in the portrayal of the erotic crisis that this novel dramatizes, is how to render such things as incest attraction or sexual initiation without actually mentioning them. She finds a metaphorical way, specifically in Tom's handling of the sword before Maggie at Stelling's school.[20] Tom, drilled by an old soldier, bribes him into lending his great sword. Just fourteen and wanting to prove his manhood, Tom takes it into his head to "astonish" (II, IV, 156) his eleven-year-old sister. It is a very odd scene, to say the least. He makes up his face and dresses like a Byronic hero, for example, the Corsair or the Giaour—a very un-Dodson-like thing to do.[21] When Maggie laughs at him, we get this:

Tom prepared for his master-stroke. Frowning with *a double amount of intention*, . . . he (carefully) drew the sword from its sheath and pointed it at Maggie.

"O Tom, please don't," exclaimed Maggie, in a tone of suppressed dread, shrinking away from him. . . . "I *shall* scream—I'm sure I shall! O don't. I wish I'd never come up-stairs!"

. . . Slowly he let down the scabbard . . . and then said, sternly,—
"I'm the Duke of Wellington! March!" . . . the sword still pointing towards Maggie, who, trembling, and with tear-filled eyes, got upon the bed, as the only means of widening the space between them. . . .
"Tom, I *will not* bear it—I *will* scream," said Maggie at the first movement of the sword. "You'll hurt yourself. . . ."
"One—two," said Tom, resolutely. . . . "Three," came more slowly, and with it the sword swung downwards, and Maggie gave a loud shriek. The sword had fallen, with its edge on Tom's foot. . . . Maggie leaped from the bed, still shrieking. . . . [Mr. Stelling] found both the children on the floor. Tom had fainted, and Maggie was shaking him . . . , screaming, with wild eyes. . . . In another minute she was sobbing with joy . . . —it seemed as if all happiness lay in his being alive. [II, V, 160–61]

Here, à la Wallace Stevens's blackbird, are thirteen ways of looking at this scene: 1) Behavior after puberty may reflect prepubescent behavior. 2) Sexual development in Eliot's world evokes thoughts and images of danger and violence: sex is frightening. 3) Sexuality is inseparable from displays of power, and the desires surrounding power and power relationships often grow out of particular relationships in families. 4) A pubescent boy, in the costume of Byron, haplessly wielding a sword to terrify and delight a bright, naive, emotional younger sister and impress her feelings and force his will upon her, bringing them both to faintly ridiculous grief—that could be a wise Victorian woman's metaphorical vision for the history of the sexes. 5) A girl or boy may learn her or his deepest and most long-lasting erotic lessons from the sexual behavior of a sibling; what seems erotically "right" and a pattern for the libido may depend upon a particular sexually charged experience with a relation. 6) Blood draws blood. 7) A comic little contretemps from adolescence may in fact be a trauma that shapes a whole love life. 8) Phallic pride can be very silly. 9) Broad sexual and social patterns of great weight and consequence often show up in apparently trivial incidents of commonplace lives. 10) Sexual imagery eroticizes Victorian fiction. 11) Victorian novelists found ways to talk about sex, and the language and methods that they used could be, as Eliot's are here, both very crude and very subtle. 12) The primal erotic desire in this novel is for connection, and connection is reached through suffering and trial, not pleasure. 13) One more subjective observation: you may try to win your love by telling her you'll do anything to make her happy, but she may be longing to hear, "I'm the Duke of Wellington! March!"

VII

Blocked from anatomy, Eliot, like so many Victorian writers, describes landscape amorously and draws implicit comparisons between it and the erotic body. Maggie haunts "the Red Deeps," the fertile area of hollows, mounds, and beautiful foliage, in her seventeenth year when she comes into her womanhood (Tom had introduced her to this area as a child [V, I, 260]). It is a place of secrecy and vague shame but also of exciting new experience—the location of first adult love. Here she holds rendezvous with the son of the family enemy, aesthetic Philip Wakem, who falls in love with her and for whom she comes to care lovingly.

The Red Deeps episode conveys the intense incestuous pressure of Maggie's—and Eliot's—world. Philip, alienated, all mind with a twisted body, brings to Maggie the joys of intelligence and rich liberal culture. Loving her beauty and idealistic kindness, he gives her more understanding and affection than does anyone else in the novel. Her attachment to him is a way of opening up and learning, of breaking out of the blinkered Dodson life into an engagement with the future. But the past recaptures. This couple brings home the irony in starting up what is called in our time "a new relationship."

Lovers sometimes look into their beloved's eyes and see those eyes years off looking back at some distant familial figure who looms larger than they ever will. Maggie tells Philip "what a dear, good brother" (V, III, 287) he would have been and how he loves her as she always wanted Tom to love her. Poor Philip, confused, says he will not give her up unless it is true that she only cares for him like a brother. She replies, in essence, *that's how I do care for you, and what more could you want? If I love you like my brother, that's as much as I can*: "What happiness have I ever had so great as being with you?—since I was a little girl—the days Tom was good to me" (V, IV, 294).

A brooding, unspoken reason for the fear and censoring of sex in Victorian fiction and life was the dread of premarital pregnancy. In Eliot's *Adam Bede*, it is just this figurative area of the red deeps where Hetty Sorel gets in trouble. One goal of the moralized, desexualized spirit of incest is surely birth control. Tony Tanner, thinking of *The Mill on the Floss*, writes, "There are cases when the bourgeois novel avoids adultery only by permitting and even pursuing something that is very close to incest." [22] When we think of the bastards and fallen women in Eliot's novels, "pregnancy" rather than "adultery" might be the more appropriate word.

The incestuous bias, however, goes wrong in this novel. It controls desire all right, but it skews it in perverse ways so that it fails to fulfill its cultural purpose—to promote marriages of positive filial feeling and kindred responsibility. It moves from social purpose to a metaphysical dead end. The familial system works to keep Maggie from red-deep activity; Tom, insensitive and self-righteous, intervenes brutally, using coercion and kin loyalty to break up Maggie's relationship with Philip. Eliot imagines for her the get-thee-to-a-nunnery treatment that a latter-day Ophelia might expect, but obviously the brother is a much greater threat than the supposed seducer. The centripetal force of Tulliver-Dodson life works against the liberating, progressive forces of free inquiry and tolerance that might bring to the family the resources and flexibility it needs to survive. Instead of concentrating power in the family and family ideals, as it was supposed to do, the incestuous bias in this novel dissolves the future of the family.

The sibling incest impulse, where it has reportedly flourished—for example, among deities, Egyptian royalty, exotic tribes, Romantic poets, hillbilly half-wits, and in Victorian culture and novels—seems to have a built-in bias towards the male: the sister, either hoping to abrogate feminine disability and identify totally with male ambition and power, or else somehow coerced into making herself one with the male, typically loses herself in the brother; the male makes the sister contributing subject to his power (cf. the Wordsworths). A bitter ex-change exposes terrible sexism: when Tom smugly criticizes her, she says, "[Y]ou are a man, Tom, and have power, and can do something in the world." He replies, "Then, if you can do nothing, submit to those that can" (V, V, 304). For a female, the genesis, appeal, and failure of loving one's brother both as oneself and as a mate all pulse in those words.

Maggie, strangely silent while Tom berates and bullies Philip, bursts out with a startlingly naked form of speech: "I have promised, I have vowed solemnly, that we will not have any intercourse without my brother's knowledge" (V, V, 303). Later, though, when alone with her brother, she attacks self-serving "moral-majority" presumption—that perennial outrage of dirty pots calling kettles black. She seems to break Tom's hold over her, asserting her sympathy for the artist-intellectual Philip.

And yet—an ironical "And yet . . ." is how this chapter ends: "And yet, how was it that she was now and then conscious of a certain dim background of relief in the forced separation from Philip? Surely it was only because the sense of a deliverance from concealment was welcome at any cost" (V, V, 305). Philip is compared to a "cloven tree" (V, IV, 293). His trunk is not sound. They cannot come together physically. Earlier Eliot describes how Maggie, at the end of one of their trysts, "stooped her tall head to kiss the pale face that was full of plead-ing, timid love—like a woman's" (V, IV, 295). She is assuming the masculine role, and Eliot's language shows telltale gender anxiety as she unconsciously disdains the feminine in the man. Loving Philip means sacrifice, and that tem-porarily pleases her religious nature. But she has a prior engagement. The hold of the Red Deeps, the reality of erotic attraction and sex, matter to her, try though she will to suppress them, and she associates them first of all with Tom.

Tanner, referring to brother-sister relationships in fiction, including this novel, writes, "This desire to replace the problematical contract of man and wife with the intrafamilial union of brother and sister reveals a latent, if faint, yearning for an incestuous relationship to avoid an adulterous one."[23] That is an illuminating remark, but with regard to *The Mill on the Floss*, it gets things backwards. The nineteenth century, as we have seen in Dickens and Thackeray as well as Eliot, promoted familial love shorn of sexual content for social and moral good; it was, however, asking too much to expect erotic repression to be successful. Sexual envy, desire, and jealousy would inevitably color family relationships. Maggie's need and longing for Tom's love is the primary desire for relationship in the novel, and her yearning for a clandestine affair and even a possible marriage with Philip, and later for a semi-adulterous, passionate liaison with Stephen, would seem to be reactions against the sin of incestuous impulse. The psychology of this novel shows how incestuous feeling and its inevitable frustration might provoke adulterous yearning and behavior: the image of Tom blots out Philip and leaves the way open for Stephen, whose force resembles Tom's.

VIII

Maggie's romance with Stephen has provoked critical disapproval and moral outrage, but it is one of the novel's successes, a well-wrought episode about falling in love and the thrill of sexual attraction. Its seeming dislocation—like most surprising outbreaks of eroticism—is only superficially arbitrary. All the life that Eliot has imagined for Maggie has prepared her for this affair. Her sensual nature which leads her to regard her engagement to Philip as duty rather than desire, her naiveté, her susceptibility to touch, and her need to attach herself to male power, come into play. So do Stephen's looks, manner, talents, and position, her resentment against provincialism, her fascination with the forbidden, and motives from childhood that might push her to take Lucy Deane's lover away. In fact, with its sexual tension, its feeling for the vertigo of eros, its public settings filled with music and dance, its aura of glamor in the otherwise mundane life of an oppressed young woman, Maggie's love affair with Stephen stands as a classic expression of erotic desire in Victorian life.

Why has it not been so recognized? One reason is that it got Eliot into a dilemma she could only solve by the magic of the flood at the end, and that tends to wash the relationship with Stephen right out of mind. Another is that Maggie turns him down, denigrating his significance. Also the narrative turn and structure shocked readers: many felt that this love story did not belong in the kind of novel Eliot was writing in the first two volumes. (In fact Eliot carefully relates the experiences of growing up to Maggie's actions and life in the final third. The trouble with almost all biographies is that they cannot give us what we need to understand a life: two volumes of childhood for one of maturity.) Joined to that notion of imbalance, but more important, I think, was many readers' resentment at the assault that the last volume made on their faith in Maggie's innocence, the innocence of girlhood, and their own conventional judgments about erotic morality and behavior.

Some reaction to the grown-up life of Maggie Tulliver has the desperate flavor of the response to Freud's theories of infantile sexuality. Swinburne, for example, though he loves the novel, grows apoplectic on the subject. He shows, as more temperate reviewers and critics do not, how much is at stake in the Stephen-Maggie section: "The first two-thirds of the book suffice to compose perhaps the very noblest . . . of humorous prose idylls in the language. . . . But who can forget the horror of inward collapse, the sickness of spiritual reaction, the reluctant incredulous rage of disenchantment and disgust, with which he first came upon the thrice unhappy third part?" His prose gets funnier and further out:

> If we are really to take it on trust . . . , resting our reluctant faith on the authority of so great a female writer, that a woman of Maggie Tulliver's kind can be moved to any sense but that of bitter disgust and sickening disdain by a thing—I will not write, a man—[like Stephen Guest] . . . the last abyss of cynicism has surely been sounded and laid bare. . . .
> The hideous transformation by which Maggie is debased—were it but for an hour—into the willing or yielding companion of Stephen's flight would probably and deservedly have been resented as a brutal and vulgar outrage on the part of a male novelist. But the man never lived . . . who could make for the first time the acquaintance of Mr. Stephen Guest with no incipient sense of a twitching in his fingers and a tingling in his toes at the notion of any contact between Maggie Tulliver and a cur so far beneath the chance of promotion to the notice of his horsewhip, or elevation to the level of his boot.[24]

Part of the frenzy here comes from the fear of female sexuality—the idea that a nice girl could really grow up to be overwhelmed by desire and swept away by an erotically appealing, morally suspect man. Swinburne, like Tom Dodson (and like that other hostile critic John Ruskin, the unhappy husband in an unconsummated marriage to a woman whose relationship to John Millais was at first not all that different from Maggie's to Stephen), intuitively understands that the issue in this romance is sex, and he finds it shocking that that struggling tomboy should grow up to care about it and live panting in its tide, so to speak. Why must these feminine icons of sympathy, idealism, and faith have bodies and libido?

Deep resentment for the seducer is traditional, but exaggeration like Swinburne's shows that it is not only the act of seduction—taking advantage of a woman—that is despised; the very order of values of the lover who puts women and the enjoyment of love above all other concerns also maddens people. Stephen makes love his highest priority, which means a woman is the center of focus and being. Male chauvinism, sadly, even more than morality, first brought about contempt for "the ladies' man."

Eliot imagines that arousing and then starving a romantic, sensual girl's hunger for affection, as Maggie's relationship with Tom does, makes an outburst of physical eroticism not only plausible, but virtually inevitable. If Maggie were a case study, Tom's strength, robust nature, and condemnation of Philip's weakness would almost ensure psychologically that she would fall for Stephen or someone like him. The girl has no way out of her bind. The pattern of her life, formed on the model of incestuous desire and taboo, is relationship followed by renunciation; and for Eliot Maggie's is a representative life.[25] The early relationship is so strong that it stimulates erotic feelings, floods them with guilt, and paralyzes other relationships.

But that is in the long run. The only way out of the stifling atmosphere for certain temperaments like Maggie's is love and romantic passion. Eliot, in the Stephen section, does create a sauna of sensual innuendo and attraction, a miniature of that well-known Victorian world where the very censoring of impulse and speech eroticizes gesture and vision. Look at this libidinous description of Maggie's arm, as Stephen sees it: "Who has not felt the beauty of a woman's arm?—the unspeakable suggestions of tenderness that lie in the dimpled elbow, and all the varied gently-lessening curves down to the delicate wrist, with its tiniest, almost imperceptible nicks in the firm softness" (VI, X, 387).

Maggie's liaison with Stephen is sexual, though the literal facts of the narrative preserve the facade of her virginity. Eliot lays sex between the lines in describing their water journey. The spirit of that ride—its rhythms, its imagery, the changing emotional states of the two—and of its aftermath conveys irrevocable erotic experience. Eliot's problem was how to represent them making love without actually doing so—how to have sex in the novel without having it. What is fascinating is that the artistic dilemma is just like the depicted personal dilemma: to face the power and ineluctable presence of sexual desire and activity while suppressing them. Sexual fulfillment of desire must be shown by mood, by association, by image and metaphor, but it cannot be openly articulated; carnal knowledge is private, not public. What happens in the novelist's art is itself a trope for sex and its place in Victorian life: sexual acts take place, but polite discourse about them is renounced, and precise knowledge about sexual consummation is diffused with mystery. The heroine, the author, the society are fascinated by erotic relationship, but they hold sex in such awe that, like the ancient Hebrews with God, they are afraid to inscribe and pronounce its name.

Eliot renders the sexual intercourse (nice, ambiguous, proper Victorian word) of Maggie and Stephen, for those who care to infer it, by literally imagining stock phrases and situations that convey erotic transgression. For example, Stephen leads Maggie "down the garden path"; she gets "carried away"; they "go too far"; they "spend the night together"; they face "the morning after"; her "reputation is ruined." The mood of their voyage is one of sensuous abandon and sexual oblivion. The entendre in this episode is hardly even double. Trying to render sexual conflict, activity, satisfaction, even ecstasy—and to put them in rational perspective—all without directly saying sex: that challenges a novelist, and it brings home the high sexual tension and critical contradictions of erotic life that animate and disrupt Victorian texts.

Eliot here expresses an almost desperate longing for an existence in which sexuality would not have to be renounced: "He murmured forth in fragmentary sentences his happiness—his adoration—his tenderness. . . . Such things, uttered in low broken tones by the one voice that has first stirred the fibre of young passion. . . . To poor Maggie . . . they were like nectar . . . : there was, there *must* be, then, a life for mortals here below which was not hard and chill—in which affection would no longer be self-sacrifice" (VI, XIII, 411). This passionate desire, that a cultural frigidity would *not* be required of humanity, takes hold and must be recognized. It inspires, for good or ill, almost all of D. H. Lawrence's work, for example, as well as hundreds of other artists of the following century.

IX

Here is Eliot struggling to render the realm of Venus for Maggie: "[T]he clouds rolled off to the horizon again, making the great purple rampart and long purple isles of that wondrous land which reveals itself to us when the sun goes down—the land that the evening star watches over" (VI, XIII, 411). It is easy enough to parody such "purple" prose, as Joyce would do, and to commercialize it, as countless hacks have done, but it expresses the Victorian need and aspiration to talk about sex. Eliot needed to get this obsessive area of life somehow into the discourse of representation and, at the same time, to break simplistic formulas equating sex and sin. The intention behind such language seems to be to make sex beautiful by spiritualizing it and showing it as something more than gross physical desire. Her impatience with symbolism and sly verbal mediation, "O . . . that intelligence so rarely shows itself in speech without metaphor,—that we can so seldom declare what a thing is, except by saying it is something else" (II, I, 124), speaks for the myriad artists of all kinds who have filled their pages and frames with swords, pokers, mossy hollows, crackling flames, rampant horses, fireworks, and fadeouts after burning kisses, in order to render sex figuratively while keeping the option of denying its literal presence. The complaint also sums up a social and historical predicament, but it reflects too the pride of the author, weaver of connections.

Sexual intercourse, more than any other human act, is commonly marked by a forgetting and a shutting out of everything else, a collapsing of *before* and *after* into *now*. It sometimes brings an intimacy with otherness that for many men and women is the greatest they ever know. People have compared it to death and to heaven because, in its ecstasies, it can obliterate chronology and the alienation of normal consciousness. It becomes a real but alternative world, where self and the object of desire fuse in a spot of timelessness. But when the act is done, that other, public world and its troubles begin to seep into mind and flood it. Everyone recognizes this phenomenon, and its rhythm and pattern conclusively mark the sexual nature of Maggie's trip: "Behind all the delicious visions . . . there was the dim consciousness that . . . there were thoughts which would presently avenge themselves for this oblivion. But now nothing was distinct to her: she was being lulled to sleep with that soft stream still flowing over her" (VI, XIII, 412). The transparent but conventionally deniable eroticism of the prose bespeaks the quandary of a culture and a personality that cannot repress what they are required to repress, that must renounce what they do not wish to renounce.

Notice that Maggie does not really give up sexuality with Stephen until after the fact: what she gives up is marriage to him. Tom's unrelenting anger towards her makes no sense except as revulsion against sex. Who actually condemns Maggie? Only her brother and "the world's wife" (VII, II, 428), that fickle entity having no more substance than a morning fog. The other characters about her—her mother, Aunt Glegg, Philip, and even Lucy, her supposed victim—all forgive her and rally to her with support. It is certain, though unprovable, that Eliot rendered Tom's vehemence because her own brother Isaac severed ties with her when she moved in with George Henry Lewes, a married man.[26] Tom's "repulsion towards Maggie . . . derived its very intensity from their early childish love" (VII, III, 437). In other words, Tom's rejection is based on incestuous jealousy and taboo against sex, and on an actual case of disapproval of immoral sexual behavior by Victorian standards.

In starchy religious circles, *The Mill on the Floss* was considered sinful. Girls in strict families were not allowed to read it. The sex-fearing knew eroticism when they read it, and no casuistry on Eliot's part, no pretense at maintaining the letter of Maggie's sexual purity could obscure for them the spirit of sexual consummation in the abortive elopement, or the novel's heterodox purport.[27]

It would be hard, now, to deny that the last part of the novel, with its erotic emphasis and crosscurrents, is, in implication and effect, an affront to Victorian moral orthodoxy. And in it the critical appeal to George Eliot's imagination of breaking sexual taboos becomes obvious.

X

The ending is remarkable any way you look at it and full of very troublesome questions. What does it mean? What is the purpose of Maggie's continued renunciation? Why refrain from marrying a desirable man in order to wind up in the fatal but somehow happy embrace with the beloved brother? Eliot is trying to create a new image of sacrifice for the world, but there are too many strands of thought, too many conflicts and contradictory aims to allow for satisfying answers or a coherent, convincing resolution. No doubt Eliot's vision helped to shape the Freudian commonplace that all culture is built on renunciation, since it is a theme in this book and all her work; but what is being renounced exactly? Erotic love? Selfish desire? Impossible social pressures brought to bear upon hapless human nature? Incest? Obsession with the dominant male? An unworkable, historically doomed separation of the sexes? Soul-killing renunciation itself? Undoubtedly she would have loved to inscribe and diffuse for the common good all these things and more.

The conclusion reveals and reflects the oceanic cravings of erotic consciousness. In it we can plausibly read connotations of incestuous consummation. Here is the end when a huge mass of wreckage looms down on Tom and Maggie in the flood: "'It is coming, Maggie!' Tom said, in a deep hoarse voice, loosing the oars, and clasping her. . . . brother and sister had gone down in an embrace never to be parted: living through again *in one supreme moment* the days when they had clasped their little hands in love, and roamed the daisied fields together" (VII, V, 456; italics mine). The "supreme moment" marks the climax, and in context suggests the mood of orgasm.

Even Wagner, maestro of the romantic death wish in *Tristan und Isolde* and the wave of incestuous passion in *Die Walküre*, did not combine the two as George Eliot does here. In the moment of death, the peremptory human taboo on the oldest and what is often the most threatening sexual desire of all dissipates. This last embrace is an incestuous *Liebestod*[28] that combines the drive for sexual fulfillment with the enduring, lifelong influence of blood kinship, moral justification in eternity, and the end to the restriction of individual, separate consciousness that death promises.

The idea of a supreme moment here, the astounding claim of the narrator to know of both the existence and the contents of such a time, depends upon the erotic nature of perception. The concept of a "supreme moment" joins psychology to the biology of orgasm, and imagining such a supreme moment depends upon the metaphorical mind playing over erotic experience and longing.

Maybe the last scenes are a logical mess because, for any given person at any given time in history, love and its desires are a logical mess. Both George Eliot and Charlotte Brontë, for instance, in their most autobiographical novels drown representations of the men they loved best in life, identify with them in the moment of drowning, and diffuse their memories in narrative art that seems to depend on their power to transcend this very erotic fixation. At the same time their texts make it clear that to have their love appreciated, vindicated, and requited by these men who rejected them was, for both of them, by far the deepest wish and greatest blessing imaginable.

To recapitulate: The ending with Tom parallels the sexual ride of Maggie and Stephen; it and its tone seem close to an apotheosis of incestuous feeling. The last embrace has an electric emotional charge. Incest taboos mean that there are desires that must be renounced. With that renunciation or sublimation of desire for closer and closer bonding with relatives, the people first known, comes pain, conflict, complexity, and fate. An end to that renouncing emotion—the conflict between instinct and culture, between libido and morality—may be seen and felt as a great relief, but it may also mean the deluge. Eliot's psychological make-up drew her to create a flood that would merge both moral imperative and incestuous longing. A novelist who could render, drown, and dissolve both incest and the incest ban might work to transcend the stagnation of nineteenth-century emotional life and develop both erotic faith and the moral power of novels.

XI

In light of *The Mill on the Floss*, I want to reconsider briefly two features of nineteenth-century British fiction: the emphasis placed on familial relationships and the absence of depicted sex. Stress on kin closeness, we have seen, can stimulate incestuous impulses and so feed the moral imperative to suppress sexual feeling by censoring it; but the ban, and the diffusion of the sexual libido into the rest of life, may be much less evasive and distorting than we tend to think. Victorian literary custom, with its displaced sexual focus, its disguises and substitutions, may be a perfect symbol for the pattern and history of civilization in which repression and postponement of instinctual, immediate gratification lead to a species-affirming diffusion of desire and to some general measure of progress and cultural satisfaction. But neither the abstract good of the race nor sublimated pleasures can ever completely curb the drive to lose oneself in the rushing, joyful shake-up of sexual union, nor can they alleviate the agonies of loneliness.

Look how powerful the image and concept of embracing are in Victorian novels. I may have seemed to be saying that the embrace of Maggie and Tom, or earlier, the embraces between Pip and Miss Havisham and between Heathcliff and the dying Cathy, were symbolic sexual acts; but though they are, that is not quite all that I meant or even what I most want to convey. It may be that the reverse is closer to the truth and that sexual intercourse, as we commonly think about it and feel its significance (in the twentieth-century Western world at least) is an acted-out attempt and metaphor for what these fictional scenes of embracement try to represent: the passionate desire to create relationship, to find family with nature and impulse, to merge with the other and embrace the death of all otherness, to find a respite from renunciation, from particularity, and from conflicting wants and loves—in other words, the vital longing never to have been and never to be separate. These scenes and novels scream out what Victorian society and human nature have sometimes tried to muffle: the primal yearning to be at one with—and in—the body of another who is no longer another.

Eliot calls the last section "The Final Rescue," an ironic title but one that makes sense if we understand that drowning the merged figures and transmuting them to memory is, for that loving narrative consciousness, an imagined rescue from the power of obsession. Eliot seems to have needed and found catharsis in imagining that Maggie (so like Mary Anne Evans) on her watery "ride" (so like adultery) with Stephen Guest (so like John Chapman) was only rehearsing and imitating the final "ride" she wished most to take (so like incest) with Tom (so like Isaac Evans), a ride in which, at the moment of climax, she is alone in the dying physical embrace of her brother with no thought of anything or anyone but him and their past.[29] For her, as Leavis and others have noted, it is lovely wish fulfillment, "the dreamed-of perfect accident . . . the dreamed-of heroic act."[30] But Eliot sees and shows something else: compulsive devotion to the brother for such a girl means renunciation of the self and dissolution of personality. Maggie alive could never become George Eliot. The birth of the novelist rests on the sacrifice of the former self.

Eliot made the epitaph for drowned brother and sister—"In their death they were not divided"—the epigraph for the novel as a whole. The words, in which a union becomes an inscribed memory, are taken from the Bible (II Samuel 1:23) and claim continuity with the moral authority of the scriptural tradition, giving the text a religious cast. Human love supplants God's love in the novel, and Maggie, in the steadfastness of her love for her brother and in her final decision not to put her love for Stephen ahead of Philip's love for her or Lucy's love for Stephen, becomes a sacrificial emblem for erotic faith.

Or so Eliot hopes. Her creed seems confused. She does, in the end, mythologize Maggie, who after all causes great turmoil before her demise. No simple paragon, she is capable of loving three men at the same time and delighting in the sheer vanity of being lovable. What she can do is *embody* faith in the mind and memory of others. But in the moral scheme, her renunciation and death, the equivalent of a modern Passion, bring the power of the love faith to Philip, to Stephen and Lucy who come as a couple long afterwards to visit her tomb (as if it were a sacred shrine), and to the narrator, who seems to find in her watery fate the medium of transubstantiation whereby moistness becomes the blessed sign and substance of love flowing into the enterprise of the novel and the world.

XII

Philip Wakem's letter to Maggie (VII, III, 439–41), a clear testament of Victorian erotic faith, expresses the moral ideal of love that Eliot intended. In the language of religious conversion he tells her how her goodness and his love for her have become a new gospel: "in loving you, I have had, and still have, *what reconciles me to life. . . . The new life* I have found in caring for your joy and sorrow more than for what is directly my own, has transformed the spirit of rebellious murmuring into that willing endurance which is the birth of strong sympathy. . . . *this gift of transferred life* which has come to me in loving you, may be a new power to me" (VII, III, 440; italics mine).[31] The message is that love, like Jesus for some, saves.

Philip's creed, dispersing his bitterness, also offers an apparent way out for Eliot in dealing with contradictions in the narrative and her own ideas. Problematic though Maggie's erotic character might be, she would serve to inspire in others living faith in love. Renouncing her own love, as she *seems* to do, not only vindicates her but brings about her virtual canonization in a new faith.

The issues Eliot faces and forces, however, are ones that swirl in the modern experience of love relationships. When Stephen pleads with Maggie to put her faith in the present love they feel for one another, not in the vows of the past which they no longer believe in, she goes to the heart of the conflict for millions in the era since this novel was written—that is, the age of divorce: "the real tie lies in the feelings and expectations we have raised in other minds. Else all pledges might be broken, when there was no outward penalty. There would be no such thing as faithfulness" (VI, XI, 394). Being true to those who love you seems here to be the essence of erotic faith. Behind these words, though, you can sense the sacramental quality of erotic relationship giving way to the strictly secular, utilitarian basis for love and marriage. No-fault dissolution is hurrying near.

Only those who cannot see the critical social dilemma Maggie poses or Eliot's subtle characterization of her here would call her speech sentimental.

It seems right to me sometimes that we should follow our strongest feelings;—but then, such feelings continually come across the ties that all our former life has made for us. . . . If life were quite easy and simple, as it might have been in paradise, and we could always see that one being first towards whom. . . . [author's ellipsis] I mean, if life did not make duties for us before love comes, love would be a sign that two people ought to belong to each other. But I see—I feel it is not so now: there are things we must renounce in life; some of us must resign love. . . . Don't urge me; help me—help me, *because* I love you." [VI, XI, 394]

Her logic says that if people are to have faith in love, it must not appear to be changeable, capricious, or self-seeking; the person who believes most strongly in love must be willing to give up individual desire so that the general faith in love will flourish. Maggie elevates love—meaning a lasting attachment to others—into an emphatic belief worth sacrificing for.

But the speech, in its artistry, and Eliot, in her honesty, actually betray the rifts that were breaching the idealistic concept of erotic love. *The Mill on the Floss* offers both the sacrificial ideal and the sacrifice of the idealization of sacrifice. Maggie's refusal of Stephen does not have the practical moral purpose she claims. It smacks of futility. Personal erotic desire, in fact, taints Maggie's doctrine of renunciation and her treatment of Stephen. We have seen, for example, that before she renounces Stephen, she goes off with him in ecstasy. Even more revealing, however, is the fact that "that one being first towards whom" Maggie felt love, whom she first remembers, with whom a childish moment of union was a paradise, the thought of whom she tries so hard here to repress, is, as the narrator has taken pains to show, *her brother*. She really does fulfill her deepest individual erotic desire, and in all her moralizing and in her Christian stoicism, there lurks an incestuous motive. From another point of view, embracing the brother, whose whole being is renunciation, is embracing renunciation. To embrace the family is to embrace sexual taboo. One way of looking at Maggie in the end is to see her, like Millais's Ophelia, as a beautiful figure of sacrifice. Another is to see her, like that Ophelia, caught in the morbid wash of the past, dying in deceivingly attractive fashion for an irrelevant and suicidal ideal. Eliot knew better than anyone that clinging to the brother was death.

The trouble with idealizing love and with erotic renunciation is, of course, the sheer force of physical desire and the personal and social distortions that repressing or dismissing sensual need create. The world has accepted Stephen's hedonistic point of view rather than Maggie's, not just because the world is a sleazy fellow, but because what Maggie preaches (preaches, but does not exactly practice) is often just too hard for people and maims their natures. Philip plays a key role in the narrative contradiction. Maggie, who supposedly puts Philip's attachment to her and Lucy's to Stephen above the mutual love between Stephen and herself, assures herself that Stephen will one day go back to Lucy and marry her, but she has no thought of ever marrying Philip. Sauce for the gander is not sauce for the goose. His deformity haunts Maggie and the novel.

Why is Philip a cripple? Eliot based him in part on the deformed D'Albert,[32] an early admirer who first made her feel lovable, but that fact does not really tell us why she chose to make the most intelligent and faithful lover in the book a neurasthenic hunchback. She may have felt growing social dangers from the mind-body split and realized that spiritualized erotic faith, noble as it could be, might take distorted forms.

Philip, alienated freethinking aesthete, disdainer of machismo and the brutal materialism of his father, is a character whose significance goes far beyond the pages of this novel. Eliot has created a prototype of the fin-de-siècle and twentieth-century artist. Marcel Proust, like the narrator a devotee of involuntary memory, read and loved *The Mill on the Floss*,[33] and why not? A description of love-obsessed Philip seems to invent and characterize Proust and his work: "Jealousy is never satisfied with anything short of an omniscience that would detect the subtlest fold of the heart" (VI, X, 389). Love and personal relationship push Philip to become an omniscient narrator of the heart—as they did his creator and her distinguished follower.

Philip's letter touches on the attraction between Maggie and Stephen: "I believe now, that the strong attraction which drew you together proceeded only from one side of your characters, and belonged to that partial, divided action of our nature which makes half the tragedy of the human lot" (VII, III, 439). That both recognizes and primly deplores the power of sex over lives, but notice that it is his and not the narrator's expression. She never can mount much enthusiasm for asexual ideals—or neurotic men—nor does she ever deny the appeal of sensuality for Maggie. Philip finds Stephen crude, but adds, "[P]erhaps I am wrong; perhaps I feel about you as the artist does about the scene over which his soul has brooded with love: he . . . would never believe that it could bear for another all the meaning and the beauty it bears for him" (VII, III, 439). Victorian erotic desire is becoming aestheticized; the art of love, pressed into queer shapes, is becoming the love of art. Erotic faith is spawning aesthetic faith, Walter Pater, Bloomsbury, and Virginia Woolf on the one hand, and, on the other, sexual revolution and the reaction of a Lawrence.

XIII

The novel is full of the love faith, but it lacks erotic wholeness. The people Maggie loves—Tom, Philip, and Stephen—are one-sided: Eliot cannot finally imagine a viable love relationship, a life of integrity, or a vocation for her heroine with any or all of them. The vision of love that she desires can only come into being by somehow unifying the artistic moral intelligence and sexual force with the conscious memory and knowledge of the imperatives of the past. She, rather than Maggie, becomes the best emblem for erotic faith in the novel. In her own particular life, as in her century, the flourishing of love and the creation of novels go together.

Love is born in the hardness of the past, but love, though perilous, can sometimes dissolve the hardness of the past in the flow of consciousness—or such is the faith of the novel maker who, with Maggie's inundation somewhere in mind, utters, "I am in love with moistness." The intelligence that could imagine and compose such a phrase must have learned to perceive love and the inclusive relationship of things through the drowning and dispersal of many selves, many dreams, many righteous, misunderstood, martyred sentiments and affections.

The moral of *The Mill on the Floss*: we know nothing unless we know that we can drown in the past and in love—nothing unless we know the story, form, and relationship of erotic desire and love in our lives.

But, true as that is, it sounds somehow so pious and smooth compared to the perilous mystery that love is in George Eliot, that I want to end with one of those farcical, coincidental tricks that fate plays on dignity. How unlike Maggie Tulliver, after all, is that magisterial narrator of Eliot's fiction and that tough, demanding woman who pursued life and love on her own terms! After living happily in what was, strictly speaking, adultery with Lewes for a quarter of a century until his death, George Eliot, an older woman but still passionate, took a handsome young husband, John Cross, more than twenty years her junior. Over a lifetime, her role in the homely Victorian version of erotic myth evolved from Electra desiring Orestes to Jocasta wanting Oedipus. On their honeymoon in Venice, the new spouse of the author of Maggie Tulliver's libidinous drowning threw himself madly out of their hotel room into the Grand Canal, evidently trying to commit suicide. We will never know why or what the exact circumstances were when he plunged into that most romantic of settings.[34] Frivolously, I want to believe that hanging in the Adriatic air that night was the sentiment, "I am in love with moistness."

A gondolier fished him out, not seriously harmed. Within the year she died, and he lived to write her biography, a secular saint's life and a testament of his love.[35] The power of her writing, the power of her love, "the effect of her being on those around her," was "incalculably diffusive."

8 The Mirror of Desire: Anthony Trollope's *Phineas Finn/Phineas Redux* (1869–74)

Love is the principle of existence and its only end.
BENJAMIN DISRAELI[1]

I

Anthony Trollope wrote that "a novel can hardly be made interesting or successful without love" (*Autobiography*, XII, 192) because he did not imagine that *life* could be made interesting or successful without love. His own great novels *Phineas Finn* and *Phineas Redux*—as he insisted, they are two halves of one novel (*Autobiography*, XVII, 274)—render exactly what Leopold Bloom in Joyce's *Ulysses* says of love, that "for men and women" it "really is life."[2] Neither Trollope's words nor mine about them are quite so commonplace or sentimental as they may seem. He was a very worldly, ambitious man who could be found in clubs and offices, at hunts, or globe-trotting—someone very interested in power, success, work, and the functioning of patriarchal institutions, such as church and government; he was a shrewd observer and participant in the bureaucratic revolution that would change, then rule, modern life. If he says that the genre of the novel has become virtually inseparable from the representation of love and if he, as a writer, places the highest value on love, he is telling us important things about his world. He claims that the most consequential human relationships are erotic, and that the so-called woman's sphere of love matters as much as *or more than* the so-called male sphere of politics and vocational endeavor.[3] His fiction shows that, in fact, they are merging into one sphere. Nothing counts more in *Phineas* than love life.

It may help to understand the resonance of the novel if we think of it as central in the Don Juan tradition—that is, as a Victorian prose-narrative version of Don Juan, the myth that explores the history of an amorous man and treats the volatile social energy his shifting erotic desire sets loose in the world. Phineas Finn is carefully defined by his desires and by the desires he arouses in others, and the consequences of these mingling desires form the novel. The Don Juan myth stresses the public implications of sexual desire and the way society organizes relationships between men and women. At its core lies a basic conflict between license and repression, between personal and communal desires. It expresses the unresolved tension between the male ego's desire for unlimited sexual freedom and gratification and society's need to regulate sexual behavior and protect itself against the anarchy of exploitative sexual lust. Love, the emotion that conveys affection and intense valuing of another, and a sense of responsibility for the well-being of that person, as well as sexual desire, develops historically as a mediator in this conflict. Redemption of Don Juan only becomes possible if and when he can fall in love and find an erotic faith.[4]

Phineas Finn/Redux plunges into sexual politics and imagines what love means and how it works in a corporate society and particularly in the life of one reflexive figure. For Trollope the nature of being in love is dialectical and evolutionary, both personally and socially. It is intimate and private, but it is also insistently political, as Trollope makes clear by centering his book on Phineas Finn, a young politician whose love life and political career are inextricably bound together. And love again emerges as a faith. It is all that Phineas believes in at the end.

II

In Velázquez's *The Toilette of Venus* ("The Rokeby Venus," c. 1650; fig. 5),[5] you do not see the goddess face to face. Her luminescent young body, somehow both slender and voluptuous, reclining on a soft couch amid satin-rich, harmoniously colored materials, glows with beauty; but the averted pose does not allow direct *confrontation* with the visage and form of erotic desire. Instead, Cupid holds up a mirror, rather than a bow or barbs, and that vanity of love mediates her image. When you look at it, Venus seems to catch your eye.

The mirror and the merging of vision portray a conception of love as reciprocal process rather than fixed desire. They define intercourse as something more than a transaction of the flesh and suggest interaction rather than a static subject-object relationship. They tend to make love social, even political—a mutual watching, a fusion of multiple desires through vanity and all that the word *vanity* implies. The psychological transaction being depicted is amazingly complex and yet basic. In the artist's mirror, a narcissistic encounter takes place between the viewer's eye and the face of love. Since the title is *The Toilette of Venus*, Eros would seem to be holding the glass so that the goddess can see her appearance; however, the optics are such that she could only be looking at the spectator and not her own face. That must mean that the viewer is part of her "toilette," that is, part of Venus's milieu. Through the reflecting medium there is a continuity between personal vision and the vision of love. The painting proclaims love as at once a personal and a social deity, both creator and creation of humanity. In the milieu of this work of art, to be is to perceive and be perceived by love.

The capacity for reflection shapes humanity. In this painting, you can only see the features of love and desire where they are reflected; here reflection means that the head and the physique of love undergo division and a mutual displacement. The portrait of Venus sets up a dynamic reverberation between erotic subject and object. It implies a continual diffusion and re-fusion of desire. Love is of the body and of the mind's eye too. On the bed, just above the curve of the thigh and the erogenous crease, the glass shows a blurred, appealing representation of love's countenance. The picture separates the expression of love from the body of love, but places that expression very close to sexuality. Reflection has its focus just above the seat of amorous instinct.

Move in front of the picture, change position, and Venus's gaze will seem to follow you. The process of making out the features and the meaning of the expression seems ongoing, variable, and subjective. "We are all, each of us," says a critic, "left to fill in the features of the face in the mirror."[6] The love relationship always takes place through the instrument of reflection. The only way you can find out what love looks like is to perceive it vaguely in the tool of speculation which is controlled by desire and formed by art. The expression of love in this work is a mutual reflection. The mirror is the mirror of love and the mirror of art. It is a way of seeing. And in the structure of this vision of love, the form of reflection is the place and the means of dialogue. Stendhal, in a famous metaphor, called the novel "a mirror in the roadway."[7] In light of Velázquez, I see the nineteenth-century novel in general, and Trollope's *Phineas Finn/Redux* in particular, as the mirror of Eros.

Phineas is one of the remarkable achievements in English fiction, and "The Rokeby Venus" may help bring into focus its distinguishing qualities—its political erotics and its erotic politics. Both painting and novel put love at the center of life, represent it as a mediating process, and concern themselves with *image*. There is no essence of love, or of the self desiring love, without a reflected image. Image means social being, even if it comes out of narcissism. To have an image that you care about, to watch the image of the self and the self's deified desire, and to see the image of another—all that implies multiple focus, several points of view, and public identity: reflections of and on love. Reflect on the complicated subject of this painting and you can see it as ineluctably political as well as erotic—like Trollope's novel. The subject of the art is not only love and its beauty, but love's subjectivity: how love is seen, how it is defined and mediated, how it affects the viewer, how it informs vision and shapes identity.

"Venus," we said, takes the form of a woman, and, unlike most deities, she is most often depicted as, in herself, a beautiful object of direct desire. The erotic feminine divinity—more human and personal than most divinities—not only arouses desire but suggests the possibility of possession. Her sex and representation mean that the erotic has traditionally been conceived of as a province where active, devoted male desire for a woman holds sway. Love is womanly, but it is man who seeks venereal love. An ambiguity clings to the love goddess as she has usually been imagined; she is icon and emblem of generative force and desire, but a female also. "The Rokeby Venus" stresses the womanly nature of the figure over the supernatural; and, with the eye that catches the eye of the beholder, it conveys the idea of the female as active desiring lover. This *Venus* moves beyond the conventional erotic frame to suggest, with its reflexiveness, a supposed male admirer and devotee as the object of love. Just so, Phineas Finn gazes at Lady Laura or Madame Max with longing and devotion, but at the same time he has become the object of their active love and need. The implications in Velázquez's mirror of the erotic subject oscillating between the genders and of the focus of meaning as erotic reciprocity become explicit in Trollope's narrative.

Both painting and novel do their best to render the power of love. Cupid, holding the mirror, is the agent for focusing desire and making it mutual; but in this use of cultural artifice, there is always the possibility that reflection will shift and erotic connection be lost. Meeting another's gaze in Eros's glass is a lovely symbol for "being in love," but like that phrase, it suggests the possibility of being out of love when the focus changes. The soft flesh of the goddess, the highlights and shadows of the materials that surround her, the play of eye and thought, the mirror image and the separate body—all convey a fluidity of love and the erotic process, a fluidity that has much in common with Trollope's *Phineas* world. In love, in politics, in this picture, in the Phineas novel, the center of attention is always shifting, and relationships—between figures, between spectators and participants, between points of view—are dynamic.

Velázquez's painting conveys a sense of sumptuousness that often accompanies visions of love. Erotic desire and libido inhere not only in the flesh and reflection of Venus, but also in the luxurious trappings of red velvet, light satins, and dark mahogany. The place of love is not nature, but urbane culture, and the setting conveys a sense of the subtle relationship between economics and erotics that also comes through in *Phineas*. Both works amorously involve feelings and thoughts about class and wealth. "It was May now," writes Trollope, "the latter end of May . . . and the charm of London,—what London can be to the rich,— was at its height."[8] Here is how he sets a scene for erotic encounter in a drawing room: "It may almost be said that there could be no prettier room in all London. . . . everything in that bower was rich and rare; and there was nothing there which annoyed. . . . Two or three gems of English art were hung upon the walls, and could be seen backwards and forwards in the mirrors. . . . Phineas already knew enough of the art of living to be aware that the woman who had made that room what it was, had charms to add a beauty to everything she touched" (PF, LXXII). Trollope, like Velázquez, gets at the sweet voluptuousness of the world, but the world, sooner or later, means gender, politics, and money.

III

"The toilette of Venus": that is, the art of calling into play erotic desire, the eroticization of appearances, the preparations for love. Keeping in mind the spirit and the complex transaction of the "The Rokeby Venus"—what it suggests about the uncertain mediations involved in falling in love—I want to concentrate on Trollope's art in one specific scene, the first meeting between Phineas Finn and the foreign parvenu Marie (Madame Max) Goesler, the hero and heroine of the whole double-novel. The passage shows how important and culturally definitive a phenomenon like Venus's "toilette" becomes when imagined in particular lives and in the social processes of desire. When Phineas, at the cabinet minister Palliser's table, finds himself seated next to Madame Max (PF, XL), Trollope, like a skillful fashion reporter, lavishes a detailed description on her. This portrait makes clear how pervasive and various in Victorian civilization are the modes of stimulating desire, how suffused in subtle eroticism representations of that society are, and how complicated a role it is to act as both subject and object of sexual attraction.

She had thick black hair, which she wore in curls,—unlike anybody else in the world,—in curls which hung down low beneath her face, covering, and perhaps intended to cover, a certain thinness in her cheeks. . . . Her eyes were large, of a dark blue colour, and very bright,—and she used them in a manner which is as yet hardly common with Englishwomen. She seemed to intend that you should know that she employed them to conquer you. . . . She always wore her dress close up to her neck, and never showed the bareness of her arms. . . . [H]er apparel was so rich and quaint as to make inattention to it impossible. The observer . . . would perceive that Madame Max Goesler's dress was unlike the dress of other women, but seeing that it was unlike in make, unlike in colour, and unlike in material, the ordinary observer would not see also that it was unlike in form for any other purpose than that of maintaining its general peculiarity of character. In colour she was abundant, and yet the fabric of her garment was always black. My pen may not dare to describe the traceries of yellow and ruby silk which went in and out through the black lace, across her bosom, and round her neck, and over her shoulders, and along her arms, and down to the very ground at her feet, robbing the black stuff of all its sombre solemnity, and producing a brightness in which there was nothing gaudy. . . . And the lace sleeves of her dress, with their bright . . . silk, were fitted close to her arms. . . . And she had rubies in her ears, and a ruby brooch, and rubies in the bracelets on her arms. Such, as regarded the outward woman, was Madame Max Goesler. [PF, XL]

"The outward woman": the object of appraisal, the subject of provocation, she ambivalently reflects a tangle of desire—crass and sublime, direct and indirect, social and personal. She is both the created artifact of society and self-generated. The very existence of this creature of decoration means that certain aesthetic functions have been attributed to, and appropriated by, the female. She becomes metaphor and embodiment of color, riches, design, precious unique- ness, and fascination. "The outward woman" proves that there is no hard de- marcation between aesthetic desire, material desire, and erotic desire. She means and is meant to tantalize: Does the outward woman reflect the inner woman? Does the outside graceful beauty indicate something more, something that can only be had by erotically possessing such a being, and yet something beyond objectivity and physical possession? One of Trollope's insistent topics is the problematic relation between outer and inner life, the awful difficulty of know- ing anything about the inward life of any other person.

To put it in crude terms, "the outward woman" may rightly be seen as a sex object and a reification of surplus value, but only those who have never felt the tremendous rush of power, energy, self-esteem, and consciousness-raising po- tential that often comes from *being* the object of erotic desire, can leave it at that and miss the promising possibilities latent in Trollope's description. The thoughtful creation of the external woman indicates a subjective being, an in- exhaustible subject who thinks, who tries—and is socially coerced—to reflect the value of her inward self and her culture in her appearance, but who also tries to escape the secondary role of her sex and accrue power through imagination and intelligence. "The outward woman" may be the fixed object of description but also an active subject who describes and manipulates the desire of others.

Trollope also imagines "the outward man," and women who are interested in male beauty. Of Finn, he says, "Nature had been very good to him, making him comely inside and out,—and with this comeliness he had crept into popularity" (PF, XL); the appeal of "this comeliness" to women is what gets him into the exclusive party. People get ready for love by looking, listening, and talking. Phineas and Marie Goesler are set to begin their relationship amidst the vanity of society, and to reflect on each other in the mirror of dialogue.

Dialogue is what makes Trollope's fiction so subtle, so full of intelligent nu- ance, so much more sophisticated than the narrative commentary would sug- gest.[9] It assumes a high critical awareness for judging the consequence of a thing said. He usually leaves it to his audience to infer the full import of people's talk, and that is what sometimes gives his fiction the illusion of being unmediated. Nothing seems to stand between reader and character. Trollope understates the significance of his dialogue, and rhetorically this understatement works to put readers in the position of characters, trying to make out the immediacy of their world and the person before them.

The talk of Phineas and Marie generates feeling for one another and deter- mines the possibility of their falling in love. Through conversation and its gestures, Trollope makes us experience the outward personality and wonder about the inner psychology of each and the meaning of their interaction. The mirror of dialogue is where potentially erotic subjects and objects come into focus. Phineas, Trollope says, has two things near his heart at this point: political patronage and his suit of the wealthy Violet Effingham. Madame Max manages to touch on both. They begin by talking politics, and in words that suggest one of the great themes of the whole novel, she remarks,

> "The one great drawback to the life of women is that they cannot act in politics."
> "And which side would you take?"
> ". . . Indeed, it is hard to say. Politically, I should want to . . . vote for everything that could be voted for,—ballot, manhood suffrage, womanhood suffrage, unlimited right of strik-ing, tenant right, education of everybody, annual parliaments, and the abolition of at least the bench of bishops."
> "That is a strong programme," said Phineas.
> "It is strong, . . . but that's what I should like. . . . But then, Mr. Finn, there is such a difference between life and theory;—is there not?"
> "And it is so comfortable to have theories that one is not bound to carry out," said Phineas. [PF, XL]

That is refreshing talk in a Victorian novel. The outward woman comes with a mind, candor, a practical sense of female disabilities, ideas about politics and political progress, and shared vocational interests with men. And she exists and speaks in the context of personal, felt life. Phineas's irony could be male conde-scension and the smug platitude of a young ass; Madame Max, in more table talk, immediately tests him to find out what he is made of, addressing his su-perior:

> "Mr. Palliser, do you live up to your political theories? . . . Your House of Commons theories, I mean. . . . Mr. Finn is saying that it is very well to have far-advanced ideas,—it does not matter how far advanced,—because one is never called upon to act upon them practically."
> "That is a dangerous doctrine, I think," said Mr. Palliser.
> "But pleasant,—so at least Mr. Finn says."
> "It is at least very common," said Phineas, not caring to protect himself by a contradiction. [PF, XL]

In the odd arena of social intercourse, he touches her and proves himself by letting her put him in a bad light before someone on whom he depends, without bothering to protest or in any way embarrass her. Shortly after, she tests him again, knowing that he has fought a duel with Lord Chiltern over Violet. As this dialogue goes on, Phineas appears reasonably honest, but protective of a woman's (Violet's) privacy and feelings: charming, but somewhat young. He seems to have a lot of maturing to do before he can be a match for the worldly

Madame Max, and of course that is to be the plot of their extended relationship. Their whole long first conversation shows Phineas's talent for pleasing, his respect for women's feelings, and his ability to win their trust and to touch an erotic, maternal chord in them. Madame Max responds to a sweetness in him, youthful beauty, and signs of a gift for intimacy. He really does engage in dialogue with women, and that is why he is popular. The same could be said of his author.

IV

From Trollope's *Autobiography* it appears that Phineas Finn was a fantasy alter ego and a reflection of his desire. Phineas gets the affection from women and the easy access to Parliament that his author longed for. As a boy, Trollope felt himself deprived of his mother's love; and until he went to Ireland, his youth was an ugly duckling's floundering. What he wanted was to be a charming but good man and to move along the corridors of power among influential politicians and extraordinary women. He describes how, as a lonely adolescent and youth, he imagined for years ongoing tales, realistic in detail: "I myself was . . . my own hero. . . . But I never became a king, or a duke. . . . I never was a learned man, nor even a philosopher. But I was a very clever person, and beautiful young women used to be fond of me" (*Autobiography*, III, 37). Young Anthony told a jeering uncle, just at the time he was building his youthful love-castles, that he wanted most of all to be in Parliament (XVI, 250). Phineas is everything that Trollope wanted to be as a young man. Even what the *Autobiography* calls the "blunder" of making Finn come from Ireland and having him marry a "simple pretty Irish girl" (XVII, 272–73) looks like straight projection: Trollope was first appreciated in Ireland, married the Irish Rose Heseltine about whom he is almost mute, and came back from Ireland to make his reputation. Running together in Phineas Finn the character, in *Phineas* the fiction, and in Trollope the author are the fascination with love, with parliamentary politics, and with their connection to each other and to the novelistic imagination.

In the world of this novel, a lover is a politician. Both occupations are fiercely competitive, and require for success—besides lots of luck—the special skills of arousing interest, pleasing others, and sympathizing with them. That is also true of novelists. Like Trollope the novelist of negative capability, Phineas the character gives shape and definition to the figures he touches. They both seem to play the part of a wonderfully empathic audience that brings out the life of others. Think again of author and character in the context of "The Rokeby Venus": the artist has posed the female model so that her eye catches his and he seems an audience for her gaze. Audience, art, artist, subject, and the social form of love seem to blend and diffuse, join and dissolve easily in a remarkable, but unaccented, process.

Anyone—and no one better than Trollope—can see why faith in love can seem irrational. Love is often unrequited; violent passions—such as jealousy— surround it; it fades; people and desires change; sexual urges subside; marriage saps libido; men and women get tired of each other; the one you adore may whine, get fat, or lose a good job. You may fall in love, marry, fall out of love and resent, hate, or—even worse sometimes—ignore your spouse. Love, we know, can be a trap, particularly for women, who historically have taken their fate from the men they wed. Love seems to belong especially to youth, and youth's the stuff will not endure. All these calamities and many more befall lovers in *Phineas*. And yet, even in this novel that renders the disillusioning process of getting older, love—the outflow of sympathy and desire—stands as the best thing life has to offer. *Phineas*, like the genre of the novel in general for Trollope, exists to explore love, tell stories of love, and finally, unsentimentally, to affirm it.

Trollope names love as a necessary subject for novels "because the passion is one which interests or has interested all," and in doing so he proclaims the catholicity of both erotic love and the novel. He sees the historical debate about the moral and intellectual status of the novel as a quarrel about whether and how love should be treated in fiction and what erotic influence and consequences novels have (See *Autobiography*, XII, 186–94). He may write with a seeming matter-of-factness, e.g., "Very much of a novelist's work must appertain to the intercourse between young men and young women" (XII, 192), but he is actually asserting a faith and describing a rhetorical, moral instrument for its propagation.

> If the novelist . . . can so handle the subject as to do good by his handling, as to teach wholesome lessons in regard to love, the good which he does will be very wide. If I can teach politicians that they can do their business better by truth than by falsehood, I do a great service; but it is done to a limited number of persons. But if I can make young men and women believe that truth in love will make them happy, then, if my writings be popular, I shall have a very large class of pupils. [XII, 192–93]

Notice how love fuses in Trollope's mind with the novelist's calling, politics, and a pastoral vocation. In his art of love, desire is always political and has public consequences. He sees the evolving human condition as one and inseparable with a public and private dialogue featuring erotic desire; life and the novel are both a continuing synthesis of voices and erotics—often incongruous voices and erotics—within the community and within the self. A great advantage of the novel as a form, as Trollope discusses it, is that it is *popular*—that is, novels appeal to the public, influence the actions of the public, and *are* public. His novel focuses on love in the world, insists upon its contextuality, shows how love is mediated in the lives of several different kinds of characters by social circumstances.

The quality of life, for Trollope, is to be found, known, and judged in personal relationships, and he calls the novelist's vocation "the fabrication of love-stories" (XIX, 294). It has been said that "love is Trollope's favorite metaphor for what the novelist does and what novels ought to be,"[10] but the reverse of that statement is nearer the truth: the novel for him is a metaphor for love (in the same manner as, for some, a church is a metaphor for religion). In the Barsetshire series dealing with clerics, clerical families, and their love lives, you can almost see him—through the agency of fiction—disestablishing the Church of England and establishing erotic faith—or at least the Novel of Erotic Faith.[11] Such faith, however, as *Phineas* and the rest of his "Palliser" novels show, is hard won and very much a social, political phenomenon.

V

Being in love in *Phineas Finn/Redux* means desire, devotion, and consolation, but desire, devotion, and consolation of multiple, sometimes conflicting kinds. During the course of the novel, Phineas himself is in love with four women, Mary Flood Jones, Lady Laura Kennedy née Standish, Violet Effingham, and Madame Max Goesler; and all, except Violet, are deeply in love with him. And besides these figures Trollope imagines Lord Chiltern, Robert Kennedy, the old Duke of Omnium, Gerald Maule, Adelaide Palliser, Glencora and Plantagenet Palliser, and other figures, all in various states and stages of love. These loves play off one another—shape and reshape each other—forming the image of personality and society that emerges in the book. But Phineas is at the heart of erotic reflection in the text.

Desire, love, identity: Trollope imagines them running together in youth, but remaining fluid, not fixed. Desire may cause one to fall in love and find the self-image of a lovable identity reflected in the wide eyes of a beloved; and being in love may focus and define desire. *Phineas* obviously bears out the idea that in love, "the object serves as a substitute for some unobtainable ego ideal of our own,"[12] but it also shows that love choice may form the ego and the self. Love may change as the self changes, and if and when love changes, the self's ideals and goals may change too.

Let us look at Phineas Finn and some key passages in his love life.

No;—he was not in love with Lady Laura Standish. . . . He supposed that he was in love with his darling little Mary,—after a fashion. [PF, IV]

He had often told himself that he was not in love with Laura Standish;—but why should he not now tell himself that he was in love with her? . . . Simply as an introduction into official life nothing could be more conducive to chances of success than a matrimonial alliance with Lady Laura. Not that he would have thought of such a thing on that account! No;—he thought of it because he loved her. [PF, V]

Since he had heard that Lord Chiltern was in love with Miss Effingham, he did not like Lord Chiltern quite as well as he had done before. . . . It was not that Phineas was in love with Miss Effingham himself. As he was still violently in love with Lady Laura, any other love was of course impossible. [PF, XVII]

He was thinking of his life, and trying to calculate whether the wonderful success which he had achieved would ever be of permanent value to him. . . . And then he thought of Violet Effingham, and was angry with himself for remembering at that moment that Violet Effingham was the mistress of a large fortune. [PF, XXXII]

He felt that he had two identities,—that he was, as it were, two separate persons,—and that he could, without any real faithlessness, be very much in love with Violet Effingham in his position of man of fashion and member of Parliament in England, and also warmly attached to dear little Mary Flood Jones as an Irishman of Killaloe. [PF, XXXV]

Then there came upon him a sudden ambition,—that he would like to "cut out" the Duke of Omnium in the estimation of Madame Max Goesler. [PF, XLVIII]

Phineas was not in love with Mary Flood Jones; but he would have liked to take her in his arms and kiss her; . . . he would have liked to have an episode. [PF, L]

Now,—now at this moment, he told himself with oaths that he had never loved any one but Violet Effingham. [PF, LIII]

"Love [says Phineas to Mary] is involuntary. . . . I have told you my history as far as it is concerned with Violet Effingham. I did love her very dearly. . . . Is there any inconstancy in ceasing to love when one is not loved?" [PF, LXVI]

But, after all, Violet lacked that sweet, clinging, feminine softness which made Mary Flood Jones so pre-eminently the most charming of her sex. [PF, LXVIII]

Phineas Finn . . . was very sore and unhappy at this time, and . . . consequently was much in love with purity. [PR, XLIV]

"I have come to tell you [says Phineas to Madame Max] that I love you." [PR, LXXIX]

Trollope is dealing with that loaded social subject—more relevant than ever for moderns—the reality and practice of serial love, and he wants to treat the changing, developing erotic life of Phineas frankly, and without satire or facile moralism. If Phineas were merely a caddish adventurer, his love history would be amusing, but easy to dismiss; and if he were simply faithful to one being from start to finish, we would not know the erotic politics and tensions in Trollope's world. He shows how the nature of love changes in one man's experience, but he is also showing, through Phineas, who is both the desiring subject and the catalytic object of others' desire, how the nature of love might change in the world.

Proverbially, timing in love is everything, and this famous timing depends on how desire sparks in the milieu of a potential lover and beloved at a given moment. For instance, after Violet finally rejects Phineas, he soon finds himself in Ireland under the loving eye of Mary, and he proposes. Madame Max offers herself to Phineas, but not until he is engaged to Mary. Later when he and Laura, who loves him, are both widowed, he sees her in her faded state just before he meets again the vibrant Marie. A variegated love life signifies not only the force but also the chronology and breadth of desire.

Exploring through Phineas the consequences of active male desire for women and what they represent, Trollope also renders active female desire encountering in Phineas male passivity. The women project their desires onto him and read them as his character, for example, political promise for Laura, sincerity for Madame Max. Phineas, reflector *of* and *on* desire, is one of the most delicate portraits of a lover in Victorian fiction.

Being in love for him offers opportunities, as it does for others, to fulfill his desires. As Dickens shows with Pip, the love object becomes both the embodiment and metaphor for what he wants, and a means to get it. Trollope, in the passages I cited, is sometimes making ironic fun of Finn's unconscious self-seeking and self-contradictions in love, but the irony is not simple or aimed merely at youthful callowness. Love, meaning many things, some of them contradictory, is itself ironical. Phineas, the good-natured, ambitious provincial, wants knowledge of the world, promotion, and success. He wants to stand well in the eyes of others—to have what they desire—and he wants to merge with that which is pleasing in his surroundings, whatever they may be. He wants the political independence that money can bring him, and he wants very much to be good—to have moral integrity. He also wants possession of another and unconditional love. He wants, among other things, respect, constancy, variety, pleasure, sexual gratification, and continual assurance that he is lovable.

For Phineas, being in love with Laura Standish offers the chance for power and advancement; being in love with Violet Effingham offers a chance for wealth and independence; being in love with Mary Jones offers an opportunity for unconditional love and devotion, for nearly absolute power over another, and for vindication of personal honor and integrity; being in love with Madame Max offers the chance of winning wealth, approbation, intelligent and joyous companionship, and the elegancies of cultured life. Winning each would also mean to him getting something, or attaching himself to qualities, that others desire.

VI

Phineas wanting to rise, in the first half of the novel especially, reflects the reason for political agitation in his world. Love is a way of advancement and a sign of personal distinction. Trollope is a master at describing mimetic, triangular desire, the desire that imitates the desire of another lover in order to appropriate for the self the qualities of the desiring other.[13] He carefully plots Phineas's erotic history and rising ambition by giving him a specific rival for each of the women he loves, and these suitors, each of whom triggers in Phineas a competitive will to win that particular woman's love, have an ascending social prominence. One reason why Phineas wants to win Violet from Lord Chiltern, and Marie Goesler from the Duke of Omnium, is that he imagines the qualities these nobles have—power, rank, influence, and sexual magnetism—and conjoins them with the women they love.

Mimetic desire, as Trollope renders it, proves the triumph of individualism and the political force of the ideal of personal success. It flows out of a world, the historical world of Victorian individualism, where erotic love, meaning the possession of the affections and the person of the beloved, can be the sign and essence of personal success—like the direct accumulation of money. Trollope's personal history with his mother, who slighted him and admired his older brother, may have led him to displace a very strong sibling rivalry into Phineas's competitive erotic life; but what is striking about this triangular desire in its political context is that it lets us see how such concepts as sibling and Oedipal rivalry, or love choice as metaphor for missing ego-ideal, might come into being as displacements and projections of an ideology of competition. Dickens and Eliot insist on the shaping of love by the familial past, but Trollope renders love as a longed-for mode of transcending the past. Where love is both a prize in life and a way of competing in the social order, there theories stressing erotic rivalry and value-seeking will abound. Love is, among other things in Trollope, the extension of individualist politics and diplomacy by other means.

Moreover, though love, meaning the mutual requital of desire and affectionate concern, can be an end in itself, behind the manners and decorum of the pursuit of love and beyond the beautiful settings that appear as both the bowers and rewards of love in the novel, there lies the same potential for violence, the same sort of determined, sometimes ruthless conflict of wills that exist in political and economic life. Trollope wrote *Phineas Finn* in 1867, when public opinion caused the second Reform Bill to be passed, and everything in both parts of the novel takes place against a background of social agitation and the impetus for democratic individualism. Things threaten to get out of hand. A rather matter-of-fact passage gives an idea of the pent-up, assertive emotions abroad in the novel's world.

> When Phineas got back to London . . . there was already a great political commotion. . . .
> Phineas . . . found that the town had been in a state of ferment . . . and that the police had
> been forced to interfere,—and that worse was expected.
>   . . . In the course of the evening three or four companies of the Guards . . . had some
> rough work to do. . . . and before the night was over all the hoardings around the new

Government offices had been pulled down. The windows also of certain obnoxious members of Parliament were broken. . . . One gentleman who unfortunately . . . was said to have said that the ballot was the resort of cowards, fared very badly;—for his windows were not only broken, but his furniture and mirrors were destroyed by the stones that were thrown. [PF, XXV]

What's love got to do with it? Almost everything. The driving social energies, the will to equality, the expectations and drives for *entry* and *access*, the passionate hope that one may "count" as much as another and that life can be reformed so as to bless and dignify the individual—the political realities that such a passage shows—reflect and are reflected in Phineas's erotic desires and those of other characters as well. He is part of a process of movement towards greater equality and a lessening of class distinction.

Whom you can love and whose love you can win tell you a lot about the political realities of your world. Shakespeare's Malvolio makes a fool of himself in loving Olivia, but middle-class Phineas, with no wealth, can aspire to marry a nobleman's daughter or a rich heiress. Love can become a matter of personal wooing and choice in the new world of individualism; in fact the stress on the pursuit of happiness through love is one of the chief and defining characteristics of individualism. Where people can go, there they can fall in love, but you can only be in love with someone you can meet and see: if Phineas can go to Lady Laura's home, he can propose to her. His desire and successful efforts in getting through the doors of the aristocratic and the rich mirror the desire and efforts of reformers to open up doors of equal opportunity.

Politics, for Trollope, ought to be an art of the possible, an art of conciliation and successful improvising that opens, or keeps open, the possibilities of betterment for people.[14] He imagines Phineas as a politician of love, not love's priest or soldier. In the first half of the double-novel, Finn competes for love, but if he does not find it requited, he recovers and moves on until he succeeds; he is touched, but not corrupted, by vanity. An ingratiating, talented member of Parliament and the government, he is, despite flaws, an honorable figure who, in both politics and love, can keep his word under temptation and bounce back from failure with a generous spirit. Whether he wins or loses in either, he is a progressive who does not get stuck. In Trollope's unsentimental vision, erotic desires, like political ideals, may be compromised—in fact, they almost certainly must be—but that does not impeach love as a faith (not, that is, for a man) any more than the conciliation and trimming that build coalitions in politics dim faith in social progress.

In *Phineas Redux* Trollope's vision is darker. Love is all that sustains faith, but it is not first love and it comes out of politically mediated desire that seeks an efficient and intelligently accomplished woman who has been around, rather than a young virgin. Phineas now reveals also, though not as fully as the female characters, what René Girard calls "metaphysical desire,"[15] the desire for transcendence from the material self and physical longing, a transcendence that lovers sometimes identify with a love choice. In the latter part of the novel, Finn, disillusioned and almost driven mad, needs to find and prove through love moral value in the world. Phineas decides that if he died there would be no gap in any man's life—not an uncommon thought (PR, LXXVIII). Only women, he thinks, only those he has loved, would care. The question of what will remain of your life, and where and in whom something of it might stay, has a way of focusing values and faith—if you can find any. The implicit belief that Trollope gives Phineas, that he is permanently connected to humanity only through love, has become a very common one.

I want to stress how Finn the outward and inward man shares, reflects, and assumes the desires and traits of his different loves. According to Trollope, to generalize from Finn, a person is both a product and a continuing process of sexual politics and the interaction of the genders. That reciprocity makes for the richness of Phineas's understated character, but it also shows a dialectics of gender operating in this political novel. It is as if Trollope were rendering the women as personified emotional colonies out of which the male draws the raw materials to build a strong personality and satisfy his wants. And he makes Phineas a mirror for the particular desires of various women. They find in him, as he finds in them, the image of love they each long for.

VII

Let us look at the possibilities for fulfilling desires in love for the five characters closest to Phineas.

1. For Lord Chiltern, Laura's fierce brother, being in love with Violet gives him a chance—his only chance, since he despises the compromises and the curbs of political life and social organization—for positive and lasting connection with the world. It is all that allows him to find the capacity for affection and responsibility in himself. Without Violet, he would be a barbarian. With her, he can become a family man and a settled master of the hunt, finding in his dislike of bourgeois civilization a ritualistic discipline that lets him get rid of his aggression in relatively positive fashion.

The sincere commonplace that he utters to Violet, "I could not live without you" (PF, LXXIII), means in effect, as that exclamation always does, that *you are the only thing that makes me at all approve of and value myself and the world I live in, and without you I would not have the identity I do but some other identity which I scorn.* Chiltern tells Phineas that to lose Violet would be as if someone were to take "my own heart out of me" (PF, XXIV). This basing of one's whole being and identity on the beloved is what makes romantic desire so dangerous and jealousy-ridden. Losing love can mean losing the self. Being in love can lead to murderous savagery, as the attempts to shoot Phineas by both Chiltern and Laura's husband Robert Kennedy show. But it can disarm too, as Chiltern's domestic fate—husband, father, property owner—also shows.

The undercurrent of Chiltern's forceful desire is primitive eroticism, and he is amazingly like a figure out of D. H. Lawrence. Everything about him connotes sexuality; Violet says of him, "Your brother, Laura, is dangerous. He is like the bad ice in the parks where they stick up the poles. He has had a pole stuck upon him ever since he was a boy" (PF, LII). Like Mellors in *Lady Chatterley*, he devotes his life to a woman and to looking after sport and game; and erotic love for him—sexual desire focused on Violet—becomes compulsive. The erotic, in the communal and increasingly collective world, strikes many as one of the few things left that seems vital and unalienated. Ironically only the politics of love—the desire to have and hold the love and respect of a good and rich woman—not the laws and mores of the *polis*, can control Chiltern's will to violence, find him vocation, and lead him to act responsibly.

2. For the orphan heiress Violet Effingham, being in love gives her the chance to abandon her caution and her strategic superficiality. Trollope imagines it allowing her to fulfill her desire for purpose and integrity. She associates the love between Chiltern and herself with childhood experience, and her treasuring of that early love makes sense in one who looks for emotional continuity. Of Violet, Trollope writes, "Love had not conquered her, but had been taken into her service" (PF, LXXI). She is to Chiltern as Botticelli's Venus is to Mars, but more joyful. As a target for fortune hunters, she has grown careful and a bit cynical. She needs passion: "It has been difficult with me to love. The difficulty with most girls, I fancy, is not to love" (PF, LXXI). What pushes her to love Chiltern—she can not quite love Phineas because he is for her too politic, "too much a friend to everybody"—is both his passionate, sexual nature, which fascinates her, and also her will to make him better.

Women, in Trollope, often desire the qualities and opportunities of male life, sometimes saying they want to act like men. (His men love and admire women, but they do not want to have the lives of women.) Violet expresses a dilemma that is more than personal: When Laura tells her that she could save Chiltern by marrying him, Violet replies, "I sometimes think that I shall have quite enough to do to save myself. It is strange what a propensity I feel for the wrong side of the post," which shows her empathy for Chiltern. But she goes on, "I prefer men who are improper, and all that sort of thing. If I were a man myself I should go in for everything I ought to leave alone. . . . But you see,—I'm not a man, and I must take care of myself. The wrong side of a post for a woman is so very much the wrong side. I like a fast man, but I know that I must not dare to marry the sort of man that I like" (PF, X). Trollope is showing a woman's desire for the transgressive flash of sex, but he is also getting at the problem of the double standard and the wife's awful vulnerability to a husband. In *Phineas Redux* Trollope gives Violet what he calls "a happy, motherly life" with Chiltern, but this match is not a piece of Biedermeier trivia. He has imagined Violet as a blessed creature (comparable to Austen's Elizabeth Bennet) who has been able to take love into her service because she has fulfilled two of the great feminine desires of the age: identification and union with the supposed forcefulness—including sexual forcefulness—of male being; and the power of moral reform—partial, at least—of destructive male will through superior moral agency and sexual magnetism.

3. For Lady Laura, being in love, even if it is a sad extramarital love, at least gives her the chance, by staying true to Phineas in her heart, to redeem the integrity she lost in marrying Kennedy. Revealingly, this being in love, though it victimizes her, also provides a chance for revenge against a patriarchal husband and society that stifle her talents and her passion.

She first sees in Phineas an appealing young man who needs help and tutoring. A mirror of innocence and hope, he is like a walking paragon to her of the romantic dream of liberalism where beautiful people make the world better and better. During most of the novel, she finds in him an outlet for her repressed maternalism; he is someone with whom she wants to identify and whose interests she wants to promote. Trollope calls Lady Laura "the best character" (*Autobiography*, XVII, 274) in the novel, which is odd but telling. She is the most tragic, the most conflict-ridden. The book shows what a prisoner of public opinion a woman is and how much Laura has in common with that energetic mass of people looking for rights and power. She draws, especially in *Phineas Finn*, sympathy for feminine courage and nerve in the face of conventional repression.

One of Trollope's great virtues is that he can create personalities strong enough to overwhelm his own opinions and desires. In Laura, he gets deeply into the politics of gender. What happens to her is a more significant political matter than the party maneuvering and the ostensible issues, votes, and debates in the novel's male Parliament. She is not pert and sexy, like Violet, nor seductive and charming, like Madame Max, nor soft and yielding, like Mary. Unlike her intellectual zero of a father and her government-hating brother, she is a born politician: she longs to wield influence and be close to the male world. "It was her ambition to be brought as near to political action as was possible for a woman without surrendering any of the privileges of feminine inaction. That women should even wish to have votes at parliamentary elections was to her abominable, and the cause of the Rights of Women generally was odious to her; but, nevertheless, for herself, she delighted in hoping that she too . . . was perhaps, in some degree, politically powerful" (PF, X). We could say that she identifies with "the oppressor," and that "the patriarchy" stifles her, keeping her from her natural vocation—though such language is too crude for the subtle grace of her characterization. Her dismal fate shows the flagellant side of the love faith and more than one reason for the rise of feminism. It even implies the problematic nature of romantic love in feminist thought. Instead of a skillful political operative, she becomes in the end the sacrificial scapegoat in the love life of the novel and a representation of the nineteenth-century career closed to talent. At one point she says, "[I]t is a great curse to have been born a woman" (PF, XXXII).

Much in *Phineas* contradicts any totalizing theories about male homosocial conspiracy to maintain and advance the interests of men against women—for example, the harmful intensity of male rivalry, Trollope's vision of women as morally better and more interesting than men, his grudging realization that women absolutely need to develop greater independence.[16] Regarding Laura, however, there is a male lack of sympathy for her, beginning with Trollope himself, that reeks of institutionalized sexism. Women in this novel are not supposed to fall in and out of love; they are supposed to love their husbands, and to love wholeheartedly only once.

In the *Autobiography* Trollope states coldly that "the tragic misery of Lady Laura . . . was . . . due to the sale she made of herself in her wretched marriage" (XVIII, 274). He omits to say that he had her marry the Calvinist soul-tyrant Kennedy because she used up her fortune paying the debts of her Byronic brother, and because she wants to be in a position to use political influence for good causes and for those people about whom she cares. She breaks the prime commandment of Victorian erotic faith by marrying a man she does not love and loving a man she does not marry. (Ironically, Trollope exposes the rifts and conflicts in such axioms of the faith: Madame Max, for instance, got her fortune without penalty from marrying a man she did not love.) Laura is allowed no room for error. Even after her lunatic husband dies, her brother condemns her love for Phineas as shameful, and the press attacks her; worst of all, Phineas, whose career from the beginning she has made possible, dreads her sad passion. Generous-spirited and self-sacrificing, she ends up alone, gloomy, barren, and prematurely aged. Her being and history express the ruthless prejudice that a wife finally must be seen to love, honor, and obey.

Two major calamities of the love faith are that time and change can kill love and that unrequited love can mean agony. When Laura is young and eligible, she seems everything that Phineas wants, but he does not know that she loves him—and it is not clear that she does. Later when her marriage fails, the strength of her love for Phineas comes, as the strength of religion so often does, as a compensating vocation in the face of personal misery. When she has lost her charm and her power, then she tells Phineas she loves him, but he no longer loves her at all. Trollope very delicately shows changes in them both: Laura really does act at times the neurotic hag, and Phineas, always polite and considerate to her, nevertheless looks upon a dutiful visit to her—whom he wanted so to marry and whose permission to visit her determined the opportunity and fate of his life—the way a guilty man might regard visiting his parent in a seedy home for the senile.

The last meeting of the two speaks explicitly of faith. At the news that he is to remarry, Laura echoes Cardinal Wolsey in a ghastly but brilliant speech that combines a melodramatic touch of falsity with sincere religiosity: "Oh Phineas, . . . Oh, my darling! My idol that I have worshipped when I should have worshipped my God!" She goes on to tell him they must of course part, but says, "When we are both old, if I should live, we may meet again" (PR, LXXVIII). That wish to renew intimacies in old age bespeaks what so often sustains erotic faith even in the hard awareness of lost or unreturned love: the living memory of the past, and love projected up to and beyond coming death. She continues, "Of course it has been my fault. . . . When I was younger I did not understand how strong the heart can be. I should have known it, and I pay for my ignorance with the penalty of my whole life." She makes herself at last a martyr for faith, like those Tudor churchmen.

Laura's assertion of her love for Phineas, even against the duties and the sanctity of marriage, has political significance and implies a desire for social change in the relationship between men and women—even though that desire contradicts the author's own conscious wishes. Trollope, insistently throughout the whole long novel, lets his reflections on the political world and the erotic world play off each other. Here, in words that recall Laura's match, he writes of the uncertainties of matrimony and of the reality that for women, all in all, love and marriage matter more than for men because they risk so much more. How, he wonders, does a woman have the audacity to decide to accept someone she knows hardly at all: "He means to be master, and, by the very nature of the joint life they propose to lead, must take her to his sphere of life, not bind himself to hers. . . . But she, knowing nothing, takes a monstrous leap in the dark, in which everything is to be changed, and in which everything is trusted to chance" (PR, XVIII). It seems he is simply pronouncing on female vulnerability and on a fixed state of marital affairs: that is, *I am stating a home truth on how marriage always has been and will be.* And yet the "leap in the dark" sets off historic reverberations. "Leap in the dark" was the epithet for the Reform Bill,[17] and Trollope's choice of imagery works to tie the fact of female subordination in marriage to the pressure for social reform and progress.

4. For Mary Flood Jones, being in love can offer a reflected identity and fulfill passive-aggressive desires to conquer by self-abnegation, as the title of the chapter "Victrix" (PF, LXVI), in which she wins Phineas's proposal, shows. Trollope, criticizing himself later, said that he made a mistake having Finn marry her; he did not much like her, and, because of her vacuousness, almost no one else has either. She does, however, embody an important male erotic fantasy and has her place in the Victorian mirror of love.

Her desire is to stand by her man, no matter what, to cling to him, to be used, to accept anything: "she had a look about her which seemed to ask to be devoured" (PF, II). Trollope, imagining her as an item for erotic consumption, compares her to "plovers' eggs" and to "cigars when one is out in the autumn" (PF, II). Mary compares herself to Tennyson's "Mariana at the Grange" (which Phineas gave her to read, presumably trying to mold her intellect on the model of this Shakespearean wronged woman whom Victorian sensibility turned into a saint of erotic faith[18]). Here is how she talks: "Do whatever you like best. . . . I do not care. . . . Though to love you and to have your love is all the world to me, . . . I would sooner give up that than be a clog on you" (PF, LXVI). She plays a familiar role of woman as safety net for the ambitious man, and her appeal fits Meredith's epigram for the male egoist: "Possession without obligation to the object possessed approaches felicity."[19] But slavishness soon bores or—what is worse—brings out sadism. Trollope happily slaughters her.

The celebrated BBC television adaptation of the Palliser novels egregiously distorts the book by having Phineas marry Mary because he gets her pregnant. Actually, Trollope associates her specifically with the "Virgin" (see PF, II); she is a kind of icon of premarital desire. In fact, Mary stands as an emblem of the now-notorious Victorian virgin-maid figure, and once she is had as a wife, she is gone, like virginity; there is simply nothing to her and she dies.

Something a bit sinister taints this character and her demise. Her disposability is the point. We find this idealized figure and her appeal all through nineteenth-century culture. She embodied—and probably, in much of the world, still symbolically embodies—a significant cultural ideal. She is woman as God's gift to a man, the woman that popes, mullahs, and rabbis praise, the selfless feminine being who is to be the antidote to the excesses of individualism and doctrines of progress, the woman who is imagined and willed to suppress selfish desire in a man's world. But a being that exists only to serve others is not a person but a wish fulfillment, and to believe in love, finally, there must be some independent entity there to love and to love you back.

Within the structure of the novel, Mary exists to test Phineas's moral faith and worth. Her desire that he keep his word to marry her is the moral imperative of *Phineas Finn*, and he passes the test, but even here we have the woman portrayed as a wholly relative figure. She exists not as a person in her own right but as a mere cipher to prove the worth or corruption of a man—something to be true to, like a flag. The phenomenon of this pretty image in the mirror of male desire has a rather ugly aura about it. She is like the figure in "The Rokeby Venus," but without a glass, unable to look back, there for the taking, only an object of desire, not a subject.

But I may be unfair to innocuous Mary, to Trollope, and to the complex social psychology that went into the imaginative creation of the passive, accepting nineteenth-century virgin. Her death marks her as a figure of transition in the progress of love. To compare her to another painted image, she is a secularized Victorian version of a conventional Renaissance Virgin of Annunciation, the instrument, according to an implicit male sentimentality, of some benevolent, divinely erotic plan. Nonetheless, her appeal has fled.

5. For Madame Max Goesler, being in love means a chance to satisfy her natural, sexual desires ("She had never yet known what it was to have anything of the pleasure of love" [PF, LX]), and also to find moral purpose and value in her social career. It allows her to change for the better. Unlikely as it seems, Trollope makes Marie, the wealthy, social-climbing, reputedly Jewish widow of an Austrian banker, the heroine, in the end, of *Phineas Finn/Redux*. Anything but a conventional house-angel, she becomes the novel's most eloquent defender of erotic faith.

Her ambition, her quick rise to the top, her worry over compromising herself to please a dubious public opinion, and her growing disillusion with success closely parallel Phineas's political career. Also, in a novel that fictionalizes Disraeli as the shrewd Conservative leader Daubeny, Trollope boldly makes Madame Max, with her Semitic looks, her brains, aesthetic taste, and touch of the exotic, the Disraeli of Society. Their parallel maneuverings in their respective milieus sharpen perspective on the driving public ambitions of men and women in the age of great expectations. The ultimate political choice of bourgeois individualism, however, is the pursuit of private happiness. In the end Trollope makes Madame Max and her progress into erotic faith transcend parties and politicians in significance. Her desire shifts. The novel repeatedly speaks of success and the obsessive middle-class desire for it, but it finally renders success as private and erotic.

Madame Max, in Trollope's vision, counts for more than the fictional Daubeny or the real-life Disraeli. She begins by manipulating people and public opinion like a party leader: "she was highly ambitious, and she played her game with great skill and great caution. Her doors were not open to all callers;—. . . were shut occasionally to those whom she most specially wished to see within them. She knew how to allure by denying, and to make the gift rich by delaying it" (PF, LVII). "Public estimation," as Trollope puts it, regards the old Duke of Omnium as the pinnacle of society, and Marie campaigns to win him like a brilliant candidate going after high office. Speaking like a Disraeli reformer, she tells the duke, "take a leap in the dark" (PF, LX), and he proposes. But already she is changing and doubting, "ever discontented with herself": "And what if she caught this old man, and became herself a duchess" (PF, LX). In *Phineas Redux*, after the duke has died, she muses on her three years in England: "And yet she hardly knew what were her desires, and had never quite defined her intentions. . . . Dukes and duchesses, dinner-parties and drawing-rooms,— what did they all amount to? What was it that she wanted? She was ashamed to tell herself that it was love" (PR, XXX). But it is.

VIII

Phineas Finn/Redux articulates the need, in a materialistic time, to preserve and find a place for reverence and religious feeling—qualities that very possibly civilization cannot do without. One of the greatest desires in love is devotion, not only the desire for devotion *from* another, but also the powerful desire of the self to offer devotion *to* another. Trollope, revealing his own desire, imagines that women as different as Mary Jones and Madame Max want to devote them- selves to men, and do so. That wish may say something about a nineteenth- century masculine hope to institutionalize love as a sort of network of spiritual service stations using women to keep men running smoothly down the grooves of change, but it expresses something more important even than just a common personal and cultural spot of sexism.

The Victorian impulse to psychologize and spiritualize desire and make a creed of love figures crucially in the language of Marie Goesler as she continues her rather embarrassed musing about her desire for loving purpose:

> She was ashamed to tell herself that it was love. But she knew this,—that it was necessary for her happiness that she should devote herself to some one. All the elegancies and outward charms of life were delightful, if only they could be used as the means to some end. . . . After that she reflected whether it might not be best for her to become a devotee,—it did not matter much in what branch of the Christian religion, so that she could assume some form of faith. The sour strictness of the confident Calvinist or the asceticism of St. Francis might suit her equally,—if she could only believe in Calvin or in St. Francis. She had tried to believe in the Duke of Omnium, but there she had failed. There had been a saint at whose shrine she thought she could have worshipped with a constant and happy devotion, but that saint had repulsed her from his altar. [PR, XXX]

That is the will to erotic faith. The religious vocabulary may seem over- wrought—even mushy—but it expresses a momentous need for faith in the world of doubt. No wonder that Trollope would imagine women of leisure and ability, like Laura and Madame Max, who are childless and lack opportunities for professional vocation, looking for vocation in love. Devotion might console disappointment by engaging one's spiritual yearning. Devotees do not doubt the purpose or true value of existence, even though their own lives are sometimes unhappy and incomplete.

The practice of erotic devotion and vocation in this novel is—at least in the long run, after a man has obtained the love and body of a woman—limited to women. On the face of it, men's idea of women's superior devotion—the idea that Trollope, Phineas, and so many Victorians shared—is as constricting in what it implies about feminine freedom as is, say, the custom of primogeniture. That devotion, however, to the *idea* of devotion gives strong evidence of a desire to locate faith and a reason for it here on earth. The idea and the reality of devoted love support the belief that people may be blessed to receive more than they morally deserve, and that is a ground for hope in *Phineas*.

But Trollope's idolization of women's love for men and his effort to give it a cast of inviolability show signs of cultural desperation. The logic seems to be, *if God is not the all-forgiving other, maybe women can fill the bill: let's try to mold them into morally beautiful house-angels.* Three reasons make this strategic line more plausible and effective than it sounds when put so baldly: gender attitudes and behavior *can* be inculcated (by novels, for example); the role of devotee and morally superior being has its pleasurable psychic rewards, especially for the relatively powerless (as the history of religion shows); and great numbers of men and women in bourgeois society of the last two centuries, because of the historical strengthening of the maternal tie, actually do seem to have felt that women are ethically better than men and capable of greater, more sustained love.

Anyone who seriously reads *Phineas Redux* can see that its self-important "world of men," i.e., the world of government, party politics, professional ethics, law, clubs, and the like—with all of its inherent fascination and its mix of good and bad—is judged calmly, and therefore all the more damagingly, to be at bottom unworthy of faith. Trollope may appear a reactionary, in feminist lights, by seeming to prescribe for women a fixed role of subservient devotion to men; but he can also look like a progressive by finding in the relationships, the loyalties, the thoughtful feeling, and the wit of his imagined women, the faith on which to build the future.

He tries to show the superiority of women's love and devotion by imagining that they can and ought truly to love only one man in their lives, but his novel contradicts its teller. Near the end, for instance, Marie Goesler tells Phineas, "[Y]ou are the only man I ever loved" (PR, LXXIX). In contrast, Phineas has loved many; but so, it might seem (see PR, XLVII and LVII), has Madame Max.

At the very least she has had amorous encounters with several men. And the two women whom Trollope expressly points out as being unable to "transfer" their "hearts," do not come across as good role models (Mary simply expires, and the late-blooming devotee Laura turns neurotic and self-lacerating). Against his conscious intention, the book suggests that a woman's idealization of one man can be destructive as well as positive—the reverse side of the coin of male libertinage. Obsessive devotion and obsessive seduction, activities that tend to ignore the particular selfhood of other people, reflect upon each other: both manifest insatiable demands on reality and often mask hostility and a sub-limated spirit of vengeance against the other sex and the world. Trollope's fiction often embraces the ideal of devotion, but it also often shows how an excess of pointless abstract devotion can hurt both the self and others—like any religious fanaticism.

Also, the narrative, daringly for Victorian times, seems to offer something hopeful in Finn's love life and in Marie Goesler's amorous experience that cul-minates in her rational choice of erotic devotion. Trollope affirms—he certainly does not condemn—Phineas's career of serial love, and he shares with both Marie and Glencora Palliser a history of changing, developing love desire. The Don Juan myth appears to have come full circle, for the variety of desire and love can be seen to temper with experience dangers of an idealized devotion that risks suicidal fixation and the negation of social values. The novel (but not the narrator) distinguishes between thoughtless devotion to a love (e.g., Mary Jones), and the rational need, will, and desire to be devoted unselfishly to an-other (e.g., Marie Goesler); and out of the mixing of desire and devotion can come consolations of maturity.

IX

Being in love is the beginning of consolation in a fickle world. Whenever Phineas gets a blow, he turns to a woman and love. Rejected by Laura, he falls in love with Violet; losing her and public office, he marries Mary. For two-thirds of the whole novel, whenever things go wrong, he has Marie Goesler to console him and work actively for him. When bad luck and the legal system almost hang him for Bonteen's murder, he finds that only love rouses him from anguish and depression. Power, reputation, and will collapse, but the loving relationship of an assertive woman holds.

The graceful chapter "Consolation" (PF, LIV) sets the pattern for the entire novel. After Violet rejects Phineas for Chiltern, Madame Max pets and cheers him. "'A man's a man for a' that,' she said. . . . 'Even though he cannot get the special bit of painted Eve's flesh for which his heart has had a craving. . . . And if you are down in the mouth, come to me, and I will sing you a Scotch song'"

(PF, LIV). Marie has the charm of Venus making ready here, and a thousand pages later we find that this was the time when she was falling in love with him and that that love helps save his life and make him whole again.

Love, like any religion, serves as consolation for something missing or lost. *Phineas Finn/Redux* narrates the glamorous appeal of the secular world and then a chilling disillusionment with it. Modern creative imagination, unable to see the face of a God who would choose the self for personal salvation, makes out the face of love in the mirror of desire. Imagine the following figures: 1) the open-hearted Phineas before the loveliness and magnanimity of Madame Max; 2) Trollope, with quiet moral courage, taking the stock figure of the worldly-wise, demirep European courtesan, turning her against all convention into the consoling, thoughtful heroine of his novel; and 3) the admiring beholder before the beauty of "The Rokeby Venus." Thinking of each brings to mind the power and will to believe in erotic faith.

But the course of this huge novel with its subdued ending cannot sustain the buoyancy of triumphant visions of love or inspire any easy faith. Trollope achieves with the two halves of the novel a doubling and disillusioned reassessment of experience and events. *Phineas Redux* is a mirror on *Phineas Finn*, but a chapter title, "The World Grows Cold," epitomizes the change between the two. In the first part, Trollope catches the glory of a world hot with energy for a good young man on the make. Later Trollope makes him learn the appalling human indifference, the injustices, and the moral deteriorations that characterize his or anyone else's world. Love in *Phineas Redux* comes as the consolation prize for life's recurrent iciness and the fading of early hopes.

The entire novel, in fact, depicts a surprising amount of violence, envy, spite, and murderous obsession that can and do grow out of love, political rivalry, and economic competition. With all the decay and sorrow in the narrative's life, however, still men and women in love or falling in love give examples of their best selves and can come to esteem one another with the attribute that Trollope, describing Phineas, finely calls "a grateful mind" (PR, LXVIII). He sees a dignity and fertile conduct born of love, and he composes joyful, coupling dialogues between lovers that convey, despite strong shades of melancholy, sweetness and richness in the life the novel portrays.

X

Phineas Finn/Redux is not sanguine about the force of love, but in it, being in love gives form and meaning to desire, devotion, and consolation. It generates those specific dialogues of the heart by which humanity, often foolishly and torturously, tries to know, perpetuate, and cherish itself.

Dialogue of the genders: that is what the novel means for Trollope. It's still a man's world in his fiction, but not irredeemably so; there is hope in the progress of love for Phineas. Marie Goesler may in part be a male fantasy blending the perfect mother and lover, but she is a desiring subject too. Phineas is in love at the beginning and the end of the book, but the object of love changes from Mary, the transparent drop of Irish dew—a watery mirror for male narcissism—to Marie, a cosmopolitan woman with a lively mind and an erotic history. The human heart in love might grow and engage the devotion and desire of *another person*, rather than merely cherish the delusive projection of his majesty the baby's lordly ego. In the end, though to the outward world she will seem to dwindle into a wife as she gives up wealth and independence to Phineas, the balance of power in their relationship seems to lie with her. Without denigrating or criticizing them for their evolved and evolving personalities, Trollope gives Phineas, judged by the usual Victorian criteria, the more womanly nature, and Madame Max the more masculine.

"Heart"[20] is the magic word in Trollope. It has primacy, as Lady Laura says, and its strength is a political as well as a personal fact. Nothing matters more in his vision than the individual experience of love from which all generation and all knowledge of mutuality must flow. That may sound banal or naive as a general proposition, but, in context, the long narrative of the inevitable fusion of love and politics, of the historic intermingling of the spheres of men and the spheres of women, and of the power of frustrated desire gives it persuasive force. This novel is a mirror held in place and angled by the force that being in love generates.

Phineas shows the power of love; but, in the end, I do not want to play down its subliminal darker reflections of the fragility of love, the hostility that unmet desire can let loose, or the suffering that women and men undergo in seeking love and satisfying the demands of sexual politics. Lady Laura, who, from her false perch of privilege, early on disdained women's rights, shows not only how strong the heart can be, but how great is her own deprivation. The meaning and emphasis of Trollope's fiction is not fixed, but dialogical.

Let me return to my comparison between the Velázquez *Venus* and Trollope's novel. In a time of popular political agitation for power, someone remarks that "our House of Commons should be the mirror of the people" (PF, XXXV), but Mr. Monk, Phineas's political mentor, says the House should be the people's miniature: "And let the artist be careful to put in every line of the expression of that ever-moving face. To do this is a great work, and the artist must know his trade well. . . . The true portrait should represent more than the body" (PF, XXXV).[21] The spirit of what people want, the soul of their desire, must somehow be reflected. Set this mirror-and-art simile next to the mob that breaks the member of Parliament's mirrors. When people lack social instruments through which they can connect with their desires and ways of imagining themselves loving and lovable, then they want to break things.

If you remain separated from loving grace and cannot see your way clear to what you want, you might try to smash the mirroring icon of a faith badly out of focus. In March 1914, on the eve of the Great War and the true end of the Victorian world, a long generation after the time of the fictional Laura Kennedy and the violent lovers and political agitators of *Phineas*, a real suffragette named Mary Richardson walked into the London National Gallery, pulled out a chopper and slashed the painted flesh of Velázquez's Venus six or seven times. Her statement to the authorities reads as follows:

> I have tried to destroy the picture of the most beautiful woman in mythological history as a protest against the government for destroying Mrs. Pankhurst, who is the most beautiful character in modern history. Justice is an element of beauty as much as colour and outline on canvas. Mrs. Pankhurst seeks to procure justice for womanhood and for this she is being slowly murdered by a Government of Iscariot politicians. If there is an outcry against my deed, let every one remember that such an outcry is an hypocrisy so long as they allow the destruction of Mrs. Pankhurst and other beautiful women.[22]

The government that locked up Emmeline Pankhurst sounds suspiciously like the government that locked up Phineas, and like the politicians who exhibit such sexist bias in *Phineas Redux*. Notice that what Mary Richardson says confirms the power of love. Her words are erotic as well as political. Anyone can see that the sentiment of love for a woman—for women—overshadows everything else in the statement. Think of her standing before the masterpiece planning the attack on Venus. In her crazy subjectivity, if she could not make out the face of Mrs. Pankhurst in the mirror of art, maybe she could sense the outline of her own desire, devotion, and consolation in a politics of love that attacked the old representation of love.

9 Pastoral Erotics: Thomas Hardy's *Far from the Madding Crowd* (1874)

The Lord is my shepherd; I shall not want.
PSALM 23:1

There's a somebody I'm longing to see
I hope that he
Turns out to be
Someone to watch over me.
I'm a little lamb who's lost in the wood;
I know I could
Always be good
To one who'll watch over me.
IRA GERSHWIN[1]

The Cyprian Queen, my children, is not only the Cyprian; there are many other names she bears. She is Death; she is imperishable force; she is raving madness; she is untempered longing; she is lamentation. Nothing that works or is quiet, nothing that drives to violence, but as she wills. Her impress sinks into the mould of all things whose life is in their breath. Who must not yield to this goddess? She enters into every fish that swims; she is in every four-footed breed upon the land; among the birds everywhere is the beating of her wings; in beasts, in mortal men, and in the gods above. . . . There is no design of mortal or of god that is not cut short by love.
SOPHOCLES[2]

I

Claude Lorrain's *Judgment of Paris* (c. 1645–46; fig. 19),[3] like Hardy's *Far from the Madding Crowd*, shows a tenuous balance of forces and a living, but menaced faith in a still harmonious world. Both represent the choosing of love as the essence of human life, but each conveys the disruption and terror that may lurk in that choice. The tension of the picture lies in the contrast between the equanimity of natural rightness of being in Claude's wide pastoral vision and the potential strife and devastation that the figures of the myth presage. On one side, the long view with enduring, stretching fertile space and the implied consciousness to perceive it gratefully; on the other, an individualizing narrative vision featuring the inaugural discord of amorous folly and tragedy. But in both painting and novel an overall serenity about life and love prevails. The sheer largeness of nature—its depths and rhythms—swallows and in perspective diminishes even the direst human experience.

Nothing could make clearer Hardy's feeling for nature and his own pastoral relationship to his subject matter than his reminiscence of how he wrote the book: "So Hardy went on writing *Far from the Madding Crowd*—sometimes indoors, sometimes out—when he would occasionally find himself without a scrap of paper at the very moment that he felt volumes. In such circumstances he would use large dead leaves, white chips left by the wood-cutters, or pieces of stone or slate that came to hand."[4] Apocryphal or not, the story makes him seem like a character in his own fiction inscribing the novel as a labor of love to, in, about, and on nature.

Pastoral love and imagery, the basis for faith in Hardy's novel, have deep roots in human culture. Somehow the pastoral vocation and heritage lend themselves to metaphorical evocation of the most profound feelings that men and women have had about love, labor, religion, and being in the world. These run from the sublime—Christ as the "good shepherd"—to the ridiculous—the comedian as sheep lover. In Woody Allen's movie *Everything You Always Wanted to Know about Sex (but Were Afraid to Ask)* (1972), a psychiatrist falls madly in love with a sheep. The episode offers a farcical example of erotic desire blowing away distinctions between pastoral concern and libido. The joke depends on the absurdity of bestial love in an up-to-date urban milieu and more subtly on the graphic force of the film medium to mock the stale pastoral imagery that resides in our discourse. Beneath the incongruity, though, lies the complex comedy of the relationship between the object of vocation and erotic drive—not to mention the sheer zaninesss of personal desire.

The real joke may be that the linguistic analogy between sheep and humankind, especially the persistent comparison of women to sheep and lambs, really has something to do with sex and power; and people, queasy about their animality, try to laugh off the subject. Notice the endurance of "crude" sexual jokes about sheep, from the parody of the Nativity in *The Second Shepherd's Play*, to obscene "sheepherder" stories and to the ultimate in modern sexism: *Why did God make women? Because sheep can't type.* There may be something uncivilized and vaguely revolting in the merging of pastoral love and carnal desire, but the place of sheep in narrative and figurative language, gamy subject that it is, lets us infer a good deal about our culture, imagination, and work.

The pastoral conceit is that life is like sheep and shepherds in their setting. Hardy tries to realize in *Far from the Madding Crowd* what is living in the

tradition of pastoral and to use it to fuse erotics, economics, and religious meaning for his world.[5] "Shepherd Oak," says a perceptive critic, "appears as the high
priest of both love and work."[6] Hardy sets love and humanity in the long historical perspective of pastoral space, time, and vocation.

II

I want to juxtapose the following items and consider how they bear on the new
pastoralism of *Far from the Madding Crowd*:

1. In Hardy's later days he recalled one of his first memories: As a child,
"crossing the ewelease . . . , he went on hands and knees and pretended to eat
grass in order to see what the sheep would do. Presently he looked up and found
them gathered around in a close ring, gazing at him with astonished faces."[7]

2. When Strife, at a wedding, tosses among the gods the golden apple bearing the words "to the fairest," and Hera, Athena, and Aphrodite squabble for it,
Zeus, via Hermes, sends them off to the Mount Ida countryside for the herdsman Paris to decide the issue. In early versions of the story, they are clothed
when Paris judges them; in later versions, they disrobe in order to show their
full beauty.[8] In Claude's painting, Hera, disputing the shepherd judge, stands
fully garbed—even seeming to carry a billowing pack on her back—at the center of the group; the other goddesses and Eros, as well as Paris, are nude except
for wisps of drapery.

3. In the King James Bible, the allegorizing headnote to chapter 1 of the Song
of Solomon begins, "The church's love unto Christ," and glosses verses 7 and 8:
"7 and [she] prayeth to be directed to his flock. 8 Christ directeth her to the
shepherds' tents." These verses proper read: "(7) Tell me, O thou whom my
soul loveth, where thou feedest, where thou makest thy flock to rest at noon;
for why should I be as one that turneth aside by the flocks of thy companions?
(8) If thou know not, O thou fairest among women, go thy way forth by the
footsteps of the flock, and feed thy kids beside the shepherds' tents."

4. In Hardy's novel, Gabriel Oak shears a ewe while the owner whom he
loves, Bathsheba Everdene, looks on: "The clean, sleek creature arose from its
fleece—how perfectly like Aphrodite rising from the foam should have been
seen to be realized—looking startled and shy at the loss of its garment, which
lay on the floor in one soft cloud."[9] (Say "Bathsheba" aloud and you can hear
both the bleat and the name of the pastoral animal.)

The first item suggests that Hardy, besides being a quirky child, might have
had a unique curiosity about the pastoral process. That this comic incident stuck
in his mind for eighty years or so, testifies to its importance. It suggests such
messages as these: "I am like a sheep"; "Sheep react like people"; "I can aston-

ish them"; "Sheep are my audience"; and "Human consciousness may be a freak of nature." Implicitly it also proclaims, "Watch this creature; he has a pastoral imagination."

The Judgment of Paris legend, which makes a shepherd the arbiter of divine beauty and precipitator of the fall of dynasties, brings out the prominence of herding in early history and the resultant traces of pastoral memory that have shaped how we think and live.[10] The choice of love over dominant political power, military prowess, and superhuman wisdom asserts the full force of erotic desire. Why is Paris a herdsman? It may well be that somewhere in the origin of this myth lies the practice of sacrifice and the substitution of animal for human victims (e.g., the substitution of a ram for Isaac in Genesis). The shepherd is not only a key man in the economy on which culture was built, he is also a key figure in the custom of religious ritual. Different deities try to gain the allegiance of the pastor. This tie between Aphrodite and Paris the keeper of flocks joins the erotic to the pastoral.

An especially puzzling feature is the disrobing part of the story, which Claude's painting features. No doubt the force of love first sparks with looking, but from where does the idea come that the shepherd has the power and privilege of having the goddesses appear naked before him? If we conjoin the image of deities unclothed with Hardy's simile of Bathsheba's newly shorn ewe as Aphrodite rising out of the foam, we might find a clue. Some esoteric, dark connection may exist between the sheep's bounty to the shepherd and the undressed goddesses' bounteous offerings to Paris. If the male is to choose a woman and love as the most tempting of prizes, then femininity, no matter how powerful, must uncover. Is it too farfetched to suppose some link exists between the shearing of sheep and the uncovering of divine beauty? What *is* sure is that from earliest times the spirit of divinity and religion, like the spirit of generation, has been felt to infuse the pastoral vocation.

The Scripture and its prefatory gloss from the Song of Solomon show this mutuality. The commentary epitomizes the drive of Judeo-Christian monotheism to incorporate and sublimate love and sexual desire. It tries to moralize and spiritualize volatile erotic passion. The Bible shows the continuing but evolving metaphorical identity between human life and the pastoral enterprise. No line from the novel seems more provocative by modern lights than Bathsheba's statement, "It is difficult for a woman to define her feelings in language which is chiefly made by men to express theirs" (LI, 270). Essential to pastoral thinking is the idea of caring love and the image of all people, male or female, as potential members of the flock; but built into the traditions of language and thought are the identification of women with sheep and the potential role of men as shepherds. An ancient analogy persists right down to the Gershwins'

"Someone to Watch over Me," between the pastoral condition and gender roles in love life; but notice certain slippages between the Scripture I cite and its commentary. In the Song of Solomon the voice of the woman sounds out boldly. Unrestrainedly in love, she is close to—part of—the work of men; love, lover, and beloved are not abstract, but personal and immediate. Love is a whole-hearted faith, unmediated by the "church" of the gloss. An unorthodox admirer of the Bible, Hardy was eager to convey the relevance of scriptural life and language that the clerisy could obscure by bracketing them off from the people and appropriating their interpretation. He was trying to recover lost ground in *Far from the Madding Crowd.*

Set my fourth item, the newly shorn sheep and the birth of Aphrodite, next to the first, and you can see how natural it is that Hardy should have composed that simile and yet how wonderful a revelation it is. No other novelist before him knew both sheepshearing and Aphrodite so well or would have seen and felt the one in the other. What the figure in context and the novel as a whole suggest is the knowledge that the goddess of love may be reborn fresh and beautiful—or terrible as death—in anyone's experience. A man and a woman may be laboring together at some mundane task when suddenly their common vocation turns into a vocation of love. Venus, a living deity reborn millions of times a day, lurks everywhere, ready to possess, ready for epiphany.

III

Hardy's pastoral is both very old and very new. Steeped in Ecclesiastes—"to everything there is a season and a time to every purpose"—as well as in George Eliot (when it came out anonymously, the *Spectator* guessed that she wrote it, and Hardy's autobiography shows how that rankled him[11]), *Far from the Madding Crowd* offers a vision and a love that show people both their continuity with the earth and the past, and a hope for the future. Like Eliot in her novels, Hardy assumes the pastoral role of Ecclesiastes: "wise, he still taught the people knowledge. . . . even words of truth. The words of the wise are as goads . . . which are given from one shepherd." (When very young—vanity of vanities!—he had tried to turn Ecclesiastes into Spenserian stanzas.) What is new—new to the Victorian reading public at least—is the place of common experience and a modern sense of vocation as a basis for flowering love between men and women. Near the book's end, Hardy describes in a passage of great significance the possibility of erotic faith in a new—or renewed—pastoralism:

> He accompanied her up the hill, explaining to her the details of his forthcoming tenure of the other farm. They spoke very little of their mutual feelings; pretty phrases and warm expressions being probably unnecessary between such tried friends. Theirs was that substantial affection which arises (if any arises at all) when the two who are thrown together begin

first by knowing the rougher sides of each other's character, and not the best till further on, the romance growing up in the interstices of a mass of hard prosaic reality. This good-fellowship—*camaraderie*—usually occurring through similarity of pursuits, is unfortunately seldom superadded to love between the sexes, because men and women associate, not in their labours, but in their pleasures merely. Where, however, happy circumstance permits its development, the compounded feeling proves itself to be the only love which is strong as death—that love which many waters cannot quench, nor the floods drown, beside which the passion usually called by the name is evanescent as steam. [LVI, 303–4]

Hardy, in this muted climax to the love story of Oak and Bathsheba, with its "mass of hard prosaic reality" and the flooding waters of the last sentence, must somehow have had the end of *The Mill on the Floss* in mind. The rich, problematic paragraph says that both idealized, romantic love and sexual love are transient—"evanescent." Shared work, friendship, common physical relationship to the abiding reality of the world can help to bind a couple with love till death. This attachment to one another and to the earth means that they participate creatively in what endures and revives. Hardy, here, chooses to evoke the most erotic part of the Bible, with its religious connotations ("Many waters cannot quench love, neither can the floods drown it," Song of Solomon 8:7), in his new pastoral love. He wants to bring together sexual love and vocation in its old and new sense (holy calling and significant work). He does *not* say that "romance" and sex, which I infer as part of the meaning of the phrase "love between the sexes," are not necessary or, for joy or woe, sure to happen. Steam, after all, has moved the world's population. At its best, love is a compound. The passage has both an idyllic and an after-the-Fall flavor. It recognizes the need to accept flaws and the damage of experience, and it allows for historical as well as personal change. One of the lessons that modern life, with the widespread employment of women as well as men, keeps repeating is that shared labor sooner or later breeds love.

The most arresting words are "strong as death." Love is not "stronger than death," but, at its best, it has the inevitability and impact of death. It gives the couple a share in the eternal, ongoing processes of life and death, for the consequences of labor and love are endless. If we put that prose from the end together with an excerpt from the beginning of the novel, we get at Hardy's vision of love's potential in the novel. In the early passage, Hardy assumes the pastoral function and even the cadences and periods of the George Eliot narrator, and yet he achieves his own sweeping, but finely sensed perspective: "The poetry of motion is a phrase much in use, and to enjoy the epic form of that gratification it is necessary to stand on a hill at a small hour of the night, and, having first expanded with a sense of difference from the mass of civilized mankind, who are dreamwrapt and disregardful of all such proceedings at this time, long and quietly watch your stately progress through the stars" (II, 12).

Human life for Hardy often has the futility of a shepherd trying to herd stars, but this astronomical view has potential comfort: to integrate the self into the majestic universe and consciously feel a part of it would be a way to be "strong as death." The pastoral love that Hardy is trying to imagine would include and blend erotic love, care for another person, and the self's intimate involvement with, and feeling for, the natural cosmos and its regenerative force. His project is to awaken and uncover a few of "the mass of civilized mankind" to consciousness of their cosmic ride, to humanity's preoccupation with erotic desire, and to restorative, faithful love.

IV

Let us look again at Claude's *Judgment* and compare it to Hardy's novel. A fateful decision for humanity is being made in a quiet, shadowed corner of a twilight world. Central to the painting, as Oak is central to the novel, and dominating it, along with the sky opening out to the vast spaces on the right, is a large, handsome tree. Reaching up almost to the top, looming over the figures competing for preeminence below, it is apparently rooted in the Idalian rock— like Oak and his romance, "growing up in the interstices of a mass of hard prosaic reality." The foliage of the tree occupies a much greater area than the group in the middle distance, and it holds focus. Its somber color, its large oval-like shape, and its position roughly at the heart of the canvas suggest that whatever the vicissitudes of fortune, history, and even religion, life revolves about mysterious, unpossessable nature.

Paris and the goddesses look small. If you casually focus on them, your eye is liable to be taken up into the dark shape of the tree or, following the source of light on the figures, out into expansive, beautifully lit reaches of the river, lands, far-off bodies of water, mountains, late-day sky, golden boughs, and the deep horizons beyond the clouds. Something Bathsheba says in the novel gets at Claude's effect perfectly: "I'll try to think . . . if I can think out of doors; my mind spreads away so" (IV, 27). The tree spreads, the sky spreads, and they convey a greater importance and sense of permanence in this vision than the grouped figures. Behind Paris, who sits on a rock in front of a cavern, rises a firm, rugged cliff topped with tree growth and golden-leaved branches; above Aphrodite and Eros a waterfall pours down the mountainside; Pallas sits on a green bank; just above Hera's head and her imperious finger pointing upward, a narrow tree thrusts straight up into the sky, the dimension of its long slender trunk faintly mocking the gesture of the goddess by making it look so petty. And just in back of her lies the darkest part of the large tree's shadow. The animals of the herd, on which human sustenance depends, sprawl in the foreground and down the slope, blending into the landscape. The herdsman who must choose, and the deities of power, wisdom, and love and pleasure, are all contained by the existential conditions of flora, fauna, rocks, soil, mountains, water, air, weather, sun, and darkness. The imperative upon humanity is not to rule this immense landscape, the notion of which Claude's vision makes ridiculous, but to fit in, to understand it, and to harmonize consciousness and human nature to its rhythms and reality. The effect of Claude's space is very much like Hardy's ride through the stars: it undercuts pride.

The representation of the shepherd hero and the deities, though their traditional stature dwindles in the pastoral setting, has important implications. Handsome Paris, here the lone shepherd, cut off from Troy and kin, looks vulnerable to love. Hera, the embodiment of worldly power, stands centrally in the group. Admonishing Paris, her finger-pointing image conflicts with all her surroundings as well as with the other figures. Her fine raiment, like her proud peacock—whose useless gaudiness contrasts completely with the muted colors of the herd animals—seems out of place. Her unwillingness to undress, the portrayed clash of wills with the shepherd, and the power, wealth, and ambition symbolized by both her pose and clothes all mark her as the foe of pastoral life. By contrast, little pride at all shows forth in Aphrodite, Athena, or Eros. Pallas, busy with her sandal, her spear looking much like a shepherd's staff, her discarded robe matching almost exactly Paris's country garb, has the casual, undaunting form of a pastoral citizen. As for the unpretentious love goddess, intently watching Hera, she does not seem more beautiful or erotic than her rivals. Her son Cupid looks rather like a rustic's thin child—graphic evidence that love is fragile. The whole group, except for regal Juno, has undergone a pastoralization process. Majesty and divinity would seem to lie not in the separate figures, but in the rich landscape, and the fusion of consciousness and the subject of love into it. Claude's composition and *Far from the Madding Crowd* imply the same thing: *Take the long view.*

The picture, like the novel, displays spaciousness almost to infinity. It features a vision of *uncovering*, an opening up and out so that everything may be seen and known. This is a world without walls where, as in Hardy, the trappings of interiority and compartmentalized culture do not obscure the ecological sight lines. The high, wheeling birds lift the mind to what Hardy calls, describing Oak's vision of Bathsheba, "a bird's-eye view, as Milton's Satan first saw Paradise" (II, 16). "E. M. Forster remarked that Hardy conceived his novels from a great height, but his females are drawn from very close up." [12] That kind of panoramic sweep, close-in focus, and intimation of relationship between the immediate and the distant—the flowing vista along with the telling detail of a particular life—make Claude "one of the unseen presences" in *Far from the Madding Crowd*. [13]

But Claude's painting, like Hardy's novel, has a more sinister side. The very peacefulness of the scene shows how close nemesis may be, how helpless people are when the gods single them out. The divine visit to the serene countryside renders the arbitrariness of fate. For Paris tending his flock, for Boldwood managing his farm, hard times and frightful chance happeneth and nothing can save them. Even Oak, the good shepherd, at the whim of fate loses his herd over a cliff.

The logic of Claude's choice of subject makes obvious one more thing: the decision of Paris for love means that the fact and nature of love are just as consequential and determining in human life as the tangible, visibly represented environment of the painting. The uncontrollable force of love, like an unseen wind, is part of the nature that fills that space and makes the picture. And power, armed wisdom, voluptuous desire—all the goddesses, all their jealousies, all that they represent—all the forces and matter of the universe, all human nature will be involved in the course of love. Of the five main characters in *Far from the Madding Crowd*, all of whom fall in love, two die horribly, one ends up in prison, and all suffer. Within the pastoral world of these two works, erotic desire means destruction and death as well as restoration.

V

Hardy—the Peeping Tom of novelists—has the libidinous curiosity of the voyeur. He combines visual intimacy and detail with far-reaching perspective, like a hawk that can see a mouse a mile away. He wants to visualize the fatal moments in life, show the spatial arrangements and details that compose critical moments in destiny. There is more, though: a fascination with *exposing the other*, with invading privacy and imaging scenes that have an aura of taboo about them. The voyeur turns his gaze on, not away from, the vulnerability and the secrets of others.

In discussing *Villette*, I said that the voyeuristic imagination, closely tied to artistic impulse, not only appropriates vicariously its desire, it also projects its obsessions onto what it sees. With Hardy no boundary exists between the erotic and the nonerotic. Judging by this novel, any reader can see that the outcome of Victorian repression is not the removal of sex from discourse, but a pressure that infuses eroticism into everything. We read a description of the countryside and suddenly we are seeing a woman's body; a sheep is shorn, and Hardy makes us think of a sexual deflowering. The erotic effect is rather like that of Sergeant Troy's phallic "blade," "which seemed everywhere at once and yet nowhere especially" (XXVIII, 144). Venereal force and desire infuse and suffuse the novel's descriptions of nature and the subsurfaces of its text. Its ruling deity is the Sophoclean Cyprian.

Not for nothing did Hardy name his heroine Bathsheba and begin his novel with Gabriel Oak, like King David, looking down upon her from a "point of espial" (I, 10). One of the fathers of the cinematic consciousness, Hardy composes like a master of focus. He reveals casually both his own aesthetic passion and his erotic feeling for life when he remarks that Oak's "delight" in visualizing Bathsheba "effaced for the time his perception of the great difference between seeing and possessing" (VIII, 59). The distinction is telling. Hardy, like his hero, is possessed by what he sees—by love possessed; and the narrative explores what it might mean both to possess, and to be possessed by, love. But until the triumph of pastoral love in the end, those who possess love cannot see, and those who see do not possess love.

Love proverbially first begins with sight, and the author's voyeuristic point of view works to generate pastoral love. Drenched in the spirit of Ecclesiastes, the book opens by comparing Gabriel's smiling eyes and face to the rising sun (which "also riseth"); and Oak the shepherd, whose first action is to spy leisurely on Bathsheba looking at herself in a mirror, pronounces the final word of the first chapter, "Vanity" (I, 11). Likening Oak to the sun, giving him the name of a sturdy tree, Hardy means to create a man close to nature—to minimize the gap between what people think of as "nature" on the one hand and "human nature" on the other. He imagines Gabriel watching Bathsheba and guessing her mind as she smiles to herself: "She simply observed herself as a fair product of Nature in the feminine kind, her thoughts seeming to glide into far-off though likely dramas in which men would play a part—vistas of probable triumphs—the smiles being of a phase suggesting that hearts were imagined as lost and won" (I, 10). When she haggles about a road toll, Gabriel shows himself and pays it for her. Life in the novel begins with a vision of desire, a relationship between man and woman, thoughts of love, and an act of charity inspired by beauty and erotic longing.

Hardy establishes the pastoral milieu and continues to describe the force of Venus. Soon Oak's eye sweeps to the stars and then back to earth, peeking again through a roof down into an interior upon Bathsheba assisting at the birth of a calf. The shepherd, like his creator, gazing into space and feeling depths of space in himself, uses his eye to find his desire: "Having . . . known the want of a satisfactory form to fill an increasing void within him, . . . he painted her a beauty" (II, 17).

In the next chapter, Oak again spies on Bathsheba, now riding a horse. As she passes under some branches, she drops "backwards flat upon the pony's back, her head over its tail, her feet against its shoulders, and her eyes to the sky" (III, 18). (An iconographic axiom for Victorian fiction: if a woman appears on or near a horse, or talks of horses, look for sex and assessment of her sexual nature.) Bathsheba on her back, feet spread, with knees up and the horse between her legs—that's a suggestive position, to say the least; Gabriel is "amused" and "astonished" (III, 18). By the end of the chapter, having been saved by Bathsheba from suffocation in his hut, his head rests in that very "lap" that straddled the horse, and he finds himself totally in love. Voyeurism and vulnerability, both forms of intimacy, work like love potions.

I dwell on the early scenes of Oak's spying to stress that the pastor is a watcher and that this version of pastoral love is highly sensual. Oak prizes and respects Bathsheba's sexuality. Hardy's imagination, like that of Dickens, insists on the interflow of erotic emotion between a desired being and her (his) surroundings. Instead of purging sexuality from the text, Hardy stands Victorian literary decorum on its head and makes the primacy of erotic life—its drives, its desires, its varied, sometimes sublimated forms—absorb and sexualize the physical details, descriptions, incidents, and even the dialogue of the book. He uses the pastoral in much the same way as Freud would use the dream: as an acceptable, rhetorically distancing means to put before a sexually repressed and repressive audience the erotic forces that shape it.

When Bathsheba comes each day to milk a cow, Hardy conveys through Gabriel what it is like to fall in love: "By making inquiries he found that the girl's name was Bathsheba Everdene, and that the cow would go dry in about seven days. He dreaded the eighth day" (IV, 24). Those deceptively simple words— think how deftly they characterize—indicate how erotic desire is integrated with the world in Oak's character and Hardy's vision. They express a fresh mode of perception in fiction: romantic, but matter-of-fact, full of candor and peasant shrewdness, aware of how the ridiculous turns into love. Steeped in the conditions of rural life, Hardy brings out in an image or phrase personal drama and the enduring patterns of humanity trying to find both love and a living in nature.

"Love," says the narrator, "is a possible strength in an actual weakness" (IV, 24). Substitute "devotion to God" or "duty" for "love" and you can see how the principle of erotic faith ties in with religious faith or faith in labor. Hardy would lose his erotic faith as he had his Christian faith (again and again he would later imagine love as a probable *disaster* in an actual weakness!), but in this novel it holds—just barely. It depends on Oak's steadiness and commitment to "the secret fusion of himself in Bathsheba" (V, 30), which I read as an expression of the religious mystery of erotic love.

VI

The crucial wooing scene between Oak and Bathsheba (IV) has embarrassed some readers with its emotional nakedness. What has been called the "stylized," disturbing quality of the chapter[14] comes from Hardy's effort to have the man and the woman speak exactly as they might think and feel, something that rarely happens in life or fiction. Using the pastoral tradition, he tries to break through the wall of manners in courtship and, through the guilelessness of his characters, get at the irresistible, sometimes demeaning power of love and its uncertainties. The interview has the flavor of old ballads or of biblical stories that omit analysis and sharply truncate time in order to emphasize characteristic patterns, cycles, desires, and symbols of life. Candor, as the scene shows, often has great charm and force, but it can also disturb, making an audience face things it might wish to avoid.

Dressed up in his Sunday best, his hair slicked down, the pastoral lover lays bare his feelings when he calls on Bathsheba and finds her aunt instead: "I've brought a lamb for Miss Everdene. I thought she might like one to rear; girls do. . . . In short, I was going to ask her if she'd like to be married. . . . D'ye know if she's got any other young man hanging about her at all?" When the aunt, playing the game, tells him yes, Gabriel says, "I'm only an every-day sort of man, and my only chance was in being the first comer" (IV, 26). He leaves, but Bathsheba comes running after him in a sweat to say, "I haven't a sweetheart at all—and I never had one, and I thought that, as times go with women, it was *such* a pity to send you away thinking that I had several" (IV, 26–27). "I *hate*," she adds, "to be thought men's property in that way."

Behind the naiveté, Hardy is pushing his readers to focus on traditional courting practices that modern individualism tends to obscure: a man will try to smooth himself for a woman. The young woman is a totem lamb, the object of concern and sometimes of barter. Hers is the favor to grant, for which she is beseeched. She must wait, and that is hard, but when she is desired, she has great power over the male. A man's sense that he must compete for a woman's favor throbs fearfully in his early life, and he thinks about his attractiveness when compared with other men. The "times"—that is, for all intents and purposes here in the nineteenth century, *all human history*—are such that a woman cannot afford to take lightly a lover or an offer. The need to preserve choice and keep options open, plus the sheer love of being loved, may lead her to great exertion and *coqueterie*.

Notice that this scene takes place outside with no relatives around—man and woman isolated in nature—and also that none of the five principal figures, all swept up in love, have any close living relatives. Hardy's new pastoral imagines characters far from the madding crowd of family as well as urban society. What he later says of Boldwood holds for Oak: "No mother existed to absorb his devotion, no sister for his tenderness, no idle ties for sense. He became surcharged with the compound, which was genuine lover's love" (XVIII, 97). No mixture of incest taboo, incest desire, or direct Oedipal conflict mediates the erotic drama in the novel.[15] Oak presses:

"Come . . . think a minute or two. I'll wait a while, Miss Everdene. Will you marry me? Do, Bathsheba. I love you far more than common! . . . I can make you happy. . . . You shall have a piano in a year or two . . . and. . . . one of those little ten-pound gigs for market— and nice flowers, and birds—cocks and hens I mean, because they be useful," continued Gabriel. . . .

"I should like it very much. . . ."

"And when the wedding was over, we'd have it put in the newspaper list of marriages."

"Dearly I should like that!"

"And the babies in the births—every man jack of 'em! And at home by the fire, whenever you look up, there I shall be—and whenever I look up, there will be you."

"Wait, wait, and don't be improper!"

Her countenance fell, and she was silent awhile. He regarded the red berries between them over and over again, to such an extent that holly seemed in his after life to be a cypher signifying a proposal of marriage. . . .

"No; 'tis no use," she said. "I don't want to marry you."

"Try."

"I've tried hard. . . . But a husband—. . . . Why, he'd always be there, as you say; whenever I looked up, there he'd be. . . . I shouldn't mind being a bride at a wedding, if I could be one without having a husband. . . ."

"Why won't you have me?" he appealed. . . .

"Because I don't love you. . . ."

"But I love you—and, as for myself, I am content to be liked."

"O Mr. Oak—that's very fine! You'd get to despise me."

"Never," said Mr. Oak so earnestly that he seemed to be coming, by the force of his words, straight through the bush and into her arms. "I shall do one thing in this life—one thing certain—that is, love you, and long for you, and *keep wanting you* till I die."

". . . It wouldn't do, Mr. Oak. I want somebody to tame me; I am too independent; and you would never be able to, I know. . . . I am better educated than you—and I don't love you a bit."

". . . Very well," said Oak firmly, with the bearing of one who was going to give his days and nights to Ecclesiastes for ever. "Then I'll ask you no more." [IV, 27–30]

This minimalist art dissolves pretenses that surround courting men and women. It liberates: "I'm only an every-day sort of man," "I am content to be liked," "I am better educated than you," "I don't love you." These common feelings and ideas that women and men often try to hide come across here as straight facts of life. In Hardy there is sometimes a lifting of moral responsibility that accounts for moments of subversive, odd buoyancy—even in his gloomiest work: You cannot help it that you do not love some deserving person, that you have flaws, that your moral code does not jibe with reality, that you are a creature of desire and chance, that love and virtue may diverge. Life is hard enough without pretending that you want only what is good or that you are not hopelessly in love with some frustrating being who is bound to cause you grief.

The suddenness of Oak's proposal, the brevity of their acquaintance, his intensity, and Bathsheba's candid wonder about whether to take up the offer and then her refusal all point up how arbitrary love and marriage are. Shear away the superfluities of wooing, and you see that people, like Oak or Bathsheba, by love possessed or trying dimly to see their own good, make the fatal decisions of their love lives from quick impressions and moody impulses. Behind its pastoral rhetoric, the scene is very sophisticated about the ways of love and of men and women. If love rules the world, it is as likely as not to be unrequited love. Characters in Hardy may decide to take love, give themselves, or marry out of calculation, but they cannot decide to be in love. People may want flamboyance rather than kind devotion in love. With any couple, there is liable to be an imbalance of desire, and the beloved wields shattering power. The one who loves less may win—*in the short run.*

On the other side, erotic desire can give shape and purpose to a whole life. As novels keep saying, lovers may be more interested in their own fidelity and the defining force of their devotion than in the character of those they love. Oak speaks the popular Victorian erotic creed: "I shall do one thing in this life . . . love you . . . *keep wanting you* till I die." Usually time proves this common sentiment false; the test of Oak's faith, then, becomes the test of erotic faith in the novel.

What do Oak and Bathsheba really want? The man seems to desire the woman's person, and she seems to desire status; but it's not that simple. When we look at how he woos her, we see that he equates the woman with the amenities of civilization: music, beauty, luxury, and, most important, regeneration. And naturally he assumes that what he wants, she would want. He is the pastor, and she, in all her beauty, is still for him a lamb. He has the craving of the good shepherd: "I will take care of you well, nourish your being, protect and love your essence, and in return I want and hope to use you for my purposes." He does not say, "I will love you, but if that does not please you, I will respect your freedom and let you go from my desire"; he wants her to know, "I will keep wanting you till I die." Pastoral love is especially unremitting and ultimately possessive.[16]

Hardy's succinct probe of desire goes deep. Oak thinks Bathsheba wants a richer life, the bourgeois dream; she does, but not nearly as much as he. She does not yet want to be settled as much as she wants passion: she wants, as strong people sometimes do, to fight a love struggle and have her independent will crossed ("I want somebody to tame me; I am too independent"). That is the key to her fall for Troy. Though Hardy and Austen would seem as different as outdoors and indoors, both imagine worlds that drive a bright, lively woman to flirt rebelliously, kicking against the social pricks. Bathsheba, when she takes up Oak's words and confesses how much she detests the idea of seeing a husband always there, like a jailer, is never more winning.

We keep seeing that the erotic dream and method of novelists are to bring together those who talk straight to each other, like Heathcliff and Cathy. Gabriel's candor is what allows Bathsheba to be honest with him and to learn her own mind. How educational it is to be rudely frank to someone who loves you. She can say anything to him; they can say anything to each other; and that experience—and memory—of being able to talk freely without penalty to a potential lover, even though things at first do not work out, can, over time, work like a slow love philter.

A quicker aphrodisiac is doubt. From start to finish, what excites Bathsheba is a love that might fly. Though she runs after Oak, once she is sure of him she feels no passion for him at all. Sexual desire may be natural, but its arousal often depends on jeopardy, novelty, and the thrill of breaking taboos. Hardy's parable about Bathsheba's father not only helps define the nature of her erotic character, it expresses perfectly the tension—tension thick in the proposal scene—and the far-reaching conflict between sex and moralized love, sex and marriage, sex and the demands of civilization.

> ". . . Miss Everdene's father—was one of the ficklest husbands alive. . . . 'Coggan,' he said, 'I could never wish for a handsomer woman than I've got, but feeling she's ticketed as my lawful wife, I can't help my wicked heart wandering, do what I will.' But at last I believe he cured it by making her take off her wedding-ring and calling her by her maiden name as they sat together . . . and so 'a would get to fancy she was only his sweetheart, and not married to him at all. And as soon as he could thoroughly fancy he was doing wrong and committing the seventh ["Thou shalt not commit adultery"], 'a got to like her as well as ever, and they lived on a perfect picture of mutel love." [VIII, 52]

That may be a desperate remedy, but all who marry ought to know about it.

Devotees of pastoral love, like Hardy and Oak, must take into account the reality that humanity is a wandering flock. Victorian and modern civilization's almost impossibly difficult project is to make love and desire, erotics and marriage, contiguous, harmonious, and whole. Hardy focuses upon that great problem in his pastoral. The tone and meaning of the wooing scene as overture come through in Gabriel's reference to Ecclesiastes and its wise pastor, who promises a time for everything under the sun, including love.

VII

All life in Hardy's art is imbued with eroticism, and the displacement of sexuality into landscape is one of its main features. As, say, Sundays and holidays are set aside from normal days, human sexuality has been abstracted, set apart, made special and "other" from "regular" life. In Hardy, the body's sexual life manifests itself and takes place in a metaphorical setting. Ironically, Hardy adapts this method to try to make eroticism integral in the life of his novel. But displacement, the solution to his artistic problem of how to express the importance of sex in a medium that represses it, shows up as a highly significant problem in itself.

His vision both counteracts repression and is itself a symptom of sexual alienation. Hardy makes perception inseparable from erotics, but because he must show the fullness of sexual being in outward nature, rather than through the inner or bodily self, the rhetoric of his novel inevitably coaxes people to look for the erotic beyond themselves, somewhere else. The trouble with displacement is that it can frustrate people erotically by locating sex everywhere, but nowhere specially. Hardy's method of sexual representation, that is, symbolic voyeurism, is part of the message. It tends to make sex metaphorical and life vicarious. Real life lies beyond the self. Hardy's imagination touches on the advent of a mass, voyeuristic, consumerist culture. His general vision carries implications that the regenerative forces of life do not lie in the person but in the fertile continuity of ongoing nature. The hope of this art is that individuals will see themselves as part of the natural continuum of being. Its drawback is that the self can seem devalued—vacuumed. Drained away from specific individuals, erotic sympathy and reverence might flow towards the macrocosm that holds the potent force and the images of sexual energy. The danger for the good shepherd, i.e., the pastoral lover, artist, or caring reader, is that personal life and being will become both idealized and fetishized in the object of desire. Pastoral love, voyeurism, and the phenomenon of the novel have much in common.

Hardy's much-praised renderings of the countryside, the famous sword-practice episode and its complement, the storm-thatching scene, show how his pastoral voyeurism works. The scene from high summer, after Bathsheba has met Troy, famously fuses human sexuality into the landscape.

The hill opposite . . . extended . . . into an uncultivated tract of land, dotted at this season with tall thickets of brake fern, plump and diaphanous from recent rapid growth. . . . At eight o'clock this midsummer evening, whilst the bristling ball of gold in the west still swept the tips of the ferns with its long, luxuriant rays, a soft brushing-by of garments might have been heard among them, and Bathsheba appeared in their midst, their soft, feathery arms caressing her up to her shoulders. . . . She reached the verge of a pit in the middle of the ferns. . . . The pit was a saucer-shaped concave. . . . The middle within the belt of verdure was floored with a thick flossy carpet of moss and grass intermingled, so yielding that the foot was half-buried within it. [XXVIII, 142–43]

Hardy is describing a midsummer night's dream where Bathsheba erotically opens to Troy.

In autumn, we see the exact same place, after Troy has married and betrayed her. She spends the night amid the ferns, and in the morning she sees seasonal changes:

[T]he ground sloped downwards to a hollow, in which was a species of swamp, dotted with fungi. . . . From its moist and poisonous coat seemed to be exhaled the essences of evil things. . . . The fungi grew in all manner of positions from rotting leaves and tree stumps, some exhibiting to her listless gaze their clammy tops, others their oozing gills. Some were marked with great splotches, red as arterial blood, others were saffron yellow, and others tall and attenuated, with stems like macaroni. Some were leathery and of richest browns. The hollow seemed a nursery of pestilences small and great. [XLIV, 232–33]

The fall landscape renders the sexual fall and the shame of Bathsheba. And in hindsight, we can see that the effects of the revolving year on the land reflect exactly Bathsheba's changing erotic condition. Hardy's seasonal visions of nature serve to objectify her libido and the emotional rhythms of her sexual life.

Why beat around the bush, to adopt his mode? His sensibility seems at times to turn nature into pornography. The uncanny precision of these descriptions—such passages in the novel could be multiplied again and again—shows his own libido fully engaged. It is as if Wessex itself were a great woman and the surface of the earth were her flesh. This kind of sensual prose vision reminds me again of David looking at Bathsheba, or of the elders looking at Susannah. Hardy has the same caressing eye, the same voyeuristic desire to possess the erotic in the act of exposure. The absorbing vision of this novel sometimes makes it clear how nature in the nineteenth century—and other times as well—could and did become a grand erotic fetish.

The sword-practice scene in "The Hollow amid the Ferns" (XXVIII), one of the most celebrated sexual passages in respectable Victorian fiction, epitomizes and vindicates Hardy's double-entendre method. In the setting and context of Bathsheba's inner sexual flowering and the outward fecundity of her surroundings, it remains vivid:

"Now," said Troy, producing the sword, which, as he raised it into the sunlight, gleamed a sort of greeting, like a living thing. . . . "The thrusts are these: one, two, three, four. . . . Now I'll be more interesting, and let you see some loose play . . . quicker than lightning, and as promiscuously". . . .

He flourished the sword . . . , and the next thing of which she was conscious was that the point and blade of the sword were darting with a gleam towards her left side, just above her hip; then of their reappearance on her right side . . . having apparently passed through her body. . . . All was as quick as electricity.

"Oh! . . . Have you run me through?—no, you have not! Whatever have you done!" . . .

In an instant the atmosphere was transformed to Bathsheba's eyes. Beams of light caught from the low sun's rays, above, around, in front of her, well-nigh shut out earth and heaven—all emitted in the marvellous evolutions of Troy's reflecting blade. . . . These circling gleams were accompanied by a keen rush that was almost a whistling—also springing from all sides of her at once. In short, she was enclosed in a firmament of light, and of sharp hisses, resembling a sky-full of meteors close at hand. . . .

That minute's interval had brought the blood beating into her face, set her stinging as if aflame to the very hollows of her feet, and enlarged emotion to a compass which quite swamped thought. It had brought upon her a stroke resulting, as did that of Moses in Horeb, in a liquid stream—here a stream of tears. She felt like one who has sinned a great sin. [XXVIII, 143–46]

Bathsheba, ravished in this way by Troy, falls in love for the first time. She is already loved by two devoted men, Oak and Boldwood, but now she feels an ecstasy that Hardy describes as the surge of orgasm. Troy, a soldier, menaces her with his sword. The kinship of sex to violence, to danger, to sublimated cruelty, to mastery and surrender of will, to flaunting physical show, and escape from ordinary life jumps off the page. It simply will not do to moralize smoothly on this chapter, as many have done, and deplore Bathsheba's reaction to Troy as "self-destructive,"[17] misguided, or tragic. To do so misses the point, slighting and cheapening the soul-shaking power of the erotic.

If the new pastoral love is to have any value and win any credence, it must allow for and include the force and even the joy of sexuality that traditional morality calls "error" or "sin." According to Hardy, we live in an old world where a David's erotic desire causes him to take a Bathsheba wrongfully and a Bathsheba's erotic drive causes her to take a Troy thoughtlessly. Libidinous love is the way of this world, and life does not just end for these figures when they follow their erotic drives into suffering. Straying sheep test faith and pastoral love, and *everyone* is a straying sheep.

VIII

The sword-flash scene is the one every reader of the novel remembers, but just as important—in fact, conjoined to it, like the panel of a diptych—is the storm scene with Oak and Bathsheba together working to save the harvest (XXXVII). Hardy imagines in this climactic passage a love that brings together devotion to a beloved's well-being, concern for the common good, mutual purpose, shared work, affection, and potent sexuality—in short, love's old dream of combining moral responsibility and the stunning force of the erotic.

Far from the Madding Crowd does not deny the ecstasy of being carried away by first love, nor the sweeping thrill of the fern-pit experience, but it works to integrate eroticism into a larger perspective. Hardy, getting at the ubiquity of the sexual imagination and his own habits of mind and art, says, "[M]an, even to himself, is a palimpsest, having an ostensible writing, and another beneath the lines" (XXXVI, 189). The context for that remark and the storm that follows is this: after the harvest and wedding celebration, which ends with Troy, newly married to Bathsheba, getting himself and all the farmhands helplessly drunk, Oak, alert, feels a ruinous storm approaching and, calculating exactly the monetary damage it will do to the unprotected grain, decides to try to save the crop. Hardy, referring to "man" as a text of hidden meanings, then writes, "It is possible that there was this golden legend under the utilitarian one: 'I will help to my last effort the woman I have loved so dearly'" (XXXVI, 189). The spirit of courtly love filters downward into society, blending with practical economics and the eroticization of nature to generate a new pastoral.

The novel portrays Oak, "the faithful man" (XXXVI, 190), acting out his love for—and with—Bathsheba in circumstances that contrast with Troy in the hollow and that put the narrative in a new light. Instead of a sword, Gabriel's instrument, that he keeps sticking in the "stack" to thatch, is "his ricking-rod, or poniard, as it was indifferently called—a long iron lance, . . . polished by handling" (XXXVII, 192). Hardy flaunts his symbolism. Bathsheba and "the stack" become one: "Oak looked up. . . . Bathsheba was sitting almost on the apex of the stack, her feet gathered up beneath her" (XXXVII, 195). Instead of ferns, we have Bathsheba's sheaves of grain. Instead of glinting summer sunlight and movement *like* electricity, we get real electricity in a dramatic lightning storm. Instead of "loose play," we have work; instead of feminine passivity, we have the mistress laboring with the man. Instead of the seducer, we have the unrequited lover risking his life for a woman. Instead of nature as backdrop for human sexuality, we have a vision of nature's full potency, sexual force, and engulfing qualities—its power to bind a man and a woman together in a closeness that mocks the looseness of infatuation and even the relative impotence of the social marriage contract. Instead of a virgin closed to the good shepherd but ready to unclose to the scarlet soldier, we have a woman who, without being conscious of it, is beginning now to open herself to the pastoral lover.

As the lightning gets closer and the man uses his rod to thatch, the woman joins him, and they work alone in harmony in the storm, he for her future good. Instead of Bathsheba's enclosure in the "firmament" of light from Troy's phallic sword, we have Bathsheba and Oak enclosed in this primal scene of cosmic sex:

[T]here came a burst of light.

"Hold on!" said Gabriel, taking the sheaf from her shoulder, and grasping her arm again.

Heaven opened then, indeed. The flash was almost too novel for its inexpressibly dangerous nature to be at once realized, and they could only comprehend the magnificence of its beauty. It sprang from east, west, north, south, and was a perfect dance of death. The forms of skeletons appeared in the air, shaped with blue fire for bones—dancing, leaping, striding, racing around, and mingling altogether in unparalleled confusion. With these were intertwined undulating snakes of green, and behind these was a broad mass of lesser light. Simultaneously came from every part of the tumbling sky what may be called a shout. . . . In the meantime one of the grisly forms had alighted upon the point of Gabriel's rod, to run invisibly down it, down the chain, and into the earth. Gabriel was almost blinded, and he could feel Bathsheba's warm arm tremble in his hand—a sensation novel and thrilling enough; but love, life, everything human, seemed small and trifling in such close juxtaposition with an infuriated universe. . . .

Bathsheba said nothing; but he could distinctly hear her rhythmical pants, and the recurrent rustle of the sheaf beside her in response to her frightened pulsations. [XXXVII, 193–94]

That sexual displacement is also erotic sublimation on a superhuman scale. Sources as diverse as popular mythology, the *Bhagavad-Gita*, Vico, James Joyce, and Jerome Kern as sung and danced by Fred Astaire in *Top Hat*,[18] locate the beginning of all eroticism and fertility in the Promethean spark of lightning, the generative heavenly act. In Hardy's storm, it is as if the arrows of blind Eros were made into Zeus's thunderbolts. Oak and Bathsheba share a time of primitive intimacy—a time, the imagery shows, of intense sexuality. What these two are made to see, feel, and share of lightning here, they are made to know in their lives of love's fiery beauty, its ominous potential for annihilation, its randomness, and the amazingly varied, fateful reactions it calls forth. Hardy represents them finding that love is not merely personal, though it is seen and experienced personally. It is set in and against the power of the impersonal—that is the meaning of Oak's experiencing the thrill of Bathsheba's touch just at the moment when nature is dwarfing to insignificance individual human emotions and concerns. This moment exposes a deep conflict in Hardy and in modern feelings about love generally.[19] One person's erotic passion may seem—and, in fact, *be*—trivial and ineluctably doomed when set against the universe's furious energy or even against the full range of human life; but without that spark of love there is no worth or meaning in life—no perception, even, according to this text, of the universe. Human love, according to Hardy, is what makes the novelist and characters see what they see. Imagining a new pastoral love, epitomized by Oak and his actions in this scene, is an attempt to reconcile the contradiction between flashing nature as both source and destroyer of love and life. The storm episode constitutes the experience and vision on which he bases his summary words about the pastoral love "strong as death" and the final union of Oak and Bathsheba. The rest of the novel elaborates the metaphorical implications of this scene.

Bathsheba's thoughts of Gabriel after the death of Fanny Robin mark the progress of her growing love.

> She suddenly felt a longing to speak to some one stronger than herself, and so get strength. . . . What a way Oak had, she thought, of enduring things. . . . [A]mong the multitude of interests by which he was surrounded, those which affected his personal well-being were not the most absorbing and important in his eyes. Oak meditatively looked upon the horizon of circumstances without any special regard to his own standpoint in the midst. That was how she would wish to be. [XLIII, 226]

No doubt that was also how Hardy himself wished to be, and, as a writer, sometimes saw himself. His own vision and desire obviously mingle here with Bathsheba's reflection. The passage claims for Oak and his pastoral outlook sweeping powers of perception unlimited by the ego's focus. Behind the modesty that she ascribes to the shepherd lies an unselfconscious pride that can make dazzling assumptions—assumptions on which the whole practice of the nineteenth-century novel may rest: first, that he can know and enter helpfully into the interests and circumstances of others; and, second, that he is so strong, competent, and farseeing that he can transcend normal self-interest. Hardy's imagination fused the identities of pastor, lover, and novelist, but so in effect did most distinguished Victorian fiction.

The wellspring of Oak's pastoralism is erotic, not ethical or conventionally religious, and that is what keeps him, the faithful shepherd, from being a sentimental or self-righteous figure. Hardy calls him, in all that he does, "the love-led man" (XXI, 112). The reward for his commitment would seem to come, after all, in the loving regard of the woman he is strong enough to love unrequitedly. Erotic desire may help stimulate a pastoral love that in turn may finally stimulate erotic desire in the other. That is the hope of this perilous world. Hardy imagines that someone could love another better than oneself, and do so effectively; erotic feeling, not God, first inspires Oak. This matters: the basis of pastoral love in *Far from the Madding Crowd* is not maternal or paternal feeling, not infantile memory, not God, not supernatural awe, not utilitarian drive or material necessity, but sexual attraction—erotic desire.

Oak is a symbolic act of faith in the novel, an ideal pastoral lover rooted in his love for the other. His rod is "grounded," unlike Troy's sword or Boldwood's gun. He can make us see the crudeness of reductive, totalizing notions of a phallocentric sexuality, a phallocentric society, *the phallus*. All phallic symbols, all phallic acts, are not the same. Gabriel wields the lance to save the lives of the bloated sheep, he plays the flute for pleasure, and he plies his rod to preserve the grain. Whatever tool or instrument he touches, he uses to serve and enrich the woman's life and space and to bring human consciousness into harmony with natural force. Odd irony that the most notoriously pessimistic of nineteenth-century English novelists should have imagined the successful good shepherd of Aphrodite.

IX

Love is the fate, test, god, and desire of the four other figures besides Oak who make the plot. They are what John Bayley, playing on the relationship between writing and emotional life, calls "characters of love."[20]

Bathsheba: A heroine with staying power, she is both the "new" woman and the old, both conventional female "life force" and uncategorizable individual.[21] Like her biblical namesake she becomes a fatal object of desire. She plays the roles of a Ruth, an Esther, and a Queen of Sheba, but she also moves and acts with restless modern subjectivity. Hardy wants to see her as a typical female partaking of a common, timeless femininity; but, knowing life as he does, he also imagines something new in history. The narrator describes her near the end: "She was of the stuff of which great men's mothers are made. She was indispensable to high generation, hated at tea parties, feared in shops, and loved at crises" (LIV, 291). That hints at her richness, shows how she has developed since Oak first wooed her, but it underscores the tensions in her characterization and indirectly points up the way she eludes even thoughtful generalization. The male author's urge to classify the female by biological function and delimit roles for even the most vital of women can nettle feminist nerves. But Hardy's sexist tic of saying, in effect, "just like a woman," or fitting Bathsheba, from time to time, into a male-defined mold of female nature, ought not to obscure her complexity and consequence as a fictional figure. Inheriting and running a large farm, knowing and accepting three very different men as mates, she works and loves as most Victorians would expect only a man could. A problematic figure, she is not yet a pastor herself, like Oak. But she shows, as she participates in Hardy's new pastoralism, that the social and novelistic imagination is moving towards the conception of woman as an active pastoral figure.

Range of emotion and action, fluidity of libido, and frankness characterize Bathsheba. She has what Hardy calls "general intensity of . . . nature" and a proportionate "capacity for intense feeling" (XLIII, 230). Look at what she does: boldly commands the men of the farm; laughs at Gabriel, but holds his love; plays girlishly with her maid Liddy and sends Boldwood the fatal valentine; meets Troy alone in the hollow; elopes; braves the lightning with Oak; opens the coffin of Fanny and her baby; lays flowers about the dead girl's head; abases herself horribly with a husband whom she loves but despises; works with Oak to decorate her rival's grave; goes to the circus; agrees to marry Boldwood out of guilt for having led him on; tries bravely to staunch the wound of her dying husband; virtually proposes to another man (Oak) when she's hardly out of mourning; loves chastity, sex, work, music, her own beauty, stoicism, and agriculture; acts with contradictory cruelty and kindness; loves and resents male strength; ends up having chosen all of her suitors.

Hardy tries to express painful truths through her that most people would like to deny. Near the end, for instance, she says to Oak with an awful matter-of-factness: "I have thought so much more of you since I fancied you did not want even to see me again" (LVI, 303). After all they have gone through, this sympathetic being nevertheless tells him in effect: *To arouse my desire and win me, don't be nice; be mean. Threaten me with loss.* Cupid is an imp of the perverse. Hardy, through Bathsheba's amorous response to indifference and the threat of loss, *is* getting at something deep about the feminine push for independence. A buried resentment wells up in her—and in other high-spirited nineteenth-century heroines, like Emma Bovary, Anna Karenina, Natasha Rostov, and Meredith's Clara Middleton—against being fixed as an *object* of desire by a conventionally good man, rather than acting herself as a desiring entity. To be put on a pedestal, to be idolized, means becoming inert, losing selfhood, as does having to admire what is conventionally respectable. To follow desire, no matter how ill-chosen, is to begin to assume full individuality.

Hardy, through Bathsheba, is candid about the abasement of love. When Troy proves a bad husband, she scorns him in her heart; but then she opens the coffin of his dead lover Fanny and sees her with the stillborn child. At Troy's return, Bathsheba's revulsion for him fades in a moment. She knows, as he kisses the dead woman, how absolute his betrayal has been, but all her feelings coalesce. Grabbing him she screams, "from the deepest deep of her heart—'Don't—don't kiss them. O, Frank, I can't bear it—I can't! I love you better than she did: kiss me too, Frank—kiss me! *You will, Frank, kiss me too!'*" (XLIII, 230).

Not much has been said about this scene. It may be shocking and melodramatic, but only someone who has never felt a hint of the power of love to debase—never felt the impulse to hang on at all costs, never seen the execution of the abandoned self in the cold eyes of a beloved—could miss the emotional force of this passage. Many want to forget the abjection that can come with erotic desire. Surely, however, there is something soothing in the resilience of Hardy's own creative imagination when he makes this figure cry out the truth of the agonizing vulnerability of being in love—"Loving is a misery for women always. I shall never forgive God for making me a woman" (XXX, 154)—but then goes on to describe the delight and promise with which she marries Oak.

Let us return to Bathsheba's remark, when Boldwood badgers her about what exactly she feels for him: "It is difficult for a woman to define her feelings in language which is chiefly made by men to express theirs." Hardy, in representing this woman, is trying to realize that insight. Bathsheba avoids fixity, she points to and sometimes embodies a protean way of being that resists the structure of definition. When Troy refuses her that kiss, she rushes away into the autumnal fern hollow turned as rank as festering eroticism. Hardy, through Bathsheba, is figuring in the text an intuition that resists abstraction and may lend itself to charges of sentimentalization and "pathetic fallacy." This creative perception works as art but tends to fade when we try to describe it in the categorizing language made chiefly by men.

But let me try: Bathsheba is not a symbol of nature or natural existence, but neither is she separable from nature. Hardy not only makes clear that her being and libido inhabit the fern hollow, he cannot imagine, in this book, that the fern hollow exists *in any conceivable form without her.* Her being, the pervasiveness of erotic desire for and by her, and the pastoral love she provokes, merge into the sheep, into the hiving bees, the landscape, the lightning, and most of the rest of what we see: her character and what is visible are not separably meaningful. The terse sentence that best epitomizes her essence opens the penultimate chapter in which, after all the calamities, she woos Oak: "Bathsheba revived with the spring" (LVI, 297). That does *not* simply say that she, being a natural creature, is influenced by the seasonal buoyancy. Hardy's insight is comparable to Botticelli's in the *Primavera*: we are wrong, we betray our real experience and perceptions of life and art, if we cannot see that the beautiful image of the woman and the reviving spring are ineluctably fused, that what we mean and understand by "spring" does not exist without that desirable configuration. It is the flow of Bathsheba's being into the world and the eye that arouses pastoral feeling for life and causes the voice of the dove to be heard in the land.

Troy: The seducer, the huckster of desire and instant gratification, the Paris of Wessex—he matters also. Lying to women, he flatters them, tells them what they want to hear, persuades them to trust and uncover. The novel makes him a Don Juan and shows in him the democratization of that mythic figure. Hardy does not moralize much on him, but in the squalid consequences of Troy's sexual victimizing he makes clear, better than most moralists, why the threat of Don Juan haunted the Western imagination and why people, though they might feel some envy and admiration for him, were so sincerely ready to damn and hate him.

A bastard born of erotic desire, the progeny of a lord and a maid—noblesse oblige and servitude—Troy seeks to replicate explosive moments of erotic euphoria. Unable to defer satisfaction, he acts out of impulse, makes sudden, splashy gestures, and embodies a nasty version of the romantic temper, which has always been conjoined with the thrill and menace of sexual attraction. He personifies at moments pure sexuality, without past or future, that loose phallic cannon on the ship of civilization. All time is *now* for him, and such people, though exciting, are dangerous: "He was a man to whom memories were an incumbrance, and anticipations a superfluity. Simply feeling, considering, and caring for what was before his eyes, he was vulnerable only in the present" (XXV, 130). Hardy goes on to say that Troy can be considered lucky, since recall often works like a disease, and absolute faith, the only comfortable form of looking ahead, is practically impossible for a contemporary human being.

As Bathsheba's first love, he has a feeling for what will touch and move her. In his early scenes with her, we get the gaiety—as we do not elsewhere—in the flirting ways of men and maids. He brings erotic desire into her ken; Troy knows what people like. The trouble is, what they like may not be good for them. Master of swordplay, he is not really a soldier, but a showman and a salesman. In terms of the plot, he helps make possible the flourishing of Oak's love; pastoralism needs erotic flash. But pastoral love, to endure, must keep the inevitable fall of Troy in perspective.

Boldwood: Love comes to him like syphilis to the South Sea islanders. More than a figure of aberrant psychology, he manifests important tendencies in erotic history. A devotee to a terrible internalized love deity, he appears as a familiar enough creature of the Victorian age: a love-struck man whose regard turns a woman into an object—not a sex object but a religious icon on whom he projects all meaning and value.

The valentine Bathsheba sends out of mischief and chance hits him like the heart attack it is and turns him into a scary romantic-obsessive. Over forty, and never having been in love, he becomes abject and compulsive. At first, his condition resembles Oak's and, later, Bathsheba's: "[H]e was now," says Hardy, in memorable words about what being in love feels like, "living outside his defences for the first time, and with a fearful sense of exposure" (XVIII, 96–97). But Boldwood, unlike Oak, cannot really see or know *the other*, the woman Bathsheba. He is like Pip, who, fixated, fetishizes Estella; except that Boldwood is middle-aged and inflexible. Symbolically, his fate is told in the vision of him staring at Bathsheba's valentine: "Here the bachelor's gaze was continually fastening itself, till the large red seal became as a blot of blood on the retina of his eye; and as he ate and drank he still read in fancy the words thereon . . . — 'MARRY ME'" (XIV, 80). In his solipsistic fixation, the blot on his retina stays permanently, and when he gazes at the card, "The vision of the woman writing, as a supplement to the words written, had no individuality" (XIV, 81). Bathsheba is a romantic injunction and fantasy inscribed in his mind, not an independent woman. And when, with this new shaft of love in him, he walks out to look at the morning, he sees "over the snowy down . . . the only half of the sun yet visible . . . like a red and flameless fire shining over a white hearthstone" (XIV, 81). The bloody-looking valentine expands to become his heart, his world, and the whole spectacle of his life.

How fitting that Boldwood turns out to be an actual fetishist, with a locked-away horde of ladies' dresses, jewelry, and the like, "brought home by stealth," neatly packaged and marked "Bathsheba Boldwood" (LV, 294). He has made a fetish of her, calling her life. He wants to own her and cherish her as a wonderful possession—a self-possession; and proof that she is an object shows through in his indifference to the fact that she does not at all love him. Love can be— often is—a fetishism of one's self, one's emotions, one's desire. Fetishism develops when the thing or configuration that symbolizes and is associated with one's love itself becomes the object of erotic desire and emotion. Feelings change; it is easy to lose the symbolic flow. My love may be like a red, red rose, but then I may stop seeing or loving the woman or man and keep loving and feeling the erotic power of the rose. Or I may love the name of the rose and the narrative of love.

The fetishist, however, lacks dignity; he acts out the theme of erotic abasement. Hardy psychologizes Boldwood and makes him more introspective than any of the other characters. His mind, finally "crazed with care and love" (LV, 295), resembles the locked closet with the collection of articles that symbolize Bathsheba, but that she never sees. Boldwood loses pastoral feeling and true vocation; he can see only what is inside his head, the image of his longing. One of love's men in the dark, deranged and locked away from the light by solipsistic eroticism, he is ruled by a blind love god sprung from his own head, engendered by caprice. Imagine him alone, surreptitiously fondling and arranging the clothes, the bracelets, the golden things he has bought for Bathsheba. That is love as idolatry, a common blasphemy of the desperate idealist against life.

Fanny Robin: She is the victim of Troy's sexual sword, one for whom the Cyprian's name is Death. Her presence reminds us of why, until recently, a society could not for long sentimentalize eroticism or treat it frivolously. Like Eliot's Hetty Sorrel and Hardy's Tess of the d'Urbervilles, she embodies the doom that has always threatened to sap and spoil erotic faith: *unwanted pregnancy*.

In all of Hardy, no fate is harsher than Fanny's, no passage bleaker than her trek on the Casterbridge highway (XL). Late in her pregnancy, starving and cold, she struggles pitifully to get to the poorhouse, where she thinks Troy may meet her. Her trip is like something out of Samuel Beckett, only without the jokes: at first barely able to propel herself on homemade crutches, then not at all, she finally gets there, mostly dead, by hanging on to a huge homeless dog. Her quest of love turns her into an agonized, dumb animal; she and her baby die wretchedly.

How can Hardy maintain a hopeful equanimity or any sort of faith when his novel includes such a character and such a fate? We come back again—as we do so often in matters of faith—to the idea of sacrifice. In the religious imagination, figures often die so that others may learn and flourish in spirit (e.g., in the love religion, Lucy Ashton, Cathy Earnshaw, Heathcliff, Paul Emanuel, Miss Havisham, Maggie Tulliver). When Bathsheba confronts the corpses of Fanny and her baby, she is at first bitter: "The one feat alone—that of dying—by which a mean condition could be resolved into a grand one, Fanny had achieved" (XLIII, 228). But that transformation from "mean" to "grand" is not limited to the self. As Bathsheba changes and warms, those words on the victim's death take on a redemptive, even religious, meaning. The sacrifice of Fanny helps move the narrative and Bathsheba out of erotic chaos towards a new kind of love.

Hardy, looking for a living creed in the world, imagines one more important "character" that makes his pastoral come alive: the chorus of country folk. If all flesh is grass, that at least means that flesh will always be. These people exist collectively in vocational relationship to nature and to each other; they constitute a kind of human landscape, a continuous entity that is the mortal equivalent of nature's revolving, returning year. In essence, they personify "good nature" and its communal voice, distilling erotic wisdom in a vivid comic *poetry of the flock*. Again and again we get language such as this by a servant bewailing her single state: "what between the poor men I won't have, and the rich men who won't have me, I stand as a pelican in the wilderness" (IX, 63).

X

Orthodox religion counts for little in the novel, except as a tradition that induces ritual habits and as Scripture, which serves as a body of common knowledge and a source of analogues that brings continuity to people's daily experience. The novel's pastoral love seems to antedate and outlast the Christian model of pastoralism, which appears here as a historical variety of something larger. Before the priest, there was the love-dazed shepherd; before the congregation, the flock. The great barn, which he describes famously in chapter XXII as the temple of the sheepshearing and the religion of "daily bread," is more holy than the church and, in its form, older.

Consider the sentence, "The defence and salvation of the body by daily bread is still a study, a religion, and a desire" (XXII, 114). Though the novel stresses and honors the vocation of gaining the sustenance to support life, "daily bread" is neither the subject nor the savior in the book. If we say the defence and salvation of the body by *love* is *still* a study, a religion, and a desire, we describe the pastoral activity and faith of Oak and the point of view of "Hardy," and we characterize *Far from the Madding Crowd* generally.

Claude's *Judgment of Paris* can again help in reading the narrative and seeing its meaning. Look, if you can find it, at Paris's golden apple and what the painting does to it. That idol of fetishistic beauty, sexual yearning, and inert mammonism—so prominent in Bronzino's view of corrupted love—is lost in the expanse and flow of nature, diminished almost to nothing by the tree and its connotations. Hardy chooses to end his novel with these words of Joseph Poorgrass, on leaving the newly wedded Bathsheba and Oak: "I wish him joy o' her; though I were once or twice upon saying to-day with holy Hosea, in my scripture manner . . . , 'Ephraim is joined to idols; let him alone.' [4:17] But since 'tis as 'tis, why, it might have been worse, and I feel my thanks accordingly" (LVII, 308).[22] That is puzzling until we go to Hosea and its final chapter. There idolatry ends and growth returns in a way that exactly parallels the novel. From "Ephraim is joined to idols" the prophet moves to this: "His branches shall spread. . . . They that dwell under his shadow shall return; they shall revive as the corn, and grow as the vine: the scent thereof shall be as the wine of Lebanon. Ephraim shall say, What have I to do any more with idols? . . . I am like a green fir tree. From me is thy fruit found." Oak, who embodies and shades amorous desire and pastoral love in this landmark vision of erotic faith, rises like the tree in Claude Lorrain, like the tree in Hosea.

10 Tristan Is Sold: The Joyce of Love and the Language of Flow(er)s (1904–39)

I am nauseated by their lying drivel about pure men and pure women and spiritual love and love for ever: blatant lying in the face of the truth. I don't know much about the 'saince' of the subject, but I presume there are very few mortals in Europe who are not in danger of waking some morning and finding themselves syphilitic. . . . Perhaps my view of life is too cynical but it seems to me that a lot of this talk about love is nonsense.

JAMES JOYCE[1]

If we consider the book [Ulysses] as a whole, the theme of love will seem to pervade it.

RICHARD ELLMANN[2]

I

If love is a religion, then James Joyce is a defender of the faith.[3] This comedian and skeptic, who wrote the taunting sentence, "Love loves to love love," mocked sentimental love fiction and doubted love's value and very existence; nevertheless he appears in his fashion as a devoted scribe of Venus. I want to show what happens to love, the staple of the nineteenth-century novel, in the prose of this most avant-garde and influential of early twentieth-century novelists writing in English. Specifically, I mean to look at instances of the word "love" and at love passages in Joyce to see how his erotic sense evolved and gave shape to the two great works of his maturity, *Ulysses* (1922) and *Finnegans Wake* (1939).

One outcome of the nineteenth-century fusion of love and the novel (and of the aesthetic movement) might be an art that makes language itself the erotic subject and object. Love has been called the word of all work, but, as George Eliot indicated, it may be asking too much of it to express all the myriad modes of mutual attraction. Joyce was caught up by the many meanings, contradictions, and effects of *love*, and he tried to inscribe, in his two epics, a whole complex tragicomedy of desire and affection that infuses human life and language. From his early life, from Ireland, from Victorian culture and English letters, he inherited what he considered a debased and exploited idealism of love and an insidious commercialization of the term. Love was going dead, killing the flesh and spoiling the word, when it was supposed to be the force by which the word can become flesh and the flesh word. In his youth and early works,

Joyce often worries that he cannot know love, feel it, or express it as it was conventionally understood. He has to find new ways of writing love, and so he comes to insist on and render its sexual, biological basis, its joyful, plural, and bizarre qualities, and—radically—its unity with the nature of language itself.

II

Odilon Redon's *The Birth of Venus* and *Pandora* (1910–12; figs. 20 and 6), paintings done at almost the same time that Joyce was finishing *A Portrait of the Artist* and beginning *Ulysses*, blend neatly with the erotics of Joycean art.[4] The myth of Pandora with her fatal box and the myth of the birth of Venus—that is, the miraculous appearance out of the sea of an immortal woman embodying the power of generation and creativity—seduced Joyce's imagination. Thematic variations on them appear again and again in his prose. Redon helps illustrate those erotic discourses in Joyce on which I will focus: Stephen Dedalus's seaside epiphany, the feminine voices of Gerty MacDowell and Molly Bloom in *Ulysses*, and the language of Issy, the washerwomen, and ALP in *Finnegans Wake*.

In Redon we can also see the art of love moving from the nineteenth to the twentieth century. Like Joyce, he appropriated myth and fed it into his medium for aesthetic ends, fell early under the spell of Flaubert and the Flaubertian ethic of devotion to art as the highest value, and was fascinated as a creator by dream states and dreamlike vision.[5] He took pride in having created—again like the later Joyce—"an expressive, suggestive, indeterminate art,"[6] which means that his paintings involve and make great interpretive demands on his audience. His *Venus*, like Joyce's writing, functions dialogically in the context of an artistic and historical tradition. It assumes a knowledge of other representations of Venus, such as Botticelli's, Titian's, or Velázquez's. His art, like Joyce's, *discovers* previous art, revealing the codes and evasions of earlier works and artists.

Like Joyce's later work, this picture features and pays homage to biological sex. Redon's "shell" dominates the painting, stresses the female sexual body, and interprets the distancing symbolism of the traditional venereal scallop. The picture blatantly appears to set the goddess of love in a vagina, and it diminishes the comparative stature of Venus so that she almost seems a mere attribute of the opening from which she rises. It implies that sex gives birth to sacred love, that desire for the female sexual organ gives rise to beauty. If the conventional Venus can be seen to stand on a shell of Christian Neoplatonism and to subordinate physical beauty and the senses to divine, imperishable beauty,[7] then Redon folds and incarnates the shell. He makes Venus, with her handsome figure, her sweet face, and all the radiance and heavenly light about her head and upper body, the child of mothering anatomy and erotic desire. The image says our life originates in a woman, not in God: deity is born of woman.

Redon does not deny idealism and the creative colorings of the imagination—he insists on them—but he grounds them in physical being. Venus is set in and against the flesh, but she is also set in an impressionistic seaside scene with striking water, wave, reed, and cloud images, muted sun and rainbow effects, shore colors of blue, green, purple, violet, and white, and a sense of oceanic fluidity and expansiveness. In the hues of the upper half of the picture towards and through which the goddess rises, we can read the meaning of Venus, who ascends from the sexual opening, as the birth of the very media of this art: color and distinct form.

It is possible to see in the positioning of Venus a figure that bridges and unites the earthy flesh-mass with the ethereality of spirit. The creature of this birth, emerging from indistinct plastic shapes, has human form and countenance; she looks to be both product and symbol of artistic inspiration. Venus, mature at birth, suggests the work of imagination that parallels parturition but issues in a finished figure. Male fantasy is operating. The artist, it seems, can imagine, even as he acknowledges the power of female genitality, a miraculous birth: a glorious Venus springs from his conception and labor, like Athena springing from her father's head.[8]

The closer we look, the more the picture engages our subjectivity. We can find a mocking playfulness in it—a grotesque face, for example, in a blotch to the left of Venus's rump and, beneath the white cloud, meatlike forms in the cavity and its background that contrast with the delicacy of Venus's face. The bottom half of the picture, with its fleshy weight, seems to oppose and parody the lightness and grace of the upper part. Redon conveys the disjunctions in the nature of human love as people feel and live it, and his work even makes subtle fun of erotic pretentiousness. This *Birth of Venus* can shed particular light on the nature and sites of Joycean erotics.

III

The crucial love scenes in Joyce occur where desire and language fuse, and land, river, sea, and sky meet. One passage in *A Portrait of the Artist* (1916) is to Joyce what Pip's first visit to Miss Havisham's is to Dickens in *Great Expectations*: desire, destiny, and the psychic material out of which perception and text are formed.[9] This prose conjoins religious, aesthetic, and erotic faith in words and images that Joyce would elaborate upon for the whole of his writing life. Stephen Dedalus, going for a walk towards the sea, has just concluded that he cannot carry out the Christian "commandment . . . to love our neighbour as ourselves." Immediately, and disjunctively, he utters the phrase, "A day of dappled seaborne clouds," and then thinks that he *is* able to love language:

> Words. Was it their colours? He allowed them to glow and fade, hue after hue. . . . No, it was not their colours: it was the poise and balance of the period itself. Did he then love the rhythmic rise and fall of words better than their associations of legend and colours? Or was it that, being as weak of sight as he was shy of mind, he drew less pleasure from the reflection of the glowing sensible world through the prism of a language manycoloured and richly storied than from the contemplation of an inner world of individual emotions mirrored perfectly in a lucid supple periodic prose? [166–67]

Language, the medium of his art, has become the object of his love; but that medium he still sees as a narcissistic reflector of himself, his desire, and a preexistent reality.

Then follows the famous long purple passage enunciating the birth of Stephen's artistic vocation and his transcendent vision of the wading girl.

> His soul had arisen from the grave of boyhood, spurning her graveclothes. Yes! Yes! Yes! He would create proudly out of the freedom and power of his soul . . . a living thing, new and soaring and beautiful, impalpable, imperishable. . . .
>
> He was alone and young and wilful and wildhearted, alone amid a waste of wild air and brackish waters. . . .
>
> A girl stood before him in midstream, alone and still, gazing out to sea. . . . Her long slender bare legs were delicate as a crane's and pure save where an emerald trail of seaweed had fashioned itself as a sign upon the flesh. Her thighs, fuller and softhued as ivory, were bared almost to the hips where the white fringes of her drawers were like featherings of soft white down. Her slateblue skirts were kilted boldly about her waist and dovetailed behind her. Her bosom was as a bird's soft and slight, slight and soft as the breast of some darkplumaged dove. But her long fair hair was girlish: and girlish, and touched with the wonder of mortal beauty, her face.
>
> She was alone and still, gazing out to sea; and when she felt his presence and the worship of his eyes her eyes turned to him in quiet sufferance of his gaze. . . . Long, long she suffered his gaze and then quietly withdrew her eyes from his and bent them towards the stream, gently stirring the water with her foot hither and thither. The first faint noise of gently moving water broke the silence, low and faint and whispering, faint as the bells of sleep; hither and thither, hither and thither; and a faint flame trembled on her cheek.
>
> —Heavenly God! cried Stephen's soul, in an outburst of profane joy. [170–71]

The mixture of the religious imagery of the Annunciation with imagery hailing a new birth of Venus and creative force marks this prose: Joyce is imagining a young man's passion to unite in aesthetic faith those jealous nineteenth-century gods of Christianity and love. Unlike the vision of the goddess in Redon, the girl's figure seems a product of the young man's rapturous thought, an immaculate conception that springs alive into his mind's eye, rather than the issue of consummated sexuality and woman's flesh: "Her image had passed into his soul for ever and no word had broken the holy silence of his ecstasy. Her eyes had called him and his soul had leaped at the call. To live, to err, to fall, to triumph, to recreate life out of life!" He then lies down in a sandy nook and falls asleep.

His soul was swooning into some new world, fantastic, dim, uncertain as under sea, traversed by cloudy shapes and beings. A world, a glimmer, or a flower? Glimmering and trembling, trembling and unfolding, a breaking light, an opening flower, it spread in endless succession to itself, breaking in full crimson and unfolding and fading to palest rose, leaf by leaf and wave of light by wave of light, flooding all the heavens with its soft flushes. [172]

This odd but genuine love scene contains nearly all the elements that Joyce uses to conceive and reconceive his art of love in *Ulysses* and the *Wake*. Note the sequence of what happens: God's impossible command to love leads to the love of words and language, the calling of literature, the image of the woman in water, vague and partly sublimated sexual desire and encounter, and the sound of flowing water fusing with that female image and the artistic vocation of the word. Language, for Joyce—here and everywhere—is the matrix, medium, and evidence of our desire, and in more than a metaphorical sense it is his true love; but in his imagination, it is fused with religion, with the idea of woman and a woman's sexuality, and with water. Last comes the libidinous dream of the rose which combines, like Redon's *Venus*, the questing vision of the heavens, of divine love and beauty, with the powerful imagery of the flowering, opened female genitalia. It is, however, "an exercise in erotic displacement,"[10] sublimating direct sexuality into "the language of flowers"—what Joyce calls in his last work, the soliloquy of ALP in the *Wake* "the languo of flohs" (FW, 621.22)—and the orgasmic rhythms of the prose.

The episode intimates the potential and particulars of later Joycean love and art, that is, the libidinous feel for words, the protean nature of desire, Molly Bloom's famous affirming *yes*es, the generative name of the modern Ulysses— *Bloom* (out of Stephen's dream flower), the dream form of the *Wake* and its hydraulic voices, its kaleidoscopic patterns of perception, and its venereal avatars. What is missing as yet is the representation in words of the physical body and the reverberating senses of humor and tragedy that awareness of joy and time's doom carry. *Ulysses* and *Finnegans Wake* splice, in the mixed streams of consciousness and unconsciousness, love and death. With the new birth of Venus, the later Joyce would combine and render the new coming of Pandora: Pandora who brings to the metamorphosing trio of life, love, and language the fatal gift of mortality and the knowledge thereof.

IV

Joyce's one-word description of *Finnegans Wake*, a "collideorscape" (FW, 143.28), fits Redon's *Pandora* nicely, and so do those words about Stephen's dream: "A world, a glimmer, or a flower? . . . an opening flower . . . breaking in full crimson . . . and fading to palest rose." Pale Pandora, tinged with palest rose, is set in a glimmering world of flowers, light, and dazzling color where the large open crimson blossoms stand out. That coincidence in Redon's art can help us to see how Pandora figures in Joyce's last books.

Redon's *Pandora* is at first sight puzzling. Why did the painter choose Pandora as a subject and caption? What has his profusion of flowering color and radiant light to do with the Greek myth of the fall, that supposed genesis of human tribulations? The simplest, most common version of the legend is this: Pandora, a woman fashioned divinely with gifts from all the deities, is sent by Zeus to tempt man into dire punishment because Prometheus stole fire from heaven. Zeus gives her a box enclosing all human ills, which escape when she opens it. Hope, also in the box, remains.[11] The legend of Pandora has traditionally signified—as Joyce's Mr. Deasy puts it in *Ulysses*—that "[a] woman brought sin into the world" (29). Redon may have hoped to revise the myth and give it new life, but what continuity did he see, what connection did he wish to draw between the calamity and the vision he offers?

Pandora, woman with her enchanted "box," would seem to represent a complex range of connotations of that deceptively casual English phrase, "the facts of life," which names sexuality and gender as the basis of all things human. What she brings into the world are not just ills per se, but erotic desire and love, perishable beauty, and the consciousness of death. As Redon's decision to name his picture would indicate, she also can be understood to bring the "gift" of *generative signification*—a term I use to denote the process by which some entity can mean or translate into something else. For example, this latter "gift" of metaphor and metonym generates a cast of mind in which Pandora may signify sex, which in turn can mean a flowering as well as a deflowering; and a flower may come to symbolize the meaning of the Pandora legend and also a woman's sex. From those "gifts" flow all the sorrows and pleasures of life. Pandora's box holds and lets loose fertility, knowledge, and individuation, but such gifts inevitably include consciousness of barrenness and time's corruption. The meaning of Pandora defines the nature of human species: *double-sexed, individually perceiving, ceaselessly signifying*. She brings and represents change, mortality, corporeal being, and an endless chain of symbolic relationship.

Nevertheless, Redon's picture stresses hope, the last gift. With its title, it shows that Pandora brings color and radiant intensity to the world and that the ostensible fall is fortunate. As Joyce later said of his own version of Pandora, "All her gifts are not maladies" (*Letters*, I, 213). Color signifies humanity's sensual identity and sensuous existence, and Redon, associating it with Pandora, celebrates it.[12]

Revising the Greek legend, which sets off divine power against human weakness, Redon in his images shows reverence for mortal existence. The bare but glittering branches of a tree—the single tree of both knowledge and life—seem to grow right out of Pandora, and the profuse blossoms on either side below the tree look like both the gifts that flow from the woman and also the living progeny of the now-dead tree. They contrast with the leafless, bloomless branches, and together with those limbs they imply the alternating cyles of life and death, the seasonal time sweep that for mutable human beings marks physical existence and its alienation from the unchanging forms of supernatural idealism.

Redon's *Pandora* makes the perfect emblem for what Joyce, at the climax of his own Pandora episode in the Anna Livia chapter of *Finnegans Wake*, identifies as her principle gifts: "She gave them ilcka madre's daughter *a moonflower and a bloodvein*" (212.15, 16; italics mine), words that convey both the female reproductive cycle and the phallus. Like *The Birth of Venus*, *Pandora* too portrays and honors eroticism, as the big, reddish blossom below and the phallic tree at the top show. The very vividness of Redon's flower and the position and shape of the female figure reproduce the same pattern and imply similar meanings as the emergence of Venus out of the vaginal shell.

In Redon's two pictures and in the two major works of Joyce, the signs of sexuality figure everywhere: both artists explicitly turn into subject matter the displacement and sublimation of sexual parts; they both show how sexual anatomy impinges upon mind and perception, determining the very shape of perception and art. In Redon, the oscillating reciprocity between blood flowers, the tree, and the Pandora figure—that is, sexuality issuing in mythic image and symbol, mythic configuration issuing in the forms of sexuality—carries the Joycean vision of continual fusion, diffusion, and recycling that we find in the *Wake*: Pandora for both artists ultimately means an eroticized, protean form of imagination and existence.

The love blooms in Redon convey a gaiety, but the picture has a distinctly somber side. Notice that Pandora's figure is comparatively colorless and downcast. Pale, naked, vulnerable, she looks ephemeral, as if at the subjective center of life there is transience and a sense of loss. The picture offers a vision of fertility but also, in the introspective dejection of Pandora's pose, a consciousness of separateness, of the unrealized and unrealizable desire for permanent unity with the renewing pageant of color, light, symbolism, and sexual bloom. Hope, symbolized by finished, beautiful gestures of art, by nature, and by the continuing flow of eroticism, lives forever in the world, but not for the single self. If Redon were a sentimentalist, he might cover Pandora with flowers; as it is, she is bare, surrounded by them, but distanced from them, unable to possess them.

The contrast between the ebullience of the flowers and the sadness of the woman gives the painting its power. *Pandora*, both joyous and skeptical, renders human life and love as a magnificent displacement—both a deflowering and a blooming. The picture describes what Joyce inscribes: a failed human desire to merge with all precious things—including most especially the medium of art— but at the same time a marvelous creative power coming out of that desire. Imagine Molly Bloom lying in her weird bed, her stream of consciousness pouring forth: "I love flowers Id love to have the whole place swimming in roses . . . the day we were lying among the rhododendrons . . . yes he said I was a flower of the mountain yes so we are flowers all a womans body yes that was one true thing he said in his life and the sun shines for you today" (*Ulysses*, 642–43). That language expresses in its context something very like what Redon shows, and, like *Pandora*, it makes a woman's body the generating site of love and metaphor.

V

Love, God's first command, carried an aura of the sacred about it for the young Joyce, which meant that the word connoted something urgent and compelling for his psyche, but also something false and imprisoning against which he had to struggle. Irish culture and the Roman Catholic religion out of which he came—like the Victorian era with its dominant discourses he knew so well— tended to idealize love in theory, repress but sensationalize sex in fact, feed what I call the incestuous bias, and exacerbate the mind-body split. In practice, Irish nineteenth-century civilization, while paying lip service to love, often denigrated it, giving it over to the colonial-like province of women's imaginations and the ulterior purposes of the church. The word that he inherited and grew up with seemed to convey a selflessness and a dedication to another that he felt he could not attain. A character in *A Portrait* asks Stephen if he has "ever felt love towards anyone or anything," and he answers, "I tried to love God. . . . It seems now I failed" (240). *Love* for Stephen had been censored both of its connotations of lust for the flesh and of its passionate self-cherishing desire, emotions that roiled Joyce's young being and formed his sense of reality.

From our own fin de siècle, the early Joyce wrestling with the historical and semantic phenomenon of *love* looks very much like a representative figure at the end of the nineteenth century. He wanted, as a youth, to find in love both religious purity and blasphemous sexual transgression. His early stories and poems and the portraits of himself as Stephen Dedalus show him much concerned with love, sometimes honoring it, sometimes disparaging it, often fretting over it. He seems to have wanted to experience it as it was conventionally understood, but, filled with conflicts spawned by the complexities of his family heritage and Irish Mariolatry, he both revered and scorned women; they fascinated and alienated him. In *Stephen Hero* (1944), he writes "Love . . . is a name for something inexpressible" and "if such a passion really existed, it was incapable of being expressed."[13] *Love* echoes over and over in the lyrics of *Chamber Music* (1907), but generally as a literary convention such as we find in a Renaissance sonnet sequence. Often here, love is an abstract personification of a nebulous ideal, e.g., "Love is unhappy when love is away."[14] These lyrics show little immediate knowledge of love, but great, if suppressed, longing for it. And, like all Joyce's early work, they provide raw material that he would animadvert upon in the very different erotics of his two epics.

Dubliners (1914) articulates the paralysis of love, and features character after character who cannot feel or utter the true love that the Victorians so exalted. Joyce put much of his own erotic insecurity into Gabriel Conroy of "The Dead," who ponders on his wife's amorous history: "He thought of how she who lay beside him had locked in her heart for so many years that image of her lover's eyes when he had told her that he did not wish to live. Generous tears filled Gabriel's eyes. He had never felt like that himself towards any woman but he knew that such a feeling must be love."[15] Gabriel's response is not much different from that of the late nineteenth-century audience reacting emotionally to *Liebestod* and erotic faith in the arts. A letter to Nora Barnacle from the summer of their courtship in 1904 shows Joyce hesitating to tell her he loves her, and yet wondering obsessively about the meaning of love: "You ask me why I don't love you, but surely you must believe that I am very fond of you and if to desire to possess a person wholly, to admire and honor that person deeply, and to seek to secure that person's happiness in every way is to 'love' them, perhaps my affection for you is a kind of love" (*Letters*, II, 55). That passage defines nicely what it can feel like to fall in love, but it shows a defensive hesitancy about using the word and about committing himself to a vague concept smacking of mass credulity and illusion. Joyce's intellectual conflict about love is typical of the turn-of-the-century crisis of erotic faith.

Early in *Ulysses*, Stephen, lonely and needing love, muses, "What is that word known to all men?" (41). He, like other men, knows the word *love*, but not what the word, according to cultural convention, supposedly signifies. Joyce is portraying himself as a young man seeking knowledge of true love—not the stale cliché "true love"; he is simply trying to sort out whether love for another actually exists and can seem, by the evidence of the senses, "true to life." He sees so much "love" everywhere—even in his own mind—that is fake. In order to find faith he would have to expose and mock the falsities in love.

Growing up, the only real love Joyce saw and felt that accorded with the word's idealistic meanings seemed to be mother love. In *A Portrait* Cranly says,

"Whatever else is unsure in this stinking dunghill of a world a mother's love is not" (241–42). By now we can see what a conventional Victorian sentiment that is and recognize, I hope, what an important role the nineteenth-century novel—with its family bias, its recurrent and insistent desire for mothers, mothering, and the elusive "vertical" erotic tie between generations—had in shaping it. Stephen seems to echo Cranly in *Ulysses*, saying, "*Amor matris*, subjective and objective genitive, may be the only true thing in life" (170). Both statements are speech acts of faith, and beneath their glib contempt for the world, they show a religious—even credulous—turn of mind. The artist as a young man did so very much desire an ideal and real form of enduring virtue. Joyce's belief in the fateful love of the mother *for* the self and the love of the mother *by* the self is essential in understanding his development as a writer and the eroticism in his work.

"*Amor matris*, subjective and objective genitive," is not quite the same thing as "a mother's love." Stephen's phrase—pregnant words indeed—fuse love, human development, and generative grammar; language and reproduction merge. Notice how Joyce's new terms subtly work to lessen the gap between "a mother's love" and the verbal medium—between signified and signifying agent. We have a translation that calls attention to the linguistic system—that process of translation that is one with life—through which we know and express experience and conceive its meaning; but we also have, in the context of Stephen's cool scholasticism, a distancing form that abstracts love. The phrase displays the hold of an idealizing faith that imagines timeless essences, but at the same time it shows Joyce's rebelliousness against the world and values of the fathers—the patriarchy of priest and king. Going far beyond Stephen's ostensible meaning, Joyce would spend his maturity fleshing out the playful possibilities of the words. *Amor matris*, in light of *Finnegans Wake*, emerges as a brilliant Joycean pun, rolling into one word love for the mother, for the child, for the mistress, for the mattress with its dirty dreamy secrets, and for grammar. *Amor matris*, subjectively and objectively generative, might be made to articulate a whole panoply of incestuous dreams and erotic desires that inform, and are informed by, language and consciousness.

Joyce has been accused of being unable to unite feelings of tenderness and sensuality towards the same object.[16] I hold, on the contrary, that he directed his life and writing towards such a union, and that in his later work, at least, he renders it. The problem is one of the most serious in erotic life. The split between affection and sexual passion that we find in Joyce's youth was obviously not some personal quirk: family life, as we have seen, requires it; incest taboos demand it. Most children, as novelists like the Brontës, Dickens, and Eliot repeatedly show, get early lessons in sexual repression and the need to divide erotic desire from affection. But it was Joyce's fate, pride, and joy, much like Freud's, to imagine an erotic wonderland of sexual impulse, amorous farce, and melodrama that bubbled babblingly out of the nineteenth-century sociology and literature of family structuring and *amor matris*.

Before he could do that, however, he had to break through both personal and literary inhibitions. Joyce's candid, pornographic, silly, and splendidly moving letters to Nora in 1909 preview the fusion of love, religion, comedy, logocentrism, and sex in his later writing.[17] Scandalous private documents, they let us see into the erotics of one genius and, beyond that, into European culture at the start of this century. Joyce's young psyche was a battlefield of clashing desires, and his writings show him in love from time to time with projected versions of the three famous female stereotypes: virgin, mother, and whore. The Virgin meant the female incarnation of moral purity and the human vessel of faith; the Mother was the unselfish nurturer, devoted servant, and source of secure love, acceptance, and care; the Whore was to provide ecstatic, but forbidden, sensual pleasure. Responsive object and sexual celebrant, she assisted with the rites of transgression. One woman, Nora Barnacle, came to unite for him his love trinity.

Revisiting Ireland five years after eloping to Italy, he let loose a torrent of epistolary eroticism to her. Some sort of emotional dam seems to have broken: Joyce could now write the word *love* over and over to her without inhibition or qualification. The letters are flooded with wild oral, anal, and genital desires as well as gushes of tenderness and idealism; with his arabesque imagination, he would mine and rework their subject matter in *Ulysses* and the *Wake*. He tells her, "[M]y love for you is really a kind of adoration" (SL, 175), and asks, "Is love madness?" He writes, "One moment I see you like a virgin or madonna the next moment I see you shameless, insolent, half-naked and obscene" (SL, 166–67). These words repeat almost exactly the split desires and crazy tension between Christian and erotic faith that we saw in Lewis's *Monk* a century before, but for Joyce they are the beginning of a reconciliation.

Full of worship, confessing sexual depravity, fascinated by the taboo, Joyce moves, in his writing cure, both to heal a personal and cultural erotic schism and to open up love life. Having found the figure, he is looking for a form to express the unity of his love trinity. "You have been to my young manhood," Joyce writes, "what the idea of the Blessed Virgin was to my boyhood" (SL, 165). He calls his mate "my little mother" (195), but also "my sweet little whorish Nora" (184). More than once, he refers to her as "[M]y beautiful wild flower of the hedges" (180). In one of the rankest letters, thrilling in its fatuousness, he writes: "[I]nside of this spiritual love I have for you, there is also a wild beast-like craving for every inch of your body. . . . My love for you allows me to pray to the spirit of eternal beauty and tenderness mirrored in your eyes or to fling you down under me on that soft belly of yours and fuck you up behind, like a hog riding a sow" (181).

Outrageous. But Joyce knew what he was doing. Sexual censorship feeds the desire that eroticizes language. Breaking through false dignity and the idealism of his early training, he was trying, like some foolish Humpty-Dumpty broken into pieces on the grounds of Victorian repression, to write himself into erotic wholeness and put the body back into the lover's discourse. That may sound pretentious, since Joyce tells Nora that one goal he has in writing out his lust is what Buck Mulligan calls the "Honeymoon in the Hand" (*Ulysses*, 178). Still, even that seamy little goal counts: one of the more significant things about pornography is that it is such a clear instance of the quixotic human wish to make words not just the signs and currency of desire but its actual fulfillment. Joyce is transparently attempting to close the gap between writing and experience—trying desperately, if crudely, to make language and flesh, word and matter, one.

In such naked outpourings, however, he was coming to realize the humor of self-advertisement inherent in the language of erotic desire; he was on his way towards creating his epic human comedies of libido. "I gave others my pride and joy," he tells Nora, "to you I give my sin, my folly, my weakness and sadness" (SL, 167). He was finding out by experiment that, without wrecking his love or ceasing to be lovable, he could write out truthfully the sexual lusts and the ridiculousness—for so I interpret "sin" and "folly"—that play in and about almost any love relationship. Writing whatever he felt like, he was exploring the erotics and the lovely farce of language. He was also, whether he knew it or not, teaching himself to become the grand mocker of pornography and pornographic impulses.

These letters make clear how Joyce could identify words with sex and make writing into a fetish. Anyone who has ever sent or received love letters knows their eroticizing power, but Joyce would make special claims for the interchangeability of the written word and sexual gratification. His project would be to mediate and dissolve the nineteenth-century mind-body split in *writing*, which becomes for him part of the beloved. Language not only reports and stimulates lust, it forms it, and words themselves turn into erotic objects. He writes, for example, "There is something obscene and lecherous in the very look of the letters" (SL, 180); and "Write the dirty words big and underline them and kiss them and hold them for a moment to your sweet hot cunt" (SL, 186). If we juxtapose that obscene image with Brontë's Lucy Snowe caressing and burying her love letters in *Villette*, we can begin to comprehend the insistent erotic contents, motives, and drives that inhere in novels. Joyce's mad imperative to Nora could serve as a bizarre symbol for 1) the inevitable blurring of distinction between physical reality and language; 2) the madman and madwoman coming out of the Victorian closet determined to communicate the secrets in the nine-teenth-century house-of-love's bottom drawers; 3) the comic body-soul splicing process, by which Joyce eventually tried to forge the uncreated conscience of his race; 4) the twentieth-century comedy of the language-reality, body-writing split that is the modern descendant of the old spirit-matter dichotomy; and 5) the projection of his own erotic discourse into the sexual being and body of a woman.

VI

Anyone can see from the 1909 letters that Joyce was a perverse, narcissistic, foolish creature, that smutty language and ideas excited him, and that he was by a protean love possessed. He was, in other words, like people we know very well. What made him different was his critical and imaginative self-awareness and his ability to make comic art out of pornographic yearning. Joyce, like D. H. Lawrence, pioneered in making sex life a subject for modern fiction, but he could do so only because he had first explored and set down the farce of his own libido. A few months before he was to write the Nausicaa section of *Ulysses*, he became infatuated with Marthe Fleischman, a woman who seemed to him the reincarnation of the wading girl from *A Portrait*.[18] He wrote gushy, adoring prose of reverence to her (*Letters*, II, 426–36), greeted her in a postcard as "Nausikaa," signed himself "Odysseus" (II, 428), and even called her, remem-bering the erotic seaside dream of the love rose, "*O rosa mistica*" (II, 436). He then lampooned in "Nausicaa" the language and imagery of his erotic reli-giosity and his own desire to sanctify carnal love. The sexual fantasies and be-havior of Bloom and others in *Ulysses* both use and make devastating fun of uniting pornography and religious impulse.

But Joyce, in his comedy, is still serious about defending erotic faith. In "Cy-clops," amid the violence and power obsessions of the man's world, Bloom fa-mously proclaims the word known to all men:

—Force, hatred, history, all that. That's not life for men and women, insult and hatred. And everybody knows that it's the very opposite of that that is really life.
—What? says Alf.
—Love, says Bloom. I mean the opposite of hatred. [*Ulysses*, 273]

In the boozy context, Bloom may look ridiculous, but in *Ulysses* and *Finnegans Wake* Joyce keeps imagining why that identification of love and real life is right.

Still, love in Bloom must be mocked. For Joyce, if life and consciousness are not subjected to a comic Calvary of ridicule, personal desire and self-righteous pride will distort truth by excluding or despising parts of reality that do not fit preconceived ideals of human dignity. And without an inclusive sense of reality, life, love, and literature become crimped and debased. Gravity, not levity, pulls everything down.[19] A mocking narrative voice chimes in on Bloom's word with a grand burlesque of erotic faith.

> Love loves to love love. Nurse loves the new chemist. Constable 14 A loves Mary Kelly. Gerty MacDowell loves the boy that has the bicycle. M. B. loves a fair gentleman. Li Chi Han lovey up kissy Cha Pu Chow. Jumbo, the elephant, loves Alice, the elephant. Old Mr Verschoyle with the ear trumpet loves old Mrs Verschoyle with the turnedin eye. The man in the brown macintosh loves a lady who is dead. His Majesty the King loves Her Majesty the Queen. . . . You love a certain person. And this person loves that other person because everybody loves somebody but God loves everybody. [273]

That passage ridicules both an erotic catholicism and Christian monotheism; it mocks those who long to believe in a world ruled by love and all-pervading divine generation. It makes fun of those who abstract meaning from its existential context and idealize a word or concept. It parodies those who mouth platitudes, those who revere love, those who congratulate themselves on exquisite feelings, when, of course, their affections are predictable and their sexual desire inevitable. It satirizes those who equate their passions with some form of cosmic virtue or divine planning. It mocks those, that is, like Bloom, Joyce, and Joyce's readers.

Yet the passage does not deny love. It even manages in daffy style to universalize and glorify libido in that motley parade of couples. Note that the amorous catalogue lumps fictional with real beings and that the words point to the erotics of biology, zoology, religion, race, marriage, nationalism, class, and language itself. The sentence "Love loves to love love," an arresting linguistic arrangement if there ever was one, tersely characterizes love as both philological and narcissistic. The self-enclosed structure of the sentence says that love is subject and object of language, that language is subject and object of love, that *we* are both subjects and objects of love, and that self-regarding love and language, infusing all parts of speech and desire, form the dynamic principle of life.

"Love loves to love love" leads soon and logically to "Nausicaa," the great comic arabesque on *A Portrait*'s seaside epiphany. Joyce reworks nearly every detail from his earlier beach scene: Stephen's calling turns into Bloom's coming; his ecstasy metamorphoses into Bloom's masturbation; the wading girl becomes Gerty MacDowell, that lovelorn lame exhibitionist and creature of erotic faith; and the mystical rose turns into a religious service for the Virgin taking place in a nearby church. "Nausicaa" splits the narrative between Gerty's Victorian pop-culture prose and Bloom's internal monologue, both styles fit for the theme of self-eroticism. The chapter is not merely a clever parody of bad romantic literature and exploitive language—women's magazine prose, advertisements for the love hungry, and the like; it stands also as a satiric metaphor for the whole practice of trying to suppress and keep hidden the body and sex life in Victorian fiction.

"Nausicaa" brings together, in a union of immense significance, love, sex, religion, art, and commercialism. Joyce implied as much when he said that it is written in "a namby-pamby jammy marmalady drawsery . . . style with effects of incense, mariolatry, masturbation, stewed cockles, painter's palette, chitchat, circumlocutions etc. etc." (*Letters*, I, 135). Gerty MacDowell, muse and harbinger of the commercial culture, is Joyce's "first extended delineation of a female psyche,"[20] but this psyche is virtually devoid of free will. The sentimentalization of love, that is, turning it into conventional, intangible feelings, leads to the commercialization of love, and commercializing love leads to the victimization of women. Joyce's chief satirical target is not, however, Irish womanhood, Marthe Fleischman, hack novelists like Maria Cummins[21] whose prose he may have mocked, or any other woman whom Joyce saw, had a crush on, or read. It is, rather, eroticism and its corrupting manifestations in his world and in himself, as the "marmalady [wonderful Wakean pun!] drawsery" style, content, and skewed Mariolatry of the letters to Nora and Marthe, and the purple prose of *A Portrait* prove. Gerty and her textual milieu expressing a need for illusion are obviously ridiculous, but so are Stephen and Stephen's author, since the Gerty-talk satire also exposes the pomposity in the previous seaside passage.

Love language clusters in Gerty's daydreams; the word *love* in all its forms, for example "lovely," "loveliness," "fall in love," appears incessantly in her section. Joyce parodies nineteenth-century faith in being in love: "She would follow her dream of love . . . for love was the master guide. Nothing else mattered. Come what might she would be wild, untrammelled, free" (299). By using the language and emotional cadence of the moment of vocation in *A Portrait*, he lays bare the grandiose self-eroticism in Stephen's aesthetic faith. Gerty had lived within Joyce and his language and was born out of the sea of his lusts. When he mocks her literary pretentions, he is laughing at himself and also at the bad, deceiving art of inculcated narcissism: "she felt that she too could write poetry if she could only express herself like that poem . . . she had copied out of the newspaper. . . . *Art thou real, my ideal?*" (298). In his verbal farce, he is making the serious point that sentimental art can be immorally crippling to the imagination: by trying to hide hard truths, it may destroy a sense of mutually shared, communicable reality (the jammy love-story prose, for example, cannot express the fact that Gerty is lame).

"Nausicaa" exposes a new Pandora consumed by erotic desire and the advertising mentality, twin gifts from the box of history. Joyce imagines Gerty as a verbal territory seized by sex and commercial propaganda. The form of her consciousness shows how the deep longings for love in the modern world can and will be manipulated for profit and also how well mercantile motives mesh with the Victorian creed that "love is best."²² Various media work to form her desire: 1) novels and stories that focus on interpersonal relationships and preach women's joy and fulfillment through love; 2) Roman Catholic teaching that glamorizes the Virgin Mary and professes formally and informally that women should emulate absolutely lovable Mary, glorifying God through selfless love and service to mankind; 3) commercial rhetoric that seeks, by creating covetable images and implying that people can buy things that will make themselves desirable, to turn men and women into shopping, spending customers.

Love is mass-produced: Venus on the half shell becomes the goddess of hucksters, and Tristan is sold. Gerty is a product of makeup and design, which emphatically includes, besides cosmetics and merchandise, fiction and the motivations of designing people. Joyce imagines her as the perfect consumer of commercial language, that fiction of seduction. "Gerty was dressed simply" in a "neat blouse of electric blue . . . (because it was expected in the *Lady's Pictorial* that electric blue would be worn)" (287). Someone who buys it all, she is an author's, an adman's, a rhetorician's dream—a prophetic figure for the century of marketed mass desire.

VII

Compare the opening of "Nausicaa," "The summer evening had begun to fold the world in its mysterious embrace" (284), with George Eliot's language in the first sentence of *The Mill on the Floss*: "the broadening Floss hurries on between its green banks to the sea, and the loving tide, rushing to meet it, checks its passage with an impetuous embrace." Joyce's parody shows how the nineteenth-century novel as a medium worked to make people see love as the be-all and end-all of life. Novels gave them ready-made images, words, and phrases to form their thoughts and art, and they tended to make everything a part of, or background for, the erotic history of an individual.

The classic Victorian novel defines life in terms of personal desire. That fiction inevitably helped to shape both mass-market psychology and the modern culture of subjectivity. Earlier in *Ulysses*, when Stephen walks by the shore, Joyce broadens the scope of individual erotics to show how desire determines the way this character perceives and tries to possess the world: Stephen thinks, "These heavy sands are language tide and wind have silted here" (37). That is fresher and more sophisticated than Gerty's prose, but it still is a case of erotic desire forming the mind's reflection of nature and creating for and out of his own libido a fiction and a self-advertisement. Stephen is naming language—*his* object of desire and love—as the physical creator of his universe. What makes "Nausicaa" self-parody is its insistence that fiction is always tainted to some degree by the advertising spirit. "Nausicaa" radically portrays language as tower-of-babble masturbation—erotic urge and self-gratification in words—the love sand on which everything is so hilariously built.

Joyce puts formulaic love novels, devotional language, and commercials in exactly the same category. They all are *advertisement*, literal attempts, as the Latin roots of the word indicate, to *turn* an audience *to* or *onto* something, to focus desire. They seek to represent and stir longings in people for appealing objects and states of being, and they advertise the possibilities of attaining goals that may well be illusory. Gerty's protean language enunciates and makes interchangeable the trinity of religion, love, and commerce. Joyce in "Nausicaa" and in Gerty herself imagines that personal identity is formed out of the religious, the commercial, and the erotic intentions and contents of language, and if we want to know what is going on, we better know what designs language—that "makeup"—has on us.

Gerty-prose also satirizes fiction—or any art—that suppresses the truth of the body and its needs. Her conventional language, that is, language obeying the conventions of others, is riddled with disjunctures because it cannot articulate key facts of her life: her deformity, her sexual drive, her victimization, as well as her bitterness towards those luckier than she. Only in Bloom's unconventional, relatively free flow of linguistic consciousness can the truth of Gerty's physical condition be expressed.

The tension implicit in Gerty-prose lies in the conflict between, on the one hand, the funny, but potentially appalling, deceptions that language practices on the self, and, on the other, the power of linguistic forms to produce real satisfaction, even if based on fraud. Beneath the satire on lying prose, there lurks a contradictory and subversive meaning: sex needs fantasy; physical love needs illusion; we need advertising to live life and to love. Joyce's onanistic writing carries a tawdry poetry of pleasure that points up the erotic, narcissistic nature of literary language and faith. Look at the "climax" of Gerty's half of the chapter: "She would fain have cried to him chokingly, held out her snowy slender arms to him to come. . . . And then a rocket sprang and bang shot blind blank and O! then the Roman candle burst and it was like a sigh of O! and everyone cried O! O! in raptures and it gushed out of it a stream of rain gold hair threads and they shed and ah! they were all greeny dewy stars falling with golden, O so lovely, O, soft, sweet, soft!" (300). Somehow that mock prose really does represent the spirit and pleasure of orgasm.

The gist of "Nausicaa," however, defends erotic faith by attacking the sentimentality that threatens it. The prose of kitsch idealism tends to eliminate as subjects and objects of love such earthy, imperfect figures as halt Gerty and Bloom the public onanist, by making it seem as if they degrade the ideals of love. The Gerty-text cannot accommodate, finally, the weird and flawed who need faith, i.e., people like Leopold and Molly Bloom, Gerty, Stephen, and all others who shit, menstruate, fuck, pick noses, and live their lives in bodies and in the milieu of tricky mother tongues.

Joyce, on love, agrees with Baudelaire, who sometimes thought it a great thing but who knew how open it was to exploitation by those who would use it to promote their own power over others. Geoffrey Grigson, discussing Baudelaire, quotes him: "'[I]n love beware of the *moon* and the *stars*, beware of the Venus of Milo'—i.e., beware of whatever has become a correct, permissible, ideal image of love or beauty—'beware of lakes, guitars, rope-ladders, and all novels, even the most beautiful novel in the world, even if the author is Apollo himself.'" [23] The idea that people must find love, if they are to have it, in the living processes of their *own* bodies and their *own* use and reading of language, finds corroboration in Joyce's venereal flowers, the Blooms.

VIII

Just before the fireworks, the Gerty narrator uses a sugary cliché to generalize about love: "Love laughs at locksmiths" (298). Ironically that tells the truth for Joyce. His love language makes a huge joke out of the human effort to put a lock on love and compartmentalize it: to pretend, for example, that the love of the Virgin, the love of a mother, the love of a child, the love of words, the love of memories, the love of one's own work, the love of art, and the love of various forms of sexual gratification are separable passions that do not spill into one another. The effort to censor sexuality out of discourse and libido out of perception, to try to keep bodies, words, and affections discrete, is laughable.

Molly Bloom is a flower in two senses. Like Joyce's Nora, she is a blooming woman ("he said I was a flower of the mountain" [643]), but also a figure of speech that flows. Her continuous torrent of words, unlike the language of Gerty, articulates her love of the senses and goes to show how the generative sexual body and its functions are indivisible from the human stream of consciousness. Joyce here weaves connections among all kinds of love, but attaches them to the twin looms of the senses and language. "Id love" and "I love" become insistent in Molly's prose as the book moves to its end, and that subjective jumbling together of her desires ("Id love a big juicy pear" [641]; "I love the smell of a rich big shop" [642]; "I love flowers Id love to have the whole place swimming in roses" [642]) works to show an erotic continuum in consciousness.

The revolutionary Joyce had his radical project of trying to forge language and physical experience together in his art. If conventional fiction avoided direct representation of the sexual flesh, he would try to incarnate a woman's parts into words. In discussing "Penelope," Molly's part of the book, Joyce identifies "its four cardinal points" as "being the female breasts, arse, womb and cunt expressed by the words *because, bottom . . . , woman, yes.*"[24] Such a code may seem daft, but it shows how serious he was about imagining a verbal metamorphosis that would convey and *embody* the tangible, yet fluid sexual nature of human life. Molly he conceived as the very opposite of the kind of Victorian love heroine he mocks in "Nausicaa": in "Penelope," she seemed to him "to be perfectly sane full amoral fertilisable untrustworthy engaging shrewd limited prudent indifferent *Weib. Ich bin der Fleisch der stets bejaht* [woman. I am the flesh that always affirms]" (SL, 285). That statement has led to much of the feminist criticism of Molly and Joyce, because it seems to accept, if not prescribe, a limited role for woman. In fact, Joyce, using Molly, sought to demolish nineteenth-century sentimentality and bad faith about the erotics of women. Through her he attacks the old human propensity to spiritualize love, moralize on it, and try to make it better than flesh and blood.

Molly, the adulterer, the criticizer, the often uncharitable rough thinker, the bed-riding Bloom who farts, pisses, bleeds, and fantasizes about fucking several men, is the figure in *Ulysses* without whom love is impossible. Like Leopold Bloom in bed, Joyce turns everything upside down and sees love in "Penelope" from the bottom up. Unlike almost all previous love heroines, Molly never says "I love you" or "My love," or specifically thinks of attaching the verb *love* to her lovers. She recalls physical acts with Bloom, Mulvey, Gardner, Boylan, and other men, but her language does not acknowledge directly that she has loved them. Worse, by the standards of Victorian love ethics for women, her prose scrambles the individuality of the men, making them sex objects and indiscriminate giggling masculine pronouns, "He, he and he." She subverts the romantic mythology of one true love. And yet Joyce imagines that her physical being and her knowledge of the flesh have made and do make love a reality in the novel. From his perspective, the self-sacrificing, pure angel-in-the-house in effect denies that the fully human is lovable. Molly does not think of herself primarily as wife or mother, but as a being who can express to herself honestly her sensual desires and try to fulfill them, and life depends on such knowing and drive. The mind-forged manacles of duty, religion, a woman's role, propriety, and the rest—all those curbs that blocked the articulation of desire in nineteenth-century culture—get swamped and sent to the bottom in the river of her mind.

She may not be an intellectual, an author, a leader, a saint, or an ornament of her sex; she may be stuck on men, but her linguistic flow reports a complex, highly individualized and varied life. Joyce has given her a shocking but supple mode of being that in its recirculation allows for new forms of life and inclusiveness. Molly's prose celebrates sensual being, thus affirming that which makes anything and everything possible. She is a twentieth-century Pandora loosing the untold consequences of a female erotic desire equal to that of a man.

Nevertheless, despite all the scorn for love propaganda and false erotic consciousness that Molly shows, I maintain that the Blooms come right out of the Victorian tradition of erotic faith. They seem, like famous lovers, to have their being in the other; each is unimaginable without the other. Though Bloom is an advertising man and Molly a professional soprano, their real passion does not go into their secular callings. Joyce defines the essence of each by their personal relationship. The essence of erotic faith, in fact, is often that it makes the interpersonal tie the primary vocation in life.

Joyce chooses significantly to make the ending of the book the affirmation of their coming together. We cannot say simply that Molly and Leopold love, or are in love with, each other, like Darcy and Elizabeth, or Heathcliff and Cathy. The Blooms have so much experience of each other, of marriage, and of life, that the different streams of consciousness of the novel drown any succinct definition of love. But the rendering of their first coming together is as vivid as that of any pair of lovers in fiction, and it colors and defines any deep, responsive understanding of the novel.

A biological, loveless vision of copulation frames Bloom's memory. He is having lunch in a pub: "Stuck on the pane two flies buzzed, stuck" (144). He savors his wine and remembers being with Molly on Ben Howth overlooking Dublin Bay years before.

O wonder! . . . Ravished over her I lay, full lips full open, kissed her mouth. Yum. Softly she gave me in my mouth the seedcake warm and chewed. Mawkish pulp her mouth had mumbled sweetsour of her spittle. Joy: I ate it: joy. Young life, her lips that gave me pouting. Soft warm sticky gumjelly lips. Flowers her eyes were, take me, willing eyes. Pebbles fell. She lay still. A goat. No-one. High on Ben Howth rhododendrons a nannygoat walking surefooted, dropping currants. Screened under ferns she laughed warmfolded. Wildly I lay on her, kissed her: eyes, her lips, her stretched neck beating, woman's breasts full in her blouse of nun's veiling, fat nipples upright. Hot I tongued her. She kissed me. I was kissed. All yielding she tossed my hair. Kissed, she kissed me.
    Me. And me now.
    Stuck, the flies buzzed. [144]

No one can prove that this same memory of himself and Nora made Joyce the writer he was and *Ulysses* the book that it is, but does anyone doubt it? As surely as the Brontës, Austen, or Trollope, Joyce the iconoclastic writer saw love as crucial and made it and the novel inseparable. He imagines an extremely personal love scene: the scatological nanny goat and the mutual mouthing of the seedcake show that he was trying to break through the strains of antiphysical bias in Western thought and accept—even embrace—the full range of sensual, bodily life in the world. But Bloom shares this with figures in the Victorian novel's great erotic tradition like Heathcliff, Lucy Snowe, Maggie Tulliver, and Pip: namely, that a mentalized, immaterial image of being in love with another lives in him and becomes the defining center of self and world.

Joyce said of Molly and his book, "The last word (human, all too human) is left to Penelope. This is the indispensable countersign to Bloom's passport to eternity" (SL, 278). Without Molly and her explosion of flowering reverie at the end, Bloom's bracketed remembrance of ecstasy would leave us with the deflating irony of the futile insects stuck together: as flies to wanton *Joyce* are we to the gods. But in the end we have Molly's corresponding memory that confirms the force of the experience for both. Molly may conflate the passion on Howth with her lovemaking on Gibraltar, and she may not romanticize Bloom, but that does not alter the strange beauty and permanence of this love encounter. Joy and excitement come through in the rhythms and imagery of her prose, and so do the surprising, simultaneous mutuality and individuality of her feeling in the end:

[T]he sun shines for you he said the day we were lying among the rhododendrons on Howth head . . . the day I got him to propose to me yes first I gave him the bit of seedcake out of my mouth . . . my God after that long kiss I near lost my breath yes he said I was a flower of the mountain yes so are we flowers all . . . and I thought well as well him as another and then I asked him with my eyes to ask again yes and then he asked me would I yes to say yes my mountain flower and first I put my arms around him yes and drew him down to me so he could feel my breasts all perfume yes and his heart was going like mad and yes I said yes I will Yes. [643–44]

This prose, then, is the validating countersign to Bloom's vision.[25]

Ulysses ends with a meeting of erotic minds, bodies, and memories in the transubstantiating medium of language. Notice, however, that this meeting exists in the past. Their intercourse lives in the novel, but only through the mystical transformation of the past into the present. Neither Joyce nor the book can or does portray the end of nineteenth-century duality, much as we might wish they did. Bloom and Molly resemble Victorian characters in this: that mind and flesh, in their discourse, ineluctably divide. Joyce might have ended the book by having them make love, or he might have had Molly specifically imagine fucking Bloom, as she imagines fucking Boylan. Instead, almost like Charlotte Brontë with Lucy Snowe, he makes their *engagement* to love and marry both the generating moment of their language and character and, in effect, a meta-physical climax of their desire. The mutual erotic experience is a religious communion of sorts.

IX

Often in *Ulysses* and especially at the end of "Penelope," the text seems to convey the excitement and rush of sexual attraction on which all creation depends. In "Circe," kisses—those gestures and signifiers of love and sex—can talk to Bloom: "Icky licky micky sticky for Leo! (*cooing*) Coo coocoo! Yummyyum, Womwom! (*warbling*) Big comebig! Pirouette! Leopopold! (*twittering*) Leeolee! (*warbling*) O Leo!" (387). That voice is meant both to *say* and to *be* sexuality and desire. Joyce wanted a language that would not only communicate but form eroticism. In *Finnegans Wake* he achieves it in the words that Issy uses.

The seductive dream language that both utters and is uttered by Issy, this wet-dream girl, temptress, daughter, sexpot, vagina, verbal fetish of incestuous desire, and rain cloud, has many sources. It grows out of those "Circe" kisses which in turn grow out of a key primal memory in *A Portrait* that eroticized both mother love and words for Joyce-Dedalus, mind-forging their link: "What did that mean, to kiss? . . . His mother put her lips on his cheek; her lips were soft and they wetted his cheek; and they made a tiny little noise: kiss" (15). It develops from that time by the sea when Stephen, saying "clouds," knows he loves words, and associates them with a girl, water, and erotic voyeurism. It comes out of the punning title of the book of poems *Chamber Music*, Molly Bloom's chamber pot, and Joyce's private sexual fantasies about micturation; out of Bloom's masturbatory urge before a younger woman; and out of the whole jelly hymn to orgasm and mankind's love of love and lies that "Nausicaa" is. It grows out of the kiss of Bloom and Molly on Howth and out of Joyce's comic vision on the great European love myth of Tristan and the two Isoldes. It comes out of his love and repressed desire for his own daughter Lucia, with her split personality and her chaotically free, brilliant, crazy language that proved so seductive to him as the artist of the *Wake*.[26] It develops in the history of sexual repression and out of the passion to put into literature the ridiculous, deadly, incestuous, world-shaking whispers of nineteenth- and twentieth-century libido. In her name, being, and voice, Joyce puns, among other things, on kisses, Narcissus, Isolde, piss, Isah (Adam's name for Eve), Swift's Vanessa, Alice Liddell of looking-glass fame and her Carrollian double *Isa* Bowman, Isis the goddess of regeneration, Venus, incest, and the *is* of existence.

A question is posed to introduce Issy: "What bitter's love but yurning, what sour lovemutch but a bref burning till shee that drawes dothe smoake retourne?" (FW, 143.29, 30). That Joycean dream question imagines love as a Pandora's gift. It expresses a bitter cynicism and implies most of the critical arguments against eroticism: What good is love when it just means yearning and bitter desire for a person who is other and not oneself, when it can lead to erotic perversity and venereal disease, when it shows the unbridgeable gap between "I" and "you"? Isn't this supposedly grand passion and ecstasy a sour thing when we realize that it lasts about as long, and matters about as much, as the flame that lights a cigarette? Since we know of life's brevity and our coming death (the burial urn and mourning of mortality lurk in the word "yurning"), how can we enjoy a love we will soon lose? Isn't love merely a matter of hot pants (pun—implicit in Joyce's *bref* which includes both *breath* and *briefs*— intended) for the time it takes a woman to pull up her dress, quickly copulate, then straighten her smock? How can love be glorified when it's situated in the place of excreta and when it may lead to venereal disease?

Issy's reply to the rhetorical question (143.31–148.32) makes love a question of rhetoric. One of the more remarkable soliloquies in the literature of love, it works expressively, like the "Circe" kisses, to connote the appeal of Eros: "Answer: I know, pepette, of course, dear, but listen, precious! Thanks, pette, those are lovely, pitounette, delicious! But mind the wind, sweet! What exquisite hands you have, you angiol. . . . I bet you use her best Perisian smear off her vanity table to make them look so rosetop glowstop nostop" (143.31– 144.1). Issy, in narcissistic *love*-stuffed dialogue with her protean water-mirrored image, discourses on such a range of libidinous practices that it would tax Krafft-Ebing, Havelock Ellis, Freud, and Kinsey to catalogue them. In the provoking rhythms of sexual excitement, she lisps and gasps "the languo of flohs" (621.22)—what she calls "the linguo to melt" (147.34). Her onomatopoeic accents and anatomical puns—comic, sensual, and romantic at the same time—are addressed to an alter ego who can change sex, to her brothers, to her father, to older men and lovers, to historical figures, to general readers—in short, to a fluid but erotically fixated audience.

Not only is anatomy destiny in Joyce's epics, it is also speech. If, like kisses in "Circe," genitalia and sexual intercourse could talk, they might say something like this:

Stoop alittle closer, fealse! Delightsome simply! Like Jolio and Romeune. I haven't fell so turkish for ages and ages! Mine's me of squisious, the chocolate with a soul. Extraordinary! . . . Thats rights, hold it steady! Leg me pull. Pu! Come big to Iran. Poo! What are you nudging for? No, I just thought you were. Listen, lovliest! Of course it was *too* kind of you, miser, to remember my sighs in shockings. . . . Ha! O mind you poo tickly. Sall I puhim in momou. Mummum. Funny spot to have a fingey! . . . Angst so mush. . . . Transname me loveliness, now and here me for all times! [144.13–145.21]

Joyce seems to have poured into her voice all the repressed sexuality, all the latent incestuous feeling of family life, all the loves that dared not speak their name, and all the joyous, perilous allure of erotic desire that he could summon up and imagine from his personal and cultural history. He has her say later, "Nircississies are as the doaters of inversion" (526.34–35), which, among a hundred things it may mean, suggests that the nursery of nineteenth-century sexual repression, investigation, and control is the necessary mother of the erotic obsessions, perversions, inversions, animadversions, advertisements, and appeals to narcissism that have flooded print, electronic media, and conscious-ness, making people dote on sex.

Something parallel Issy says, speaking of parents, also helps to understand her: "Whoses wishes is the farther to my thoughts" (147.19–20). In the whole of the *Wake*, she is the child of the male dreamer's multiple, sometimes contra-dictory desires, and that is why she speaks in different voices, has a split person-ality, plays the parts of wanton slut and pure daughter, nymphomaniac and vir-gin. But "Whoses" also plays on "Moses" and on his role as the bearer of the inscribed wishes of the great Unknown, the Omnipotent Whoses: Yahweh, God, the Word. Both daughter of God's plan and rebel against "Whoses wishes," Issy, the speaking proof of the desire for, and pleasure in, the flesh, is the necessary child who, in the generational cycle, mothers the mother of all creation. Sex leads to the fall but also the rise of man. Against taboo, Issy liberates an anarchic pleasure principle, the corollary of which is that if the body were not a source of joy, if there were no teasing, galling desire for sensual delight, there would be no body.[27]

Lacking stable focus and identity, a moral threat to family, state, and civiliza-tion, she is nevertheless Joyce's choice to reply to the question, "Why love?" and the question behind it, "Why life?" The starting point for an answer to such questions—the starting point, that is, for faith—lies, for the Joyce of this book, in the gist of Issy's talk: *Because it feels good! Because it's fun!* That naked sentiment is what has been missing from English fiction. Look again at Cara-vaggio's scandalous masterpiece of love *Amor Vincit Omnia*. There is hardly anything like its free, amorally joyous spirit of polymorphous love in British literature until the flow of Issy's language.

Joyce associates her with beginnings, with budding youth, with clouds and rain that start the flow of earthly life, with what unfolds and brings the future. Sexually she articulates the spirit and feeling of foreplay. Temporally, she rep-resents the twenty-eight days that make up the menses-governing moon cycle of fertility. Essentially, she metamorphoses into material to rouse and delectate the five senses: she becomes the rainbow, dividing into the seven prismatic col-ors; she merges with flowers, with sweet-tasting things, with glittering jewels, with fabrics, with the graceful movements of dance, with pleasant odors, with music. But nothing is more revealing about her—or, for that matter, about her author—than the fact that he identifies her, among all her protean forms, as the raw material of writing, the alphabet.

Joyce, this Alphabet Souperman,[28] imagines the letters as feminized objects of desire and Issy's sexual play. Listen to her speech conjoining writing and eroticism: "And my waiting twenty classbirds [i.e., twenty-eight], sitting on their stiles! Let me finger their eurhythmytic. And you'll see if I'm selfthought. They're all of them out to please. . . . There's Ada, Bett, Celia, Delia, Ena, Fretta, Gilda, Hilda, Ita, Jess, Katty, Lou, (they make me cough as sure as I read them) Mina, Nippa, Opsy, Poll, Queeniee, Ruth, Saucy, Trix, Una, Vela, Wanda, Xenia, Yva, Zulma, Phoebe, Thelma. And Mee!" (147.7–15). At this point in the text, she is surrounded with the conventional trappings of Venus: myrtle, doves, roses, the wind, love, and fluttering garments.[29] Letters and the goddess of love emerge at the same time, and literature is the product of their generation.

Pandora and Venus come together in Issy's prose. Issy sometimes articulates the whorish world of pornographic commerce and an amoral, Darwinian view of human nature governed by eroticism ("O, you mean the strangle for love and the sowiveall of the prettiest?" [145.26–27]), but she renders the beautiful world of flowering Aphrodite also. In the dream work and fantasy projections of the *Wake*'s sleeper, the language of Issy seethes with an erotic drive and desire so insistent that it can make all the reiterated rational and moral criticisms of love by the wise men and women of the ages seem as futile as ordering the tide to stop, or the menstrual cycle and masturbation to cease.

Bright pigeons all over the whirrld will fly with my mistletoe-message round their loverib-boned necks and a crumb of my cake for each chasta dieva. . . . Now open, pet, your lips, pepette, like I used my sweet parted lipsabuss . . . *pipetta mia*, when you learned me the linguo to melt. . . . Are you enjoying, this same little me, my life, my love? Why do you like my whisping? Is it not divinely deluscious? But in't it bafforyou? *Misi, misi*! Tell me till my thrillme comes! . . . Your delighted lips, love, be careful! Mind my duvetyne dress above all! It's golded silvy, the newest sextones with the princess effect. . . . As I'd live to, O, I'd love to! Liss, liss I muss whiss! . . . With my whiteness I thee woo and bind my silk breasths I thee bound! Always, Amory, amor andmore! Till always, thou lovest! Shshshsh! So long as the lucksmith. Laughs! [147.22–148.32]

I take the end of that speech as a playful but conclusive assertion by Joyce of his own erotic faith, even though he laughs at, and with, love: Love, he says in this conflation of Gerty's "love laughs at locksmiths" and Stephen's words at the end of *A Portrait* ("I go to encounter for the millionth time the reality of experience and to forge in the smithy of my soul the uncreated conscience of my race"[252–53]), will last as long as the lucky smith, who is forging in "the smithy" of his "soul the uncreated conscience" of his "race," laughs. In other words, love is recursive and joyful as long as the will to love and to create an art of human comedy can be combined. Joyce and Issy sum up one important meaning of the nineteenth-century novel: love and literature are interdependent constructs of language and consciousness.

X

Other versions of love, however, appear—and reappear—to mock and confound the lucksmith who gives way to the sentimentalities of sanguine individualism or romantic humanism. Love is death-bringer as well as life-giver. In the night of *Finnegans Wake* all figures merge in the sleeper and the constituent elements to which he regresses.[30] Issy, daughter and tease, Anna Livia Plurabelle, mature woman, wife, and mother, and all the feminine variations on them, flow together, separate, and "reamalgamerge" in endless recirculation of life and death, like the water whose forms they also assume. Neither deadly Pandora nor fertile Aphrodite exists without the other.

In the great "Anna Livia" chapter (196.1–216.5), Joyce explicitly fuses the two figures. He narrates the history of the river-woman Anna in the dialogue of washerwomen laying out humanity's dirty linen. Here one of them, telling of the forms and avatars Anna takes, describes, with help from Botticelli, the birth and toilet of Venus (Ophelia and Maggie are there too): "First she let her hair fall and down it flussed to her feet its teviots winding coils. Then, mother-naked, she sampooed herself with galawater and fraguant pistania mud. . . . allover her little mary. Peeld gold of waxwork her jellybelly. . . . And after that she wove a garland for her hair. She pleated it. She plaited it. Of meadowgrass and riverflags, the bulrush and waterweed, and of fallen griefs and weeping willow" (206.29–207.4).

This figure, "Anna was, Livia is, Plurabelle's to be" (215.24), containing Issy now, moves out, transmuted into a flowing Pandora to give all her gifts from "under one crinoline envelope" (212.22–23)—i.e., her genital, sexual being—to all the figures in and out of the novel: the gifts of disease, of private fate and personal death, of language, of myth, legend, and history—the whole universal human catalogue of turbulence and woe.

ALP-Pandora's list contains a précis or résumé of everything that happens in the book, including Joyce's often cynical treatment of love and his satire on its commercial debasement. He puts into the *Wake* ribald versions of the Don Juan and Tristan myths, but the essence of his vision shows through in the gifts ALP gives them: "a stonecold shoulder for Don Joe Vance" (211.32) and "a change of naves and joys of ills for Armoricus Tristram Amoor" (211.25–26). "A change of naves" combines religious, linguistic, and erotic mutability (e.g., the shift from Christian faith and a cathedral as the site of reverence to love faith and the written text); "joys of ills" brings together the names and roles of author and lover, and the elevated passion, the farce, and the "mixed bag" of love. Joyce's Pandora lets loose prurient love corrupted by hypocrisy and prostitution, but she also carries hope into the world. The inventory of gifts ends with her presents of the flower and fruit of sexuality: "She gave them ilcka madre's daughter a moonflower and a bloodvein: but the grapes that ripe before reason to them that devide the vinedress" (212.15–17). Love and language, which fertilize hope, come together in Anna-Venus-Pandora's erotic daughter and phallic-writing son: "So on Izzy, her shamemaid, love shone befond her tears as from Shem, her penmight, life past befoul his prime" (212.17–19). Like the nineteenth-century novel, Joyce's apotheosis of life, love, and language is a family affair. It is an irony that the most avant-garde twentieth-century "novel" reflects so fully the erotic and incestuous bias of nineteenth-century British fiction.

Finnegans Wake ends with Anna's powerful meditation on dying, on rejuvenation, and on the enduring, changing world. Issy notes earlier, "there's a key in my kiss" (279, n. 1), and it turns out to be, in spite of all, the key to life. In the end, the voice of the daughter, the cloud of desire and young love, becomes one with the mother. But the union does not take place without great pain. As the water-woman moves to the sea, she talks to her man-land mate:

Yes, you're changing, sonhusband, and you're turning, I can feel you, for a daughterwife from the hills again. . . . And she is coming. Swimming in my hindmoist. . . . Just a whisk brisk sly spry spink spank sprint of a thing theresomere, saultering. Saltarella come to her own. . . . For she'll be sweet for you as I was sweet when I came down out of me mother. My great blue bedroom, the air so quiet, scarce a cloud. . . . I could have stayed up there for always only. It's something fails us. First we feel. Then we fall. . . . Anyway let her rain for my time is come. . . . A hundred cares, a tithe of troubles and is there one who understands me? . . . All me life I have lived among them but now they are becoming lothed to me. . . . How small it's all! . . . But I'm loothing them that's here and all I lothe. Loonely in me loneness. . . . I am passing out. O bitter ending! [627.1–35]

We are back to the question that set off Issy's love-talk: "What bitters love . . . ?" There is in the Joycean text a way of transnaming "lothe" into the force of love, of changing Pandora to "Dora Riparia Hopeandwater" (211.10), whose last gift is the hope and reproduction of Venus out of the "hitherandthithering waters of" (216.4–5).

Reproduction: Joyce presents through ALP the desire of death-fated consciousness to recreate life and the self. The feeling of the text, as in Molly Bloom's stream of words, passes through negativity and denial to affirm regeneration. The incestuous urges of family, the anthropomorphosing powers of the human mind, the metamorphosing medium of language, the perception of nature and its cycles, the erotic desires and resources of word-wielding, *written woman*, become part of Joyce's vision of creation sustained beyond personal death. Biology, geology, meteorology, narratology, and all kinds of love again blend into this speech. Joyce unites *amor matris*, sexual ecstasy, and the love of words, *amor verborum*, subjective and objective genitive.

The end of the book brings back Issy's regenerative, erotic voice: "Bussoftlhee, mememormee! Till thousendsthee! Lps. The keys to. Given! A way a lone a last a loved a long the" (628.14–16). That ending reiterates Issy's earlier words. The lips, the kiss, the key that makes love laugh at locksmiths, and the key word *love* reappear; and as the passing mother fades into the living daughter, so the renewed rhythms of breathy love return.

On the last page of the *Wake*, Anna Livia exclaims the single truncated syllable "Lff!" LFF: That ecological pun, joining the waters of the Liffey with love, laugh, and life in a single word, might stand as Joyce's vowel-less inscribed name for the god of his new testament of love and comic faith, as Y*W*W stood for the God of the Old Testament. The Joyce of love, subjective and objective genitive, lives in the language of *flowers*, some of which are novels.

11 The Prophet of Love and the Resurrection of the Body: D. H. Lawrence's *Lady Chatterley's Lover* (1928)

The loins are the place of the last judgement.
WILLIAM BLAKE[1]

Today it is sex that serves as a support for the ancient form—so familiar and important in the West—of preaching.
MICHEL FOUCAULT[2]

He said it with some bitterness, and no doubt it contains the real germ of truth. The mode of putting it, however, is neither delicate nor respectable.
D. H. LAWRENCE[3]

I

Love has no end, but in the novel, love as erotic faith may be said to reach a climax with Lawrence. In *Lady Chatterley's Lover* he preaches redemption through tender, physical love, and that love specifically includes and depends upon what he provocatively calls "cunt-awareness" (XVIII, 301), the "bridge" of "the phallus" (VII, 77), "the democracy of touch" (VII, 78), and "the resurrection of the body" (VII, 78). For him the novelist is the new pastor, the sexual body is the new pastoral site, and the novel is the religious instrument of prophetic revelation: "And here lies the vast importance of the novel, properly handled. It can inform and lead into new places the flow of our sympathetic consciousness, and it can lead our sympathy away in recoil from things gone dead. Therefore, the novel, properly handled, can reveal the most secret places of life: for it is in the *passional* secret places of life, above all, that the tide of sensitive awareness needs to ebb and flow, cleansing and freshening" (IX, 106).

Passional, the crucial word, combines and fuses for Lawrence the old Christian sense of the word *passion* as holy, with its erotic connotations. Having searched all his own passionate life for something worthy to believe in, he imagines the erotic relationship between two people in *Lady Chatterley's Lover* as a religious mystery. To do that, however, he had, like Joyce, to try to change conceptions of what *is* religious, to break down the still surviving orthodox distinctions between sacred and profane, mind and body, soul and sensuality. Harrowing Victorian hell, he reclaims the condemned flesh, proclaims sex to the

279

heavens, and turns it into a rite of faith. He becomes very dogmatic about sex, as true believers do about religious matters, moralizing it, as the Victorians moralized love. Preaching salvation through sexual healing may be, unto the conventionally righteous, a stumbling block and, unto the worldly-wise, a foolishness; but Lawrence knows he is a true prophet, even if he rails in a wilderness.

He is the Heathcliff of novelists. A scary, romantic underdog, tormented by his demons, he lashes out and, going too far, sooner or later says terrible things about everyone. No one would deny that there are deeply offensive passages and poses in his work,[4] but as a child of the Victorian age, he needs to be seen in historical perspective. A visionary, he longs for the liberation of human possibilities, and he sees English cultural decorum and understatement stifling the chances for freedom. He faces up to hard issues of modern secularism and tries to expose the usual shams and pieties of privilege and control. Full of cranky rant, he rattles the cages of class and sexual repression, hating the smug little egotisms and evasions of polite and not-so-polite society. His trying vocation is to both erotic tenderness and writing.

II

Lady Chatterley grows out of nineteenth-century homage to love, Victorian sexual repression and obsession, and the unimaginable destruction of flesh that was World War I. For Lawrence the war was a historical product of abstract thinking, alienated from the blood quickness of the senses. To understand his talk of "the resurrection of the body," we need to see what happens in the novel. It begins with a piece of wistful generalizing ("Ours is essentially a tragic age") and physical mutilation ("She married Clifford Chatterley in 1917. . . . Then he went back to Flanders: to be shipped over to England again six months later, more or less in bits" [I, 1]). It ends with Mellors in a letter to Connie giving the comic last word to his personified, metonymized cock: "John Thomas says good night to Lady Jane, a little droopingly, but with a hopeful heart" (XIX, 328). From the tragedy of history and Clifford's emasculating wound to "John Thomas" is resurrection indeed. The body, lost in mentalizing, scorned by idealisms, torn apart by mechanical, impersonal forces, reasserts its primacy. It finds its enduring rhythms and even a voice—the cock may sometimes droop, but it talks and it even possesses a Victorian heart!

Sexual conversation is meant to regenerate erotic faith. The novel's last sentence stands the project of spiritualizing love on its head: not intertwined souls, but speaking genitalia. The words also express the great tension in Lawrence and his world between fateful class consciousness ("*Lady* Jane") and the knowledge that in our physical being we are, or aspire to be, all one flesh—equal citizens in the democracy of touch. Biology—Lawrence's conception of genital, sexual identity—both does and does not reproduce sociology: the John Thomas–Lady Jane configuration equals and does not equal Oliver Mellors–Lady Chatterley. Notice that we can infer from the word *Lady* that gender is a social as well as a biological fact. Erotic, anatomical being, in Lawrence's sexual synecdoche, contains emotions, articulates relationship, makes clear even complex class feelings and gender relationships. Essential personality and social reality can and do speak through the erotic experience of individual men and women.

Lady Chatterley's Lover is about fucking—"warm-hearted" fucking. All who look into the book soon see this—which is of course why so many people *do* look into it—but I mention the obvious for three reasons:

1. For Lawrence, being able to fuck warmheartedly, the redemptive act of life, is inevitably related to breaking through taboos and being able to say and think about the forbidden word with pride and joy. He is like a semantic missionary going out to save *fuck* from damnation and redeem it as a living word of love. Anthony Burgess, slighting *Lady Chatterley* and calling the use of *fuck* an aesthetic "gaffe," reveals exactly the condition Lawrence deplored and what is at issue: "Lawrence believed that it [*fuck*] could be cleansed of its centuries of accumulated filth. . . . A man can fuck a whore but, unless his wife is a whore, he cannot fuck his wife. Mellors does not fuck Connie, nor do he and she fuck a flame into being. They make love. This is not a euphemism. On the other hand, *fuck* is a genuine dysphemism."[5] Quixotic Lawrence would see those sentiments as proving his case: erotic life can only be reformed by making *fuck* positive and conjoining it with *love*.

Despite Lawrence, Freud, and TV talk shows, most people still do not easily communicate in public discourse about personal sexual behavior and desire. The old idea, that we best keep silent about a body whose functions are somehow shameful, hangs on, as does the reverse attitude that what is sacred is best kept hidden. Early in the novel, Tommy Dukes puts forth Lawrence's latter-day creed: "Oh, intellectually I believe in having a good heart, a chirpy penis, a lively intelligence, and the courage to say 'shit!' in front of a lady" (IV, 40). His words epitomize the book's moral creed and its reclamation project for the body.

With all that has been written about *Lady Chatterley*, the point, as it were, still gets blunted. It may be plausible—even helpful and convincing—to say, as excellent critics recently have, that Lawrence's novel addresses itself to "the illustration and enactment of the practice of writing,"[6] and that it takes its place in the context of the traditional literary pastoral;[7] but to do so, and leave the emphasis on "writing" or "the pastoral," somehow reduces the power of the text and skews the force that made (and makes) it scandalous. "And this is the real point of the book," said Lawrence famously; "I want men and women to be able to think sex, fully, completely, honestly, and cleanly."[8]

How the characters fuck, why they fuck, and what they and the narrator think about fucking raise issues of the greatest personal, historical, and literary significance. And what is more, the fucking—the human experience that for Lawrence fuses most intensely our sensual, linguistic, and moral consciousness and imagination—not only demands from each reader a strong response, it really seems to *get* it, be it disgust, pleasure, anger, embarrassment, release, mockery, or venereal pontificating. That emotional reaction, I believe, colors even the most detached, abstract views of this novel and so teaches us not merely the subjectivity of reader response, which is a cliché, but the practical inseparability of our erotic nature from our critical perceptions. The novel is meant to reveal and clarify our own eroticism.

2. Representing sexual acts openly and in detail, celebrating them extensively, giving them moral and religious importance—these features are what made *Lady Chatterley* new, or "novel," in English. As I have tried to make clear, what's missing in nineteenth-century novels is the direct rendering of those moments of high intimacy and religious oneness that sexual intercourse can bring. Lawrence wants to move beyond the metaphorical representation of sexuality—that common mode of Victorian and later art—and also to obviate the desire for, and practice of, pornography. The habit of sublimating sex, treating it with euphemism, or thinking of it as dirty, he sees as dangerous—even deadly. His novel seeks to rescue sex from alienation, taboo, and obscenity, and to reintegrate it into moral life.

3. Fucking in *Lady Chatterley's Lover* is the sacred ritual that can make life and love appear holy; it can end the repression of the body that kills the spirit and turns the material world ugly. Mellors pours out a typical Lawrentian *profession de foi*: "I believe in being warm-hearted. I believe especially in being warm-hearted in love, in fucking with a warm heart. I believe if men could fuck with warm hearts, and the women take it warm-heartedly, everything would come all right. It's all this cold-hearted fucking that is death and idiocy" (XIV, 222).[9] For Lawrence, hoping to transcend the Victorian world and novel, no true love or marriage, no effective faith, hope, or charity, no good world, without warm, tenderhearted fucking. It seems a simple idea, but to take it seriously and put faith in it, as he and his novel did, is to try to shake the temple, the palace, the bank, the office building, the academy, the fortress, and even the men's club.

III

Gustav Klimt's popular painting *The Kiss* (1908; fig. 8), reproductions of which hang like icons in late twentieth-century bedrooms, illustrates the spirit and even particular details of *Lady Chatterley's* eroticism. Instead of Shakespeare's slighting description of sexual intercourse as "the beast with two backs," which neatly sums up the idea that sex reduces people to animals, *The Kiss* renders just what Lawrence honors: the beautiful, blooming man-and-woman with two backs.

Lawrence and Klimt had much in common. Both were charismatic, both worked at shaping a new art for a new century, both had utopian ideals and ran afoul of officialdom and censorship.[10] Both were deeply touched by the intellectual currents of the late nineteenth- and early twentieth-century "erotic movement" in Germany and Austria.[11] Both sought to represent the connection between social dissolution and regeneration; both were fascinated by sexuality and the world of women; both had profound matriarchal allegiances, as well as great fears of female emasculating power; both moved up from modest class origins through sexual magnetism as well as artistic prowess; and both, losing illusions about possibilities of the public redemption of society, sought to depict earthly salvation in the glory of erotic union.

The Kiss celebrates eroticism—private eroticism. It portrays a withdrawal from the world into amorous, pastoral bliss. Like Lawrence's novel and like much religious art, it bestows about its figures the sense of election—in this case *erotic election*: these lovers are among the chosen few. The vision is intimate, yet lonely; tender, yet full of force and vulnerability. The figures merge in a womblike oasis of love. They are paradoxically both unified and highly distinct. The costumes, decorated with the rectangular and circular patterns of their respective gender symbols, stress masculinity, femininity, and sexual differentiation; but one single vision fuses and holds both woman and man. Klimt expresses joy and fertility in their raiment, in the round floral designs of the enveloping space, and above all in the field of brightly colored flowers beneath them that lights up the painting and contrasts with the monotone background. Compare Lawrence: "Even the flowers are fucked into being" (XIX, 328).

In *The Kiss*, sexual imagery, replicated in almost every detail and feature, defines the picture and gives it life. Klimt represents "the mystery of the phallus" (XIV, 227), as Lawrence puts it, but like Lawrence, he just as obviously pays homage to the womb and the genital power of woman. The male image, squeezed between the female and the edge of the containing form, fills up all the available room on his side of the lovers' space and rises straight up to the long, overarching neck. The figure with its hairy head looks masterly, potent, aroused; there is just a faint hint of the vampire about it. None of his flesh shows except for the long fingers, the neck and the edge of the face beneath the dark hair. The plethora of white and black vertical rectangles on his garb conveys a sense of upward motion, but also strength and rigidity—thrusting energy. As for the woman, her eyes are closed, her white face a mask of passive rapture. She seems caught in erotic surrender, her expression molded into quiet ecstasy by the force of male sexuality.

In neither this picture nor Lawrence's novel, however, does the male sexual symbol of the phallus dominate. Klimt makes just as prominent, if not more so, the sexual imagery of flowering, ovular shapes, and the enveloping curved space. The uterine form encloses the male, and both male and female are enfolded in the symbolically feminine site of coming together and regeneration. If you follow the line between man and woman down to the genital level, you see how it flows into an erotic fusion of shapes, color, and—miraculously—vaginal with phallic form and function. That ingenious design makes a good visual symbol for the Lawrentian mystery of sexual intercourse in which male and female flesh become one and yet remain individual. If anything Klimt's uterine imagery seems to absorb and transform the phallic symbolism and turn its rectangularity circular.[12]

The desire generating a painting like *The Kiss* or a book like *Lady Chatterley* is surely to liberate sexual awareness. These works, whatever we may think of them, were designed to make their audience positively sex conscious. Just because we have no easy adjective like "phallic," no simple imagistic concept like the male flesh-stick, to describe women's sexuality and the female organs, with their complicated, expandable inner space of reproduction, does not mean that the urge somehow to represent female sexual being is any less pervasive in the creative imagination. The impetus of the erotic movement to preach the new resurrection of the sexual body depends equally upon both female and male delight in and reverence for the flesh. Artists like Klimt and Lawrence, and others who grew up amid the increasing might of impersonal political and corporate entities, longed to throw off Western culture's fig leaf and show the rapture of sexual activity for both genders.

In *The Kiss*, the male figure flows up out of the line that defines the bare flesh of the woman's legs and feet. Those feet break the contained symmetry of the lovers' space, as if male being were based upon and engendered by the female's physical being, which is directly in touch with ground, cosmos, and the mutable, evolving forms of life. If you look at the symbolic shapes of the picture—for example, the womb of love penetrated by the kneeling legs—and think of *Lady Chatterley* as well, you can see that for these artists phallic power is not something exclusively male, but that it comes from the mutuality of erotic love. The small squares and rectangles in the outer empty space to the right of the woman reiterate the patterns of masculinity in the man's attire, as if the brown-gold murk were the proverbial man's world without eroticism. Lawrence says explicitly that the lifeless, cold space—that nightmare of colorless industrialism—enclosing and pressing on the fertile wood of his lovers is the sterile vacuum of men.

The Kiss suggests the transfiguring nature of the erotic connection. With its gold, its bejeweled mosaic quality, its formal, halolike arrangement of the woman's hair with flower-stars and a seeming crown, as well as the majesty of the man's robe, the picture has strong affinities to Byzantine religious art. The effect is to fuse sexual love into a holy tradition and to propagate an erotic faith. The painting also implies, like Lawrence's novel, that when you are in love—making love—you may be blessed: in that time out of time, you can live in your own space, emancipated, ennobled—lords and ladies of creation.

IV

The love novel can be a hunt for a disappearing God, a new way to find or define God, or a means of overthrowing God. If Lawrence did not exist, he might have been invented from the raw material and implications of nineteenth-century fiction. *Lady Chatterley's Lover* relates dialectically on almost every page to other English novels and novelists in the tradition of erotic faith; they held dialogue with Lawrence's imagination.

Take Austen: he abuses her in "A Propos of *Lady Chatterley's Lover*," calling her "mean" and "English in the bad, mean, snobbish sense of the word," "knowing in apartness instead of knowing in togetherness" (357). Yet they have a lot in common, and he doth protest too much. Like her, troubled and fascinated by class and gender problems, he uses the novel as an instrument of love; you can see *Lady Chatterley* as a male variation a century later of *Pride and Prejudice*. Both betray the same plaintive English dream that love might be stronger than class, and each features the erotic redemption of an upper-class figure—Darcy and Connie respectively. They both insist that true love must be an equilibrium of vital, distinctive beings, not an absorption process. Both locate hope in the coming together of man and woman, but each arrives at an erotic faith only after much soul-searching and inner conflict—even pain—and with full awareness of love's agonies and idiocies.

In fact, Austen's vision helps us to see and grasp Lawrence's book, with its moral insistence on "a lively intelligence," a woman's freedom of erotic choice, and a love that fuses tenderness and desire as cornerstones of faith. Like her he refuses to take the conventional "man's world" more seriously than erotic relationship. Lawrence, however, filled with anxiety about his working-class origins and his own sexuality, misreads Austen as a sexless snob, and his quarrel runs deep. Attacking in her what he calls "personality," he goes on to say that his Sir Clifford Chatterley, without heart and warmth, is "purely a personality" ("A Propos," 357), having lost all connection with men and women—lost, that is, "blood-warmth" and the ability to make love: "He was not in actual touch with anybody" (II, 13). For Lawrence, "personality" means a psychological fetish of disconnected individualism. The abstract idealization of a self-identity threatens the natural flow of being.

Both write Cinderella stories, but they differ sharply. Austen's heroine gets a chance, through love, to be rich and to extend the scope of her power and consciousness. Lawrence's heroine, who is rich, comes to love through passionate and full sexual life with her poor lover; she has the chance to experience redeeming sexual intimacy, to be with him and bear their child. The difference points up the force of Lawrence's critical vision and desire. He holds the absurd credo—absurd in the way that a religious credo so often appears to rational, quantifying minds—that lovely fucking might matter more than status, money, celebrity, and social power.

He abhors in Austen the smooth blending of morals with assets and the idea of love as a meeting of minds, rather than bodies. He does not believe that personalities and minds, madly working away at calculation, self-projection, and rationalizing processes that distance the flesh and blood of others, *do* meet and connect. Writing in the wake of industrialization and international mass slaughter, he deplores what "civilized" reason can plan for—and do to—corporeal being. Minds, he thinks, love ideas, and ideas turn human bodies into classes, statistics, cannon fodder, immortal souls, and such like, maiming life. Meanly, Lawrence calls Austen an "old maid" ("A Propos," 357)—for him, one who is untouched and does not touch.

The awakening-to-love moments from their novels get at the essence and difference of their erotic faiths. Love for her can offer a bright woman a chance, narrow though it may be, for distinction and personal dignity; but, she imagines, for a girl or woman to succumb to sexual desire almost always means victimization. Elizabeth consciously warms to Darcy when she views his estate and senses how much its valuable harmonies could mean to her. Later, "gratitude and esteem" move her to love. Lawrence, on the other hand, would scoff at the idea of a stately home or "gratitude" as good bases for love. He sees the "bitch-goddess, Success" (III, 26) sacrificing love or capturing it and claiming it as a sterile rite of homage.

Connie begins to open to Mellors when she sees him naked, bathing.

[I]n some curious way it was a visionary experience: it had hit her in the middle of the body. She saw the clumsy breeches slipping down over the pure, delicate, white loins. . . . contours that one might touch: a body!

Connie had received the shock of vision in her womb, and she knew it; it lay inside her. But with her mind she was inclined to ridicule. A man washing himself in a backyard! [VI, 68]

History of white flesh in the English novel: now you see it, now you don't, now you do. Remember that Austen, reacting to Henry Fielding and his passage in *Tom Jones* about identifying love with the desire for "delicate white flesh," had banished that sexual image from her own similar meditation on love (see above, chapter 2, pp. 49–52). *Imaginary dialogue*: Austen: "Vulgar, mortifying! Believe in rationality. That sorry instinct for the flesh forms the Lydias and Wickhams of the world and the misery they bring. Manners, propriety, *sublimated* sexual desire turning to affection and generous esteem: they are all that stand between people—particularly women—and savagery. The dignity of life and positive, affectionate love depend upon the distinction of *personality*, not animal impulse."

Lawrence: "No. Not personality with its insidious alienation, but the mutual interflow of life and humanity matter. Love is of the body; because the flow of sexual sympathy and desire—that longing for touch—drives people to want and try to connect with others; it gets them to care about and cherish life beyond themselves. The appeal and touch of the body are, and ought to be, holy."

Chatterley, with whom he associates Austen, dins on to Connie, "It's the lifelong companionship that matters. . . . The long, slow, enduring thing . . . [author's ellipsis] that's what we live by . . . [author's ellipsis] not the occasional spasm of any sort" (V, 44–45). But she rebels: "The human body is only just coming to real life. With the Greeks it gave a lovely flicker, then Plato and Aristotle killed it, and Jesus finished it off. But now the body is coming really to life, it is really rising from the tomb" (XVI, 254). Lawrence's vocation, then, is to pursue "the life of the human body" (XVI, 254) in the novel, a tricky calling.

V

Lady Chatterley follows patterns in *The Bride of Lammermoor* that assert the primacy of love and imbue the sex act with a new sanctity. Like Scott, Lawrence sees love as a potential refuge from social warfare and enmities of the past. Each renders abominable a marriage that thwarts a woman's erotic hope. And Scott's historicism contributed to Lawrence's cultural perspectivism. Scott, however, believed in historical progress and collective values, despite his nostalgic portrayals of glamorous lost causes. His antiquarianism is very different from Lawrence's primitivism, which delights in the body. Subtly idealistic about the past, Scott uses it to feed readers' longing for an epic sense of being and a living relationship with what has preceded them. History is a text in which to sublimate and fulfill desire.

For Lawrence history has failed: "This is history. . . . The industrial England blots out the agricultural England. One meaning blots out another. The new England blots out the old England. And the continuity is not organic, but mechanical" (XI, 167–68). Lawrence wants an end to the history that defines itself as collective, social, chronological, readily transcribable, economic, and grandiosely oriented towards future goals. Such history means the new empire of Midas that turns blood to machinery grease: "mechanised greed or . . . greedy mechanism" (X, 128). For him, the modern era has brought the deadly glorification of abstractions on the one hand (*nationalism, progress,* and *civilization*), and, on the other, inanimate matter (minerals, weapons, money). To counteract the ravages of idealizing, mechanizing history, he writes a history of particular lovers' sexual flesh.

Lawrence's famous symbol for the modern epic of mutilating war and dehumanizing industrialism is Sir Clifford's mechanized wheelchair that squashes the hyacinths and bluebells in the spring countryside and then breaks down, injuring Mellors. Where Scott found in his narrative a historical moment when marriage without love and against the woman's desire becomes rape, Lawrence, in his eroticized world, finds that conventional history itself has become an institutionalized, social rape of nature and organic humanity. Stressing the horror of coercing a woman to submit her body to a man she does not want, Scott honors the intangibility of love. A century later, Lawrence *embodies* love, emphasizing a woman's right to put her body in touch with a man who can cherish her flesh.

VI

If Lawrence tries to make peace with the flesh, Emily Brontë, his great predecessor in rendering love as a calling, often looks to be waging all-out war on it. Few novelists, though, are closer in spirit than these two. Like *Wuthering Heights,* his fiction conveys the animism of the common world and gets at people's startling mood swings: the intensity and discontinuities of emotions within short periods of their daily life. Both were haunted by the menace of the disease that would kill them. Their novels show their rage for a love more powerful than death. "Tenderness," his alternative title for *Lady Chatterley,* fits neither her world nor his.

Lawrence senses, as do Emily Brontë and Dickens, how under-class resentment might feed erotic hunger and how love can become a means of class warfare. The Mellors–Connie–Sir Clifford triangle recalls Heathcliff, Cathy, and Edgar Linton. If we set Mellors next to Heathcliff, we can better understand Lawrence's gamekeeper and his diatribes. Each has a sadistic verbal streak that scourges the world for blocking his erotic vision. Lady Chatterley's lover, in his most miserable moments, rages wildly: "When I'm with a woman who's really Lesbian, I fairly howl in my soul, wanting to kill her" (XIV, 219). That kind of bullying pose, taken out of context, makes Lawrence an irresistible target: the pig you love to hate. But notice how close it is to a hyperbolic cruelty we have heard before: "I have no pity! The more the worms writhe, the more I yearn to crush out their entrails! It is a moral teething," cries Heathcliff.

Bad as they are, Mellors's ugly words, so much in Heathcliff's style, are a symptom, not a cause, of the sickness and enmity in the novel. Each of these characters, like "a broken-backed snake" (XIV, 222), lashes out poisonously, frustrated in his drive to be in touch with love. Both novelists want to take their audience beyond accepted wisdom, ethical platitudes, and the easy opportunities for self-congratulation that fiction offers. For both, the world is full of the most excruciating pain; things are unfair, all people are dying, and nothing redeems life but the virtually unrealizable connection of passionate love, which lovers with terrible moral failings must define for themselves and then seek, like the blind looking for beauty. Against such visions, moral criticisms of their protagonists read like attacks on early Christians for being bigoted fanatics—possibly true but beside the point.

Lawrence, like Emily Brontë, loves fiercely the growing things of the earth, especially flowers. It is as if their strong erotic natures, so tormented by the frailty of the flesh and their own bad health, seized on the recurring beauty and fertility of the countryside and tried to inscribe in it their will to faith. But Lawrence, coming later, sees the widening despoliation of the English countryside and cannot take its lovely continuity for granted. Somehow, like the flowers, the human spirit and body must be rejuvenated if nature itself is to be saved.

Compare the most famous eruptions of flora in *Wuthering Heights* and *Lady Chatterley*: in Brontë the flesh passes into foliage, but in Lawrence the flowers pass into flesh. She wants to diffuse love; he wants to concentrate it. The blooming harebells, heath, and grass on the grave of Cathy and Heathcliff transform the personal vocation of love and life into an endless flowering process, a metamorphosis of desire into a continuum of love, language, and nature: the round of eternity. Here, in contrast, is Mellors's notorious floral decoration in Lawrence: "He fastened fluffy young oak-sprays round her breasts, sticking in tufts of bluebells and campion: and in her navel he poised a pink campion flower, and in her maiden-hair were forget-me-nots and woodruff. . . . And he . . . wound a bit of creeping-jenny round his penis, and stuck a single bell of a hyacinth in his navel" (XV, 246).

Nothing in *Lady Chatterley* has set off more critical jeering, but it is just as essential to his love vision as Emily Brontë's final scene is to hers. In one way, Lawrence was simply letting a puss out of the nineteenth-century literary bag: all those flowers in Romantic poetry, all those blooming landscapes in Victorian fiction are in part eroticism diffused into nature—roses that dare not speak their name. But the flowers, for him, really are elements in a holy ceremony. He means them to adorn and celebrate the creative burst of fecundity that is—or ought to be—sexual intercourse, without which nothing would exist; Emily Brontë wants to comprehend death in living nature. Lawrence wants to lose death for a while by reveling in the ecstatic, timeless moment of creation. No matter how ridiculous the floral scene may seem in a buttoned-up mood, we need to see that the impulse that causes Lawrence and his characters to entwine flowers on the sexual body is like the exuberance that led people to decorate their churches with rose windows. Those plucked blossoms are for him what the mystical Rose was to medieval Christians, or Aphrodite's roses were to her devotees: symbolic homage to the mystery, genesis, and goodness of being—the sacred generative force. Remember that Lawrence came out of an age and language in which the first sexual act was routinely called a *de*flowering. Social life had gone bad because of such habits of mind. He sought a private ritual of *en*flowering.

Oddly enough, he is also celebrating aestheticism along with eroticism. He employs, in a basic mode, both art (i.e., adornment with materials arranged for aesthetic purposes) and metaphorical thinking (e.g., my love is like a red, red rose; flowers = fertility) to represent the reality of joyful fucking and to transfer to the bodies and their genital parts the qualities that flowers suggest. Mellors decorating the body with flowers is to making love what Lawrence writing sensitively about an orgasm is to fucking. Looking at this flower scene, we could say, adapting Kristeva, that out of the corporeal *jouissance* of the body in love comes the impetus to metaphor, art, and religion.

VII

At the novel's close, Mellors writes to Connie as they wait to be together: "Well, so many words, because I can't touch you. If I could sleep with my arms round you, the ink could stay in the bottle" (XIX, 328). These lines open up brilliantly the relation between erotic sublimation, displacement, and nineteenth-century fiction, or any imaginative literature; in particular they make a perfect epigraph for Lucy Snowe and *Villette*. Charlotte Brontë, like Lawrence, is obsessed by the relationship between love and language. Both want the ink in the bottle to become a genie out of the bottle that can enchant and bring faith to their hard worlds. The main difference between them would seem to be that she embraces the sublimation of touch into word, while he detests and fights it, longing for the word to become flesh. He wants to get to a saving sexuality beyond language.

The love-letter—or the love narrative—means for her the lover gone, but the love present. For the nineteenth-century woman the displacement of the body into the "heretic narrative" might help bring a new empowerment of imagination and self-conception. A text could be a means and area to connect with the god of creation. For the post–World War I man, the love letter, no matter how fine, signifies the lack of touch, and it is in physical knowledge, in what intercourse might be, that Lawrence finds his religious faith—a potential assumption of the mortal self and the abstracting word into erotic beatitude: "That exquisite and immortal moment of a man's entry into the woman of his desire."[13]

From a woman's perspective, that might seem like male heaven in a man's world—not nearly as good for her as for him. Lawrence, however, fears the loss and dispersal of vital, physical being in mentalizations, including writing. The doubt that there is anything real or of value beyond the ink comes close to driving him mad. He lives in terror that the ink genie is really his master and that he is an impotent word-fucker, like the writer Sir Clifford. Caught up in a contradiction, Lawrence broadcasts in a novel, "Not words but fucking!"

Yet he, differing from Charlotte Brontë about the primacy of word or flesh, shares with her the evangelical temperament. (Lawrence, the sexual puritan moralizing on "good" and "bad" sex, is like Protestant Charlotte assessing the religious practice of others.) Both are prickly, intense beings who love to preach and denounce. They each express great moral concern, but no one would call their voices especially magnanimous or merciful. Neither can stomach ideas or works that separate the world of art from the real world, and they both imagine themselves as the authors of "heretic" narratives, writing in praise of erotic passion against tepid convention and the shriveling hypocrisies of orthodoxy.

VIII

Among the many things that the burning of Miss Havisham in Dickens's *Great Expectations* could be made to symbolize, one might be the relationship between Lawrence and his mother. He omits or suppresses in Mellors those staples of nineteenth-century fiction: childhood, incestuous impulses, and the drama (trauma) of transference; but in *Sons and Lovers* he had imagined from the start his autobiographical Paul Morel's crucial relationship to the mother, with its Oedipal overtones. Lawrence realized there what Dickens especially, but other Victorians too, had rendered: that compulsive incestuous feeling, with its inhibition etched in the psyche, made adult eroticism problematic and full of conflict.

It is hardly an exaggeration to say that Dickens made the symbolic choice of family over sex in his fiction—mother and sister over lover—and that Lawrence found himself in a terrible war against that Victorian syndrome. Dickens idealizes proper love between men and women into something like kindly, asexual affection among chaste family members. For Lawrence, reading the deadly strains in modern history and his own boiling mind, such conjoining of incest bias and sexual repression had worked to criminalize the body, make love a jail keeper, and fragment the psyche. *Lady Chatterley* is meant to redeem sex from its taint of criminal guilt.

The novel with its ballyhoo about fucking will seem misconceived if we do not see how bleak Lawrence thought social circumstances had become, and also why. For him, displacing sexuality, as Dickens and the Victorians had done, teaches that real life is elsewhere. Without adult genital desire and satisfaction, a person's love is disembodied and the present is devalued. Libido repression leaves the inner self a dreaming child caught in the neurotic trap of early sorrow and need; it makes the outer self a social robot going through motions planned by others, "out of touch."

For most commonsense people who think in the usual conventions of linear time (i.e., their own spans of fourscore years, the long epochs of human history, the geological and astronomical eons), preaching a creed of erotic love and warmhearted fucking will seem a dubious proposition at best.[14] Sex seems such an instinctual thing: it's over so fast and accounts for such a relatively small amount of experience, most of which takes place in only three or four decades of the normal life span. But here the temporal implications of *Great Expectations* help with the rationale of Lawrence's faith. Dickens imagines that the usual sense of linear time is wrong: children are fixated with programs of desire. When they fetishize—say, a person, money, or writing—or sublimate themselves in national identity or religious ideals, they lose touch with the vulnerable reality of the senses, and the world turns murderous. Therefore, it seemed to Lawrence and many of his generation that something was needed to break through the abstract programs of the past and make life *immediate*. The narrator of *Lady Chatterley* wants a dissolution of psychological and historical determinism, and passionate eroticism is the only way he sees of getting into a true time current and moving on to a better future. Wrong or not, he is neither crazy nor mindless.

Great Expectations can help us see why Lawrence is so keen on "the democracy of touch." Like Dickens, he uses in his dialogue both standard English and dialect to show up the British class system and the way it divides people from one another and themselves. In *Lady Chatterley*, Connie at first can barely understand Mellors when he speaks the vernacular, which he does out of mixed motives—to be natural, to underline class and sexual hostility, and to achieve a kind of earthy intimacy. Lawrence imagines a world of upper-class and lower-class talk: the one, the speech of the dominant will in society; the other, that of the laboring body. The only way he imagines of harmonizing the two languages and the two nations for which they stand is through erotic touch rendered in the form of his novel.

His grandiose linguistic reclamation project is to wed body and soul, bridge the class gap, make dirty words clean, bring down the artificial Victorian wall between male and female discourse, and point the way to a potential new wholeness for humanity. That is exactly what he is trying to do in this conversation between his lovers:

> "It heals it all up, that I can go into thee. I love thee that tha opened to me. . . ."
> "But you do believe I love you?" she said.
> "Tha loved me just now, wider than iver tha thout tha would. . . ."
> "Ay!" she said, imitating the dialect sound. . . .
> He laughed. Her attempts at the dialect were so ludicrous, somehow.
> "Coom then, tha mun goo!" he said.
> "Mun I?" she said.
> "Maun Ah!" he corrected.
> "Why should I say *maun* when you say *mun*," she protested. "You're not playing fair."
> "Arena Ah! . . . Th'art good cunt, though, aren't ter? . . ."
> "What is cunt?" she said.
> "An' doesn't ter know? Cunt! It's thee down theer; an' what I get when I'm i'side thee; it's a' as it is, all on't."
> "All on't," she teased. "Cunt! It's like fuck then."
> "Nay nay! Fuck's only what you do. Animals fuck. But cunt's a lot more than that. It's thee, dost see: an' tha'rt a lot beside an animal, aren't ter? even ter fuck! Cunt! Eh, that's the beauty o' thee, lass." [XII, 190–91]

Such dialogue brings out the silly—even insulting—audacity of Lawrence, and the impossibility of his project: it shows how deep and various are the differences between people and the conflicts in the single self. But the writing may also arouse some tenderness towards poor, struggling men and women who must try to touch one another in the exciting, uncontrollable media of language, class, and sex.

IX

When Lawrence compares Clifford's garrulous nurse Mrs. Bolton to George Eliot and then to the phenomena of gossip and the novel (IX, 105), he intimates how much in *Lady Chatterley* relates to Eliot and to the text of eroticism that *The Mill on the Floss* offers. He is steeped in her moral seriousness, her sympathy for common life, and her feeling for the flow of libido in everyday experience. He also manifests George Eliot's sense of erotic crisis. The title of one study of Lawrence, *River of Dissolution*,[15] points to his kinship with Maggie and the flood. For both novelists, the ego, trapped in history and tormenting cultural imperatives, must be dissolved and diffused in an overwhelming flood of love.

After comparing George Eliot to the gossipy Mrs. Bolton, Lawrence writes, "But the novel, like gossip, can also excite spurious sympathies and recoils. . . . so long as they are *conventionally* 'pure.' Then the novel, like gossip, becomes at last vicious . . . because it is . . . ostensibly on the side of the angels" (IX, 106). He hates the doctrine of renunciation and the sacrifice of the flesh that he thinks Eliot's side-of-the-angels idealism finally endorses. Maggie Tulliver begs Stephen to help her renounce him *"because* I love you." The gist of her prayer, *help me to resign a life together with you and your touch, because I love you,* is mystical; it seeks to replace eroticism with religious idealism. But the prayer leads to death, not life. Loyalty to Philip (forerunner of emasculated Chatterley), all mind and no body, and to the sexually taboo brother, means the squandering of human flesh.

Renunciation of adult physical love might be on the side of the angels, but it does not blunt the force of erotic desire: what Maggie wants most is the approval of, and union with, the powerful male family member—identification with the masculine deity of the past. She dies ecstatically, her soul content, her body at last free from the profound inhibition against the incestuous embrace, but only by virtue of ceasing to be.

Set next to Maggie's drowning this notorious scene between Connie and Mellors—egregiously on the side of the devils:

The sun . . . lit up . . . the erect phallus rising darkish and hot-looking from the little cloud of vivid gold-red hair. She was startled and afraid.

"How strange! . . . Now I know why men are so overbearing! But he's lovely, *really.* Like another being! . . ."

"Ay ma lad! . . . Theer on thy own. . . . John Thomas. Art boss? of me? . . . Dost want *her?* . . . Ax Lady Jane! Say: Lift up your heads o' ye gates, that the king of glory may come in. . . ."

And afterwards . . . the woman had to uncover the man again, to look at the mystery of the phallus. . . . taking the soft small penis in her hand. "Isn't he somehow lovely! so on his own, so strange! And *so* innocent! And he comes so far into me! . . . He's mine too. He's not only yours. He's mine! . . ."

He laughed.

"Blest be the tie that binds our hearts in kindred love," he said. [XIV, 226–27]

That is the Lawrence that can make people wince and snicker: the prophet of pubic faith. But he felt in his marrow that men and women had a radical need to relearn physical pride. Equal time and fair play for the body as well as the soul, male beauty as well as female beauty, man as erotic object of desire and adoration as well as woman. The mutilation of Clifford Chatterley, of Hemingway's Jake Barnes, and of millions of real men in World War I make the phallic point of Lawrence's logic plain. Better to celebrate a penis or an orgasm than a tragic drowning or the guns of August. Pompous and ridiculous as Mellors and Connie are, they are playfully loving. Homoerotic homage to the phallus may swell the scene, but Connie does not show envy or feel any deprivation at not being a man. The phallus belongs to her as well as to Mellors, and there is nothing in their relationship like the abjection and suicidal *ressentiment* of Maggie in her dealings with Tom and other men. Sensual pleasure for Connie is good and exists for the taking.

Lawrence literally tries to give a voice to the long-muted body, but he can by no means imagine the end of the mind-body split. In fact, the passage assumes alienation of flesh and spirit just as surely as the drowning in *The Mill on the Floss* does. What is radically new is that Lawrence refuses to privilege the mind over the body. John Thomas becomes a character, and even gets his own personality and dialogue. The novelist, like the contemporary scientists who were developing their modes of specialization for analyzing particular parts and functions of the body, seeks to put the body and its sexuality in touch with linguistic consciousness. Ironically Lawrence's narrative of bodies in love shows how erotic faith might later evolve into a "sexology" that tries to say how people should "have sex." Popularized scientific eroticism would privilege the alienated flesh, try to teach ecstasy out of handbooks, and make Eros an acrobat of technique rather than a personal god.

X

Anthony Trollope and D. H. Lawrence would seem as different as men could be, but almost no other Victorian novel comes closer than *Phineas Finn/Redux* to Lawrence's view of the absolute need for erotic faith to counteract the failures of modern public life. Trollope renders a curious hollowness in the men of the ruling classes and an unfulfilled desire in the women that, by the time of *Lady Chatterley*, Lawrence sees as endemic.

Of Connie before she knows Mellors, Lawrence writes, "[E]verything in her world and life seemed worn out" (V, 49). Near the end of the book, Mellors says, "Well! . . . The world is a raving idiot, and no man can kill it. . . . We must rescue ourselves as best we can" (XVIII, 310). They could be repeating the sentiments of Madame Max and Phineas Finn after they spend their youth chasing the bitch-goddess. It is not far from Madame Max longing for a love she can believe in or from Laura Kennedy bewailing her infertile life and body, to Connie, neurotic and ill, "crying blindly" (X, 122) just before her first sexual intercourse with Mellors.

The potentially dangerous split in Trollope between erotics and politics that can lead to the eruption of violence by those who are "out of touch" becomes in Lawrence a disaster. His heavy stress on erotic life comes about because the possibilities of public life seem to have collapsed entirely; but Trollope's narrative had already shown how men and women, seeing the despair of politics, find it easy to believe that real life is love life. In *Phineas*, Trollope actually did create a genuinely Lawrentian figure in Lord Chiltern, who detests politics and, à la Mellors, marries out of sexual passion and becomes a gamekeeper. Lawrence, on the potential of such eroticism and a love of the outdoors, would try to build faith and reverence into the secular world.

Small wonder then that Thomas Hardy, with his vision of nature, meant more than any other novelist to Lawrence.[16] The scene that begins the lovemaking of Connie and Mellors definitely shows the older writer feeding the younger's imagination. She goes forlorn in the flowering spring to see the hatching of the new birds. With the keeper, who touches the hens and chicks tenderly, she looks "in a sort of ecstasy" at one tiny prancing little creature: "Life, life! Pure, sparky, fearless new life! New life! . . . Even when it . . . disappeared under the hen's feathers in answer to the mother hen's wild alarm-cries, it was not really frightened; it took it as a game, the game of living. For in a moment a tiny sharp head was poking through the gold-brown feathers of the hen, and eyeing the Cosmos" (X, 120–21). Moved, she begins weeping, Mellors touches *her* tenderly, and soon he is inside her.

The chick peeking at the cosmos is pure Hardy. The image situates humanity amidst all kinds of cyclical, pulsing erotics of the universe, and it stresses *consciousness* of the gaping difference between the smallness of individual being and the infinite largeness of regenerative nature.

Lawrence needed Hardy's earthiness and took to heart his rendering of the problems, for a post-Christian intelligence, of faith and religious longing and his direct stress on erotic drive and crisis in the lives of men and women. But he had to fight shy of Hardy's influence, too, and find his own vision—as his *Study of Thomas Hardy* proves. Ostensibly a monograph on Hardy, the *Study* is really a wide-ranging speculation on artistic and religious problems, and in it Lawrence formulates a theory that turns religion into an erotic faith: "By 'religious' he suggests a deep desire in man and woman to meet in physical and spiritual fulfilment. . . . Lawrence sees that when art can truthfully express the achieved equilibrium between man and woman . . . then it is the hour of joyful or 'religious art.'"[17] But Lawrence dislikes Hardy's distancing fatalism and the split he reads in Hardy between lust and spiritual aspiration: these things destroy the chance for genuine religious passion between women and men.

Far from the Madding Crowd is the Hardy novel closest to *Lady Chatterley*. Lawrence clearly means Mellors to be a pastoral figure of sorts, but if we compare him to Gabriel Oak, we see how narrow the pastoral possibilities have become in Lawrence and consequently how much more is at stake for Mellors in his erotic relationship. The idyllic setting—the place where open, loving relationship may occur and where nature banishes the artificial—has diminished by the end of the novel to the space of the human body, sanctuary of the post-industrial age.

Lawrence, like Hardy, tries for a new pastoral. Mellors has many of Oak's traits and virtues, but in a claustrophobic world where commerce surrounds and dooms the wood, the keeper's life lacks the scope of the shepherd's. Without passion a sacred sense of life fades, and by "passion" I mean the example of a mysterious, transcendent, or sacrificial act of devotion that transgresses worldliness and "common sense" on behalf of what might be called "a higher power." Lawrence, believing in the resurrection of the body as the only basis for religious feeling in his time, needs to combine pastoral feeling with passion. He wants, in Mellors, to fuse both Oak, the staff of goodness, and Troy, the transgressive sword of sex. "I came," says Christ, "not to send peace, but a sword" (Matthew 10:34); but Lawrence, playing off that verse, reverses Scripture in Connie's passion: "It might come with the thrust of a sword in her softly-opened body, and that would be death. . . . But it came with a strange slow thrust of peace . . . such as made the world in the beginning" (XII, 186). The only place where the urge to violent passion can be accommodated and pacified too is the eroticized body. The new pastor, to resurrect it, must not only care for it, he must arouse, thrill, and penetrate the senses. In Hardy the "salvation of the body" is "still a study, a religion, and a desire." In *Lady Chatterley* the salvation of religion *by the body* is now a study and a desire.

XI

Vocation: How in a secular age can men and women find a passionate, moral calling that brings faith in life? Hardy, Trollope, and the Brontës explicitly, Dickens and Eliot implicitly, deal with this question—an awful one for Lawrence. For him, vocation without passionate love is unholy. In satirizing Clifford, he connects the incestuous, Oedipal Victorian social strategy with the loveless practice of vocation. Victorian ethics united and glorified Christian, commercial, and family values, but Lawrence renders a corrupt alliance of erotic impotence, mammon worship, and infantile self-indulgence. When Clifford breaks down sobbing after Connie tells him about Mellors, the novel makes sinister and obscene the incest bias of nineteenth-century British fiction.

Clifford became like a child with Mrs. Bolton. . . . And he would gaze on her with wide, childish eyes, in a relaxation of madonna-worship. . . . letting go all his manhood, and sinking back to a childish position that was really perverse. And then he would put his hand into her bosom and feel her breasts, and kiss them in exaltation, the exaltation of perversity, of being a child when he was a man . . . almost like a religious exaltation: the perverse and literal rendering of: "except ye become again as a little child."—While she was the Magna Mater, full of power and potency. . . .

The curious thing was that when this child-man . . . emerged into the world, he was much sharper. . . . This perverted child-man was now a *real* business man. . . . It was as if his very passivity and prostitution to the Magna Mater gave him insight into material business affairs, and lent him . . . inhuman force. [XIX, 316–17]

That passage symbolizes for Lawrence the Victorians' bargain with the devil and explains why *Lady Chatterley* makes a vocation out of fucking. In just over a century, the novel has come full circle from Monk Lewis's Madonna, who assaults faith with the lure of sex. Magna Mater now promises that if you give up, displace, or denigrate genital desire you can win the power and glory of *this* world.

Sex, therefore, must be a vocation to save the world from faithlessness, but Lawrence's dilemma is that it cannot be a lasting or satisfactory one in itself. A pastoral vocation, sooner or later, means language and profession, even if it consecrates the body. Since writing inevitably privileges mind, Lawrence gets himself into an impossible position. What is Mellors to do? He frets, "A man must offer a woman *some* meaning in his life. . . . I'm not just my lady's fucker, after all." Connie's reply is devastating: "What else are you?" (XVIII, 300). Much as Lawrence wishes it were otherwise, the vocation of the new pastor is to shepherd with words as well as touch. Mellors's long speeches, the narrator's words about the moral function of the novel, the symposium scenes, and the eloquent letter that ends the book, all go to show the sexual vocation turning into preaching and writing. T. H. Adamowski describes Lawrence's religious aspiration as the "impossible ideal of desire . . . to overcome isolation by having consciousness touch consciousness at the very instant when each of the partners is reduced to flesh" (never mind the very un-Lawrentian connotations of "reduced").[18] But that incarnation is not a stable condition. Consciousness and bodies divide, and words have to be used to point to the holiness of the body and tender touch, even though they cannot be that sacred flesh.

Lydia Blanchard, discussing the relation of language and sexuality in *Lady Chatterley*, asserts that, "[W]hen we are truly together, the ink *can* stay in the bottle."[19] But people are almost never, if ever, "truly together"; therefore the ink, which signifies separation, must flow to sanctify touch. The ending, Mellors's letter to Connie, reflects "the very brilliance of the novel" in creating, ironically, "a language of love, a lover's discourse"[20] that describes the subordination of words to mingling flesh and fucking: "So I believe in the little flame between us. . . . It's my Pentecost. . . . The old Pentecost isn't quite right. Me and God is a bit uppish, somehow. But the little forked flame between me and you: there you are!" (XIX, 327). Since Pentecost is the coming of the Holy Ghost to the Apostles, the logic of the language says that Mellors's vocation, like his author's, is to be an apostle writing.

Religious faith and the soul, then, lie in, and arise out of, the physical act of love between two human beings: "I love this chastity, which is the pause of peace of our fucking, between us now like a snowdrop of forked white fire" (XIX, 328). Lawrence here comes close to justifying his vocation as a writer. Chastity, in his creed, is the time of homage to the faith that has sprung into being from the body. The words are a substitute for touch, but they come out of a chastity that is the beatitude of fucking, and therefore part of the sacred connection.

Not wanting to end with anything that exalts spirit and language over flesh, he then concludes, "John Thomas says good night to Lady Jane, a little droopingly, but with a hopeful heart." That sentence stresses and personifies sex, makes the subject and object of language genital, and gives the last word to the body. It testifies that metonym, metaphor, synecdoche, and all figures of language are interfused—and *con*fused—with somatic, erotic reality.

XII

James Joyce, having fought to get free of the church, had little sympathy for priests and prophets—even prophets of love. He ticked off *Lady Chatterley* as "a piece of propaganda in favour of something which, outside of D. H. L.'s country at any rate, makes all the propaganda for itself." To the nude, flower-decorating scene, he responded, "Lush!" Lawrence, in turn, called Molly's section of *Ulysses* "the dirtiest, most indecent, obscene thing ever written. . . . filthy."[21] And yet, on love, these modern masters have much in common. For both, *love* is a suspect term. Each frets that the nineteenth century killed love with Christian kindness and commercialization, but both reembody it in their last work. If the novel is to erotic faith what the New Testament is to Christian faith, then Joyce and Lawrence are like two great theologians at odds: arrogantly scornful, but joined almost against their will in the larger faith.

In historical perspective, their sexual candor unites them, and both imagine that erotic faith depends on giving voice to the sexual body, with its rhythms and desires.[22] One critic rightly compares Lawrence to Don Quixote and Joyce to Sancho Panza,[23] but, just as in Cervantes the two characters come sometimes to take on the world view of the other, so it is with Joyce and Lawrence: the end of *Lady Chatterley* seems positively Joycean (Leopold Bloom also says good night a little droopingly), and Molly's final effusion of flowers and sex is positively Lawrentian. It's easy, living in the era of Foucault, call-in sex-talk shows, and AIDS publicity, to forget how original and influential Joyce and Lawrence were in putting sexuality and bodily organs into serious fiction (just as, in the age of Freud, it was easy to take for granted what Dickens and George Eliot had done in putting childhood experience into the novel).

Joyce's "propaganda" witticism can actually tell us a lot not only about his relationship to Lawrence, but also about *Lady Chatterley*. Joyce thinks the proper function of the novel is to produce a radiant aesthetic effect, which may ultimately be religious as well. It brings the pleasure of contemplation and the satisfaction—rather than the arousal—of desire. For Lawrence, the purpose of art is moral and rhetorical. The novel should be just what Joyce thinks it should not: "kinetic"; it can and should direct the flow of passion. In effect he would say that in neither *his* country nor Joyce's had tenderhearted fucking and the resurrection of the body through love *had* good "propaganda." Why, for example, was *fuck* dirty, *Ulysses* not for sale, and most popular "love" fiction trash? Why was Bloom impotent with Molly, and why were masses of people more interested in money than their own love lives? Propagation of erotic faith was exactly what was needed.

From another perspective, however, Lawrence would agree with Joyce. In Connie's drive through the industrial squalor of the Midlands, she notes, "[A]ll went by, ugly, ugly, ugly, followed by the plaster-and-gilt horror of the cinema with its wet picture announcements, 'A Woman's Love!'" (XI, 163). (Imagine the irony if Lawrence had lived to see steamy pictures outside moviehouses in Nottingham or Detroit advertising "hot, sexy" *Women in Love*.) The spirit of Joyce's Gerty MacDowell satire on the sleazy business of love informs *Lady Chatterley* on almost every page. Lawrence's whole intention in the novel is to try to break free of propaganda mentality and be honest about eroticism.

Naturally he often fails, but surprisingly, *Lady Chatterley*'s foolish moments can make us see how alive the spirit of Leopold Bloom is in Lawrence. When Bloom professes his creed of love in the bar, the Citizen's insult to him fits Lawrence's critical plight: "A new apostle to the gentiles. . . . Love, moya! He's a nice pattern of a Romeo and Juliet" (*Ulysses*, 273). To be ridiculous, to seem weird, to get didactic, to fall into unwitting comedy—such things are unavoidable when you're preaching love (and not just love but holy fucking) to a worldly-wise audience in a materialistic age. But like poor Bloom, an apostle can make a fool of himself—in fact he must continually risk doing so—and still be faithful in his fashion.

XIII

Lawrence tries to make the novel, the medium of erotic faith, a means and form to constitute sanctified sex. Around their fucking, he centers the narrative and moral vision, and he sets himself the job of representing seriously the developing sex life of his lovers. How successful is he? Because sexuality is so subjective, there can be no normative answer about it in *Lady Chatterley*. Lawrence, however, despite his follies and lapses, did well for his time and beyond in writing about intercourse, much better than most critics have seen, and the sex in this book has helped to shape and profoundly influence the climate of modern erotic opinion and expectations.[24]

People glibly talk of making love, but when Connie gives herself to a German youth, when she honeymoons with Clifford, when she fucks Michaelis, she does not make love. For Lawrence, Mellors is her only lover. Love is made by using and combining all kinds of physical and mental resources, especially the sensitive touch of the body, tenderness, and the skills of imagination and language. That is not a new idea, but what is novel is trying to show seriously the development and quality of love by concentrating on repeated sexual experience. The eight sexual encounters between Connie and Mellors all relate to the kind of faith the novel forms and the story it tells.[25]

Lawrence imagines the abrupt first copulation happening because Connie and Mellors, looking at the new birds, so need to be touched (both physically and mentally) and because she *is* touched.

And slowly, softly, with sure gentle fingers, he felt among the old bird's feathers and drew out a faintly-peeping chick. . . . Suddenly he saw a tear fall on to her wrist.
. . . Her face was averted, and she was crying blindly, in all the anguish of her generation's forlornness. His heart melted suddenly, like a drop of fire, and he put out his hand and laid his fingers on her knee.
"You shouldn't cry," he said softly. . . .
He laid his hand on her shoulder, and softly, gently, it began to travel down the curve of her back, blindly, with a blind stroking motion, to the curve of her crouching loins. And there his hand softly, softly, stroked the curve of her flank, in the blind instinctive caress. [X, 122–23]

That is the beginning, an annunciatory soft touch for the sexual reformation of faith. The gamekeeper touches her gently and with compassion, and then moves irresistibly to fuck her. (Lawrence wants to overcome the kind of jarring disjunction signified by the end of my sentence; his passion, hopeless no doubt, is to join integrally *compassion* with *a passion to fuck*.) What creates the possibility for this experience and what matters so much for Lawrence is the intercourse between poetic awareness and body consciousness. Something about the man's touch of the hen, something about the hen with the chick suddenly symbolizes and defines her terrible sexual need, and something about her tear and all that it might mean becomes a metaphor that sets off his erotic desire.

The scene has been pilloried: not enough foreplay (just one kiss on her navel); Mellors moves too fast, is too much the boss; Connie obeys him too passively and does not have an orgasm.[26] Given the context of her life and, what is more, the individual contingency of every lover and act of love, such criticism hardly seems fair. It tends to make sex and life abstract, reductive, and formulaic. But Lawrence does so himself when, supposedly in her thoughts, he says with depersonalizing sexism that her "modern-woman's brain still had no rest" (X, 124). He recovers, however, and has her then think, "She was to be had for the taking. To be had for the taking" (X, 124). It is just the right phrase for her to play with. Has she lost her independence? Is she just sluttish prey? Other voices, word scraps, and phrases come to mind at the time of new openness, as people, surprised by the power of their own erotic desire, try to figure out who they are and what is going on. She tries to imagine what he is thinking, realizes she doesn't know, and ponders on his separateness, as women and men, shocked into an extraordinary interest in one another by sex, often do. The dialogue of their bodies inaugurates the dialogue of their whole being. Fucking is a new beginning, a new chance for the regeneration of "the novel" in all senses of the word.

> ". . . I thought I'd done with it all. Now I've begun again."
> "Begun what?"
> "Life."
> "Life!" she re-echoed, with a queer thrill.
> "It's life," he said. "There's no keeping clear. . . . So if I've got to be broken open again, I have." . . .
> "It's just love," she said cheerfully.
> "Whatever that may be," he replied. [X, 125]

Their lovemaking is described mainly from Connie's point of view, but sometimes from Mellors's too, with the narrator, like some imaginative composite of Pandarus, double-sexed Tiresias, Kierkegaard, and Wilhelm Reich, hovering about, ready to comment. Their second intercourse shows Mellors touching "her living secret body" (X, 133) with his face and mouth, finding beauty in her, and stirring her. But Connie cannot yet feel the "ecstasy" and "live beauty of contact" (X, 133), or the passion that makes it possible. She stays distant, detached from her body, her sex consciousness remaining cerebral. She dwells on gender, gender difference, and gender chauvinism, as all sometimes must, even in times of intimacy—maybe most significantly then. Crying in her aloneness, she articulates silently, "Stranger! Stranger!" (X, 134). Thinking of his class and dialect, she wanders in the hierarchy of thought, not yet able to embrace the democracy of touch. But this also is part of the process of lovemaking, not necessarily failed sex or sad experience. She knows now how the touch of her body inspires rapture in him and remembers how his face on her begins to arouse her. The man's head moves to the woman's flesh. For Lawrence, symbolically, that is the beginning of the way to salvation.

Their next encounter has the surprise of passion in it: After avoiding him, she meets him by chance, and almost brutishly he takes her out in the open wood, she lying down "like an animal" (X, 141). And yet she reaches climax, they come simultaneously and conceive a child. Lawrence is asserting the power of whole, organic desire—full body consciousness over false consciousness. He tries for a language here that will represent the magnetic rhythm and epiphany of orgasm for woman as well as man: "Rippling, rippling, rippling . . . soft as feathers, running to points of brilliance, exquisite, exquisite and melting her all molten inside. It was like bells rippling up and up to culmination" (X, 141–42). His success here is doubtful, but what does come through is a male's drive to empathize with a woman and know, as they say, the opposite sex. The text keeps asserting that it is in sexual intercourse, not in detached speculation, that men and women become most interested in one another and can most fully imagine *being* the other. After climax, they drift back to individuality, and Mellors says, "We came off together that time" (X, 143). Let us trust the slang for the meaning of the desire: "coming together" can mean not only temporary unity with another person, another "generation," and, miraculously, the cosmos, but a momentary end of gender division, that awful burden of being a member of a sex cut off from the other half of the world.

Their next intercourse brings out the vicissitudes of their relationship and the strains that social concerns put on sex life. With thoughts of the future and a possible child, with their uncertainty about each other and the special English agony over class bothering them, sex this time becomes a grotesque comedy. Lawrence imagines for Connie the disembodiment of self from sex and shows how it threatens love. Using what he calls "double-consciousness," he gets in her head while Mellors is in her body: "the sort of anxiety of his penis to come to its little evacuating crisis seemed farcical. Yes, this was love, this ridiculous bouncing of the buttocks, and wilting of the poor insignificant, moist little penis. This was the divine love!" (XII, 184). (Woody Allen, in his movie *Annie Hall*, borrows from Lawrence when he has the split image of Annie get up in the middle of sex and go about other business.) That vision contains in it the gist of nineteenth-century scientific rationalism's critique of love, and twentieth-century skepticism about the value of the whole erotic enterprise.

Connie then weeps, badly failing, she thinks, the test of faith. In her head, she decides she cannot love him, and her idealistic moral will does not help her. But Mellors tells her not to fret or force herself, and at last she relaxes, letting go of the conventional imperative to put the mind's romantic, rational love before the body. Lawrence again uses oceanic imagery to express Connie's coming, and according to Lydia Blanchard, this sea language was, and still is, the way many women express their sexuality.[27] To me it reads like stale Molly-Bloom prose set in a cosmic dishwasher: "Oh, and far down inside her the deeps parted and rolled asunder, in long, far-travelling billows. . . ." But he redeems himself at the end of the passage, "suddenly, in a soft, shuddering convulsion, the quick of all her plasm was touched, she knew herself touched, the consummation was upon her, and she was gone. She was gone, she was not, and she was born: a woman" (XII, 187). Lawrence's holy erotic mystery—the dying to consciousness, the resurrection of the body, and the sex-induced sense of being a gendered mortal being at one with rhythms of rebirth—comes through. She begins to find, in the merging of separate flesh and in the loss of her fixed personality, intimations of an end to loneliness.

When their lovemaking continues in two encounters at the keeper's cottage, Mellors feels frustrated at the normal apartness that flows back into life. For Lawrence, however, the confidence from mutual orgasm and fertility lets you confess the pain and craziness of consciousness to someone you have a tangible faith in. Sexual trust and intimacy mean you can show all of yourself and still feel you can come together again. Lawrence now has the semi-autobiographical Mellors spew out vile prejudices and misogynist gripes, amid his savage insights into political, social, and gender relations. The lovers quarrel and Connie stands up to his selfishness. But all the talk and mind-fucking only serves to frame the joyous exploration of their physical selves. The fifth tryst features that personification and mythologizing of "John Thomas" and of "Lady Jane" in a private lovers' language that makes them for the moment—like all couples who speak in erotic tongues—conspirators against a world of infidels.

Next follows the notorious pubic flower show. Flaunting bourgeois propriety, that passage signifies a return to the joys of polymorphous perversity that growing up represses, but with fully mature sexual consciousness: Cathy and Heathcliff romping as big kids. For Lawrence, the flower-bedecked intercourse is a real wedding, a spontaneous, affirming ceremony of innocence that asserts the unity of crocuses, sexual bodies, and love, fusing their signifying power.

The penultimate fornication scene is historically significant but a botch as art. Until now, Lawrence has conveyed the particular, personal quality of sex between Connie and Mellors. Here, he tries to integrate with the tenderness of touch a very aggressive, willful sensuality and willess sexual surrender in an act of sodomy; but, for whatever reason—fear of the law, conflicts about his own sexual bent, or worry about reputation—he does not write with his usual candor. A confused message comes through that it is beautiful and noble to do what is too disgusting and dangerous actually to say. He wants to portray anal intercourse as a final, full acceptance of the body, "Burning out the shames, the deepest, oldest shames, in the most secret places" (XVI, 267);[28] but he cannot render convincingly the characters' feelings in the act. He only sermonizes, gloats, conceals, and reveals in disingenuous puns ("At the bottom of her soul, fundamentally, she had needed this phallic hunting out" [XVI, 268]).

The prose is embarrassing: "She had to be a passive, consenting thing, like a slave, a physical slave. . . . she really thought she was dying: yet a poignant, marvellous death. She had often wondered what Abélard meant, when he said that in their year of love he and Heloise had passed through all the stages and refinements of passion" (XVI, 267).

"Poignant"? "Often"? And yet, bad as it is, the passage matters. It has an intentional religious resonance. Echoes of Joan of Arc and Saint Theresa as well as Héloïse and Abelard rise here as Lawrence tries to combine ecstasy and religious martyrdom with passion and sexual transgression. The passage focuses on the necessity of opening the self completely to the lover's flesh. Salvation depends on giving up "self-important mentalities" (XIII, 209), the defensive will, and the old, ethereal soul.

But all the surrender is the woman's; that whole experience is hers. Lawrence, locked into his own "self-important" mentality and fragile masculinity, does not—*cannot*—imagine the man abandoning his will. In *Lady Chatterley* the male is the good pastor who shepherds and brings out the female's eroticism.[29] There are, however, important contradictions and multiple levels in the text. In the sex scenes, the narrator identifies much more closely with the woman than with the man. Lawrence imagines himself as the erotic lamb. In the anal intercourse, the emotions, the observation, and the ideas that are being attributed to Connie's point of view and experience seem almost wholly the unintegrated commentary of the author. The narrator may identify in part—in *small* part— with the male phallic hunter, but much more significant is his wish-fulfilling identification with the woman. On one plane, Lawrence's novel obviously presents the sexual dominance of the male and the relative passivity of the female, but on a deeper level, it offers another much more subversive meaning: you may, as a man, assume the traditional role of a woman, or you may, as a human being, follow erotic redemption and resurrection of the body in any way passion takes you. Sexual identity lives in the fluid, mutable imagining of the self's erotic body, and Lawrence's fictional sodomy assumes a Dionysian, highly perilous right to use the flesh to love in any way you want.

XIV

The last coming together of Mellors and Connie is the most comic, and it changes the novel, making it both more traditional and more original. Assuming Mellors's point of view almost exclusively for once, Lawrence takes the edge off his fierceness and prepares us for the humanism of the concluding letter. Before, the man has not been able to take any joy in the woman's pregnancy, nor speak the usual assurances of love; but now when she tells him that his tenderness makes the child's future, he, in "sheer love for the woman," kisses "her belly and her mound of Venus . . . close to the womb and the foetus within the womb" (XVIII, 302). He enters her with love, and Lawrence astonishingly writes this:

"I stand for the touch of bodily awareness between human beings," he said to himself, "and the touch of tenderness. And she is my mate. And it is a battle against the money, and the machine, and the insentient ideal monkeyishness of the world. And she will stand behind me there. Thank God I've got a woman! Thank God I've got a woman who is with me, and tender and aware of me. Thank God she's not a bully, nor a fool. Thank God she's a tender, aware woman." And as his seed sprang in her, his soul sprang towards her too, in the creative act that is far more than procreative. [XVIII, 302–3]

That is a ridiculous and sublime moment in fiction, Lawrence at his most endearing, daring, irritating, and laughable: a holy fool. We have both a private discourse, getting at the strange personality of the novel's protagonist, and a public discourse too. Think of it: a man is fucking a woman and speaking, in this ludicrous interior monologue, a profession of his erotic faith.[30] Two bodies and sexes are joined together in mutual love, but the man who adores the woman for not being a man is talking to himself and an idealized public. Such language in such a context, however, will seem unlikely only to those who hold superficial notions about sex and love. Mellors's words are just the sort of subjective, pompous, silly eloquence and wisdom that might be popping in the mind of some happily fucking human being. "I stand for the touch of bodily awareness between human beings": that *is* what making love can make you feel.

Moreover the passage proclaims the Lawrentian moment of vocation; good fucking leads to the prophetic calling of the novelist. The words represent an act of faith in the future, but they go back to the past, expressing an almost Victorian vision of what marriage ought to be—except that this whole sentiment is now depicted as rooted in the flesh. The dialectic of love speaks here out of neither the idealized body of Plato nor the crucified body of Christ but the copulating bodies of two lovers. The history of sex in this narrative culminates with Lawrence bringing his gospel of erotic faith to us in a blasphemous Second Coming. It is wonderful and foolish, like people's continuing, troubled, comic faith in love.

Shortly after the publication and suppression of this novel, Edward VIII gave up his throne to marry "the woman I love." As Connie says near the end, "But don't you see, . . . I *must* live with the man I love" (XIX, 321). If love is the word known to all men and women, the heritage of erotic faith in Lawrence and in British fiction had helped to spread that word.

Epilogue: The Art of Love and Love among the Ruins

Every limit is a beginning as well as an ending.
GEORGE ELIOT[1]

The union of love and the novel has continued to generate diverse and important meanings, forms of art, and patterns of desire. For Lawrence, the course of true love from the nineteenth to the twentieth century flows to the sexual body; for Virginia Woolf it runs to creative vocation for a woman; for Samuel Beckett it leads to an absurdist sanctity of utter humility. Erotic faith can become sexual faith, aesthetic faith, feminist faith, faith in vocation, even a tragicomic faith in defiant nihilism and the continuing play of consciousness.

I began with erotically charged paintings and images, and I will end with a painting in Woolf's *To the Lighthouse* and a bizarre religious image of love in Beckett's *Malone Dies*. Both writers move far beyond the conventions of nineteenth-century love stories, but each makes clear the determining effects that the fusion of being-in-love in novels and erotic faith has had on the evolving shapes of the modern imagination.

I

In *The Monk* a picture of the Madonna provokes desire and spoils a holy vocation. In *To the Lighthouse* the erotic feelings that surround and are aroused by a secular madonna figure lead to the vocation of art that confirms and renews love. The central character in Woolf's narrative changes from Mrs. Ramsay—mother, wife, hostess, weaver of erotic relationships, and subject of love—to Lily Briscoe, the unmarried artist. The book concludes when Lily finishes her painting and fulfills her "vision" (310).

Near the end, Lily thinks, "Love had a thousand shapes. There might be lovers whose gift it was to choose out the elements of things and place them together and so, giving them a wholeness not theirs in life, make of some scene, or meeting of people (all now gone and separate), one of those globed compacted things over which thought lingers, and love plays" (286). Woolf is here imagining erotic faith as both a source and end of art. The words equate the artist with a lover, sanction the spreading diversity of erotic activity, and show how the narrative and pictorial imaginations may, *in effect*, be joined. They indicate

how a special erotics—the emotional field of drives, longings, and goals surrounding the creation and experience of artworks—can describe art as surely as
traditional aesthetic and generic classification. The significance of specific paintings and novels, for example, may fuse in the erotic desires that give them
impetus and that they satisfy, or that they define. In Woolf's novel and in Lily's
painting, love becomes art, but then art becomes the possible occasion to set love
flowing again.

We first learn of the picture through Mrs. Ramsay, who sits framed and posed
in a drawing-room window. She thinks of Lily's "puckered-up" (29) face and
supposes that she won't marry; she can't take Lily's painting seriously. The antifeminist sentiment uttered by an intellectual boor, "Women can't paint, women
can't write" (75), gnaws at Lily and makes one goal of the plot her completion
of the picture.

Few characters show more overtly the influence of being in love and of erotic
faith than Lily Briscoe, but none is so definitively distanced from the traditional
models of erotic relationship. Like Lucy Snowe, whom she so much resembles,
Lily, as she begins her work, is "in love"—in love with the Ramsay life and
household, "in love with them all, in love with this world" (37). "What she
called 'being in love'" (72) floods her feelings. As she pauses in her painting,
she sees Bankes, a sixty-year-old scientist, gazing in a rapture of love at Mrs.
Ramsay, and his disinterested devotion helps give Lily faith in life. She thinks
of a time when Mrs. Ramsay told her that an unmarried woman misses "the
best of life" (77), and when Lily had impulsively laid her head in the uncompre-
hending older woman's lap, loving her and wanting passionately perfect "intimacy itself" (79) with her. Lily seeks that erotic intimacy in her creative art.
Working towards her vision, she tries, like Mrs. Ramsay, but "in another
sphere," "to make of the moment something permanent" (241), to join with
her in saying and somehow achieving the imperative, "Life stand still here"
(240).

The move from Mrs. Ramsay—mediator of love and the incarnation of what
wise Victorians would have meant by the angel-in-the-house—to Lily, the post–
World War I, "post-Impressionist"[2] creator, would seem to represent a shift
from erotic to aesthetic faith and, more broadly, away from a woman's vocation
of heterosexual love—away, that is, from the social and psychological female
identity determined by the title *Mrs.* ("Mrs." Ramsay has no proper name of
her own) to other more varied callings and passions.

But it is not so simple. Mrs. Ramsay is, all in one, the past transcended, the
past recaptured, the past mourned, and the past made present. One of Woolf's
themes is Lily's emotional bond with her, but another is the break between
them. The inspiration for Lily's painting is explicitly Mrs. Ramsay and the love

she sparks. Lily begins the picture and then finishes it ten years later because she is in love with Mrs. Ramsay herself. The gift for life and the inimitable richness of the older woman's being are what make Lily's art possible; but Lily cannot complete her picture until Mrs. Ramsay dies, time passes, and the man-slaughtering world war has come and gone. The novel renders both the sharply differing natures of Mrs. Ramsay and Lily, and the flow of Mrs. Ramsay's identity into Lily's consciousness and art. It contrasts, balances, and finally connects "the fluidity of life" and "the concentration" of art (237), but it also points to the concentration of life and the fluidity of art.

Famously Virginia Woolf portrays in Mrs. Ramsay her mother; Joyce's "*amor matris*, subjective and objective genitive," animates the book. Why didn't Woolf, literary artist and sister to the painter Vanessa Bell, make Lily a daughter of Mrs. and Mr. Ramsay, as might appear natural in such an autobiographical novel? Apparently, she felt the need to diffuse the power of the mother that protected the rule of the father, and to break with the patterns of the prescribed familial erotics that so predominated in Victorian life and literature. The novel shows both the full attractive force of nineteenth-century erotic faith with its incestuous biases, and the passionate urge, especially for women, to expand its stifling limits. Woolf imagines a beautiful woman as another admirable woman's love object. She sets love free to assume a thousand shapes.

Bankes the Victorian looks at the first version of Lily's picture with scientific curiosity. "Mother and child then—objects of universal veneration . . . — might be reduced to a purple shadow without irreverence" (81–82). Her picture, she tells him, is not "of them" (mother and child), at least "not in his sense. There were other senses too in which one might reverence them" (81). Lily's picture, like Monk Lewis's, carries one away from the Madonna, but by the end she comes back to a spirit of reverence. The worship of the Madonna passes into the process and form of making art, which in this novel is an act of faith.

To the Lighthouse shows erotic sublimation driving the artist's passion for work, but it does not denigrate art by rendering it a mere substitute for love or family. Woolf is wonderful at showing how art means choice and choice means freedom, even though free choice can be agony. A key moment in the novel comes when Lily feels the power of Paul Rayley's love for Minta Doyle and, very much attracted to him herself, senses "the heat of love, its horror, its cruelty, its unscrupulosity" (154). Just then she sees a reminder of her painting-in-progress and tells herself, "she need not marry, thank Heaven: she need not undergo that degradation. . . . She would move the tree rather more to the middle" (154). Years after, working on the final version of the painting, she thinks of Mrs. Ramsay's mania for making marriages, and remembers the force of Paul's love for Minta and her own strange passion for him, and feeling again in her mind the fire of being in love, she reflects, like a Brontë, that "for a sight, for a glory, it surpassed everything" (261–62).

Nevertheless, Woolf, a female artist writing about a female artist, does not turn art into sublimation for sexuality, as did much contemporary theory, oriented as it was towards male forms of eroticism. She is trying for an art that stretches the erotic imagination beyond the conventional libido. Art is creative love here, and even though Lily's love may move her to paint, it does not lead her to an art of representation that tries to copy the beloved. Her work is creation, not imitation, and the last part of the narrative that describes Lily finishing her painting does not speak of what the picture is about, but of how it is made, what problems it presents, what emotions and intentions go into it, and what it is like for this dedicated woman to follow her career.

Yeats said that one must choose between the perfection of life and the perfection of art, but for Woolf the choice is false, since the desire for each depends on the other, and the drive to make and have love has come to suffuse and motivate the idea of both. No one can perceive and hold onto perfect moments of life without art, and excellent art can come only with the erotic turmoil of living. In the light of *To the Lighthouse*, the mother is the artist of the artist, and the artist is mother to the mother, and the lover is mate, progenitor, child, and *semblable* of each.

To the Lighthouse does not repudiate either the erotic faith of Victorian novels or its basis in the romantic eroticization of the family and vocation. Instead Woolf claims the continuity of that fiction with the shapes and forms of love and art to come. Lily thinks of her vision and of Mrs. Ramsay together: "she owed it all to her" (241). The life of Mrs. Ramsay can and must be subsumed into the life of the present and future. Here again is Lily's assessment of love: "there is nothing more tedious, puerile, and inhumane than this [love]; yet it is also beautiful and necessary" (155).

II

Beckett, a monk of postmodernism and a man for all seasons (except spring and summer), might seem the ultimate antiromantic novelist, the writer who most devastatingly mocks the illusions and credulous sentimentalities of faith, including the love faith. His characters, caught in the same boat of failing flesh, must ride a stream of deceiving consciousness through life's verbal desert mirages towards an imaginary sea of death. And yet in the brief love story of Macmann and Moll in *Malone Dies*, he shows, as well as anyone has, the hold of eros on the modern psyche and the persistent drive to bring together and utter in the art of fiction aesthetic, religious, and erotic desire.

Everyman-and-woman as novelist and lover: Malone dying, making up stories for himself, imagines a series of apparent alter egos who live out what seem to be different parts of his life. One is Macmann, aging derelict, inmate of an asylum, "the House of Saint John of God" (84). There he has a keeper, Moll, a little old, ill-favored woman who "wore by way of ear-rings two long ivory crucifixes which swayed wildly at the least movement of her head" (86). Soon, says the narrator, there sprang up between them "a kind of intimacy which, at a given moment, led them to lie together and copulate as best they could" (89). The grotesque eroticism of these aged ones parodies the legends of all the passionate lovers from Tristan and Isolde to Lady Chatterley and *her* keeper: "The spectacle was then offered of Macmann trying to bundle his sex into his partner's like a pillow into a pillow-slip, folding it in two and stuffing it in with his fingers. . . . And though both were completely impotent they finally succeeded, summoning to their aid all the resources of the skin, the mucous and the imagination, in striking from their dry and feeble clips a kind of sombre gratification" (89).

Beckett, stressing the farcical split between physical reality and the idealizing bent of human language and desire, imagines how this pathetic, ridiculous sex turns literary, and issues in a surprising love: "It was also the occasion of his penetrating into the enchanted world of reading, thanks to the inflammatory letters which Moll brought and put into his hands" (89). Since erotic cynicism and deflation mewl everywhere in Beckett, the lyrical pathos of Moll's love letters comes through all the more powerfully.

Example. Sweetheart, Not one day goes by that I do not give thanks to God, on my bended knees, for having found you, before I die. For we shall soon die, you and I, that is obvious. . . . Consider moreover that the flesh is not the end-all and be-all, especially at our age, and name me the lovers who can do with their eyes what we can do with ours. . . . Moral, for us at last it is the season of love. . . . Let us think of the hours when, spent, we lie twined together in the dark, our hearts laboring as one, and listen to the wind saying what it is to be abroad, at night, in winter, and what it is to have been what we have been, and sink together, in an unhappiness that has no name." [90–91]

It is as if this mocking novelist of the post-God, post-nuclear world were writing against himself; the impulse to love pushes through any muck.

Macmann, who at first despises Moll, at last responds to her writing with his own acid lyricism; falling in love, for Beckett, as for so many others, seems *a literal thing*:

[H]e began to compose brief rimes of curious structure. . . . Example:

> Hairy Mac and Sucky Molly
> In the ending days and nights
> Of unending melancholy
> Love it is at last unites.

Other Example.

> To the lifelong promised land
> Of the nearest cemetery
> With his Sucky hand in hand
> Love it is at last leads Hairy.

He had time to compose ten or twelve more or less in this vein, all remarkable for their exaltation of love regarded as a kind of lethal glue, a conception frequently to be met within mystic texts. [91–92]

That passage savages the romanticizing of love, and yet still manages to exalt it mystically and show its tenacity. The humble scholar of love in the novel is tempted to repeat after Macmann's verse, the words of Malone and Beckett, "I am lost. Not a word" (92). But there follows, in this love among twentieth-century ruins, the image that stays in the mind of everyone who reads *Malone Dies*. One day Macmann, still wary of Moll's passion, tries to distract her ardor by asking about her earrings:

Why two Christs?, implying that in his opinion one was more than sufficient. To which she made the absurd reply, Why two ears? . . . Besides they are the thieves, Christ is in my mouth. Then parting her jaws and pulling down her blobber-lip she discovered, breaking with its solitary fang the monotony of the gums, a long yellow canine bared to the roots and carved . . . to represent the celebrated sacrifice. . . . This incident made a strong impression on Macmann and Moll rose with a bound in his affections. And in the pleasure he was later to enjoy, when he put his tongue in her mouth and let it wander over her gums, this rotten crucifix had assuredly its part. But from these harmless aids what love is free? [93]

The heart bows down, as Joyce and Lawrence might say, even while it gags. Though Beckett makes fun of love, religion, and art, he also celebrates their wild communion in the novel. Let the conjunction of lovers' being, God, representative form, and the verbal collage of passions in bodies and texts stand as a symbol for the lasting power and absurd glory of erotic faith in fiction.

Amen. And ah women.

Notes

Chapter One

1. *Evagatorium in Terrae Sanctae, Arabiae et Egypti Peregrinationem*, trans. J. M. Clifton-Everest, in *The Tragedy of Knighthood: Origins of the Tannhauser Legend*, J. M. Clifton-Everest (Oxford, 1979), p. 143.

2. Samuel Beckett, *Malone Dies* (New York, 1956, reprinted 1977), p. 34.

3. Norman Mailer, *The Executioner's Song* (Boston and Toronto, 1979), p. 473.

4. Lawrence Stone, *The Family, Sex, and Marriage in England, 1500–1800* (New York, 1977), p. 272. This work is invaluable for its information and suggestiveness about changing erotic life, romantic feeling, and mating practices in England, particularly among the middle and upper classes, in the era preceding the nineteenth century. See especially Chapter 6, "The Growth of Affective Individualism," pp. 221–69, and Chapter 7, "Mating Arrangements," pp. 270–324.

5. Anthony Trollope, *An Autobiography* (London, 1953), World's Classics edition, chap. 12, p. 192. All subsequent citations, by chapter and page, are to this edition.

6. I use the term "novelization" to indicate traits of narrative, characterization, and the like that are conventionally ascribed to the traditional novel; but I also use it in Bakhtin's sense of the term that stresses, in John Bender's words, "the novel's capacity to set . . . genres into 'dialogic' commerce with one another and, in the process, to establish a 'zone of contact' between the literary work and the social practices that inform daily life" (*Imagining the Penitentiary: Fiction and the Architecture of the Mind in Eighteenth-Century England* [Chicago and London, 1987], pp. 89–90). For pertinent discussion of "novelization" see Mikhail M. Bakhtin, *The Dialogic Imagination*, ed. Michael Holquist, trans. Caryl Emerson and Michael Holquist (Austin, Tex., 1981), pp. 5–7; and Bender, pp. 89–90, pp. 279–80 n. 6.

7. See Robert M. Polhemus, *Comic Faith* (Chicago, 1980), especially pp. 3–23.

8. See ibid., p. 5.

9. Of the making of books on love, there is no end. My study lays stress on particular novels as acts, causes, and effects of erotic faith that feature the state of being in love. Indispensable to me, among many invaluable works, in forming my understanding of love and the relationship of religious feeling, erotic love, and artistic expression have been Irving Singer's monumental, ongoing work *The Nature of Love* (Chicago, 1966–88), Paul Friedrich's *The Meaning of Aphrodite* (Chicago, 1978), and Jean Hagstrum's *Sex and Sensibility* (Chicago, 1980). Peter Gay's *The Tender Passion* (New York and Oxford, 1986), the second volume of *The Bourgeois Experience: Victoria to Freud*, and Joseph A. Boone's *Tradition Counter Tradition: Love and the Form of Fiction* (Chicago, 1987) did not appear until this book was substantially written, but both are works of the highest worth to scholars of love and the nineteenth century. Peter Gay's work is the fullest account we have of middle-class attitudes towards love and sexuality in Europe during the Victorian period. Boone's study contains an excellent and wide-ranging investigation of the subjects of marriage, love, and the question of marital destination in post-eighteenth-century British and American fiction. It emphasizes the dialectic, or tradition and counter- tradition, of the marriage plot in novels. His second chapter, "The Emergence of a Literary Ideal of Romantic Marriage: A Historical Perspective," is a fine and useful short summary of the historical and literary context that led to the love marriage as subject and plot in nineteenth-century English fiction.

10. Geoffrey Grigson, *The Goddess of Love* (London, 1976), p. 36: "Edgar Snow has written . . . of seeing a colour-print of Botticelli's Venus pinned up in the flat of a Chinese steel-worker, in a town near the Great Wall."

11. Ronald Lightbrown, *Sandro Botticelli, Life and Work*, vol. 1, Berkeley and Los Angeles, 1978, p. 88.

12. Michael Levey, "Botticelli and Nineteenth-Century England," *Journal of the Warburg and Courtauld Institutes*, vol. 31 (1968): 291–306.

13. E. H. Gombrich, *Symbolic Images* (London, 1972), p. 64.

14. *Fors Clavigera: Letters to the Workmen and Labourers of Great Britain* (Boston, no date), Letter 22, vol. 1, p. 288.

15. Walter Pater, *The Renaissance: Studies in Art and Poetry*, the 1893 text, edited, with textual and explanatory notes, by Donald Hill (Berkeley, 1980), p. 46.

16. J. A. Symonds, quoting a friend, noted the painting's "echo of a beautiful, lapsed mythology" (*The Renaissance in Italy* [New York, 1888], vol. 3, *The Fine Arts*, p. 250 n. 1). D. H. Lawrence, who used the art of the novel as a means to promote erotic faith, writes of Botticelli's image: "It is the utterance of complete, perfect religious art. . . . the heart is satisfied for the moment, there is a moment of perfect being" (*Study of Thomas Hardy and Other Essays*, edited by Bruce Steele [Cambridge, 1985], p. 69).

17. See Yukio Yashiro, *Sandro Botticelli and the Florentine Renaissance* (London, 1929), pp. 134–35, who also quotes Bernard Berenson: "[W]hat is it that makes Sandro Botticelli so irresistible that nowadays we may have no alternative but to worship or abhor him? The secret is this, . . . he abandoned himself to presentation of those qualities alone, which in a picture are *directly* life-communicating and life-enhancing." This impulse towards "worship" and unconscious eroticism ("*directly* life-communicating") is Victorian.

18. Symonds writes a highly revealing note on Botticelli:

> In the last century and the beginning part of this, our present preoccupation with Botticelli would have passed for mild lunacy, . . . because the moment in the history of culture he so faithfully represents was then but little understood [i.e., a moment of tension between the Madonna and Venus, Christianity and erotic faith, supernaturalism and humanism—in other words a typical nineteenth-century "moment"]. The prophecy of Mr. Ruskin, the tendencies of our best contemporary art in Mr. Burne Jones's, the specific note of our recent fashionable poetry, and *more than all our delight in the delicately-poised psychological problem* of the middle Renaissance have evoked a kind of hero-worship for this excellent artist and *true poet*. [vol. 3, p. 249, n. 1; italics mine]

Such a passage lets us infer that the novel's lessons of historicism, its psychological penetration into the relations of the individual and society, and its preoccupation with love prepared the way for the pre-Pre-Raphaelite Botticelli and the *Birth of Venus*.

19. For discussion and summary of textual influences on the *Birth of Venus*, see Lightbrown, pp. 73–90; Gombrich, "Botticelli's Mythologies," in *Symbolic Images*, pp. 31–81; and *The Complete Paintings of Botticelli, introduction by Michael Levey, notes and catalogue by Gabriele Mandel* (Harmondsworth, England, 1985), pp. 96–97.

20. See Gombrich, *Symbolic Images*, p. 174. On the subject of the relation of the fine arts to literature and love, besides the work of Dora and Erwin Panofsky, E. H. Gombrich, Jean Hagstrum, Bram Dijkstra, Svetlana Alpers, Edgar Wind, Leo Steinberg, and others cited

elsewhere in the notes to this chapter and in the general bibliography, I have found of great use Rudolph Arnheim, *Visual Thinking* (Berkeley, 1969); John Berger, *Ways of Seeing* (Harmondsworth, England, 1977); Anthony Blunt, *Artistic Theory in Italy: 1450–1600* (Oxford, 1940); E. H. Gombrich, *Art, Perception, and Reality* (Baltimore, 1972); Nelson Goodman, *The Languages of Art* (Indianapolis, 1968); Jean Hagstrum, *The Sister Arts* (Chicago, 1958); John D. Hunt, *Encounters: Essays on Literature and the Visual Arts* (London, 1971); Jeffrey Meyers, *Painting and the Novel* (New York, 1975); Ronald Paulson, *Emblem and Expression* (Cambridge, Mass., 1975); Wendy Steiner, *The Colors of Rhetoric* (Chicago, 1982).

21. See Lightbrown, p. 82.

22. Yashiro comments, "Only the fine genius of Botticelli, who felt the snaky charm in the hair itself, could realize the presence of . . . imaginary creatures in the daughters of Eve" (p. 124).

23. *Gombrich Symbolic Images*, p. 62.

24. D. H. Lawrence writes of this image, "Aphrodite stands there not as a force to draw all things unto her, but as the naked, almost unwilling pivot, the keystone. . . . But there is still the joy, the great motion around her, sky and sea, all the elements and living joyful forces" (*Study of Thomas Hardy*, p. 69).

25. See Cecil Gould, "Bronzino," p. 41, in *The Sixteenth-Century Italian Schools* (London, 1975). For Bronzino information, see also Charles McCorquadale, *Bronzino* (New York, 1981); Arthur McComb, *Agnolo Bronzino: His Life and Works* (Cambridge, Mass., 1928).

26. Time's threat is removed through the enduring sacrifice and sacramental reality of Christ. Bronzino has made "a parallel in visual language to the idea that the meaning of the death of Jesus is incomplete when understood as event only; the second, sacramental meaning completes the first, partial one" (Marcia B. Hall, *Renovation and Counter-Reformation* [Oxford, 1979], p. 43).

27. Thomas Sheehan, *The First Coming: How the Kingdom of God Became Christianity* (New York, 1986), p. 68.

28. James Joyce, *Finnegans Wake* (New York, 1958), p. 260, note 2. All subsequent citations to this book are to "FW," page and line.

29. Samuel Richardson, *Clarissa*, edited and with an introduction and notes by Angus Ross (Harmondsworth, England, 1985), Letter 220, Mr. Lovelace to John Belford, Esq., p. 704.

30. See Plato, *The Symposium*, trans. Walter Hamilton (Harmondsworth, England, 1951), pp. 58–65.

31. W. Arens, *The Original Sin* (New York and Oxford, 1986); Robin Fox, *The Red Lamp of Incest* (New York, 1980); James B. Twitchell, *Forbidden Partners: The Incest Taboo in Modern Culture* (New York, 1987); Michael V. Miller, "What Dracula Was Really Up To," review of *Forbidden Partners*, *New York Times Book Review*, 18 January 1987, pp. 7–8.

32. See Arens, pp. 122–56.

33. A short time later, Baglione, "in competition and emulation," completed his righteous painting *Divine Love* (fig. 12) to set against *Amor Vincit Omnia*. The two works draw the opposition between Christian and erotic faith sharply. In Baglione, Eros is tumbled on his back and looks up with fear and awe at victorious Divine Love, a large, potent figure, with huge wings, that towers over the helplessness of the vanquished trifler. Those wings proclaim the triumph of celestial might; not surprisingly the angel of Divine Love has forceful beauty, but the figure seems impersonal and unapproachable. It is not "lovable." The image works to

diminish human love and erotic longing, but next to Caravaggio's masterpiece, Baglione's painting only emphasizes the force and pull of eroticism. See *The Art of Caravaggio* (New York, 1985), pp. 90, 277–81 (Mina Gregori, contributor).

34. My understanding of Caravaggio, Botticelli, and Italian painting generally have been informed by the prescient insight and expression of Simone Di Piero.

35. For an introduction to the extensive and various scholarship and criticism of Vermeer, see *The Complete Paintings of Vermeer*, introduction by John Jacob, notes and catalogue by Piero Bianconi (London, 1987); Svetlana Alpers, *The Art of Describing* (Chicago, 1983); A. K. Wheelock, Jr., *Jan Vermeer* (London, 1981); M. Pops, *Vermeer: Consciousness and the Chamber of Being* (Ann Arbor, Mich., 1984); Edward A. Snow, *A Study of Vermeer* (Berkeley, 1979); Christopher Wright, *Vermeer* (London, 1976).

36. So I interpret the picture and so, in a methodologically suspect but, for me at least, convincing survey, did ten out of ten people I asked.

37. See Svetlana Alpers, pp. 192–207, for discussion of the connection of love and letters in Vermeer and other artists.

38. Ibid., p. 196.

39. Terry Eagleton, *The Rape of Clarissa* (Oxford, 1982), p. 45.

40. Choderlos de Laclos, *Les liaisons dangereuses*, trans. P. W. K. Stone (Harmondsworth, England, 1961), Letter 47, pp. 109–10.

41. Ibid., Letter 48, pp. 110–11.

42. Matthew Lewis, *The Monk* (Oxford, New York, etc., 1980), World's Classics edition, vol. I, chap. I, p. 7. All subsequent citations, by volume, chapter, and page, are to this edition.

43. See Judith Wilt, *Ghosts of the Gothic: Austen, Eliot, and Lawrence* (Princeton, N.J., 1980), especially the introduction, "'This Heretic Narrative': Approaches to a Gothic Theoretic."

44. See René Girard, *Violence and the Sacred*, trans. Patrick Gregory (Baltimore and London, 1977), especially chaps. 1–4.

45. See Paul Friedrich, *The Meaning of Aphrodite* (Chicago, 1978), pp. 181–91.

46. E. M. Forster, *Howards End* (London, 1973), chap. 22, p. 183.

47. Christened Robert Wiedemann Browning, the child is heard by his pen-mad parents to mispronounce his middle name as "Penini," which they conveniently decide to shorten to "Pen"—the nickname of the author-hero of their friend Thackeray's current and popular novel *Pendennis*—and then adopt for him. What's in a name? See Maisie Ward, *The Tragi-Comedy of Pen Browning (1849–1912)* (New York, 1972).

48. See Frances Donaldson, *Edward VIII* (Philadelphia and New York, 1975), p. 323; for a lively and full account of the affair, see also Stephen Birmingham, *Duchess: The Story of Wallis Warfield Windsor* (Boston, 1976).

49. Donaldson, *Edward VIII*, p. 318.

50. Ibid., *Edward VIII*, p. 314.

51. See ibid., *Edward VIII*, p. 282.

Chapter Two

1. Lionel Trilling, *Sincerity and Authenticity* (London, 1972), p. 82.

2. Marilyn Butler, *Jane Austen and the War of Ideas* (Oxford, 1975), p. 201.

3. Jane Austen, *Pride and Prejudice: An Authoritative Text, Backgrounds, Reviews, and*

Essays in Criticism, ed. Donald J. Gray (New York, 1966), Norton Critical Edition, vol. 3, chap. 18, p. 262. All subsequent citations, by volume, chapter, and page number, are to this edition.

4. In Maria Edgeworth's *Belinda* (1801) an important conversation about the bases for love and marriage and the difference between loving and being in love takes place between the wooden heroine and Lady Delacour, an appealing, witty older woman. "You may marry . . . ," says Lady Delacour, "without being in love with him." "But not without loving him," replies Belinda (London and New York, 1986), chap. 24, p. 308.

5. *Jane Austen's Letters to Her Sister Cassandra and Others*, ed. R. W. Chapman (London, 1932), 29 January 1813, vol. 2, p. 297.

6. Jane Austen, *Northanger Abbey* (New York, 1965), Signet Classic edition, Chap. 5, pp. 29–30.

7. William Shakespeare, *Much Ado about Nothing*, act 2, scene 1.

8. See Robert M. Polhemus, "Jane Austen's Comedy," in *The Jane Austen Companion*, ed. J. David Grey, A. Walton Litz, and Brian Southam (New York, 1986), p. 69. For background on Botticelli's *Venus and Mars*, see E. H. Gombrich, *Symbolic Images*, pp. 66–69, and note J. A. Symonds wrong-headed but illuminating remarks implying the similarity of spirit betwen this work of Botticelli and Austen's art: "At first sight the face and attitude of that unseductive Venus, wide awake and melancholy opposite her snoring lover, seems to symbolize the indignities which women may have to endure from insolent and sottish boys with only youth to recommend them. This interpretation, however, sounds like satire. It is more respectful to presume that Botticelli failed, partly through inadequacy of means . . . , to do the authorized version of the legend justice" (vol. 3, p. 253).

9. Fanny Burney (Arblay), *Evelina*, ed. Edward A. Bloom (London, 1968), p. 1.

10. Besides Austen, two other of Burney's most prominent immediate successors as distinguished female novelists had intensely close and problematic relationships with fathers who definitely influenced their literary bent. For detailed discussion and assessment of Maria Edgeworth's relationship to Richard Lovell Edgeworth and Mary Shelley's relationship to William Godwin see, respectively, Marilyn Butler, *Maria Edgeworth: A Literary Biography* (Oxford, 1977), and Anne K. Mellor, *Mary Shelley* (London, 1988).

11. See John Halperin, *The Life of Jane Austen* (Baltimore, 1984), pp. 63, 229–30.

12. See John Mueller, *Astaire Dancing* (London, 1986), pp. 110–12.

13. See Susan Morgan's excellent study of Austen, *In the Meantime: Character and Perception in Jane Austen's Fiction* (Chicago, 1980), pp. 92–99, for a different interpretation.

14. See Samuel Richardson, *The Rambler* 197.

15. Henry Fielding, *Tom Jones*, ed. Sheridan Baker (New York, 1973), Norton Critical Edition, book 6, chap. 1, pp. 205–6. In Edgeworth's *Belinda* (see note 4, above), Belinda tells Lady Delacour that "a great deal of esteem is the foundation for a great deal of love" (p. 309), but the wise elder woman is not so sure, and in fact Belinda does not marry the man she is discussing. Edgeworth is ambivalent.

16. Susan Morgan made this point in a talk, "Why There Is No Sex in Jane Austen," at the Modern Language Association meeting, 29 December 1986, New York; she elaborates it brilliantly in her recently published book *Sisters in Time* (New York, 1989).

17. In Edgeworth's *Belinda*, Lady Delacour remarks, in the style of Elizabeth Bennet, "We never fall in love with good qualities, except, indeed, when they are joined to an acquiline nose" (p. 309). Jane Austen wonders.

18. *Austen's Letters*, vol. 2, pp. 482–83.

Chapter Three

1. Walter Scott, *The Bride of Lammermoor* (London, 1979), Everyman's Library edition, chap. 19, p. 193. All subsequent citations, by chapter and page number, are to this edition.

2. Elizabeth Gaskell, *Wives and Daughters* (Harmondsworth, England, 1969), Penguin edition, chap. 6, p. 104.

3. Gustave Flaubert, *Madame Bovary: Backgrounds and Sources, Essays in Criticism*, edited with a substantially new translation by Paul De Man (New York, 1965), part 2, chap. 15, p. 161.

4. E. M. Forster, *Where Angels Fear to Tread* (London, 1975), chap. 6, pp. 95–96.

5. See Leo Tolstoy, *Anna Karenina: The Maude Translation: Background and Sources, Essays in Criticism*, ed. George Gibian (New York, 1970), part 5, chap. 33. According to Herbert Weinstock, Anna, defying society, sees the opera and *"Lucia* becomes part of the fabric of her sensibility and emotions" (*Donizetti* [New York, 1963], p. 112). I accept his reading: though *Lucia* is not directly mentioned, her "cavatina," to which Flaubert had referred, is; and the soprano Adelina Patti, whom Anna and Vronsky go to hear sing, was famous for her Lucia.

6. W. M. Parker, in his preface to the Everyman edition, claims that Scott "transfigured" (p. vi) the historical incidents on which he based the novel, whether or not he altered his mother's account of the doomed and broken Janet Dalrymple–Lord Rutherford troth and Janet's subsequent marriage to David Dunbar. The bride died shortly after the marriage "of a broken heart," but there is no historical allusion to the tragedy that Scott recounts in his introduction and renders in his narrative. Commentators generally make it sound as if Scott merely transcribed the basic story he heard from his mother and others; they have been too credulous of Scott's introduction to the novel. Much more of his own invention seems to have gone into the wedding-night denouement than has been assumed. The so-called events (1669) were more than a century past when Scott was born (1771). See Parker's preface (pp. v-viii) and W. S. Crockett, *The Scott Originals: An Account of Notables & Worthies, the Originals of Characters in the Waverly Novels* (London and Edinburgh, 1912), pp. 249–68.

7. See Weinstock, pp. 109–10.

8. Karl Kroeber, quoted by Francis R. Hart in his excellent study *Scott's Novels* (Charlottesville, Va., 1966), p. 24.

9. Donald Cameron, "The Web of Destiny: The Structure of *The Bride of Lammermoor*," 185–205, in *Scott's Mind and Art*, ed. Norman A. Jeffares (New York, 1970), p. 185.

10. Scott has updated his source and set the novel forward so that it occurs around, or just prior to, the date of Union, 1707. The Union and the subsequent history that issues for Scott and his audience is thus tacit vindication of the lovers and their sacrifice. See Jane Millgate, *Walter Scott: The Making of a Novelist* (Toronto, 1984), pp. 172–76, on the dating of events in *The Bride of Lammermoor* and the changes that Scott made between editions.

11. James Joyce, *Ulysses: The Corrected Text*, ed. Hans Walter Gabler with Wolfhard Steppe and Claus Melchior (New York, 1986), p. 28. All subsequent citations, by page, are to this edition.

12. See, for example, Cameron, p. 200.

13. George Eliot, *Middlemarch: An Authoritative Text, Backgrounds, Reviews and Criticism*, ed. Bert G. Hornback (New York, 1977), Prelude, p. xiii.

14. James Joyce, *A Portrait of the Artist as a Young Man: Texts, Criticism, and Notes*, ed. Chester C. Anderson (New York, 1977), p. 213. All subsequent citations are to this edition.

15. William Kennedy, *Legs* (New York, 1983), p. 113.

16. In light of Lucy's bloody insanity, we might think of all the images, incidents, and characters in Victorian fiction that betray the culture's terrors and complexes about doubtful weddings and their aftermaths, e.g., Charlotte Brontë's famous "mad woman in the attic" in *Jane Eyre*, Thackeray's drawing in *Vanity Fair* of Becky Sharp as the knife-wielding destroyer of Jos Sedley, and even George Eliot's killing off of Dorothea's husband Casaubon in *Middlemarch*. Marriage without mutual love in fiction could mean assault on the body, murder of the spirit, and the touch of lunacy.

17. In chapter 18 of *A Room with a View* (1908), E. M. Forster, holding novelistic dialogue with Scott's *The Bride of Lammermoor*, has his heroine, another Lucy, play and sing, like her namesake, "Look not thou on beauty's charming." He quotes in full that lyric, just as *his* Lucy is in the process of breaking her engagement to a man she does not desire erotically and taking one whom she loves. Forster gave her the perfect surname for a devotee of erotic faith: "Honeychurch."

18. *Memorials of Burne-Jones*, by G B-J [Georgiana Burne-Jones, the artist's wife] (New York, 1906), vol. 2, p. 194.

19. D. H. Lawrence, *Sons and Lovers* (New York, 1951), part 2, chap. 7, p. 169.

20. *The Tate Gallery: An Illustrated Companion to the National Collection of British and Modern Foreign Art* (London, 1979), p. 59.

21. See Martin Harrison and Bill Waters, *Burne-Jones* (London, 1973), pp. 139, 141–45.

22. "The Beggar Maid," *The Poems of Tennyson*, ed. Christopher Ricks (Harlow, England, 1987), vol. 1, pp. 604–5.

23. That Burne-Jones wanted to stress the religious aspect of erotic love comes clear from his parody, *King Cophetua and the Beggar Maid in the style of Rubens* (fig. 16). See Harrison and Waters, *Burne-Jones*, p. 139.

24. Pater's wonderful novelistic descriptions and readings of da Vinci's *Mona Lisa* and Botticelli's *Venus* may well owe as much to the indirect influence of Scott as to the painters. For the "enormous impact of Scott on the development" of nineteenth-century painting, see Roy Strong, *Recreating the Past: British History and the Victorian Painter* (London, 1978), pp. 30–31.

Chapter Four

1. Georges Bataille, *Erotism: Death and Sensuality* (San Francisco, 1986), p. 226.

2. Winifred Gérin, *Emily Brontë* (Oxford, 1971), p. 190.

3. J. Hillis Miller, *The Disappearance of God* (Cambridge, Mass., 1963), p. 175.

4. See Cyril W. Beaumont, *The Ballet Called Giselle* (New York, 1969).

5. Georges Bataille, "Emily Brontë and Evil," trans. Alistair Hamilton, in *Emily Brontë: A Critical Anthology*, ed. Jean-Pierre Petit, pp. 151–63 (Harmondsworth, England, 1973), p. 156.

6. Emily Brontë, *Wuthering Heights: An Authoritative Text with Essays in Criticism*, ed. William M. Sale, Jr. (New York, 1963), Norton Critical Edition, chap. 14, p. 126. All subsequent citations, by chapter and page, are to this edition.

7. Sigmund Freud, *Civilization and Its Discontents*, in *The Standard Edition of the Complete Psychological Works*, ed. and trans. James Strachey (London, 1953–66), vol. 21, p. 66.

8. Belief in ghosts, whose broad social function can in part be said to preserve and make

memorable figures, voices, and influences from the past ("beyond the grave"), ebbed as literacy spread. Writing—letters, printed material, books—gradually took over the function in the last three centuries of memorializing the past and preserving, as it were, dead voices and the reality and influence of the deceased.

9. See Dorothy Van Ghent, *The English Novel: Form and Function* (New York, 1953), pp. 160–61.

10. *The Poems of John Donne*, ed. Herbert Grierson (London, 1937), Holy Sonnet 10, p. 297.

11. See, for example, Bataille in "Emily Brontë and Evil," p. 153; Irving H. Buchen, "Emily Brontë and the Metaphysics of Childhood and Love," *Nineteenth-Century Fiction* 22 (June 1967): 63–70; Margaret Homans, *Bearing the Word: Language and Female Experience in Nineteenth-Century Women's Writing* (Chicago, 1976), pp. 73–77, who stresses the Lacanian hypothesis of child development in her reading of *Wuthering Heights*.

12. See Denis de Rougemont, *Love and Death in the Western World*, pp. 42–46, 50–53, for the counterargument.

13. See, for example, Thomas C. Moser, "What Is the Matter with Emily Jane?" *Nineteenth-Century Fiction* 17 (June 1962): 1–19.

14. Wallace Stevens, "Sunday Morning," in *The Collected Poems* (New York, 1972), pp. 66–70.

15. See, for example, de Rougemont, *Love in the Western World*; Freud, "Being in Love and Hypnosis," in *Works*, vol. 18, pp. 111–16; José Ortega y Gasset, *On Love: Aspects of a Single Theme*, trans. Tony Talbot (New York, 1958); Singer, *The Nature of Love*, vol. 2, *Courtly and Romantic*, pp. 14–15, 298, 432–87 (Singer, however, is well aware, as all his work shows, of the power, the appeal, and the emotional payoff of passionate love).

16. Edward Albee, *The Zoo Story*, in *The Plays* (New York, 1981), vol. 1, p. 44.

17. See, for example, the discussions of Thomas Moser and, in *Bearing the Word*, Margaret Homans.

18. See Moser, "What Is the Matter with Emily Jane?" and Terry Eagleton, *Myths of Power* (London, 1975).

19. See the introductory chapters in both volumes 1 and 2 of Irving Singer's *The Nature of Love*.

20. J. Hillis Miller, pp. 209–10.

21. J. Hillis Miller, p. 211.

22. See, for, example, Nina Auerbach, *Woman and the Demon: The Life of a Victorian Myth* (Cambridge, Mass., and London, 1982), and Ann Douglas, *The Feminization of American Culture* (New York, 1977).

23. "Editor's Preface to the New Edition of *Wuthering Heights* (1850)," in *Wuthering Heights*, by Emily Bronte, ed. William M. Sale, Jr., p. 12.

24. See Winifred Gérin, *Charlotte Brontë: The Evolution of Genius* (Oxford, 1967), p. 31.

25. Winifred Gérin, "Byron's Influence on the Brontës," *Keats-Shelley Memorial Bulletin* 17 (1966): 2.

26. Helen Moglen, *Charlotte Brontë: The Self Conceived* (New York, 1976), p. 29.

27. For an informative discussion of Byron, romantic love, romantic irony, and the potential influence of "Byron" in nineteenth-century erotic history, see Anne K. Mellor, *English Romantic Irony* (Cambridge, Mass., 1979), pp. 31–76.

28. See Leslie Marchand, *Byron: A Biography* (New York, 1957), vol. 1, p. 328.

29. Byron, *Don Juan*, Canto 1, stanza 194.

30. See Bataille, *Erotism: Death and Sensuality*, p. 240.

31. For discussion of Bernini's Saint Theresa, see Robert T. Petersson, *The Art of Ecstasy: Teresa, Bernini, and Crashaw* (New York, 1970); Rudolf Wittkower, *Gian Lorenzo Bernini* (London, 1966), especially pp. 216–17; Howard Hibbard, *Bernini* (Harmondsworth, England, 1965, reprinted 1976); Hans Kauffman, *Giovanni Lorenzo Bernini: Die figurlichen Kompositionen* (Berlin, 1970); Robert Wallace, *The World of Bernini: 1598–1688* (New York, 1970), especially pp. 143–48.

32. See *The Age of Caravaggio*, p. 277: "There is no figure more closely analogous to this triumphant Cupid than Bernini's smiling angel who directs his arrow towards Saint Teresa."

33. See Bataille, *Erotism*, p. 244, which cites the language of the Transverberation. See also *The Life of Saint Teresa*, trans. J. M. Cohen (Harmondsworth, England, 1957), p. 210.

34. Luis Buñuel, *Los abismos de pasion* (Produciones Tepeyac, 1954).

35. Kate Bush, "Wuthering Heights," on the album *The Kick Inside*, EMI America (Capitol) CDP7–46012–2, 1978.

Chapter Five

1. William Shakespeare, *Venus and Adonis*, line 362.

2. Charlotte Brontë, *Villette* (Harmondsworth, England, 1979), Penguin edition, ed. Mark Lilly, with an introduction by Tony Tanner, chap. 38, p. 550. All subsequent citations, by chapter and page, are to this edition.

3. *"Du Heilige, rufe dein Kind zurück, / Ich habe genossen das irdische Glück, / Ich habe gelebt und geliebet!"* from *"Des Mädchens Klage"* (The maiden's prayer).

4. Snowe versus Ashton: Brontë may have chosen the cold surname of *her* Lucy to contrast with the romantic blaze and burnout of Scott's heroine.

5. See Françoise Basch, *Relative Creatures* (New York, 1974).

6. See John Tofanelli, *The Gothic Confessional: Language and Subjectivity in the Gothic Novel, Villette,* and *Bleak House*, Ph.D. dissertation, Stanford University, 1987, for an illuminating discussion of religious language and traditions in *Villette*.

7. William Makepeace Thackeray, quoted in Gérin, *Charlotte Brontë*, p. 598.

8. Thackeray, ibid., p. 522.

9. Ibid., p. 363.

10. See ibid., pp. 467–72.

11. See above chap. 1, n. 35, for Vermeer criticism and scholarship.

12. See Gérin, *Charlotte Brontë*, p. 511.

13. See Chase, *Eros and Psyche*, pp. 84–85.

14. Freud, "On the Universal Tendency to Debasement in the Sphere of Love," in *Works*, vol. 11, p. 189.

15. Joyce, FW, 194.10.

16. See Girard, *Deceit, Desire, and the Novel*, pp. 1–52.

17. I emend the passage to change the word *from*, which all texts print, but which makes little sense and is in all likelihood a misprint, to *form*. To call God "form everlasting" fits Lucy's vision and vocation as a maker of narrative form perfectly and shows crucially how the nineteenth century was aestheticizing faith.

18. See Cyril W. Beaumont, *The Ballet Called Swan Lake* (New York, 1982).

19. Gérin, *Charlotte Brontë*, p. 232.

20. See John Maynard, *Charlotte Brontë and Sexuality* (Cambridge, 1984), p. 175, for a discussion of the implicit relationship between espionage and sexuality.

21. See Freud, "On the Universal Tendency to Debasement," pp. 184–89.

22. See Gérin, *Charlotte Brontë*, pp. 240–41.

23. See ibid., pp. 241–42.

24. See Judith Wilt, *Ghosts of the Gothic* (Princeton, N.J., 1980), pp. 7–8, where she claims the phrase "heretic narrative" "to some extent describes the important works in all the great fictional traditions of the nineteenth century."

25. See Michel Foucault, *The History of Sexuality*, trans. Robert Hurley (New York, 1978), vol. 1, p. 19.

26. I know I am making hash of the orthodox conception of the Holy Ghost, but the fact is that, even though theologians have always loved it, it has hardly been a popularly understood and passionately embraced part of the Trinity: in Catholic practice, its mediative role tended to be in effect subsumed or replaced by the Virgin Mary and in Protestant practice by the Bible. As real ghosts lost credibility with the triumph of literacy, so the Holy Ghost, in the time of widespread circulation of the Bible, became a vague, abstract concept and lost much of its meaning and credibility in the lay world.

27. Various interpretations of Lucy's role and performance in the school play abound. See, for example, Kate Millett, *Sexual Politics* (New York, 1971), p. 194, who sees Lucy's onstage lovemaking to Ginevra as "one of the most indecorous scenes one may come upon in the entire Victorian novel"; and Sandra M. Gilbert and Susan Gubar, *The Madwoman in the Attic* (New Haven and London, 1979), p. 413, who stress her cross-dressing "allowing for the freer expression of love for other women" (Lucy is generally very hostile to other women), the lack of adequate roles for her to play in life, and the idea that "this play-acting is an emblem for all role-playing."

28. Gérin, *Charlotte Brontë*, pp. 481–82.

29. Bataille, *Erotism: Death and Sensuality*, p. 11.

30. For description and identification of the paintings that Brontë saw and used to render this episode, see Gérin, *Charlotte Brontë*, pp. 209–10. Interestingly, a woman, Fanny Geefs, painted the conventional stages of "a woman's life."

31. As we have seen, the same sentiment behind Brontë's assault here shows through a generation later in Burne-Jones's satire of materialism, the parody *King Cophetua and the Beggar Maid in the style of Rubens*.

32. Winifred Gérin quotes the notice of *Villette*, *Daily News*, 3 February 1853, p. 2, in *Charlotte Brontë*, p. 598.

33. Martineau's criticism of the love in *Villette* has often been echoed and reshaped. Lucy on the interpretation couch has been analyzed as a classic example of those neurotic "women who love too much." Certain feminist commentary has stressed Lucy's three happy years of independence without Paul, running her own school (see, for instance, Nina Auerbach, *Communities of Women* [Cambridge, Mass., 1978], p. 113), and her suppressed, deflected rage at the patriarchy (see Gilbert and Gubar, p. 431). Some of it has scorned her two loves (see, for example, Patricia Beer, *Reader, I Married Him: A Study of the Women Characters of Jane Austen, Charlotte Brontë, Elizabeth Gaskell, and George Eliot* [New York, 1974], pp. 104, 126) and implied that Paul's removal is a happy ending of sorts, a necessary purging of male sexism, romantic delusion, and an obstacle to Lucy's growth as an autonomous, mature self (see Millett, pp. 192–202, especially p. 201). Brontë, however, does not seriously undercut Lucy's overall judgment that Paul and Dr. John are both admirable, principled men,

capable of love and worthy to be loved, but people who have serious faults; these figures, as products of culture and history, participate in typical Victorian sexist practices. In other words, they are morally flawed figures who do good and are good: "Magnificent-minded, grand-hearted, dear, faulty, little man," says Lucy of Paul. Readings that tend to disparage Lucy's love or minimize the agony for Lucy of Paul's death and its repression, no matter how ingenious or enlightening on historical conditions, for me have the effect of patronizing or trivializing her dedication, suffering, religious crisis, and the making of her text that Brontë represents. They tend subtly to undermine Charlotte Brontë's ordeal, the toughness of her imagination, and the historical dilemma of innumerable nineteenth-century women.

34. Mary A. (Mrs. Humphry) Ward, Introduction to *Villette*, vol. 3 of *The Life and Works of The Sisters Brontë*, Haworth edition (New York and London, 1902), pp. xxiii–xxvii.

35. Thomas J. Wise and J. A. Symington, eds., *The Brontës: Their Lives, Friendships and Correspondence* (Oxford, 1932), vol. 4, p. 41.

36. See Gérin, *Charlotte Brontë*, p. 522.

37. For evidence of Charlotte Brontë's strong effect on Virginia Woolf, see *The Diary of Virginia Woolf*, ed. Anne Olivier Bell, vol. 5, 1936–41 (London, 1984), p. 313 and note; Virginia Woolf, *Collected Essays* (New York, 1967), vol. 3, pp. 185–90; Virginia Woolf, "Charlotte Brontë," *Times Literary Supplement*, 13 April 1916.

38. *To the Lighthouse* (New York, 1955), p. 155. All subsequent citations, by page, are to this edition.

Chapter Six

1. "The Definition of Love," in *The Complete Poetry of Andrew Marvell* (New York, 1968), p. 35.

2. Charles Dickens, *Great Expectations*, ed. Angus Calder (Harmondsworth, England, 1965), Penguin edition, chap. 56, pp. 469–70. All subsequent citations, by chapter and page, are to this edition.

3. See Polhemus, *Comic Faith*, p. 95, for a similar analysis of *Great Expectations'* opening.

4. William Makepeace Thackeray, *Vanity Fair: A Novel without a Hero*, ed. Geoffrey and Kathleen Tillotson (Boston, 1963), chap. 37, p. 369.

5. See Marcel Röthlisberger, *Claude Lorrain* (New Haven, 1961), vol. 1, pp. 384–86, for discussion, background, description, and history of this painting. See also Marcel Roethlisberger (*sic*), *Im Licht von Claude Lorrain Landschaftmaler* (Munich, 1983); Michael Kitson, *The Art of Claude Lorrain* (London, 1969); *Tout l'oeuvre peint de Claude Lorrain*, Introduction and Catalogue by Marcel Röthlisberger (Paris, 1977); H. Diane Russell, *Claude Lorrain, 1600–1662* (Washington, 1982). On Cupid and Psyche, see also Jean Hagstrum, "Eros amd Psyche: Some Versions of Romantic Love and Delicacy," *Critical Inquiry* 3 (Spring 1977): 521–42.

6. See Lucius Apuleius, *The Transformations of Lucius, Otherwise known as The Golden Ass*, trans. Robert Graves (Harmondsworth, England, 1951), chaps. 7–9, pp. 114–47.

7. Stendhal, *Love*, trans. Gilbert and Suzanne Sale (Harmondsworth, England, 1975), chap. 2, p. 45.

8. Ibid., p. 45.

9. Freud, "Contributions to the Psychology of Love," II, in *Works*, vol. 11, pp. 179–90.

10. See Julian Moynahan, "The Hero's Guilt: The Case of *Great Expectations*," *Essays in*

Criticism 10 (1960): 60–79, for an excellent discussion of Pip's relation to the "id" figure Orlick.

11. Compare Pip's vision of the wedding table: "as I looked along the yellow expanse out of which I remember its seeming to grow, like a black fungus, I saw speckled-legged spiders with blotchy bodies running home to it, and running out from it, as if some circumstance of the greatest public importance had just transpired in the spider community" (11:113), with this conversation between Jaggers and Pip later: "'Pip. . . . Who's the Spider?' 'The Spider?' said I. 'The blotchy, sprawly, sulky fellow.' 'That's Bentley Drummle,' I replied" (26:234).

12. Edmund White quotes Frederick Goldin and *The Mirror of Narcissus* (Ithaca, N.Y., 1967) in "Nabokov's Passion," *New York Review of Books*, 29 March 1984, p. 39.

13. White, pp. 39–40.

14. Domenick Argento has created out of the extravagant drama of *Great Expectations* and the violent end of Miss Havisham an opera, with "libretto (after Dickens)" by John Olon-Scrymgeour. The opera takes its name from this fabulous burning: *Miss Havisham's Fire* (New York, 1979).

15. See Edgar Johnson, *Charles Dickens: His Tragedy and Triumph* (London, 1953), vol. 1, pp. 45–46; Albert D. Hutter, "Reconstructive Autobiography: The Experience at Warren's Blacking," *Dickens Studies Annual* 6 (1977): 12; Alexander Welsh, *From Copyright to Copperfield: The Identity of Charles Dickens* (Cambridge, Mass., 1987), pp. 173–81.

16. Freud, "Tendency to Debasement," p. 190.

17. Mark Spilka, "On the Enrichment of Poor Monkeys by Myth and Dream; or, How Dickens Rousseauisticized and Pre-Freudianized the Victorian View of Childhood," in *Sexuality and Victorian Literature*, ed. Don Richard Cox (Knoxville, Tenn., 1984), p. 168.

18. See Tony Tanner, *Adultery in the Novel* (Baltimore, 1979), and also Judith Armstrong, *The Novel and Adultery* (New York, 1976), especially pp. 1–56.

Chapter Seven

1. Phyllis Rose, *Parallel Lives* (New York, 1983), pp. 212–13.

2. Ruby Redinger, *George Eliot: The Emergent Self* (New York, 1975), pp. 29–30.

3. George Eliot, *The Mill on the Floss*, ed. Gordon S. Haight (Boston, 1961), Riverside edition, book 1, chap. 1, p. 8. All subsequent citations, by book, chapter, and page, are to this edition.

4. See David Carroll, ed., *George Eliot: The Critical Heritage* (New York, 1971), p. 167.

5. George Eliot, *Middlemarch: An Authoritative Text, Backgrounds, Reviews and Criticism*, ed. Bert G. Hornback (New York, 1977), book 8, "Finale," p. 578.

6. See Hugh Witemeyer, *George Eliot and the Visual Arts* (New Haven, 1979), who reports George Eliot's admiration for Millais's work, especially pp. 76, 116, 117, and 153.

7. See Elaine Showalter, "Representing Ophelia: Women, Madness, and the Responsibilities of Feminist Criticism," in *Shakespeare and the Question of Theory*, ed. Patricia Parker and Geoffrey Hartman (New York, 1985), pp. 77–94, for a discussion of the representation of Ophelia in the arts since Shakespeare's day.

8. *Middlemarch*, book 2, chap. 21, p. 146.

9. Eliot, for example, writes, "[W]e can conceive Hamlet's having married Ophelia, and got through life with a reputation of sanity, notwithstanding many soliloquies" (VI, VI, 351).

10. For bibliographical information and scholarly and critical discussion of John Millais,

see Gordon Howard Fleming, *That Ne'er Shall Meet Again: Rossetti, Millais, Hunt* (London, 1971); Timothy Hilton, *The Pre-Raphaelites* (New York and Washington, 1974); William E. Freedman, *Pre-Raphaelitism: A Bibliographical Study* (Cambridge, Mass., 1965). The most informative look at early productions of the Pre-Raphaelites is the Tate Gallery catalogue *The Pre-Raphaelites* (London, 1984); it contains a full account of Millais's *Ophelia*, pp. 96–98.

11. The story—apocryphal or not—that Elizabeth Siddal, the famous model of the Pre-Raphaelites, became ill from lying in a tub of cold water because Millais, unable to heat it properly, nevertheless kept her posing, fits the picture perfectly. That many people casually believe that this was how Siddal in fact *died* is not incidental and relates to the iconography of female sacrifice in the pictures of her.

12. Gordon S. Haight, Introduction to *The Mill on the Floss* (Boston, 1961), p. xix.

13. See Homans, *Bearing the Word* (Chicago, 1986), pp. 120–52, for an illuminating discussion of Eliot's relationship in *The Mill on the Floss* to Wordsworth. Homans uses Eliot's phrase "the mother tongue of our imagination" both to support and critique Lacanian psychology, but I see the words as much more subversive of the whole Lacanian school than does Homans: they assert the feminization and maternal role of language.

14. See Redinger, pp. 45–60.

15. "Brother and Sister," in *The Writings of George Eliot*, Warwickshire edition (Boston and New York, 1908), vol. 19, pp. 179–87, Sonnet 7, pp. 183–84. See also Redinger, p. 51.

16. Recent feminist criticism has stressed the inadequacy of older readings. See Gillian Beer, *George Eliot* (Brighton, England, 1986), chap. 1, "The 'Woman's Question,'" pp. 1–29, for a provocative and enlightening discussion and critique of various modern feminist approaches to the novel.

17. See Homans's interesting discussion of the brother-sister relationship, especially pp. 122–39. Her always stimulating argument relies heavily on a Lacanian and feminist neo-Lacanian formulation that has a tendency to turn this novel and others she discusses into Lacanian and revisionist-Lacanian allegories. *The Mill on the Floss* both supports Lacanian theory and undermines it by subverting its rigid notions of "the symbolic order" and other constructs of latter-day psychoanalytic myth-making.

18. See Tanner, pp. 66–72, for discussion of this passage.

19. See Garrett Stewart, *Death Sentences: Styles of Dying in British Fiction* (Cambridge, Mass., 1984). I read this beautifully perceptive book, which includes a picture of the Millais *Ophelia*, after completing this chapter and juxtaposing *Ophelia* with the novel. Nina Auerbach also chooses to illustrate *Woman and the Demon* with this picture. Note that Emily Brontë, in the last "supreme moment" of Cathy I, in effect has Cathy cast off Linton and embrace Heathcliff, as Maggie casts off Stephen and clasps Tom.

20. This scene very probably inspired Hardy to write one of the most blatant sexual scenes in Victorian fiction, in Sergeant Troy's sword practice in *Far from the Madding Crowd*.

21. Eliot, like Maggie, had been and was an admirer of Byron. Well aware of his scandalous history, she was made defensive and ill at ease by the attacks on him for his supposed incest, which, Redinger has shown, she subconsciously associated on more than one occasion with her own brother-sister relationship. She protested against Byron and Augusta being dragged into public notice. See Redinger, pp. 45–46.

22. Tanner, p. 72.

23. Ibid., p. 75.

24. See Carroll, pp. 163–65.

25. Gillian Beer, whose brilliant reading of *The Mill on the Floss* (pp. 82–107) I read after writing this chapter, makes this point; see especially pp. 94–95 and 104.

26. See Gordon S. Haight, *George Eliot: A Biography* (New York and Oxford, 1968), pp. 228–33, and Redinger, pp. 336–42, for accounts of Isaac Evans's definitive break-off of direct communication with his sister.

27. See Haight, Introduction, pp. xx–xxi.

28. Gillian Beer uses this term, p. 101.

29. See Haight, *George Eliot*, pp. 80–96 (especially p. 86), and Redinger, pp. 175–202, for accounts of Mary Anne Evans's relationship with John Chapman.

30. F. R. Leavis, *The Great Tradition* (London, 1948), pp. 45–46.

31. Compare Philip's letter to Darcy's stagy speech to Elizabeth in *Pride and Prejudice* (III, XVI, 255–56), and see my discussion in chapter 2 above.

32. See Haight, *George Eliot*, pp. 75–79, and Redinger, pp. 169–75, for discussion of François D'Albert Durade and his place in George Eliot's life.

33. See George Painter, *Marcel Proust*, vol. 2, *The Later Years* (Boston, 1965), p. 157: Proust, communicating to a friend, "urged her to read *The Mill on the Floss*, and added in gloomy jest, alluding to the fate of Tom and Maggie Tulliver: 'no doubt I shall be drowned soon as well!'"

34. See Haight, *George Eliot*, p. 544, and Rose, pp. 235–36, for brief accounts of this bizarre honeymoon event.

35. John W. Cross, *George Eliot's Life as Related in Her Letters and Journals* (Edinburgh and London, 1885), 3 vols.

Chapter Eight

1. See Robert C. Solomon, *Love: Emotion, Myth, and Metaphor* (Garden City, N.Y., 1981), p. xxi, who features this quotation in his thoughtful meditation on love.

2. Joyce, *Ulysses*, p. 273.

3. Portions of this chapter appeared in very different form in my article "Being in Love in *Phineas Finn/Phineas Redux*: Desire, Devotion, Consolation," *Nineteenth-Century Fiction* 37 (December 1982): 383–95.

4. Several allusions in *Phineas* suggest that Byron and his *Don Juan* were very much on Trollope's mind when he wrote his novel. Like Byron's Juan, Phineas, who also rises in the world by winning the favor of women, has an irresistibly appealing attractiveness and an easy, warm nature. Another character, Lord Chiltern, carries the more famous strain of Byronic love, that reckless passion of a Manfred, a Heathcliff, or a Byron himself in his "mad, bad, and dangerous to know" mood. To Phineas, however, Trollope has given the more passive erotic charm and sensibility of Juan or of the Byron that many friendly memoirs and some of his own letters reveal. Finn's history, like Juan's, becomes the occasion for social observation and assessment. Byron's comic epic works to civilize both Eros and Don Juan, now no longer a flagrant exploiter, as in nearly all earlier versions, but a figure who genuinely falls in love with women. Trollope continues and develops this trend of socializing the hero's erotic desire. See my article "Being in Love," pp. 385–86.

5. See for discussion of "The Rokeby Venus" and Velázquez, Jonathan Brown, *Velázquez: Painter and Courtier* (New Haven and London, 1986); Enriqueta Harris, *Velázquez* (Ithaca, N.Y., and Oxford, 1982); José Lopez-Rey, *Velázquez's Work and World* (Greenwich, Conn., 1968); Joseph-Emile Muller, *Velázquez*, trans. Jane Benton (London, 1976).

6. See Harris, p. 140.

7. See Frank O'Connor [Michael O'Donovan], *The Mirror in the Roadway* (New York, 1964), for the critical application of Stendhal's term and for a fine discussion of Trollope, "Trollope the Realist," pp. 165–83.

8. Anthony Trollope, *Phineas Finn* (London, 1973), Oxford University Press edition of the Palliser novels, chap. 57. All subsequent citations to *Phineas Finn* and *Phineas Redux* will be by chapter numbers only. Since the Oxford edition divides both *Phineas Finn* and *Phineas Redux* into two volumes with pagination beginning over and doubling in each novel, though the chapters are numbered progressively through both volumes, and since there is no standard edition (there is a good Penguin popular edition of *Phineas Finn*, edited by John Sutherland [Harmondsworth, England, 1972]), page numbers are likely to be confusing and much less helpful than chapter numbers alone. In my textual citations I will abbreviate *Phineas Finn* as PF and *Phineas Redux* as PR.

9. Robert M. Polhemus, "Trollope's Dialogue," in *Trollope: Centenary Essays*, ed. John Halperin (New York, 1982), pp. 95–108.

10. Walter Kendrick, *The Novel-Machine: The Theory and Fiction of Anthony Trollope* (Baltimore, 1980), p. 100.

11. See Polhemus, *Comic Faith*, pp. 166–203 for the elaboration of these points in the discussion of *Barchester Towers*.

12. Freud, "Being in Love and Hypnosis," vol. 18, p. 112.

13. See René Girard, *Deceit, Desire, and the Novel: Self and Other in Literary Structure*, trans. Yvonne Freccero (Baltimore, 1965), pp. 1–52.

14. See Robert M. Polhemus, *The Changing World of Anthony Trollope* (Berkeley and Los Angeles, 1968), p. 150.

15. See Girard, pp. 66–67, 83–95.

16. On the subject of male homosocial bonding and control, see Eve Kosofsky Sedgwick, *Between Men* (New York, 1985), especially the introductory first chapter.

17. Derby, the prime minister, called the reform program "the leap in the dark." See Asa Briggs, *The Age of Improvement, 1783–1867* (London, 1959), pp. 513–14.

18. See, for example, *Mariana* (Tate Gallery, London), the famous painting by John Millais (see *The Pre-Raphaelites* [London, 1984], pp. 89–90), who illustrated *Phineas Finn*.

19. George Meredith, *The Egoist* (London, 1915), chap. 14, p. 156.

20. Frank O'Connor, in *The Mirror in the Roadway*, pp. 170–71, 175, stresses the importance of "heart" in Trollope.

21. This passage was pointed out to me by Victor Luftig.

22. *The Times*, 11 March 1914.

Chapter Nine

1. George and Ira Gershwin, "Someone to Watch Over Me," from the musical *Oh, Kay!*, 1926.

2. Sophocles, fragment trans. F. W. Cornford in Gore Vidal's *The Judgment of Paris* (New York, 1952), p. 361; see *The Fragments of Sophocles*, Fragment 941, ed. Alfred C. Pearson (Cambridge, 1917).

3. For comments on the rediscovery of this painting, see John Walker, *The National Gallery of Art, Washington*, new and revised edition (New York, 1984), p. 310. See also the citations on Claude above in chap. 6, n. 5, especially Röthlisberger.

4. Florence Emily Hardy, *The Life of Thomas Hardy* (New York, 1962), p. 96. All the *Life*, except the account of the last few years, was really written by Thomas Hardy himself.

5. For authoritative discussion of pastoral modes, various definitions of the pastoral, bibliographical information on the pastoral, and broad perspective on the subject of the pastoral in literature, see Michael Squires, *The Pastoral Novel: Studies in George Eliot, Thomas Hardy, and D. H. Lawrence* (Charlottesville, Va., 1974); W. W. Greg, *Pastoral Poetry and Pastoral Drama* (1906, reprinted New York, 1959); William Empson, *Some Versions of the Pastoral* (1935, reprinted Norfolk, Conn., 1960); Thomas G. Rosenmeyer, *The Green Cabinet: Theocritus and the European Pastoral Lyric* (Berkeley and Los Angeles, 1969); Harold E. Toliver, *Pastoral Forms and Attitudes* (Berkeley and Los Angeles, 1971); Frank Kermode, ed., *English Pastoral Poetry: From the Beginnings to Marvell* (London, 1952); Renato Poggioli, "The Oaten Flute," *Harvard Library Bulletin* 11 (1957): 147–84.

6. See Susan Beegel, "Bathsheba's Lovers: Male Sexuality in *Far from the Madding Crowd*," in *Sexuality and Victorian Literature*, p. 121.

7. F. E. Hardy, p. 444.

8. See T. C. W. Stinton, *Euripides and the Judgement of Paris* (London, 1965), for a full account of the story and development of the judgment of Paris motif in the classical world. See also Karoly Kerényi, *The Heroes of the Greeks* (London, 1959), trans. H. J. Rose, p. 316, who confirms that the disrobing was a part of later versions of the legend.

9. Thomas Hardy, *Far from the Madding Crowd: An Authoritative Text, Backgrounds and Criticism*, ed. Robert C. Schweik (New York, 1986), Norton Critical Edition, chap. 22, pp. 115–16. All subsequent citations, by chapter and page, are to this edition.

10. For the prominence of herdsmen in early cultures and in myths and folk tales involving love and love's deities, see Stinton, pp. 51–63, especially p. 60.

11. F. E. Hardy, p. 98.

12. Rosalind Miles quotes E. M. Forster, "The Women of Wessex," in *The Novels of Thomas Hardy*, ed. Anne Smith (Plymouth and London, 1979), p. 31.

13. Joan Grundy, *Hardy and the Sister Arts* (London, 1979), p. 53: "Claude might be described, it seems to me, as one of the unseen presences of this novel." She speaks of Claude generally. I happily came upon this reference after I had decided to compare his *Judgment of Paris* with *Far from the Madding Crowd*.

14. Squires, p. 37.

15. One great Oedipal, incestuous complex does storm through this novel, and indeed through most of Hardy's writing: the relationship between himself and Nature and Fate, upon whom he projects the roles and attributes of Mother and Father.

16. D. H. Lawrence, whose gamekeeper, Lady Chatterley's lover, owes much to Gabriel, wickedly and—it must be said—unfairly compares Oak to "a dog that watches the bone and bides the time" (*Selected Literary Criticism*, ed. Anthony Beal [New York, 1956], p. 170).

17. Beegel, p. 113.

18. Rosalind Miles writes that Hardy "was always in love," but it never made him happy (p. 23).

19. My discussion of the storm, the sexuality in the episode, and the meaning of this and other passages has been informed by Susan Beegel's discussion, especially pp. 121–23.

20. John Bayley, *The Characters of Love* (New York, 1960).

21. See Penny Boumelha, *Thomas Hardy and Women: Sexual Ideology and Narrative Form* (Totowa, N.J., 1982), for a balanced, insightful feminist reading of Hardy's sexual ideology as it emerges in his fictional treatment of women. Boumelha implies that Bathsheba

has always been more popular with men than women, and that is probably true. She shows the contradictions in Hardy's characterization of Bathsheba, which reveal, she says, "antagonism" (p. 32) as well as sympathy. I find her a more complex figure than does Boumelha or Rosalind Miles ("Women of Wessex"), and I do not see a shrinking of potential in her; instead, stressing the vocational love passage and the relationship with Oak, I read the genuine possibility for growth. Bathsheba, in context, is not a typical Hardy heroine and ought not to be lumped together with later Hardy women.

22. See the note by Robert C. Schweik that the Poorgrass quotation from Hosea is "comically irrelevant" (*Far from the Madding Crowd*, LVII, 308, n. 5). Obviously I disagree.

Chapter Ten

1. *The Letters of James Joyce*, ed. Stuart Gilbert and Richard Ellmann (New York, 1966), vol. 2, pp. 191–92. All subsequent citations, by "*Letters*," volume, and page, are to this edition.

2. Richard Ellmann, "Preface," in *Ulysses, The Corrected Text*, ed. Hans Walter Gabler with Wolfhard Steppe and Claus Melchior (New York, 1986), p. xiii.

3. A small part of this chapter appeared in Robert M. Polhemus, "Love in Joyce," *Sequoia* (Stanford) 27, no. 3 (Autumn 1983): 39–44.

4. For commentary, criticism, and information on Redon see Roseline Bacou, *Odilon Redon: Pastels*, trans. Beatrice Rehl (New York, 1987); Penny Florence, *Mallarmé, Manet, and Redon* (Cambridge, 1986); Richard Hobbs, *Odilon Redon* (Boston, 1977); Carole Keay, *Odilon Redon* (London, 1977); Odilon Redon, *To Myself: Notes on Life, Art, and Artists*, trans. Mira Jacob and Jeanne L. Wasserman (New York, 1986); *Lettres de Odilon Redon* (Paris, 1923); John Rewald, "Odilon Redon," in *Odilon Redon, Gustave Moreau, Rodolphe Bresdin* (New York, 1961–62), pp. 9–49; Jean Selz, *Odilon Redon*, trans. Eileen B. Hennessy (New York, 1971).

5. See Rewald, p. 26.

6. Hobbs, p. 168.

7. See E. H. Gombrich, *Symbolic Images*, for a brilliant discussion of Botticelli's Venus, Neoplatonism, and a possible Neoplatonic program in the representation of Venus.

8. In a male chauvinist mood, a viewer might even deny the primacy of female sexuality by interpreting the concave shape as an ear rather than as a vagina, since medieval Catholic legend has it that "at the Conception the Word of God penetrated the Virgin Mary's ear" (Colin MacCabe, *James Joyce and the Revolution of the Word* [London, 1979], pp. 125–26, n. 2). MacCabe comments, following Lacan, that "the virgin mother bears witness to the power of the phallic wor(l)d of communication."

9. James Joyce, *A Portrait of the Artist as a Young Man: Texts, Criticism, and Notes*, ed. Chester C. Anderson (New York, 1977), pp. 166–73. "[Based on] the definitive text, corrected from the Dublin holograph by Chester C. Anderson and edited by Richard Ellmann, published in 1964." All subsequent citations are to this edition. For two other discussions of the relations between flowers and language in Joyce, see Jacqueline F. Eastman, "The Language of the Flowers: A New Source for *Lotus Eaters*," *James Joyce Quarterly* 26 (Spring 1989): 379–96; and Ramón Saldívar, *Figural Language in the Novel: The Flowers of Speech from Cervantes to Joyce* (Princeton, N.J., 1984).

10. See Suzette Henke, "Stephen Dedalus and Women: A Portrait of the Artist as a Young

Misogynist," in *Women in Joyce*, ed. Suzette Henke and Elaine Unkeless (Urbana, Ill., 1982), pp. 93–96, for a helpful reading of this scene. I am much indebted to her interpretation.

11. See Dora Panofsky, *Pandora's Box*, second edition, revised (New York, 1962), for an informative treatment of the Pandora myth and for a summary of Pandora as a subject in art.

12. Another *Pandora* (fig. 7) by Redon in the Washington National Gallery shows magnificent colors in the rocks and shapes at Pandora's feet in the foreground, but blank, colorless rocks and spaces in the background distance where her presence is lacking, thus corroborating her role and identity as color-bearer to the world.

13. James Joyce, *Stephen Hero*, ed. Theodore Spencer, revised by John J. Slocum and Herbert Cahoon (New York, 1963), p. 180.

14. James Joyce, *Chamber Music*, edited with an introduction and notes by William York Tindall (New York, 1954), IX, p. 125.

15. James Joyce, *Dubliners: Text, Criticism, and Notes*, ed. Robert Scholes and A. Walton Litz (New York, 1969), p. 223.

16. See Darcy O'Brien, *The Conscience of James Joyce* (Princeton, N.J., 1968), pp. 43–44.

17. See *Selected Letters of James Joyce*, ed. Richard Ellmann (New York, 1975), pp. 157–96. All subsequent citations, by "SL" and page, are to this edition.

18. See Richard Ellmann, *James Joyce*, new and revised edition (New York, 1982), pp. 448–52, for an account of this episode.

19. See Polhemus, *Comic Faith*, p. 297.

20. Fritz Senn, *Joyce's Dislocutions*, ed. John Paul Riquelme (Baltimore and London, 1984), p. 164. This collection of essays includes an illuminating study of "Nausicaa," pp. 160–88, that calls attention to similarities between Gerty and Molly (p. 178).

21. See Suzette Henke, "Gerty MacDowell: Joyce's Sentimental Heroine," in *Women in Joyce*, pp. 132–49, who discusses Cummins's novel *The Lamplighter* as a source of Joyce's parody. For a fine, subtle, and provocative reading of "Nausicaa" and its larger implications, see Margot Norris, "Modernism, Myth, and Desire in 'Nausicaa,'" *James Joyce Quarterly* 26 (Fall 1988): 37–50.

22. See Joseph Wood Krutch, *The Modern Temper* (New York, 1933), p. 84.

23. Quoted and discussed by Geoffrey Grigson, *The Goddess of Love*, p. 90.

24. SL, p. 285. Richard Ellmann adds a footnote: "Joyce is playing on Mephistopheles' identification of himself in Goethe's *Faust*, Act I: 'I am the spirit that always denies.'" That negative spirit is the kind Joyce saw and satirized in erotic idealism.

25. See Richard Ellmann, *Ulysses on the Liffey* (New York, 1972), pp. 159–76, especially p. 162.

26. Joyce came to ascribe to a woman the generation of language as well as life. In his most eloquent and emotional moments—for example, in the final pages of *Ulysses* and *Finnegans Wake*—he speaks in the guise of a woman. The highest form of heroism for him seems to be the act of creation, and he finds and represents the basis of creativity—the fusion of desire, flesh, and language—in a woman, not in the male God of Christianity nor the heroic male artist.

27. "In Joyce's universe," writes Shari Benstock, "sexual survival is linked with the broader concern of affirming the legitimacy of basic human needs, making sexual motivation a measure of psychological equilibrium. . . . Issy give[s] promise to yet another generation by demonstrating [her] enthusiastic acceptance of that which is 'human' through an equally

enthusiastic response in matters sexual" ("The Genuine Christine: Psychodynamics of Issy," in *Women in Joyce*, p. 190).

28. I am indebted to Susan Lowell Humphreys for this accurate Wakean coinage.

29. See Grigson.

30. See John Bishop's brilliant work of scholarship and critical acumen *Joyce's Book of the Dark* (Madison, Wis., 1986) for this idea.

Chapter Eleven

1. William Blake, "Jerusalem," in *The Complete Writings of William Blake*, ed. Geoffrey Keynes (London, 1966), plate 30, line 38, p. 656.

2. Foucault, *The History of Sexuality*, vol. 1, pp. 7–8.

3. D. H. Lawrence, *Lady Chatterley's Lover* (New York, 1968), the complete and unexpurgated 1928 Orioli edition, preface by Lawrence Durrell, edited and with an introduction by Ronald Friedland (includes "A Propos of *Lady Chatterley's Lover*"), chap. 17, p. 291. All subsequent citations, by chapter and page, are to this edition.

4. Much feminist criticism of D. H. Lawrence is compelling. The feminist case against Lawrence is put clearly and succinctly by Simone de Beauvoir (*The Second Sex* [New York, 1970], pp. 214–24). The passion and polemics that Lawrence can arouse are well illustrated by comparing Kate Millett's bitter attack on him (*Sexual Politics*, pp. 315–86) with Norman Mailer's powerful defense and spiteful counterattack on Millett (*The Prisoner of Sex* [Boston, 1971], pp. 134–60). The antifeminist aspects of *Lady Chatterley*, as I read it, do not finally cripple it either aesthetically or morally. For reasons that I hope I make clear and persuasive, I find that the main impetus of the novel ultimately and on balance promotes the development of human freedom and potential, women's as well as men's; but I do not presume to judge—and cannot judge—for those who feel themselves injured or offended by Lawrence.

5. Anthony Burgess, *The Life and Work of D. H. Lawrence: Flame into Being* (New York, 1985), pp. 238, 237.

6. Lydia Blanchard, "Lawrence, Foucault, and the Language of Sexuality," in *D. H. Lawrence's "Lady": A New Look at Lady Chatterley's Lover*, ed. Michael Squires and Dennis Jackson (Athens, Ga., 1985), p. 26.

7. See Squires, *The Pastoral Novel*.

8. Lawrence, "A Propos of *Lady Chatterley's Lover*," p. 332.

9. Readers may gag on the sexist attribution of a passive role to women in love; I wish he had written "if men and women could fuck with warm hearts." One cause of the backlash against Lawrence is his use of the verb *fuck* in the traditional way that an angry feminist slogan of the 1970s, "men fuck—women get fucked," captures. The semantic history of the word does indeed reflect gender exploitation (see Burgess, pp. 237–38). For me, however, the peculiar syntactical male chauvinist slant of Mellors's creed fades into its larger meaning; in fact, the overall logic of Lawrentian thought might well indicate that the insidious antifeminist idea that somehow nature has decreed forever that men fuck and women just take it comes precisely out of the custom he attacks: *coldhearted* fucking.

10. For discussion and critical analysis of Klimt, see Carl E. Schorske, *Fin-de-Siècle Vienna: Politics and Culture* (New York, 1980); Alessandra Comini, *Gustav Klimt* (New York, 1975); Fritz Novotny, *Gustav Klimt* (New York, 1968), with a catalogue of his painting; Werner Hofmann, *Gustav Klimt*, trans. Inge Goodwin (Greenwich, Conn., 1971); Peter Vergo, *Art in Vienna: 1898–1918* (London, 1975).

11. See Martin Green, *The Von Richtofen Sisters, the Triumphant and the Tragic Modes of Love: Else and Frieda Von Richtofen, Otto Grass, Max Weber, and D. H. Lawrence* (New York, 1974).

12. If prurience is the enemy of true piety, and eroticism the hope of life, then seeing, concentrating on, and reading into works of art the shapes of wombs, phalluses, and nipples (look carefully and you can see all three in the sheath-form holding Klimt's lovers) would be the very opposite of dirty-minded and degrading; it would be proper homage to the goodness of the body and sex. In the artistic imaginations of Klimt and Lawrence, who grew up in an era of the increasing might of impersonal political and corporate entities, it is not adoration, fascination, and desire for the genital forms of the opposite sex—or the same sex—that harm people, debase them, or make them less whole or powerful; rather, it is despising or ignoring sexuality and the erotic being of another that does that.

If there are such things as penis envy and phallic fascination, then in men's imaginations vagina envy and womb obsession just as certainly exist and affect their erotic life and symbolization. As surely as male symbolism, female sexual symbolism pervades the arts.

Look, for example, at another picture that depicts erotic relationship and the joy of falling in love, Vermeer's *The Officer and Laughing Girl* (1657; fig. 21). Anyone can see the phallic form and thrust of the officer with his arm and his tall hat, but just as significant is the sexual symbolism of the rounded glass in the girl's hand, the open window whose space the hat touches, and even the whole pregnant interior itself that holds this burst of fertile life and new energy caught in the girl's face: If towers, swords, lances, long implements, and the like become symbols that show a fixation with male sexuality, surely small containers, interiors, vessels, openings of all kinds, bodies of water, and even empty skies reveal an equal obsession with female sexuality.

13. D. H. Lawrence, *John Thomas and Lady Jane* (London, 1972), p. 114.

14. "A writer," Frederick Crews says, "whose inclination has been to confuse a damp crotch with a burning bush is likely to wake up some years later and wonder what he could possibly have had in mind" ("Mr. Updike's Planet," *New York Review of Books*, 4 December 1986, p. 10).

15. Colin Clarke, *River of Dissolution: D. H. Lawrence and English Romanticism* (New York, 1969).

16. For a helpful discussion of how Lawrence read Hardy, see Richard Swigg, *Lawrence, Hardy, and American Literature* (London, 1972), preface, pp. ix–xii.

17. Swigg, pp. 67, 68.

18. T. H. Adamowski, "The Natural Flowering of Life: The Ego, Sex, and Existentialism," in *D. H. Lawrence's "Lady,"* p. 50.

19. Blanchard, p. 32.

20. Ibid., p. 31.

21. See Ellmann, *James Joyce*, p. 615, for these reactions of Joyce and Lawrence.

22. See Zack Bowen, "*Lady Chatterley's Lover* and *Ulysses*," in *D. H. Lawrence's "Lady,"* pp. 116–35, especially p. 118.

23. Ibid., p. 134.

24. A distinguished author, critic, and feminist sent me a note about *Lady Chatterley*: "I like *Lady Chatterley*. I learned about sex from it, with my first man. Yes, I did." This testimony matches what I often hear from women and men who matured in the 1950s and 1960s; it also makes the key point that art shapes love life.

25. See Frank Kermode, *D. H. Lawrence* (New York, 1973), pp. 131–43.

26. Millett, pp. 322–23.

27. Blanchard, p. 28.

28. Frank Kermode has made a convincing case about how important to Lawrence's meta-physic was "this reconciliation of dissolution and creation in anal sex" (*D. H. Lawrence*, p. 142).

29. See Squires, pp. 196–212, for a discussion of *Lady Chatterley* as a novel in a traditional pastoral mode.

30. The situation, many women say, is definitely not gender-specific.

Epilogue

1. George Eliot, *Middlemarch*, "Finale," p. 573.

2. See Sharon Proudfit, "The Fact and the Vision: Virginia Woolf and Roger Fry's Post-Impressionist Aesthetic," Ph.D. dissertation, University of Michigan, 1967, p. 224.

Select Bibliography

This bibliography lists only writings that have been of direct help to me in making this book; it is by no means a complete record of all the works and sources I have consulted and used.

1. Faith, Love, and the Art of the Novel

The following works have been instrumental in helping me to judge where and what the most important written information about love is, in formulating my own ideas on the subject, in relating love to art, fiction, religion, Great Britain, and the nineteenth century, and in writing both the introduction and, indeed, this whole study of love and novels.

Andreas Capellanus. *The Art of Courtly Love*. Trans. John Jay Parry. New York, 1964.

Ariès, Phillipe. *Centuries of Childhood: A Social History of Family Life*, trans. Robert Baldrick. New York, 1962.

Armstrong, Judith. *The Novel and Adultery*. New York, 1976.

Armstrong, Nancy. *Desire and Domestic Fiction*. Oxford, 1987.

Atkins, John. *Sex in Literature: The Erotic Impulse in Literature*. Volume 2, *The Classical Experience of the Sexual Impulse*. London, 1973.

Auerbach, Nina. *Communities of Women*. Cambridge, Mass., 1978.

———. *Woman and the Demon: The Life of a Victorian Myth*. Cambridge, Mass., and London, 1982.

———. *Romantic Imprisonment: Women and Other Glorified Outcasts*. New York, 1985.

Bailey, Derrick Sherwin. *The Mystery of Love and Marriage: A Study in the Theology of Sexual Relations*. New York, 1952.

Bakhtin, Mikhail M. *The Dialogic Imagination*. Ed. Michael Holquist. Trans. Caryl Emerson and Michael Holquist. Austin, Tex., 1981.

Barickman, Richard, Susan MacDonald, and Myra Stark. *Corrupt Relations: Dickens, Thackeray, Trollope, Collins, and the Victorian Sexual System*. New York, 1982.

Barthes, Roland. *A Lover's Discourse*. Trans. Richard Howard. New York, 1978.

Bataille, Georges. *Erotism: Death and Sensuality*. San Francisco, 1986.

Bayley, John. *The Characters of Love: A Study in the Literature of Personality*. London, 1960.

Beaty, Frederick L. *Light from Heaven: Love in British Romantic Literature*. De Kalb, Ill., 1971.

Beauvoir, Simone de. *The Second Sex*. Trans. H. M. Parshley. New York, 1970.

Beer, Gillian. *George Eliot*. Brighton, England, 1986.

Beer, Patricia. *Reader, I Married Him: A Study of the Women Characters of Jane Austen, Charlotte Brontë, Elizabeth Gaskell, and George Eliot*. New York, 1974.

Bender, John. *Imagining the Penitentiary: Fiction and the Architecture of the Mind in Eighteenth-Century England*. Chicago and London, 1987.

Bersani, Leo. *A Future for Astyanax: Character and Desire in Literature*. Boston, 1976.

Blake, Kathleen. *Love and the Woman Question in Victorian Literature: The Art of Self-Postponement*. Totowa, N.J., 1983.

Boone, Joseph A. *Tradition Counter Tradition: Love and the Form of Fiction*. Chicago, 1987.

Boumelha, Penny. *Thomas Hardy and Women: Sexual Ideology and Narrative Form*. Totowa, N.J., 1982.

Bowie, Malcolm. *Freud, Proust, and Lacan.* Cambridge, 1987.

Brantlinger, Patrick. *Rule of Darkness: British Literature and Imperialism, 1830–1914.* Ithaca, N.Y., 1988.

Broadbent, J. B. *Poetic Love.* London, 1964.

Brown, Nathaniel. *Sexuality and Feminism in Shelley.* Cambridge, Mass., 1979.

Brown, Norman O. *Love's Body.* New York, 1966.

Brownstein, Rachel M. *Becoming a Heroine: Reading about Women in Novels.* New York, 1982.

Burke, Kenneth. *The Rhetoric of Religion.* Berkeley, 1970.

Butler, Marilyn. *Romantics, Rebels, and Revolutionaries.* Oxford, 1982.

Calder, Jenni. *Women and Marriage in Victorian Fiction.* New York and Oxford, 1976.

Chase, Karen. *Eros and Psyche: The Representation of Personality in Charlotte Brontë, Charles Dickens, and George Eliot.* New York and London, 1984.

Chodorow, Nancy. *The Reproduction of Mothering: Psychoanalysis and the Sociology of Gender.* Berkeley, Los Angeles, and London, 1978.

Cockshut, A. O. J. *Man and Woman: A Study of Love in the Novel, 1740–1940.* London, 1977.

Cox, Don Richard, ed. *Sexuality and Victorian Literature.* Knoxville, Tenn., 1984.

Demony, A. J. *The Heresy of Courtly Love.* New York, 1947.

Dijkstra, Bram. *Idols of Perversity: Fantasies of Feminine Evil in Fin-de-Siècle Culture.* New York and Oxford, 1986.

Eco, Umberto. *The Name of the Rose.* New York, 1980.

Eigner, Edward. *The Metaphysical Novel in England and America: Dickens, Bulwer, Hawthorne, Melville.* Berkeley, 1978.

Ellis, Havelock. *Studies in the Psychology of Sex.* 4 volumes. New York, 1936.

Faderman, Lillian. *Surpassing the Love of Man: Romantic Friendship and Love between Women from the Renaissance to the Present.* New York, 1981.

Fiedler, Leslie. *Love and Death in the American Novel.* New York, 1960.

Ford, Clellan S., and Beach, Frank A. *Patterns of Sexual Behavior.* New York, 1951.

Foucault, Michel. *The History of Sexuality.* Volume 1: *An Introduction.* Volume 2: *The Uses of Pleasure.* Volume 3: *The Care of the Self.* Trans. Robert Hurley. New York, 1978–86.

Freedman, Estelle, and John D'Emilio. *Intimate Matters.* New York, 1988.

Freud, Sigmund. *The Standard Edition of the Complete Psychological Works.* 24 volumes. Ed. and trans. James Strachey. London, 1953–66. In particular, vol. 7, *Three Essays on the Theory of Sexuality;* volume 11, "Contributions to the Psychology of Love," I–III; volume 12, "Observations on Transference-Love."

Friedrich, Paul. *The Meaning of Aphrodite.* Chicago, 1978.

Gallagher, Catherine. *The Industrial Reformation of English Fiction.* Chicago, 1985.

Gay, Peter. *The Bourgeois Experience, Victoria to Freud.* Volume 1, *The Education of the Senses.* Volume 2, *The Tender Passion.* New York and Oxford, 1986.

Gilbert, Sandra M., and Susan Gubar. *The Madwoman in the Attic: The Woman Writer and the Nineteenth-Century Literary Imagination.* New Haven and London, 1979.

Gilligan, Carol. *In a Different Voice: Psychological Theory and Women's Development.* Cambridge, Mass., and London, 1982.

Girard, René. *Deceit, Desire, and the Novel: Self and Other in Literary Structure.* Trans. Yvonne Freccero. Baltimore, 1965.

———. *Violence and the Sacred.* Trans. Patrick Gregory. Baltimore and London, 1977.

Goldfarb, Russell M. *Sexual Repression and Victorian Literature*. Lewisburg, Pa., 1970.

Goody, Jack. *The Development of the Family and Marriage in Europe*. Cambridge, 1983.

———. *The Logic of Writing and the Organization of Society*. Cambridge, 1986.

Greer, Germaine. *The Female Eunuch*. New York, 1971.

Grigson, Geoffrey. *The Goddess of Love*. London, 1976.

Hagstrum, Jean. *Sex and Sensibility: Ideal and Erotic Love from Milton to Mozart*. Chicago, 1980.

———. *The Romantic Body*. Knoxville, Tenn., 1985.

Haller, John S., Jr., and Robin M. *The Physician and Sexuality in Victorian America*. Urbana, Ill., 1974.

Harrison, Fraser. *The Dark Angel: Aspects of Victorian Sexuality*. London, 1977.

Hazo, Robert G. *The Idea of Love*. New York, 1967.

Hellerstein, Erna Olafson, Leslie Parker Hume, and Karen M. Offen, eds. *Victorian Women: A Documentary Account of Women's Lives in Nineteenth-Century England, France, and the United States*. Stanford, Calif., 1981.

Houghton, Walter. *The Victorian Frame of Mind*. New Haven, 1957.

Hunt, Morton M. *The Natural History of Love*. New York, 1959.

Jacobus, Mary, ed. *Women Writing and Writing about Women*. London and New York, 1979.

Jameson, Frederic. *The Political Unconscious: Narrative as Socially Symbolic Act*. Ithaca, N.Y., 1981.

Jay, Elizabeth. *The Religion of the Heart: Anglican Evangelicalism and the Nineteenth-Century Novel*. Oxford, 1979.

Johnson, Wendell Stacy. *Sex and Marriage in Victorian Poetry*. Ithaca, N.Y., 1975.

———. *Living in Sin: The Victorian Sexual Revolution*. Chicago, 1979.

Joseph, Gerhard. *Tennysonian Love: The Strange Diagonal*. Minneapolis, Minn., 1969.

Kaplan, Fred. *Sacred Tears: Sentimentality in Victorian Literature*. Princeton, N.J., 1987.

Katchadourian, Herant. *The Fundamentals of Human Sexuality*, fourth edition. New York, 1985.

Kennard, Jean. *Victims of Convention*. Hamden, Conn., 1978.

Kennet, Wayland. *Eros Denied: Sex in Western Society*. Boston, 1964.

Kristeva, Julia. *Desire in Language*. New York, 1980.

———. *Revolution in Poetic Language*. New York, 1984.

———. *Tales of Love*. New York, 1987.

Krutch, Joseph Wood. *The Modern Temper*. New York, 1933.

Kucich, John. *Repression in Victorian Fiction*. Berkeley and Los Angeles, 1987.

Lacan, Jacques. *Speech and Language in Psychoanalysis*, trans. Anthony Wilden. Baltimore and London, 1968.

Lerner, Laurence. *Love and Marriage: Literature and its Social Context*. London and New York, 1979.

The Letters of Abelard and Heloise. Trans. C. K. Scott Moncrieff. London, 1925.

Levine, George. *The Realistic Imagination: English Fiction from Frankenstein to Lady Chatterley*. Chicago and London, 1981.

Lewis, C. S. *The Allegory of Love*. New York, 1936.

———. *The Four Loves*. New York, 1960.

Lovell, Terry. *Consuming Fiction*. London, 1987.

Mailer, Norman. *The Prisoner of Sex*. Boston, 1971.

Marcus, Steven. *The Other Victorians: A Study of Sexuality and Pornography in Mid-Nineteenth-Century England*. New York, 1967.

Marcuse, Herbert. *Eros and Civilization*. New York, 1955.

Marks, Elaine, and Isabelle de Courtivron, eds. *New French Feminisms*. New York, 1981.

Maynard, John. *Charlotte Brontë and Sexuality*. Cambridge, New York, London, Melbourne, 1984.

McGhee, Richard D. *Marriage, Duty and Desire*. Lawrence, Kans., 1980.

Mellor, Anne K. *English Romantic Irony*. Cambridge, Mass., 1979.

Millett, Kate. *Sexual Politics*. New York, 1979.

Moers, Ellen. *Literary Women: The Great Writers*. New York, 1976.

Moi, Toril. *Sexual/Textual Politics: Feminist Literary Theory*. London and New York, 1985.

Morgan, Douglas N. *Love: Plato, the Bible, and Freud*. Englewood Cliffs, N.J., 1959.

Morgan, Susan. *Sisters in Time: Imagining Gender in Nineteenth-Century British Fiction*. New York, 1989.

Neale, R. S. *Class and Ideology in the Nineteenth Century*. London, 1972.

Nygren, Andres. *Agape and Eros*. Trans. P. S. Watson. Philadelphia and New York, 1953.

Ortega y Gasset, José. *On Love: Aspects of a Single Theme*. Trans. Tony Talbot. New York, 1958.

Panofsky, Erwin. *Studies in Iconology: Humanistic Themes in the Art of the Renaissance*. New York, 1962.

Pearsall, Ronald. *The Worm in the Bud: The World of Victorian Sexuality*. Toronto, 1969.

———. *Public Purity, Private Shame: Victorian Sexuality Exposed*. London, 1976.

Plato. *The Symposium*. Trans. Walter Hamilton. Harmondsworth, England, 1951.

Polhemus, Robert M. *Comic Faith: The Great Tradition from Austen to Joyce*. Chicago, 1980.

Poovey, Mary. *Uneven Developments*. Chicago, 1988.

Praz, Mario. *The Romantic Agony*. Trans. Angus Davidson. London, 1951.

Proust, Marcel. *Remembrance of Things Past*. Trans. C. K. Scott Moncrieff and Terence Kilmartin. New York, 1981.

Rabine, Leslie. *Reading the Romantic Heroine*. Ann Arbor, Mich., 1985.

Rank, Otto. *The Don Juan Legend*. Trans. David G. Winter. Princeton, N.J., 1975.

Reade, Brian. *Sexual Heretics: Male Homosexuality in English Literature from 1850 to 1900*. London, 1970.

Robb, Nesca. *Neoplatonism of the Italian Renaissance*. New York, 1968.

Rose, Phyllis. *Parallel Lives*. New York, 1984.

Rougemont, Denis de. *Love Declared: Essays on the Myths of Love*. Trans. Richard Howard. Boston, 1963.

———. *Love in the Western World*. Trans. Montgomery Belgion, revised and augmented. Princeton, 1983.

Rover, Constance. *Love, Morals, and the Feminists*. London, 1970.

Rowse, A. L. *Homosexuals in History: A Study of Ambivalence in Society, Literature, and the Arts*. New York, 1977.

Sadoff, Dianne. *Monsters of Affection: Dickens, Eliot, and Brontë on Fatherhood*. Baltimore and London, 1982.

Sedgwick, Eve Kosofsky. *Between Men*. New York, 1985.

Showalter, Elaine. *A Literature of Their Own: British Women Novelists from Brontë to Lessing*. Princeton, N.J., 1977.

Simpson, David. *Fetishism and Imagination*. Baltimore, 1982.

Singer, Irving. *The Nature of Love.* Volume 1, *Plato to Luther.* Chicago, 1966 (revised, 1984). Volume 2, *Courtly and Romantic.* Chicago, 1984. Volume 3, *The Modern World.* Chicago, 1988.

Skura, Meredith Anne. *The Literary Use of the Psychoanalytic Process.* New Haven and London, 1981.

Smith, Peter. *Public and Private Value: Studies in the Nineteenth-Century Novel.* Cambridge, 1984.

Soble, Alan, ed. *The Philosophy of Sex: Contemporary Readings.* Totowa, N.J., 1980.

Solomon, Robert C. *Love: Emotion, Myth, and Metaphor.* Garden City, N.Y., 1981.

Stallybrass, Peter, and Allon White. *The Politics and Poetics of Transgression.* Ithaca, N.Y., 1986.

Steinberg, Leo. *The Sexuality of Christ in Renaissance Art and in Modern Oblivion.* New York, 1983.

Stendhal. *Love.* Trans. Gilbert and Suzanne Sale. Harmondsworth, England, 1975.

Stewart, Garrett. *Death Sentences: Styles of Dying in British Fiction.* Cambridge, Mass., 1984.

Stone, Donald D. *The Romantic Impulse in Victorian Fiction.* Cambridge, Mass., 1980.

Stubbs, Patricia. *Women and Fiction, Feminism and the Novel, 1880–1920.* New York, 1979.

Symons, Donald. *The Evolution of Human Sexuality.* New York and Oxford, 1979.

Tanner, Tony. *Adultery and the Novel.* Baltimore, 1979.

Taylor, Gordon Rattray. *Sex in History.* New York, 1954.

Taylor, Mark. *Shakespeare's Darker Purpose.* New York, 1982.

Trudgill, Eric. *Madonnas and Magdalens: The Origins and Development of Victorian Sexual Attitudes.* New York, 1976.

Twitchell, James B. *Forbidden Partners: The Incest Taboo in Modern Culture.* New York, 1987.

Unger, Roberto Mangabeira. *Passion: An Essay on Personality.* New York, 1986.

Valency, Maurice. *In Praise of Love: An Introduction to the Love-Poetry of the Renaissance.* New York, 1958.

Vannoy, Russell. *Sex without Love: A Philosophical Investigation.* Buffalo, N.Y., 1980.

Vicinus, Martha, ed. *Suffer and Be Still: Woman in the Victorian Age.* Bloomington, Ind., 1972.

———. *A Widening Sphere: Changing Roles of Victorian Women.* Bloomington, Ind., 1977.

Watt, Ian. *The Rise of the Novel.* Berkeley and Los Angeles, 1957.

Webb, Peter. *The Erotic Arts.* Boston, 1975.

Weeks, Jeffrey. *Sex, Politics, and Society: The Regulation of Sexuality since 1800.* London, 1981.

Wind, Edgar. *Pagan Mysteries in the Renaissance.* New Haven, 1958.

Wohl, Anthony S., ed. *The Victorian Family: Structure and Stresses.* New York, 1978.

2. Jane Austen and *Pride and Prejudice*

There is a wealth of informative, varied, and provocative critical discussion of Jane Austen in general and *Pride and Prejudice* in particular. I have found the following works helpful:

Babb, Howard S. *Jane Austen's Novels: The Fabric of Design.* Columbus, Ohio, 1973.

Duckworth, Alistair M. *The Improvement of Estate.* Baltimore, 1971.

Fergus, Jan S. *Jane Austen and the Didactic Novel.* Totowa, N.J., 1983.

Gray, Donald J., ed. *Pride and Prejudice: An Authoritative Text, Backgrounds, Reviews, and Essays in Criticism.* New York, 1966.

Grey, J. David, A. Walton Litz, and Brian C. Southam. *The Jane Austen Companion.* New York, 1986.

Halperin, John, ed. *Jane Austen: Bicentenary Essays.* Cambridge and New York, 1975.

———. *The Life of Jane Austen.* Baltimore, 1984.

Honan, Park. *Jane Austen: Her Life.* London, 1987.

Johnson, Claudia. *Jane Austen: Women, Politics, and the Novel.* Chicago, 1988.

Kirkham, Margaret. *Jane Austen, Feminism and Fiction.* Totowa, N.J., 1983.

Lascelles, Mary. *Jane Austen and Her Art.* Oxford, 1939.

Litz, A. Walton. *Jane Austen: A Study of Her Artistic Development.* London, 1965.

McMaster, Juliet. *Jane Austen on Love.* Victoria, B. C., 1978.

Monaghan, David. *Jane Austen, Structure and Social Vision.* London, 1980.

Morgan, Susan. *In the Meantime: Character and Perception in Jane Austen's Fiction.* Chicago, 1980.

Mudrick, Marvin. *Jane Austen: Irony as Defense and Discovery.* Princeton, N.J., 1952.

Poovey, Mary. *The Proper Lady and the Woman Writer: Ideology as Style in the Works of Mary Wollstonecraft, Mary Shelley and Jane Austen.* Chicago, 1984.

Reddy, T. Vasudeva. *Jane Austen: The Dialectics of Self Actualization in Her Novels.* New York, 1987.

Scott, P. J. M. *Jane Austen, A Reassessment.* London, 1982.

Smith, LeRoy W. *Jane Austen and the Drama of Woman.* London, 1983.

Southam, Brian C., ed. *Critical Essays on Jane Austen.* London, 1968.

———. *Jane Austen: The Critical Heritage.* London and New York, 1968.

Spencer, Jane. *The Rise of the Woman Novelist.* Oxford, 1986.

Spender, Dale. *Mothers of the Novel.* London, 1986.

Tanner, Tony. *Jane Austen.* Cambridge, Mass., 1986.

Tave, Stuart. *Some Words of Jane Austen.* Chicago, 1973.

Wallace, Robert K. *Jane Austen and Mozart.* Athens, Ga., 1983.

3. Walter Scott and *The Bride of Lammermoor*

I have made use of the following works in my discussion of *The Bride of Lammermoor* and have benefited from them, though my emphasis on the importance of the love story and the wedding night is greater than the general critical estimate.

Alexander, J. H., and David Hewitt, eds. *Scott and His Influence: The Papers of the Aberdeen Scott Conference, 1982.* Aberdeen, 1983.

Bos, K. *Religious Creeds . . . in Sir Walter Scott's Works.* Amsterdam, 1932.

Brown, David D. *Walter Scott and the Historical Imagination.* London, 1979.

Caserio, Robert. *Plot, Story, and the Novel.* Princeton, N.J., 1979.

Cockshut, A. O. J. *The Achievement of Sir Walter Scott.* New York, 1970.

Daiches, David. "Scott's Achievement as a Novelist." In *Literary Essays.* Edinburgh, 1956.

Davie, Donald. *The Heyday of Sir Walter Scott.* London, 1961.

Dekker, George. *The American Historical Romance.* Cambridge, 1987.

Fleishman, Avrom. *The English Historical Novel: Walter Scott to Virginia Woolf.* Baltimore, 1971.

Gordon, R. C. "*The Bride of Lammermoor*: A Novel of Tory Pessimism." *Nineteenth-Century Fiction,* 12 (September 1957): 110–24.

Hart, Francis B. *Scott's Novels.* Charlottesville, Va., 1966.

Hook, Andrew. "*The Bride of Lammermoor*: A Re-examination." *Nineteenth-Century Fiction,* 23 (September 1967): 111–26.

Jack, Ian. *Sir Walter Scott.* London, 1958.

Jeffares, Norman A., ed. *Scott's Mind and Art.* Totowa, N.J., 1970.

Johnson, Edgar. *Sir Walter Scott: The Great Unknown.* 2 volumes. London, 1970.

Kroeber, Karl. *Romantic Narrative Art.* Madison, Wis., 1960.

Lockhart, J. G. *The Life of Sir Walter Scott.* 10 volumes. Edinburgh, 1902.

Lukács, G. *The Historical Novel.* Trans. Hannah Mitchell and Stanley Mitchell. London, 1962.

Millgate, Jane. *Walter Scott: The Making of a Novelist.* Toronto, 1984.

Mitchell, Jerome. *The Walter Scott Operas.* Tuscaloosa, Ala., 1976.

Raleigh, John Henry. "What Scott Meant to the Victorians," *Victorian Studies* 7 (1963–64): 7–34.

Sandy, Stephen. *The Raveling of the Novel.* New York, 1980.

Shaw, Harry E. *The Forms of Historical Fiction.* Ithaca, N.Y., 1983.

Welsh, Alexander. *The Hero of the Waverley Novels.* New Haven, 1963.

Wilt, Judith. *Secret Leaves.* Chicago, 1985.

4. Emily Brontë and *Wuthering Heights*

The commentary on *Wuthering Heights* is immense, and, as is the case with any important subject that has been around for a good while, it is extraordinarily difficult to say anything sensible about the novel that has not been said or prefigured. Good scholarship is emerging on the criticism that the novel has spawned (see, for example, J. Hillis Miller, *Fiction and Repetition* [Cambridge, Mass., 1982], pp. 50–53). I have found the following works, along with the previously cited work by Georges Bataille, most helpful in writing this chapter:

Allott, Miriam, ed. *The Brontës: The Critical Heritage.* London, 1974.

Benvenuto, Richard. *Emily Brontë.* Boston, 1982.

Chitham, Edward. *A Life of Emily Brontë.* Oxford, 1987.

Duthie, Enid Lowry. *The Brontës and Nature.* Basingstoke, England, 1986.

Eagleton, Terry. *Myths of Power: A Marxist Study of the Brontës.* London, 1975.

Evans, Barbara Lloyd, ed. *The Scribner Companion to the Brontës.* New York, 1982.

Gérin, Winifred. *Emily Brontë: A Biography.* Oxford, 1971.

Homans, Margaret. "Repression and Sublimation of Nature in *Wuthering Heights*." *PMLA* 93, no. 1 (1978): 9–19.

———. *Bearing the Word.* Chicago and London, 1986. Especially chapter 3, "The Name of the Mother in *Wuthering Heights*."

Kavanagh, Janis. *Emily Brontë.* Oxford, 1985.

Miller, J. Hillis. "*Wuthering Heights*: Repetition and the 'Uncanny.'" In *Fiction and Repetition: Seven English Novels.* Cambridge, Mass., 1982.

Moser, Thomas C. "What Is the Matter with Emily Jane?" *Nineteenth-Century Fiction* 17 (June 1962): 1–19.

Parker, Patricia. "The (Self)-Identity of the Literary Text: Property, Proper Place, and Proper
    Name in *Wuthering Heights.*" In *Literary Fat Ladies: Rhetoric, Gender, Property.* Lon-
    don and New York, 1987.
Petit, Jean-Pierre, ed. *Emily Brontë: A Critical Anthology.* Harmondsworth, England, 1973.
Sanger, C. P. *The Structure of Wuthering Heights.* London, 1926.
Van Ghent, Dorothy. *The English Novel: Form and Function.* New York, 1953.

5. Charlotte Brontë and *Villette*

While I frequently disagree with the particular readings of *Villette* in the following works, I
have found them to be full of helpful information and suggestive insight for interpreting and
understanding Charlotte Brontë's great, indeterminate, and difficult novel:

Allott, Miriam, ed. *Charlotte Brontë: Jane Eyre and Villette, A Casebook.* London, 1973.
    (Includes important criticism of *Villette* by Robert Heilman, Roy Pascal, R. B. Martin,
    and R. A. Colby, as well as contemporary and later Victorian assessments of the novel.)
————. *The Brontës: The Critical Heritage.* London, 1974.
Auerbach, Nina. "Charlotte Brontë, the Two Countries." *University of Toronto Quarterly*
    42 (1973): 328–42.
Bledsoe, Robert. "Snow Beneath Snow: A Reconsideration of the Virgin of *Villette.*" In
    Gender and Literary Voice, ed. Janet Todd. New York and London, 1980.
Blom, Margaret. "Charlotte Brontë, Feminist *manquée.*" *Bucknell Review* 21 (Spring 1973):
    87–102.
Carlisle, Janice. "The Face in the Mirror: *Villette* and the Conventions of Autobiography."
    ELH 46 (1979): 262–89.
Duthie, Enid Lowry. *The Foreign Vision of Charlotte Brontë.* London, 1975.
Eagleton, Terry. *Myths of Power: A Marxist Study of the Brontës.* London, 1975.
Gaskell, Elizabeth. *The Life of Charlotte Brontë.* London, [1857] 1975.
Gérin, Winifred. *Charlotte Brontë: The Evolution of Genius.* Oxford, 1967.
Jacobus, Mary. "The Buried Letter, Feminism and Romanticism." In *Women Writing and
    Writing about Women.* London and New York, 1979.
Keefe, Robert. *Charlotte Brontë's World of Death.* Austin, Tex., 1979.
Martin, Robert B. *The Accents of Persuasion.* London, 1966.
Maynard, John. *Charlotte Brontë and Sexuality.* Cambridge, 1984.
Moglen, Helene. *Charlotte Brontë: The Self Conceived.* New York, 1976.
Ohmann, Carol. "Historical Reality and 'Divine Appointment' in Charlotte Brontë's Fic-
    tion." *Signs* 2 (1977), 752–78.
Peters, Margot. *Charlotte Brontë: Style in the Novel.* Madison, Wis., 1973.
————. *Unquiet Soul: A Biography of Charlotte Brontë.* New York, 1975.
Platt, Carolyn. "How Feminist Is *Villette?*" *Women and Literature* 3 (1975): 16–26.
Plotz, Judith. "Potatoes in the Cellar: Charlotte Brontë's *Villette* and the Feminized Imagi-
    nation." *Journal of Woman's Studies in Literature* 1 (1979): 74–87.
Tanner, Tony. Introduction to *Villette,* by Charlotte Brontë. Harmondsworth, England, 1979.
Tillotson, Kathleen. *Novels of the Eighteen-Forties.* Oxford, 1956.
Winnifrith, Tom. *The Brontës and Their Background.* London, 1973.
Wise, Thomas J., and J. A. Symington, eds. *The Brontës, Their Lives, Friendships and Cor-
    respondence.* 4 volumes. Oxford, 1932.

6. Charles Dickens and *Great Expectations*

The scholarly and critical discussion of *Great Expectations* is voluminous. I have found the following works relating to Dickens and this novel to be of use; but this list stresses recent work and is by no means exhaustive.

Allen, Michael. *Charles Dickens' Childhood*. Basingstoke, 1988.

Brooks, Peter. *Reading for the Plot*. New York, 1984.

Carey, John. *The Violent Effigy: A Study of Dickens' Imagination*. London, 1973.

Cockshut, A. O. J. *The Imagination of Charles Dickens*. London, 1961.

Dabney, Ross. *Love and Property in the Novels of Dickens*. Berkeley and Los Angeles, 1967.

Daldry, Graham. *Charles Dickens and the Form of the Novel*. London, 1987.

Daleski, H. M. *Dickens and the Art of Analogy*. New York, 1971.

Dunn, Albert A. "The Altered Endings of *Great Expectations*: A Note on Bibliography and First-Person Narrative." *Dickens Studies Newsletter* 9 (1978): 40–42.

Engel, Monroe. *The Maturity of Dickens*. Cambridge, Mass., 1959.

Ford, George H. *Dickens and His Readers*. Princeton, N.J., 1955.

Ford, George H., and Lauriat Lane, Jr., eds. *The Dickens Critics*. Ithaca, N.Y., 1963.

Frank, Lawrence. *Charles Dickens and the Romantic Self*. Lincoln, Nebr., 1984.

Garis, Robert. *The Dickens Theatre: A Reassessment of the Novel*. Oxford, 1965.

Hardy, Barbara. *The Moral Art of Dickens*. London, 1970.

Hornback, Bert G. *Great Expectations: A Novel of Friendship*. Boston, 1987.

Kaplan, Fred. *Charles Dickens: A Biography*. New York, 1988.

Kincaid, James R. *Dickens and the Rhetoric of Laughter*. Oxford, 1971.

Kucich, John. *Excess and Restraint in the Novels of Charles Dickens*. Athens, Ga., 1981.

———. *Repression in Victorian Fiction*. Berkeley and Los Angeles, 1987.

Leavis, Q. D., and F. R. Leavis. *Dickens the Novelist*. London, 1970.

Lettis, Richard, and William Morris. *Assessing Great Expectations*. San Francisco, 1960.

Miller, J. Hillis. *Charles Dickens: The World of His Novels*. Cambridge, Mass., 1958.

Moynahan, Julian. "The Hero's Guilt: The Case of *Great Expectations*." *Essays in Criticism* 10 (1960): 60–79.

Page, Norman. *Hard Times, Great Expectations, Our Mutual Friend: A Casebook*. London, 1979.

Sadrin, Anny. *Great Expectations*. London, 1988.

Said, Edward. *Beginnings*. New York, 1975.

Slater, Michael. *Dickens and Women*. Stanford, Calif., 1983.

Smith, Grahame. *Dickens, Money, and Society*. Berkeley and Los Angeles, 1968.

Stewart, Garrett. *Dickens and the Trials of Imagination*. Cambridge, Mass., 1974.

Stoehr, Taylor. *Dickens: The Dreamer's Stance*. Ithaca, N.Y., 1965.

7. George Eliot and *The Mill on the Floss*

In addition to the general works previously cited that refer specifically to George Eliot, the following texts contain illuminating discussions of *The Mill on the Floss* and its author.

Beer, Gillian. *George Eliot*. Brighton, England, 1986.

Bloom, Harold, ed. *Modern Critical Views: George Eliot*. New York, 1986.

Ermarth, Elizabeth D. *Realism and Consensus in the English Novel*. Princeton, N.J., 1983.

Hardy, Barbara, ed. *Critical Essays on George Eliot*. New York and London, 1970.

Hayles, N. Katherine. "Anger in Different Voices: Carol Gilligan and *The Mill on the Floss*." *Signs* 12, no. 1 (Autumn 1986): 23–39.

Hardy, Barbara, ed. *Critical Essays on George Eliot*. New York and London, 1970.

Jacobus, Mary. "The Question of Language: Men of Maxims and *The Mill on the Floss*." *Critical Inquiry* 8, no. 2 (Winter 1981): 207–22.

Knoepflmacher, U. C. *Religious Humanism in the Victorian Novel: George Eliot, Walter Pater, and Samuel Butler*. Princeton, N.J., 1965.

———. *George Eliot's Early Novels: The Limits of Realism*. Berkeley and Los Angeles, 1968.

Myers, William. *The Teaching of George Eliot*. Leicester, England, 1984.

Paris, Bernard J. "The Inner Conflicts of Maggie Tulliver." *Centennial Review* 13, no. 2 (Spring 1969): 166–99.

Welsh, Alexander. *George Eliot and Blackmail*. Cambridge, Mass., 1985.

Wiesenfarth, Joseph. *George Eliot's Mythmaking*. Heidelberg, 1977.

8. Anthony Trollope and *Phineas Finn/Redux*

The following texts present informative criticism, discussion, and scholarly material that bears on love in Trollope's fiction and his achievement in *Phineas Finn/Redux*.

apRoberts, Ruth. *The Moral Trollope*. Athens, Ohio, 1971.

Denton, Ramona L. "'That Cage' of Femininity: Trollope's Lady Laura." *The South Atlantic Bulletin* 45 (1980): 1–10.

Gilmour, Robin. *The Idea of the Gentleman in the Victorian Novel*. London, 1981.

Hall, N. John, ed. *The Letters of Anthony Trollope*. Stanford, Calif., 1983.

Halperin, John. *Trollope and Politics*. New York, 1977.

Herbert, Christopher. *Trollope and Comic Pleasure*. Chicago, 1987.

Kendrick, Walter. *The Novel-Machine: The Theory and Fiction of Anthony Trollope*. Baltimore, 1980.

Kincaid, James. *The Novels of Anthony Trollope*. Oxford, 1977.

Letwin, Shirley. *The Gentleman in Trollope: Individuality and Moral Conduct*. Cambridge, Mass., 1982.

McMaster, Juliet. *Trollope's Palliser Novels*. New York, 1978.

Morse, Deborah Denenholz. *Women in Trollope's Palliser Novels*. Ann Arbor, Mich., and London, 1987.

Nardin, Jane. *He Knew She Was Right: The Independent Woman in the Novels of Anthony Trollope*. Carbondale, Ill., 1989.

Overton, Bill. *The Unofficial Trollope*. Totowa, N.J., 1982.

Pei, Lowery. "Anthony Trollope's Palliser Novels: The Conquest of Separateness." Ph.D. dissertation, Stanford University, 1975.

Polhemus, Robert M. *The Changing World of Anthony Trollope*. Berkeley and Los Angeles, 1968.

Smalley, Donald, ed. *Trollope: The Critical Heritage*. New York, 1969.

Snow, C. P. *Trollope: His Life and Art*. New York, 1975.

Super, R. H. *The Chronicler of Barsetshire: A Life of Anthony Trollope*. Ann Arbor, Mich., and London, 1989.

Terry, R. C. *Anthony Trollope: The Artist in Hiding*. Totowa, N.J., 1977.

Tracy, Robert. *Trollope's Later Novels.* Berkeley and Los Angeles, 1978.
Wall, Stephen. *Trollope: Living with Character.* New York, 1989.

9. Thomas Hardy and *Far from the Madding Crowd*

In addition to the extremely helpful bibliographical, scholarly, and critical materials in the Norton Critical Edition of *Far from the Madding Crowd*, ed. Robert C. Schweik (New York, 1986), the following texts have been particularly useful to me in understanding *Far from the Madding Crowd.*

Beegel, Susan. "Bathsheba's Lovers: Male Sexuality in *Far from the Madding Crowd.*" In *Sexuality and Victorian Literature*, ed. Don Richard Cox. Knoxville, Tenn., 1984.
Boumelha, Penny. *Thomas Hardy and Women: Sexual Ideology and Narrative Form.* Totowa, N.J., 1982.
Carpenter, Richard C. *Thomas Hardy.* New York, 1964.
Grundy, Joan. *Hardy and the Sister Arts.* London, 1979.
Guerard, Albert J. *Thomas Hardy.* 1949; reprinted, Norfolk, Conn., 1964.
Holloway, John. *The Victorian Sage.* London, 1953.
Kramer, Dale, ed. *Critical Approaches to the Fiction of Thomas Hardy.* London, 1979.
Meisel, Perry. *Thomas Hardy: The Return of the Repressed: A Study of the Major Fiction.* New Haven, 1972.
Miles, Rosalind. "The Women of Wessex." In *The Novels of Thomas Hardy*, ed. Anne Smith. Plymouth and London, 1979.
Miller, J. Hillis. *Thomas Hardy: Distance and Desire.* Cambridge, Mass., 1970.
Vigar, Penelope. *The Novels of Thomas Hardy: Illusion and Reality.* London, 1974.
Wittenberg, Judith Bryant. "Angles of Vision and Questions of Gender in *Far from the Madding Crowd.*" *Centennial Review* 30, no. 1 (Winter 1986): 25–40.

10. James Joyce and Love

The following works are of interest or have been of use in writing on the subject of Joyce and love (two of the most provocative and informative, Richard Brown's *James Joyce and Sexuality* and Brenda Maddox's biography of Nora Joyce, I read after essentially completing this study), but by no means do they or the other texts mentioned in the notes to the Joyce chapter begin to exhaust the helpful material on these two endless subjects—no one can consume efficiently the entire output of the marvelously productive and intellectually rich "Joyce industry."

Adams, Robert Martin. *Surface and Symbol.* Oxford, 1972.
Atherton, James. *The Books at the Wake.* 1959; reprinted Carbondale, Ill., 1974.
Attridge, Derek. *Peculiar Language: Literature as Difference from the Renaissance to James Joyce.* Ithaca, N.Y., 1988.
Begnal, Michael H., and Fritz Senn, eds. *A Conceptual Guide to Finnegans Wake.* University Park, Pa., 1974.
Bishop, John. *Joyce's Book of the Dark.* Madison, Wis., 1986.
Brivic, Sheldon R. *Joyce between Freud and Jung.* Port Washington, N.Y., 1980.
Brown, Richard. *James Joyce and Sexuality.* Cambridge and London, 1985.

Budgen, Frank. *James Joyce and the Making of Ulysses and Other Writings.* London, 1972.

Cheng, Vincent. *Shakespeare and Joyce: A Study of Finnegans Wake.* University Park, Pa., and London, 1984.

Cixous, Hélène. *The Exile of James Joyce.* Trans. Sally Purcell. London, 1972.

Ellmann, Richard. *The Consciousness of Joyce.* London, 1977.

———. *Ulysses on the Liffey.* New York, 1972.

French, Marilyn. *The Book as World.* Cambridge, Mass., 1976.

Henke, Suzette. *Joyce's Moraculous Sindbook.* Columbus, Ohio, 1978.

Henke, Suzette, and Elaine Unkeless, eds. *Women in Joyce.* Urbana, Ill., 1982.

Herring, Phillip F. *Joyce's Uncertainty Principle.* Princeton, N.J., 1987.

Kenner, Hugh. *Joyce's Voices.* Berkeley and Los Angeles, 1978.

———. *Ulysses.* London, 1980.

Litz, A. Walton. *The Art of James Joyce.* New York, 1964.

MacCabe, Colin. *James Joyce and the Revolution of the Word.* London, 1979.

McGee, Patrick. *Paperspace: Style as Ideology in Joyce's Ulysses.* Lincoln, Neb., 1988.

McHugh, Roland. *Annotations to Finnegans Wake.* Baltimore and London, 1980.

Maddox, Brenda. *Nora: The Real Life of Molly Bloom.* Boston, 1988.

Norris, Margot. *The Decentered Universe of Finnegans Wake.* Baltimore and New York, 1976.

Raleigh, John Henry. *The Chronicle of Leopold and Molly Bloom.* Berkeley, 1977.

Scott, Bonnie Kime. *Joyce and Feminism.* Bloomington, Ind., 1984.

Shechner, Mark. *Joyce in Nighttown.* Berkeley and London, 1974.

———. *James Joyce.* Atlantic Highlands, N.J., 1987.

Solomon, Margaret C. *Eternal Geomater: The Sexual Universe of Finnegans Wake.* Carbondale, Ill., 1969.

Vico, Giambattista. *The New Science of Giambattista Vico.* Third edition. Trans. Thomas Goddard Bergin and Max Harold Fisch. Ithaca and London, 1984.

Wedekind, Frank. *Pandora's Box.* In *Tragedies of Sex.* Trans. Samuel A. Eliot, Jr. London, 1923.

11. D. H. Lawrence and *Lady Chatterley's Lover*

For a critical understanding of *Lady Chatterley's Lover* and D. H. Lawrence, the following texts are of great help.

Britton, Derek. *Lady Chatterley's Lover: The Making of the Novel.* London, 1988.

Clarke, Colin. *River of Dissolution: D. H. Lawrence & English Romanticism.* New York, 1969.

Daleski, H. M. *The Forked Flame: A Study of D. H. Lawrence.* Evanston, Ill., 1967.

Delaney, Paul. *D. H. Lawrence's Nightmare.* New York, 1978.

Ford, George. *Double Measure: A Study of the Novels and Stories of D. H. Lawrence.* Reprint of 1965 edition. New York, 1969.

Hinz, Evelyn J. "Pornography, Novel, Mythic Narrative: The Three Versions of *Lady Chatterley's Lover.*" In *Modernist Studies* 3, no. 1 (1979): 35–47.

Hough, Graham. *The Dark Sun: A Study of D. H. Lawrence.* New York, 1956.

Kermode, Frank. *D. H. Lawrence.* New York, 1973.

Leavis, F. R. *D. H. Lawrence: Novelist.* New York, 1955.

Rieff, Philip. *The Triumph of the Therapeutic: Uses of Faith after Freud.* New York, 1966.

Sagar, Keith M. *The Art of D. H. Lawrence.* Cambridge, 1966.

Sanders, Scott. *D. H. Lawrence: The World of the Five Major Novels.* New York, 1973.

Schneider, Daniel J. *The Consciousness of D. H. Lawrence.* Lawrence, Kansas, 1986.

Schorer, Mark. "On *Lady Chatterley's Lover.*" *Modern British Fiction*, ed. Mark Schorer. New York, 1961.

Smith, Anne, ed. *Lawrence and Women.* New York, 1978.

Spilka, Mark. *The Love Ethic of D. H. Lawrence.* Bloomington, Ind., 1955.

Squires, Michael. *The Creation of Lady Chatterley's Lover.* Baltimore and London, 1983.

Squires, Michael, and Dennis Jackson, eds. *D. H. Lawrence's "Lady": A New Look at Lady Chatterley's Lover.* Athens, Ga., 1985.

Index

Note. Fictional characters are entered under forenames, except when referred to by only one name; human individuals under surnames.